Speak to the Winds

RUTH MOORE

Speak to the Winds

ʏ ʏ

Originally Published in 1956
by William Morrow & Co.
Reprinted December 1987 By Blackberry
ISBN 0-942396-54-5

© Ruth Moore, 1987

Cover By Beth Leonard

Blackberry Books
Chimney Farm
Nobleboro, Maine 04555

Printed in the United States of America

Contents

PART ONE
MacKechnie's Kingdom
1855–1910

THE island was off the beaten track as islands go; it was four miles from the mainland, across a stretch of dangerous water. Other islands lay around it to the north and west, but to the south and east it had nothing but open ocean, the North Atlantic stretching to the sky. The islands were of all kinds, some rocky, some low-lying and green, with harbors for boats and beaches where children could play. Wherever there was a harbor not too much of a tide hole, people lived. This one, Chin Island, as it was called, had no harbor, so that for years it went uninhabited, a jutting chin of granite thrust out into the ocean, a wild three miles of rock, spruce forest and alders laced with blackberry vines.

In the very old time, an ancient race of Indians, the Paint People, went there for red ocher, which they mined on the west end of the island; at least, the ocher was there in a series of scratched, shallow pits; who made them, or when, was anybody's guess. Later, the Passamaquoddy hunters must have stopped long enough to lose an occasional arrowhead near the only place where it was possible to pull up a canoe—a small, exposed beach on the western shore, which had a fine spring of clear water running out of a split rock. They might have stayed as long as the migrating flocks of sea birds did, but no longer, for the place was unsheltered, unfriendly to humans.

Its shores came down in blocks and tiers of tumbled granite, shelving off gradually underwater, so that around three sides of the island thrust out wicked snouts of rock, on which the sea loitered with intent, even in calm weather. From tidemark, ten acres of black ledges made off to the east and south, some underwater, some just awash, at different times of tide. Over them, the sea was always in motion.

No matter how quiet the day, or how still the spruces baked in the summer sun, a slow, cool, sleepy sound hung over the island everywhere, a sound, it seemed, not so much of water as of air.

Perhaps on some such summer day, an early visitor to the coast, seeing the swirl of lazy green about the ledges, the rockweed lifting and falling like a field of grass, named the place The Pasture, though no one could say what pastured there, outside of crabs and cunners and south-flying sea birds. In winter, The Pasture was white water for weeks at a time. Big rollers lifted up green from across the gulf and smashed in on the headland, shattering the granite sometimes, shifting great boulders and changing the face of the shore. Sheets of spray roared up, twenty, forty, fifty feet high, drove in to freeze in white rime on the spruces, which on the eastern shore were stunted like trees at timber line.

The island was all granite, its peak a round hill a hundred feet high and naked as a cup. What grew there, grew where the land leveled out at the base of the hill, a wild tangle of northern coastal forest, on roots driven into the crevices of rock. Through centuries, it had made topsoil, deep enough on the island's western end to grow a little grass, and on that side, too, a half-mile back from the shore, just before the hill started to climb, was a small, deep pond in an alder swamp of almost tropical lushness.

This pond was always full; it caught the wash of rain from the hill behind it, and, besides, it was spring-fed. From the high, dry, lichened ledges, no one would suspect that the island was a watery place, but deep within it flowed never-failing streams, surfacing here at the pond and trickling down, through crevices into the sea—in summer, a slow, steady drip dampening the rocks above tide line, in winter, great waterfalls of yellow ice.

The swamp flowered all summer, no matter how dry the season. Above it, the granite crisped its lichens in the sun, baked as fiercely dry as if the heat struck outward from furnace fires within. But the growth around the pond stayed brilliant, electric green. Alders grew thick as a man's thigh, and some of the old swamp birches were three feet through at the base. Tall trees and the hill kept away the wind, so that air hung hot and still, full of jungle-rich smells of mud and moss and lush, sunny leaves. Squirrels lived in the swamp, and deer, and mink and beaver and muskrat. Hermit thrushes sang there all spring long. The trees were full of wing-flash and flutter and the four or five clear notes, repeated a thousand times, of white-throated sparrows. Ducks gathered in the pond; at fall dusk, it might be brimful of them, floating side by side. To these inhabitants, at any time of year, the swamp offered shelter, either of shade or snow.

The Indians made a few scratches on the land and went; early white settlers sailing along the coast eyed the rugged island warily. "No harbor," they said, and passed on to other islands.

One of them must have gone ashore there for a while, and built himself some kind of house on the western side by the Passama-quoddy spring, for he left a stone foundation over a shallow cellar hole, and his initial, "A," chiseled in a ledge by the shore. But no one knew what his name was, nor how long he might have stayed. When Robert MacKechnie and Ansel Gilman, early settlers, went to the island in 1855, they found the marked boulder; but "A's" cellar stones were fallen in and green with moss, his initial almost obliter-ated by the gray rosettes of the lichen that grows on granite.

Robert MacKechnie and Ansel Gilman were quarrymen—stonecut-ters by trade, looking for stone. In the cities, public edifices were building—churches and courthouses, post offices, tombs. Already in the coast country, south and west, quarries were coining money, the two and three masted schooners sailing to New York and Boston and Philadelphia loaded deck-deep with the pink-gray granite that split so straight along the grain of the stone. MacKechnie was newly over from Scotland, where his people had owned and operated quar-ries for generations. Ansel Gilman, a Connecticut man, knew a good deal about stone, too, though perhaps not by instinct and by heritage, as MacKechnie did.

From the deck of a small sloop hired for the day, they saw the granite hill on Chin Island heaved up against the bay's blue water, and MacKechnie looked and whistled. Ansel shook his head.

"I said to him," Ansel wrote in his diary, "that's the worst rock pile I ever saw and there's no landing place within forty rows of apple trees. By landing place I meant a harbor where we could load stone aboard of a vessel. But Robert kept on looking at it. I will say it was a sightly island, but I did not like the look of it from the beginning."

He also wrote, "It is a waste of time to argue with Robert, I have found out that. Because when you have got done, you find you have not changed his mind, so your time is wasted anyway."

This was the journal which did not come to light until years after Ansel's death, and then was rummaged out of a trunk in the attic of his empty house by his young grandson, Elbridge Gilman. There was little enough in it about the actual happenings of that day. Most of what took place, Elbridge got from his other grandfather, who was MacKechnie.

"Nevertheless I said to him," MacKechnie said, "that I would like to land and look it over."

They landed on Chin Island, on the beach by the stone marked "A," and hauled up their punt; and MacKechnie went as straight as a hunting dog through the tangled thickets and the swamp to what he was looking for—the high-nosed hill, rounded, polished by weather—clean outcrop, straight-grained red granite.

"He kept up with me until we came to the swamp," MacKechnie said, "and then he fell behind and didna catch up until I had been for some time on top of the hill. I thought it was the swamp that was bothering him—a stone man hates a swamp like a cup of cold poison, you have to have hard ground to move granite over; but it seems it was not that, or not that entirely."

Before they left the island that day, Ansel and Robert had a fight. They stood toe to toe on the level bank near the stone marked "A" and decided whether or not to put their money into a granite quarry on the island. Robert wanted to; Ansel didn't; and Robert won.

It was a long time afterwards and Ansel had been dead for years, before MacKechnie told his grandson, Elbridge Gilman, the grandson of them both, how the settlement on the island had begun with a fight.

"And a bloody one," MacKechnie said. "My nose bled for a week. We told the girls we'd fallen down yon mountain."

Elbridge grinned, remembering his grandmother, "Big" Sarah MacKechnie, long dead, but a power in her time. "The girls," Sarah MacKechnie and Jennie Gilman, doubtless guessed what had taken place. In a country where the custom was to tell women only what was supposed to be good for them to know, most women learned early to put two and two together. He recalled hearing Big Sarah say, once, with a snort, "The lies, for heb'm sakes, that men tell women! If 'twas only about each other, I could put up with it, makes things more fun not to have the like of that nailed down, cut and dry. But he wants to burn coal in the stove, too lazy to cut wood—so he tells me now, after fifty years, that wood will ruin the chimney!"

And indeed, it did seem to Elbridge, thinking over the lore of the country, that some of it might be based on, not lies exactly, but on men's convenience. Weeds are good for the garden, they shade the plants. Potatoes grow better on new ground if you don't shake out the turf. Cistern water is better to drink than well water; such things. Oh, yes, the girls would have guessed about the fight. Anse and Robert would not have wanted them to know that a decision which meant so much hardship and change in their lives had depended on whose husband had the toughest fists. And Anse would not have wanted anyone to know that he had been thrashed by a man half his size.

Elbridge hid his grin. No sense to stir the old man up—he looked pretty frail today; and MacKechnie went on.

"Anse hated the place from the beginning," MacKechnie said. "I never could see or find out why. He said, that day, it was Old Ellick, whatever that was. It sounded foolish to me and, at first, it was what made me mad, he a grown man letting himself be shaken in such an enterprise by the bogieman, if that was what it was; I never knew. But later on that day, I was mad because I wanted the place, and to talk to him was like talking to last year's deer hide nailed on the barn. I wanted it for the stone, though not entirely for the stone. Though it was lovely stone.

"If you could have seen yon hill that morning the way I saw it—the clean granite, none finer in Scotland or in any place in the world I ever saw, the hill itself, and the island lying there as if untouched since the start of time—I remember there away east and south was a mess of rocks and timber—plenty of poles stout enough for derricks, I noticed at once—then a black headland and a wrack of ledges breaking white, and all the sea and sky in the world. And I said, 'What a place, Ansel! Look at yon stone!' And he said, 'Considerable surf, ain't there?' and went stomping back down the hill.

"I did not go back to the boat for three hours, but spent time going over the island to see what might be done. I found it would be a tairrific job of work but could be done," said MacKechnie.

His Scottish burr was a memory, overlaid now with a Yankee twang through years of association, and his voice had always been curiously gentle for so tempestuous, though so small sized, a man.

"So I went back to the shore and there was Ansel with a face like a meat ax, because he guessed when I didna come that I was up on the hill, looking, with serious purpose in my mind. Besides, I looked as if I had swum the frog pond. My clothes were ripped from the blackberry bushes, and I had a great splat of mud across my face.

"'If a hundred-and-thirty pound man has that much trouble clawing himself down from that hill,' he says to me, 'what about loads of granite blocks weighing upwards of five tons?'

"If I hadna been already put out with him, I would have been then, as he well knew. I have never wished to be twitted about my size. So I went to the spring and washed my face without making him an answer.

"'Do you expect to drop and bounce them, maybe?' he says. 'Or dig a canal in across that swamp and sail your vessels up to the foot of the hill?'

"I said, 'We can throw a causeway across the swamp, there's a place where 'tis no a hundred feet wide, and then all downhill and hard ground to the shore,' and he snorted like a bull.

"'And what do you plan to build a causeway out of?' he said, and that was unreasonable, because he knew as well as I did, having seen it, that there was a part of the hill which could be blasted away, an overhang which would fall. I didna trouble to explain it to him, a child could have seen it. So I said in short words, as though to a child, 'Yon hill is not so steep but you could ease loaded flatcars down with winches and cables. They would roll of their own weight to the shore. You'd not need any power, even, only iron rails for the cars to roll on, and cables to ease them down.'

"'Why bother to ease them down,' Anse says. 'Take out the chocks and let them roll. They might travel fast enough to jump the gap between the shore and a vessel's hold out in the bay. Because that's the only living God's way you'd ever get a vessel loaded here. Or set your granite afloat and a man with a crowbar on each block to paddle it down to Boston. There's no harbor here. How would you load a vessel? Or have you got that figured out, too?'

"'I have,' I said. 'In Scotland, on a difficult shore, we build a break-water.'

"'Build a causeway, build a breakwater!' he says. 'There are dozens of places on the mainland where we wouldn't need to do either. Are you crazy, man?'

"So then I tried to tell him a little of what I had in mind. I did not come from Scotland, I said, to work for other men, in places they have already interfered with and chumbled over. I could have done that at home. But nobody had touched this island, and I had it in mind that we could build something lasting here on good foundations.

"He said, 'To hell with it, Robert! I have it in mind to start a stone quarry, not a kingdom. You've got bees in your bonnet. Go ahead, if you want to, but count me out,' and he started down the shore for the punt.

"It was then that I began taking off my jacket.

"I said, 'I won't quit the partnership, Anse, over this bee I've got in my bonnet, but I'll fight you for it, win, we stay, lose, we go elsewhere,' and I let him have a backhander, and we went to it, there on the shore.

"I didna know what possessed me to think I could lick him. He was a bookish man, not a fighter, perhaps that made the difference. Though do not get it into your head," MacKechnie said, peering at his grandson from under his shaggy eyebrows, "that the two cannot go together. We fought for upwards of half an hour, until he hit me on the nose and the pain was tairrific, and I butted him in the belly and knocked him head over giblets into 'A's' old cellar hole, where he stayed for some time."

"That was dirty fighting, Gramp," Elbridge said. "To butt a man in the belly."

"It was. But he was a head and a half taller and outweighed me by forty pounds. And a fight, then, was a fight, not a punching match. I would have done worse, just so I beat him that day, or any other man who came between me and what I had made up my mind to do. Bees in my bonnet, he told me, when his own was buzzing, and did so, all his life, with notions such as he could mine profit out of a trace of gold vein in the quartz, when a child would have known that the money was in cut stone. He might have buzzed his way through the earth to China or come back with the wealth of the Indies, pairhaps, but with no more gold from that vein than he found, which was enough, precisely, to make a wedding ring—"

"Now, hold on, Gramp, you're mixed up," Elbridge said. "It was Father had the gold mine. Malcolm. Remember?" and the old man stared at him testily, shifting his weight a little in the bed where he now spent his days.

"—for my daughter," he went on stubbornly, aware that he had made a mistake, not willing to admit it, passing it over quickly, as trivia from the packed trunk of his memory.

"That day, for once, I knocked the stubbornness out of him, the foolishness, the Old Ellick, whatever that was. At least, I thought I had."

Elbridge knew what "Old Ellick" was.

"It is lonesome, yes," read Anse's journal. "But so is any wild place and I have seen plenty of those. I cannot help but see how foolish I am to feel that this lonesome has anything behind it. A place is a place, no more than that. A man can do his work anywhere. But remembered when small, a time I was stealing apples and looked up to see a hairy head poked out of the bushes, old black hat, shag eyebrows and whiskers, little eyes, looking, not winking. It was only Old Ellick, he owned the orchard, a neighbor who never hurt anyone, nobody to be scared of. Yet, all of a sudden, what there was in the world to be afraid of, hidden but not seen in any dark woods or secret place, now was here. The old wild, the come-to-get-you. It is all damn foolishness to feel that a place can be your enemy. I made a bargain and I will keep it. But I do not believe that we will ever make a scratch on that island, and I told Robert so."

"I thought I had," MacKechnie went on saying. "But on that day as we were sailing home in the sloop, he looked back at the island, and said, 'It's a hell of a place, Robert, and we'll never make a scratch on it.'"

MacKechnie, in the eighty-fifth year of his life, in the year 1908, from his bed pointed out how he had been right, Anse Gilman wrong.

"As for scratches," said MacKechnie, "we made them."

THE enterprise, as MacKechnie said, in the beginning was "tair-rific." On his good days, when he felt like talking and could remember, he never tired of telling how they did, back there, when they built the quarry. If the place were an enemy, and there were times when it seemed to be, they fought it tooth and nail. Heavy equipment of all kinds, tools, wagons, forges, anvils, chains, had to be loaded aboard a vessel at a mainland wharf, sailed across, and somehow landed on the shore, from the anchorage out in the bay. The light stuff they handled in dories, and other small boats; for the heavy, they built timber rafts, loaded them deep and hauled them ashore with cables.

It took a long time; they could work only on days when the wind did not blow, and those days were few.

"It was a devilish landing place," MacKechnie said. "Boulders everywhere, even at high tide, to trip up a raft, and we waded to our shoulders in the cold water every time we brought one in."

And Anse had written in his journal, "The damn southwest wind still blows. Today we drove the horses overboard from the deck of the vessel and made them swim ashore. Robert thinking that horses might go when boats could not. We lost three."

"We lost a good deal," MacKechnie said. "Had you been able to walk on the sea bottom, you could have followed our track from the vessel to the shore, what with the bolts, tools, iron stuff, we lost over-

board; even a donkey engine. But I will say of Anse, he did not rub
it in, even when we lost the donkey."

Elbridge had seen the donkey. At low tide, on a calm day, you
could look down through the water, a hundred yards off the beach,
and see it lying there on bottom, not even rust color any more, only
a vague outline crusted with barnacles, wavering with the motion
of the water.

MacKechnie never mentioned the loss of horses, nor did he at any
time mention the loss of men. He had always been a man to cut
losses, and now his memory, searching back, cut them for him. But
Anse had been living in a present that was, more than anything, real
to him. He wrote it all down.

"Today we lost Joe Packard. Taking out the big birches on the
causeway road through the swamp. One of them fell on him, drove
him face-down into mud. We got him out quick as we could, but too
late he was gone. He was a good man and will be missed."

And later, "Teddy Winter took sick in the camp and had to be sent
home when the vessel left. I hope he is not going to have a bout of it.
We all have this cold and coughing, but his is bad."

And three days later, "Manson brought back news of Teddy Win-
ter's death, said pneumonia. I took Robert one side and tried to talk
him into quitting until spring. It is not right to keep the men here,
living the way we have to in these lean-to shacks, sleeping on the
ground and no way to dry wet clothes and boots except an outdoors
fire. But he is bound to drive through. He says I am crazy to think of
turning a gang of men loose, coming into winter, with no work, and
he is right, though he would do it, and be damned to them, if it
suited his turn. It does not suit his turn; so I have taken part of the
men off the causeway and we are building tight houses. Robert has
raved at me some, but he knows as well as I do that we will need
houses sometime if we are to bring the women over, so why not now?"

"We cleared for the houses first," MacKechnie said. "Dug cellars,
laid foundations. In December, at the end of the first year's time, we
brought the women and the young ones over, and had Christmas in
warm houses, with fires going. Most went on the vessel, with all our
stuff and things, but Anse had a dory he wanted to sail across, so he
and Jennie went in that."

"December 18, 1856," wrote Anse. "Sailed Jennie over to the island
for the first time today. It was a cold day, and ice made on the dory
and stiffened up the sail, so I had to knock some off. I was afraid she
would be cold and take harm in the state she is in, three months

along, so I bundled her up in everything we had and put in so many hot bricks that we both laughed when I had to take some out, it ballasted the dory's bow too low in the water. We had a good time going over. She tickled to death to be with me for good now, and I to have her. We have been apart the biggest part of a year now. And when we hove up under the lee of the island, she saw the big yellow icicles the springs make down over the ledges, and said it was pretty. I don't call it pretty, I call it darn cold. I hope I have not done wrong to bring her here. If anything happens to her I don't know what I would do."

And in May, 1857: "Jennie has had our baby, a fine boy. Called him Malcolm, after her father. She did not have a hard time. Was a good girl from the beginning and had it in the DAYTIME, in good weather, so it was not hard to sail over to town and fetch the doctor. I thank God."

THAT winter and spring, MacKechnie's gang swamped and cleared roads. They built a breakwater with a loading wharf at the end of it, on the northern side of the island, where the next island to the north somewhat sheltered a landing place. They built MacKechnie's causeway across the swamp, his railway running from the hill to the shore, where the loaded flatcars were to be let downhill by an ingenious system of cables and winches.

For over half a century MacKechnie and Gilman's quarry operated on the island and shipped cut stone half a world away. Five hundred people lived there in its heyday, a cross-section of nationalities, for MacKechnie imported his stonecutters, the best in the world, he said, from Italy and Scotland; and as soon as the breakwater thrust out its curve far enough to make a safe harbor for boats, the Yankee farmer-fishermen came. Schooners hauling granite down the coast had crews who might be Yankee, or Greek or Negro or Portuguese. Some stayed, brought families, or married on the island. The children had strange combinations of names: Eliseo MacGimsey, Nikolaides Pumlow—not strange at all when it was shortened, as it soon was, to Nick.

In time, the island was no longer cut off from the world. The vessels, hauling granite, sailed back and forth from the cities; twice a week a little coastwise steamer called at the wharf, bringing passengers and freight. A minister and a priest came over from the mainland periodically to hold services for those of their faiths. Summer visitors came, a few at first; or temperance speakers and debaters to talk to the Iron Clads, which was a forum; once or twice a year a stock company stopped over from the mainland and offered plays in the new town hall.

"We put up our own town buildings and took pride in them," said MacKechnie.

In spare time, the island men laid stone foundations, hewed timbers and drove nails; they built a church, a schoolhouse and a town hall, in the order of importance. Their stone foundations were a wonder to see, the big, bland, pink-gray granite blocks tailored to fit, morticed and overlapped as if they had been no more trouble to cut than so many pieces of soap.

"The men who worked for me did not need to look twice at a piece of stone to see how the grain would run. And then, too, there was consider-rable competition. A public building is something for a man to be remembered by. In time to come, a grandson might lay his hand on the stone and say, 'From here to here, my grandfather, Sherebiah MacGimsey, laid this stone; from there to the corner, Joseph Lessaro. You see there is a difference."

Yes, his grandson thought, that's true; and MacKechnie went on. "There was a difference in the work, but not in quality, only in style. It was all built to last."

The church was a bleak, rectangular box with a squat gable and a low belfry, in which hung a singularly clear-toned bell. Mac-Kechnie had sent to Scotland for the bell, having in his youth known the bellmakers. In his letter to them, he wrote that he wanted a bell which would say, "Come."

"It was only what church bells have always been supposed to say, but some do not. When it was rung for the first time, I did not have to tell anyone what to listen for. They heard the bell say, 'Come.'"

It was rung a good deal, not only for services—for gatherings of all kinds, for emergencies, at five-thirty in the morning and at six at night to mark the beginning and the end of a work day. On a still, sunny morning, or above the hoarse growl of the sea and the battering wind of a black winter's evening, the bell sounded sweet and penetrating, "Come . . . come . . . come."

The church building was white, painted with thick, almost pure white lead, thinned a little with oil. Against the greens of spring and summer, it stood out in immaculate whiteness; against snow, it looked pale blue. Its pews were bought by island families, who paid thirty dollars apiece for them, a large sum, even when the money went to support the church. They were built of solid plank, two planks to a pew. In those days of mighty trees, no one thought it remarkable that these planks should be an inch-and-a-half thick, fourteen feet long and twenty-five and thirty-five inches wide, all clear pine. They were, merely, what was practical. They did not have to be joined to make the seat wide enough or the back high; they wouldn't sag under the weight of a tall man, his substantial wife and eight or nine children. They were probably the most uncomfortable seats ever devised anywhere, the planks at stiff right angles to each other.

"But people went to church not to be comfortable but to hear the good rewarded and the sinners fry," said MacKechnie.

The walls were whitewashed between the tall, narrow windows, which were clear glass below the meeting rails and arched at the top, with small, colored, leaded panes. The pulpit was a tall box, like a coffin, of black walnut; and behind it, two Sundays in the month, oftener if he could get over from the mainland and spare the time, the Reverend Archie Snow gave forth a remarkably blazing brand of hell-fire and brimstone. It was said of him that when he really let himself go, frying the sinners, his breath would light the kerosene lamps across the church under the gallery.

"Hold on, Gramp," Elbridge said once. "The way you talk about the church, you'd think it was gone, that none of us had ever seen it. I've got a tail-ache right now, from setting on those seats. It's still there, Gramp. It's just had a new coat of paint."

"Don't talk like a cussed fool," MacKechnie said testily. "I know it's still there. And don't think I don't know how much trouble the town had to squat out enough money for that coat of paint. In my day, we did the work ourselves and it was not a chore, but a privilege. It's the men I am talking about; the men are gone. You don't have Archie Snow. You don't have Marshfield Plummer."

"No, I guess we don't," Elbridge said.

It was in his mind to start an argument about who would swallow all that hell-fire and brimstone nowadays, but the old man was going on, telling about Marshfield Plummer.

Across the road from the church and at a decent interval from it, was the town hall, and beside that, the school. The first schoolmaster who taught in the new school building was Marshfield Plummer. He was a graduate of Bowdoin College, a boy of twenty who ate his heart out because he had a gimpy leg; and then buckled down, after a while, and taught the little Gilmans and MacKechnies, and the Roccos and Lessaros; and the Cayfords and Gonzales and MacGimseys; and Erastus Mills Nikolaides, and Tilson Shepheard and Harriet Horn; and Joanna Vira and John Cloud's four mulatto children. He taught them to read and write and figure in a way they never forgot. To some he taught Greek and Latin; he was fascinated to hear modern Greek talked, tried to figure out how it joined on to the speech of ancient Homer. He was as interested in Italy and Scotland and Greece and Portugal as he was in his own home on a farm on the mainland, and knew almost as much about them, that is, what he could get out of books; he'd not traveled any then. The only difference he ever saw among his pupils was that some were boys and some girls, some smarter than others to learn.

He ended up as the president of a Midwestern university, "and, in his time was a great force for cee-valization; but never more so than here, in his first school, where he taught little Yankees and Greeks and Italians about each others' countries, and said that a colored boy was anybody with a darker tan."

BY 1874, the granite hill was bisected with quarry pits, some of them sixty feet deep. On a June morning in that year, Anse Gilman, then fifty-five years old, went down into one of them to see why a dynamite charge had not blown when the fuse was lit. Someone had to, and he would not send one of the men. The fuse had not gone out; it was smoldering slowly; the charge let go just as Anse reached the bottom of the pit. They picked up as much of him as they could find, which was not a great deal, for Jennie to take over to the mainland and bury in the cemetery with Anse's family. He had always made them promise not to bury him on the island if anything happened to him there.

"Jennie sat in the parlor, in there, and Anse's pine box on the wharf by the freight shed," MacKechnie told Elbridge. "Neither Sarah nor I knew how to comfort her; we didna know how to comfort ourselves. For the first time in my life, I, Robert MacKechnie, the great man, found myself dee-minished, walking slow, for the lack of a steady hand on my enterprise and on my heart. For nineteen years he had been at my elbow, holding back, at times, not without reason, for I was never a temperate man in my purposes, and he was —he was—"

"He had bees in his bonnet, Gramp," Elbridge reminded.

The old man's eyes flew open.

"He did indeed," he said shortly. "That gold mine. And the idea he had that whoever the island belonged to, it was not to us. That

is not to say I didna love him. For all there were times I could have
killed him, and he me, he was a—a good man and greatly missed.

"When the steamboat whistle blew in the bay that day, Jennie fell
down, fainting, and after that, she could never abide the sound
across the water, when the steamer came in. In a year's time, she
moved away and took her family with her to the mainland, where
she shortly died. All except Malcolm. Malcolm stayed."

"Malcolm," Elbridge said. "My father. He was the one had the
gold mine, Gramp. Not Anse."

"Be that as it may," said MacKechnie. "Anse did not stop him."

MALCOLM stayed, not because he wanted to quarry stone, but be-
cause he had the bee. On one of the northerly outcrops, stripped
for working and abandoned early because the stone was faulted
there, Anse and Robert had found a vein of quartz which showed
a slight trace of gold. They did not bother with it, except as a cu-
riosity, because in their experience this was not gold country. You
might run across a trace here and there, never enough worth work-
ing. The gold was in good, honest cut stone, quarried and shipped
and sold for cash; what traces might be uncovered, of gold, had to
be more than had ever showed itself to them. They used the old
quarry hole for a grout pile and forgot about the vein, except for
an occasional joke about it, might be, when times were bad.

But Malcolm was obsessed with the gold. He was a boy of eleven
when his father pointed out to him the faint, infinitesimal yellow
stain.

The coast country was walking with long strides then. It was new
enough so that no man could say, for sure, what riches it might con-
tain. Fortunes were already made out of lumber, out of lime, out of
ships and shipping, out of stone. Every little town that had a steep-to,
sheltered shore was building vessels, coasters for Boston and Virginia,
clippers for the China trade. A new atlas for the county had come
out; a copy of it was among the books at the school. One map showed
mineral deposits in the area, so far as they were known. Or guessed
at. The map was speckled over with colored dots marking the mining
districts. Blue dot for silver, red for copper; white with a cross for
tin, yellow for gold. Malcolm pored over the map, marking down
the many blue and yellow dots, and across his mind the high winds
of hope and excitement blew. The Bay View Mine—that was gold.
The White Star Mine. The Brooklin Mine. The Eastern Star Mine. The
Egypt Mine. The Cline Mine. All gold. And many others not marked

by names, only by yellow dots. And on an island at sea, not far from home, The Atlantic Silver Mine. Gold. Silver. Fortunes.

Malcolm went back after school to the quartz vein. He pounded at it with an old hammer and a cold chisel, sweating, blistering his hands. He got out a chunk of rock as big as a cup and took it to his father, who told him it was no good, but, for further assurance, to ask MacKechnie.

MacKechnie turned the chunk over in his hands.

"Ay," he said. "I don't doubt it might assay sixteen dollars to the ton. But there's no a ton of the quartz, there's not half a ton. And who's to bother to blast out this for eight dollars, and it not there?"

Malcolm told about the atlas, the mining districts.

MacKechnie already had seen the map. He shook his head.

"The country's full of hope," he said. "As well it may be. Every man has gold or silver in his back yard. He thinks. Some will be rich, some not. No one knows."

"Well, that's it," said Malcolm. "No one knows."

"This we know," MacKechnie said. "The money's in stone. Gold, silver, all right, if you find it. But the stone's already found and is there for the cutting, don't forget it."

He showed figures to Malcolm, but Malcolm still would not abandon the mine.

He did not abandon it for years, until he was a young married man with a wife and two small children; and then he gave up, only because he had to, because of circumstances beyond his control.

The pit was in his cow pasture, not a hundred feet from his house, for Malcolm had built close to it for expediency's sake; and he never bothered to put rails around it, figuring that the piles of grout heaped up near the naked hole would warn anyone that here was a hole, or keep anything from falling in. But one afternoon, a neighbor's dog chased the cow, and she, in her terror, somehow scrambled up the grout pile and fell into the pit. She lay at the bottom with all the life knocked out of her, except what could bring forth, at intervals, a hoarse, wavering bawl. Malcolm's wife, "Little" Sarah, Mac-Kechnie's daughter, heard it through her kitchen window, realizing at the same time the excited barking of a dog.

It's that darn hound of Biah's, she thought, putting on her shawl and running. He's after poor old Daze.

The hound was dancing hysterically around the edge of the pit. Little Sarah drove him away, heaving chunks of split rock from the grout pile. But it was too late to do anything for Daze.

Little Sarah leaned as far as she dared over the crumbling edge, seeing Malcolm's ladders going down to a clear, still pool of water that reflected her head and shoulders against a patch of sky with a white cloud in it, going by, gone while she looked. It was Daze, sure enough, the pale-tan, gentle cow, a shapeless gray mass at the bottom, an automatic hollow moaning coming up out of the deep and dark, like the sound of all desperation.

I've told Mal and I've told him, and now it's Daze that we can't afford to lose, but it might's well have been one of the kids, ours or someone else's.

And Little Sarah went to Mal's shed where he kept his blasting tools under lock and key, stove in the door with an ax and found his dynamite. She knew well enough how to handle it, or thought she did, having lived companions with blasting tools all her life, at Mal's house now, but first at her father's, where MacKechnie used to bring the dynamite into the kitchen on a winter's morning and put it in the oven to warm up for the day's work at the quarry, cold dynamite being hard to handle—not that warmed dynamite wasn't a chancy thing. She remembered while she hunted out cap and fuse for the pale stick, that her mother, Big Sarah, would as soon have picked up a snake; but Big Sarah, on the winter's morning when the stick of dynamite had exploded in the oven, blowing pieces of stove, fire and all, up through the ceiling, and the back wall out of the kitchen, and a piece of the oven door past MacKechnie himself, cutting off the first joint of his forefinger, Big Sarah had very little to say. She had been out taking corn and water to her hens and was walking along the frozen path from the henhouse, when the back of the kitchen came out to meet her; for a moment, she did not know who was dead and who living in the smoking house. But the children had been in the front downstairs bedroom, and MacKechnie had stepped out on the steps to look at the weather; so no one had been in the kitchen. When the fire was out, though the damage not yet counted, and Big Sarah was doing up the streaming finger, Little Sarah heard her father say, "Lucky it wasn't but one stick today, Sarah," and Big Sarah said, "Yes. Wasn't it?"

You could put up with anything, if it only had a purpose to it.

But all Little Sarah's married life had been shadowed by the deep, useless pit into which Mal put the best of himself, out of which he never took anything but odds and ends of flecked quartz rock, enough gold to make her wedding ring.

Little Sarah, in case one stick of dynamite should not be enough, put six sticks into Mal's derrick bucket and lowered the bucket to the bottom of the pit. Then, with tears of rage and pity running down her face, she held the capped stick in her hand, lit the fuse and dropped it into the pit, and ran.

Little Sarah, who was pretty and small of size, like her father, was the child of a people already become so individual that among them acts of collective violence were unknown; so that a lynching, for example, would be inconceivable, or any circumstance whereby the entire body politic got together and did revenge or harm. Their particular genius was for action taken by vote, for the ballot box, for due course of law. They were modest, no one wishing to push himself forward in the eyes of his neighbors. Thus a town meeting would be conducted by the articulate few whose duty it was, while the majority sat silent, listening; but how they listened. If, after a town meeting, two men got up and went outside and there fought, then this, too, was a part of the particular genius of this people—silence, covering up deep-down, festering anger until it burst out like pus, in an act of violence; but an act, always, of individual violence, on rare occasions so terrible that people, even looking at it, could not believe it to be true.

So Little Sarah blew up her husband's gold mine to stop a sound of suffering she could not bear to hear; but more than that to end the old battle between Malcolm and MacKechnie, between Sarah and her husband. Down into the pit, exploding in red flame and fall of rock, went all the times Mal Gilman had been laughed at, called a fool; all the times Little Sarah had run head on into the strange, unpierceable wall that was Mal's idea of himself and his gold mine; for what he was after, he could not himself have told, unless it was something more malleable, less uncompromising, more beautiful than cut granite; something that was there if he could only follow it far enough into the earth to prove all MacKechnies wrong—they who made people knuckle under, as he, Malcolm, would never do; nor to Little Sarah, either, which she knew.

The men working up at the quarries, including Mal, saw the explosion go up in the quiet afternoon, and heard it run like an earthquake tremor along the island's solid granite base. They came running. Up from the shore, from the houses clustered in the clearing, the women came running, too, not even stopping for shawls over their heads. They stood aghast, not believing the destruction which their eyes saw. Malcolm's house was in ruins—windows blown, the whole rear wall flattened in. Split rocks and raw clods lay all over what had been his green back pasture. A blackened hole was all that was left of his powder shed, for the explosion had set off what Malcolm had had stored in there—nobody but he knew how much dynamite, how many kegs of blasting powder.

At first people thought that Sarah and the children must be dead inside the house—it was already starting to burn, ignited by the fire that had been in the crushed kitchen stove. Malcolm tore in at the front door and ran all over the house like a wild man, all over, that is, the parts he could get to, for the back wall of the kitchen was down, and the kitchen was where Little Sarah and the two kids would most likely have been. When the fire really got going, which it did, fast, the neighbors had to haul Mal out of there by main strength.

He took off, then, as hard as he could run, headed for the well to fetch water. There wasn't anything handy to carry water in except an old iron kettle which Little Sarah had set out under the spout to catch rain water. The explosion or something falling on it had cracked it, and when Malcolm grabbed it, it fell apart, but he didn't seem to notice, just started running for the well, carrying half an iron kettle by the handle.

MacKechnie and some of the others took out after him—not that they could have done any good, by that time, if they had had buckets enough for a bucket line and the well had been nearer. It was a long piece down the road; one reason why people always said Mal was such a fool was because he'd built his house so far from his drinking water.

Too far from the well and too near to the powder shed, they'd said, and more than one had cautioned him about keeping dynamite in that shed, because it was dangerous.

"That cussed stuff," they said. "One day you could throw it around, jump on it, burn it up in the stove—" not that anyone ever did "— and nothing'll happen. And the next day the cat walks by the powder house and *ker-whango!*"

This was not true, only approximately. It merely gave the idea.

Nobody caught up with Mal, he was running so fast; but when they got to the well they saw him standing there, and sitting with her back to the curb, holding one little boy and the other one huddled up close to her, was Little Sarah. Her dress was in ribbons and one cheek was a mass of bloody scratches where she'd been blown face-down and scrubbed along the gravel; but she had a bucket of water out of the well, and she'd torn off a piece of her petticoat and they could see where she'd used it to sponge off a cut on the baby's head. It didn't seem to be too bad a cut.

Old MacKechnie, being small and light on his feet, had got there a little ahead of the others. He took one look at Little Sarah, and yanked off his work frock and put it around her to cover her.

"Sarah," he said. "You all right?"

"Yes, I am, Pa," she said, and she looked up, right across him, to Malcolm.

"Are the kids hurt any?" MacKechnie said.

"No."

"You'd better come home with me, then," he said. "Can you walk?"

"Yes," she said, "if you'll carry Elbridge."

And she got up and handed him the baby, and the four of them started down the road toward MacKechnie's house, leaving Malcolm, walking by him as if he hadn't been there.

Malcolm stood looking after them, not moving a muscle, his hands driven as deep as they would go into his pants pockets—they were burned some, people found out later—and his face streaming, though no one could tell whether it was sweat or tears. He didn't know yet that it wasn't the cat walking past the powder shed door, or some such thing, that had set off his dynamite, so he had only himself to blame; and most people there were dead against him, for the same reason. It had been town talk for years how close that powder shed was to his house. So the neighbors didn't say anything to Mal, either; they left him standing and went back up the hill to tend to the fire, make sure it didn't get into the woods; all except Luther MacGimsey, who was always ready to shoot his mouth off on any occasion, and who didn't keep it shut now. He shook his fist under Mal's nose and said, "Looka what you done, you careless bastard!" which seemed to be the consensus.

Nobody knew where Mal spent the night; he certainly didn't go anywhere near MacKechnie's. It turned out he'd slept at Aunt Tilson Vira's. She was a sociable soul who lived down by the wharf, always taking in strays. Along about nine o'clock that night, she saw him go by her place, "either with the blind drunks or the blind staggers, appeared to be," she said. He was headed for his skiff, which he kept tied up down by the end of the wharf, and it didn't seem to her that it was fitten to let him go out in a boat. So she went down and hauled him back and tried to make him drink some hot coffee; and when he wouldn't, she got out the jug of rum she kept for her own private use. He lowered the jug considerable, she said, and when he was dizzy enough to let her come near him, she did up his burned hands in lint and sweet oil, and put him to bed to sleep it off.

The next morning MacKechnie was down on the wharf, cocky as a bantam rooster over what Little Sarah had done. The kids had been out in the woods playing, a ways from the house, which was why they hadn't got worse hurt; and Sarah'd put enough distance between her and the blast so that she'd taken no harm except for some bruises and scratches and a headache that was already going away.

There was quite a crowd of people on the wharf, and everyone had a word to say; in fact, the only ones concerned not already heard from were Malcolm and Daze, the cow.

Aunt Tilson Vira said it was like listening to a gaggle of geese, and over it all, MacKechnie, bragging, proud as a peacock.

"By God," he said, "it takes more than dynamite to kill a Mac-Kechnie," and at that, Malcolm, who'd been sitting just inside Aunt Tilson's kitchen door, with his face driven down into the lint bandages on his hands, got up and started down the wharf.

Aunt Tilson said the gab on the wharf stopped as though someone had chopped it off with a hatchet. The men around MacKechnie stared at Mal with their jaws dropped, and then stood back, opened a way to let him through.

"He did look like the devil," Aunt Tilson said. "Part rum, a course."

He didn't even stop when he went by MacKechnie, just said over his shoulder like, "But the Gilmans blow up all over the place, don't they?"

And MacKechnie, who, apparently, had just been bragging—it was his way not to stop and think how something would sound and no one was more bowed down than he was when Ansel died—said, "Oh, Jesus. Wait, lad, you know better than that." But Malcolm had already got to the wharf ladder, and was starting down.

"Hell," he said, "there's no difference in any of you, if that's what you mean. Except you blew the house out and she blew it in," and he kept on down the ladder to his skiff, which he kept tied up there.

The last they saw of him was her sail, headed out toward the tide rips toward the mainland.

Aunt Tilson Vira told Elbridge Gilman this part of the story, in later years, after MacKechnie was dead, and Elbridge was trying to piece together what had really happened to his father.

IT was in this way that Malcolm abandoned his gold mine. Around the county, others abandoned theirs. The mines—the gold, the silver, the copper, the tin, most of which never got to be real mines anyway —wouldn't pay an honest man's wages. There remained only the hopeful map, speckled with colored dots, to remind anybody who looked into an old atlas, that, one time, the county was full of hope. Times changed, too, for the lumber people and the shipping men. The lumber was cut down and shipped away; sails changed to steam. And in the cities, cement and steel took the place of building stone.

MacKechnie kept his quarry going as long as he could. He had made money, he and Ansel, but Ansel was gone. His two grandsons, Ralph and Elbridge, brought up in MacKechnie's house, were Little Sarah's boys, not Gilmans at all, though their name was Gilman. None of Ansel's tribe had been half the man their father was, and now they were a drain. Meticulously, Robert sent half his profits to Jennie Gilman, over on the mainland; if Ansel had lived, the money could have been put back into the business. There was less and less demand for granite, fewer vessels to haul it down the coast. The quarries were getting hard to work; some of the pits were unworkable, the grout piles were so high, and seepage from the underground springs had half-filled them with deep pools of clear green water.

One by one, the pits closed down. Scottish and Italian stoneworkers packed tools and went off to other jobs. Most of the young men left for the cities, for any place where there was work. The steamboat ceased to call; the wharf fell into disrepair. On a night in an icy February, the town hall burned down. Rust ate into the tracks of the tiny, narrow-gauge railway; finally, MacKechnie, with his few remaining workmen, tore them up and sold them for junk. Elbridge Gilman remembered how his grandfather, following the last load of iron rails along the loading wharf to the vessel, had walked slow.

For the last years of his active life, MacKechnie was a stonemason. As foreman, he helped build three lighthouses, some wharves here and there; but most of his work was on foundations, stone fireplaces and chimneys and boat piers for summer cottages.

Big Sarah, his wife, died in 1900. MacKechnie himself fell from a stone pier in 1905 and damaged his spine, so that he spent the last five years he had left in bed—even flat on his back and at the small-end of his life, his grandsons thought, a little too much for any ordinary man.

MacKechnie saw to their education, not caring, "par-ticularly," he said, "for the claptrap put out in the school." There was nobody, nowadays, like Marshfield Plummer. And a boy who got an education from MacKechnie, got one not only in stoneworking and carpentry but in other things. The old man knew the Bible from end to end, and a good deal of literature, too; he kept up with what was going on in the world, and had a word to say about it; his mail was always loaded with papers and magazines. His talk about the world of affairs and the humming early days of the quarries on the island fascinated Elbridge; but Ralph was another matter. He was an active boy with many fish to fry; listening to any talk, except about his own affairs, made him fidgety.

"All that gab about the good old days gives me the pip," Ralph would say. "He thinks this place'll come back sometime, be the way it was then. Good God, look at it! It's dead as a haddock. All it's good for's to get away from. Go on in and talk to him. Remember a page of the Bible for him, or some of his goddamned old poetry. He likes you best, anyway, you freak, because you've got a memory."

And away Ralph would go on the dead run; until one day he kept on running and went over to live with his father's people on the mainland and refused to come back, and in 1917 went to war and never came back at all.

Elbridge supposed he did have a freak memory—a handy one anyway that stood him in good stead in school; but to MacKechnie, it was remarkable. He would hold up a page of the Bible, or some book or other, for Elbridge to read; and Elbridge would read it, look away from the text and repeat it; a week or a month later, he could still repeat it; MacKechnie said it was a great gift. He was puzzled as to where it could have come from.

"Not from Ansel," he said, "though you look like him, the spit and image. I always told Ansel that if he had brains to go with the rest of him, he'd be a great man," and Elbridge recalled a page in Ansel's journal, the crabbed, faded writing:

"Robert says I am a fool. But he thinks any man is a fool who does not agree with him."

My Lord, Elbridge thought, if I'm a combination of those two fellows, I ought to be in one hell of a war with myself all the time. Funny, I don't seem to be. I'm a little jealous of Ralph, I guess, off on his own like that; wish I'd been the one to think of it first. But somebody's got to stay and look after Ma and Gramp, and Ralph wouldn't have been the one to do that.

At twenty, he knew he looked like Grandfather Gilman—the spit and image, all the older people said—big frame, six foot three, shock of flaming red hair, freckles, mild inquiring blue eyes.

But I wouldn't mind looking like *him*, either, Elbridge thought, glancing at the old hawk head against the pillow, the way he was when he was young.

It was something you couldn't get away from, the feeling of continuity with the past, that he'd got from MacKechnie. Ralph didn't have it, but Ralph hadn't listened much to MacKechnie's talk; about the Red Paint People, of whom next to nothing was known, the Passamaquoddy hunters, the man whose initial had been "A;" about himself and Ansel Gilman and the people of different nationalities and color who had helped him build the quarries, and whose sons and grandsons, living, were now the people of the island.

"What we have here is a microcosm of the world," he said. "Dinna think the world grows old in three generations. She goes through foolish and nervous times, like a woman with her changes, but then she settles down and is better."

He was a stubborn man, MacKechnie. Even before he died, the interior of the island where the workings had been had gone back to wilderness. Blackberry vines covered the forges; the quick seeds of spruces rooted at the steps of the powder sheds, sending up small, fast-growing saplings. Ducks came back to the pond and muskrat and beaver to the swamp, swimming over from other islands and the mainland; but the deer did not come back, at least, not yet, for by the shore above the harbor behind the breakwater, a small community of people were left—twenty families, living here and there among many old and empty houses slowly rotting between the granite hill and the sea. But MacKechnie believed to the day of his death that the quarries would open again; that the heyday of the island, the big affairs, the crowds of men going to work, would come back. He died talking to the spirit of Ansel Gilman; or maybe it was to the twenty-year-old grandson who looked like Ansel, sitting by the bed clasping his transparent old hand.

"Ansel," he said. "You and I, we built our house upon a rock. You canna tell me that nothing will come of it. Men will not always be such fools. When the silly stuff they are using now begins to crumble, as it will, they will build their foundations of stone again."

PART TWO
Christmas

ELBRIDGE GILMAN, coming up the steps to L. MacGimsey's general-store-and-post-office, could hear Stella MacGimsey even before he opened the storm door.

". . . come right down on top of him, tooth and claw. Said, one *swipe*, and that man's face was gone."

Orin must have brought a dandy today, Elbridge thought.

Orin Vira was the mail carrier, who boated the mail over from the mainland three times a week. If there happened to be any news, Orin brought that, too.

Elbridge closed the door behind him, and Imogene Cayford, standing transfixed beside Stella's wicket, turned a glazed face toward him without, apparently, seeing him.

Inside the wicket, Stella said, "Elbridge! That fellow over to Walbrook, runs the rooming house, kept a pet bear to haul in the summer trade? He went into the pen last night, that thing jumped him."

"Did?" Elbridge said. "Hurt him?"

"Hurt him! I guess it hurt him! My Lord, there wasn't a piece of him left big enough to recognize. Said every rag he had on him was shred to thread, even to his—well, no wonder. The awful thing, his wife see it from the pantry window, she run out and round and round the pen screeching, but no livable, namable thing could she do, till the neighbors heard her and come over, and I guess he like to got two-three of them, fought him off with a shovel, till one of them thought of a gun—why they hadn't before is the God's wonder —and went and got a .30-30 rifle and shot the bear."

"Good grief!" Elbridge said, shaken. Usually he let Stella's stories roll off, for any item of news going in through the post office wicket was likely to come out different from the way it went in, like a squash seed going into the ground. "What on earth was he doing, into a pen with a bear?"

"Done it times without number," Stella said.

She reached around, without looking, for Elbridge's mail, thrust it under the wicket. "He had that bear for years, it was an attraction to his trade. Said he'd get a crowd of summer people around, then go into the pen and scratch the critter behind the ears, make everybody 'oh' and 'ah.' Never a move to touch him before, but this time, well— In he went and *out* he did not get."

"That doesn't seem surprising," Elbridge said, "if he was fool enough to do such a thing."

There was a letter from Roger, his boy working over on the mainland, he saw, thumbing through his batch of mail. He slit open the envelope, pulled out the letter.

Imogene Cayford pursed up her lips. She had stood by the wicket ever since it had opened, listening to Stell tell about the bear to different ones, watching how they took it. Addie Shepheard had turned a real green color and had to sit down, and Wid Lowden had just stood there wagging his fat head from side to side and saying, "Ain't that awful, now, ain't that awful!" But Elbridge hadn't seemed to be very interested—he wasn't a good one to tell a story to, anyway, likely to be picky—and that had thrown Stell off, so she'd left out some of the best parts.

"Tch!" Imogene said. "Said they took him out of there with a shovel. Said his wife was 'bout crazy."

"Think she might've been," Elbridge said, not looking up from his letter.

"Changing the straw in the pen this time, wasn't he, Stell?" Imogene asked.

"Oh, my Lord, Imogene, *yes*, he was," Stell said.

If there was anything Stell hated, it was to tell a story the same livelong way every time; and here was Imogene settled down for the afternoon, built her nest right outside the wicket, take the words out of your mouth if you told anything different.

"Well," she said, forestalling Imogene, "this man, Fifield or Bigler, some such name—"

"Ben Beavey," Elbridge said, absently.

He folded up his letter, stuffed it back into the envelope. He'd read enough to see that Roger was all right and would be home for Christmas. The rest he'd keep for later, with Jess, in peace and quiet.

"Beavey?" Stella said. "No, that wasn't the name. It was Fifield or Bigler, I couldn't be mistaken, odd name like that. Well, now, this Fifield, this bear, he—"

"Beavey," Elbridge said. "And it was a she-bear."

"My Lord, Elbridge, I had the word right straight from Orin. They were all talking about it over to the harbor whilst Lombard sorted the mail. I guess Orin ought to know the man's name."

"Seems as though," Elbridge agreed. "But if it was that fellow ran the rooming house over Walbrook way, kept the bear penned up in his back yard, his name was Beavey. I've seen that bear. It was an ugly critter, paced up and down the cage all day. Nobody ever went near it, except to heave meat from a distance. I guess likely if Ben Beavey went into the pen for any reason at all, he thought the critter was hibernating. Give me Miss Greenwood's mail, will you, Stella? I've got to walk over to the Point today, might as well take it along."

There was a dead silence from inside the wicket, punctuated by slapping sounds as Stella hauled mail from a pigeonhole. Then she pushed up the wicket, thrust out a pile of assorted magazines, newspapers and envelopes.

"You'll need a sled, haul this," she said icily.

She banged the wicket down and turned away, and her voice came out stridently from the interior of the post office cubicle. "It'd be a favor to me if people'd pick up their mail when it comes, not leave a mess of it around to clutter up the office. Here I am, all stuffed-up with mail-order catalogs, I don't know how them mail-order stores know, but the minute the mail's heavy or there's ice in the bay or a bad storm, there'll be catalogs unlimited for Orin to lug and me to sort. Miss Greenwood gets more mail than any other five people on the island, and she ain't got it for a week."

"I know," Elbridge said. "I met her on the way home yesterday, halfway down the Point road. There's a foot-and-a-half of snow there in the road to wallow through, and she still had a mile to go to get home. She said she was by here about one o'clock. The office was closed."

"Well!" Stella said. "Of all the gall! Now you listen to me, Elbridge Gilman. A fourth-class post office, I'll have you know, don't pay enough, most people think you get rich, but I can't afford to spend all my time in here waiting for the summer people to make up their mind to come around and pick up their mail. I've got some other fish to fry, among them the Christmas pageant, besides in here behind this wicket. The mail is a free gift from Uncle Sam, but the way some people act, you'd think they paid five dollars an hour for it and fed the mailman. If they want their mail, they can be here when I am. That's all there is to it, not go around complaining to the selectmen because I ain't in the office at their convenience."

"All right, calm down," Elbridge said. "Nobody's complained to me, far as I know. But if the mail comes at twelve-thirty and you're closed up tight at one, makes it hard for some folks to get their mail. How's Luther standing the cold weather—he any better?"

"No, he ain't. And if I ain't got my nose right down onto the cussed grindstone in this store and post office fourteen hours out of the day, I guess that some people might tumble to the idea that I was in there tending to him."

"I expect so," Elbridge said. He buttoned his mackinaw, started for the door. "Tell him I'll be around to see him, first chance I get. There's some town business I want to talk over with him."

"That so?" Stell said. She put her face up close to the wicket again. "Want me to tell him what it is?"

"Kind of complicated to explain in a few words," Elbridge said. "Luther'd know offhand, though—something none of the rest of us is old enough to remember."

"Oh, I don't want to *know*," Stella said, withdrawing again. "Only poor Grampa—" her voice came, disembodied, out of the cubicle— "only poor Grampa, he ain't got much to take up his time. If he could have it to mull about—"

"About a deed," Elbridge said. "Tell him, a land title."

He went out, closing the door firmly behind him, and grinned as he heard the spate of talk start up in full force.

". . . don't suppose someone's going to sell some more land, do you?"

". . . might be George, he's—"

Elbridge walked along the road between the windrows of old snow, toward his own house. The road was icy, packed down by sled runners and horses' hooves, and the feet of people going to and from the store and kids going to school. He kept to the side, where a little powder snow made the walking easier under his felts-and-rubbers.

Well, he'd given Stell something else to think about besides being mad with him. No sense starting a row. The Lord knew, it was easy enough to start one, let it snowball, as it would be more than likely to, especially in the winter; for however you might feel about the summer people, they gave people something to do and something to talk about. Now, everyone was odd-jobbing around the house, living on credit; the weather made fishing a chancy thing, and the snow was too deep to cut wood. Just the time for two people, say, to have a tongue-lashing; and then, in a week or so, half the families on the island wouldn't be speaking to the other half, taking sides. It seldom made much difference what the issue was—might be some little disagreement that didn't amount to a hoot. This business of Stell's closing up the office right after the mail got in, for example, not even keeping the store open from one to four in the afternoon, was causing a lot of feeling. People were used to dropping in for mail or groceries whenever they felt like it. When old Luther MacGimsey kept the store, before he had his shock and wasn't able to, his custom was to open before daylight and close when the last customer left at nine or ten in the evening. But it was different with Luther; the store was his life, he had nothing else; and Stell, as she said, had other fish to fry. She was into church work up to her ears, president of the Ladies' Aid, and of the Quilt Society; for the last three weeks she had spent her afternoons rehearsing her part in the Christmas entertainment to be given at the church.

"I will *not* set around here the whole everlasting afternoon waiting for somebody to come get a package of saleratus and an advertisement for a truss," Stell said in the post office one day.

This would have offended everybody there, if it had not been a joke on Willard Lowden, whose mail for the day was the postcard bearing the truss ad. Willard was a fat man and sensitive about it; he did not need a truss, did not want one. It was bad enough to know that some truss company thought he looked as if he needed one—at least, they'd sent him a card—without having it pointed out to a whole storeful of people. He had said nothing, merely grinned sheepishly, at the time, but Elbridge knew he was still broody. Only yesterday Willard had said to him down at the wharf, "If a man's mail ain't private, Elbridge, what is?"

And Little Sarah, Elbridge's mother, had said last night, when he'd dropped in to see if she needed anything, "Stell had better be there when I go after *my* mail, that's all."

So, what with things building up the way they were, Elbridge had decided to speak to Stell, before someone blew up and caused a real hassle. He'd figured it could be done quite naturally by mentioning Miss Greenwood; everybody knew how far she had to walk through the snow for her mail, and besides, even though she lived on the island the year round now, and had for years, she was a foreigner, she was still summer people. Them you didn't get mad at the way you did at your neighbors, at least, not to their faces. Not Stell.

As far as he himself was concerned, sometime soon, when she'd had a chance to cool off, he'd drop around and see Luther, ask the old man to help him establish the boundaries of the old John Cloud place. Not that it would do much good. Old John Cloud probably had a couple of hundred heirs, living the Lord knew where, all over the country; the only one Elbridge could pin down for sure was his own wife, Jess, who was a cousin. The old place sat up there on the edge of the village, fields full of hardhack and puckerbrush, buildings dropping down, and this fellow from away darned interested in buying it; but Elbridge doubted if it could ever be legally sold. As first selectman and tax assessor, heir to MacKechnie's records, Elbridge knew about what there was to know about island property; only Luther MacGimsey knew more.

Luther was nearly the last of the old-timers, one of MacKechnie's men, a second cousin to old Sherebiah; he carried records—family relationships, boundaries, land titles—in his memory. After the quarries petered out, he had worked, still with MacKechnie, as a stonemason; then for years, he had kept store and post office. Now he was bedridden; and his grandson Warren's wife, Stella, ran his store and took care of him, Warren being dead. Whenever Elbridge went around to the house to talk with Luther, Stella always took care to sit in on the conversation. She wasn't likely to get too seriously put out with Elbridge, unless she had a lot of reason to. She was too interested in finding out what property was being bought or sold, as, Elbridge thought soberly, who wasn't?

He had never agreed with MacKechnie about the quarries coming back, or the good times either. In his own lifetime, which was thirty-four years, he had watched the island going down. The families who lived there now hung on by the skin of their teeth. They farmed a little, fished a little, scrabbled along for nine months of the year, waiting for three months of moderate prosperity when the summer people came. The houses might be built on rock which didn't crumble; but each year paint flaked off, clapboards and sills rotted, old shingles went sailing in the wind. The young men couldn't make a living; most of them couldn't get off the island fast enough, as soon as they were grown-up enough to leave home; like Roger, Elbridge's eldest, who was only sixteen, and who had a job now in the drugstore over at the Harbor. The houses showed the lack of young blood. Elbridge and his partner, Liseo MacGimsey, kept theirs in repair and so did Willard Lowden, doing the work themselves. But the only other really spruced-up ones were the summer cottages, which ringed the island shore solidly now, on three sides of the old village.

Elbridge didn't see how any economy could possibly be healthy, or ever return to prosperity, in a place where two-thirds of the taxable property was owned by people who didn't use it for nine months out of the year. At the same time, he didn't see what else could be done. Without the fat taxes the summer people paid, and without the jobs they offered in the summer, the island would be done for. Outside of Stell's store, he and Liseo MacGimsey had the only business possible. They owned the wharf at the end of MacKechnie's old breakwater.

Ten years ago, starting on a shoestring, they had rebuilt the wharf, shingling the aged sheds and remodeling them to accommodate fishermen's gear and bait. They sold marine supplies—rope and hardware, laths and nails, sills and heads and pockets for lobster traps, work gloves, paint; and they bought lobsters and groundfish in season, which they in turn boated over to the mainland and resold to the dealers there. Once in a while, they got an order from some city construction company for a little cut granite. When they did, they hired the Lowden "boys," George and Willard, to cut and haul it down from the quarry and load it on the scow. There was never very much—a few sidewalk curbings, maybe, or blocks for a house foundation or a fireplace; and, of course, they didn't have the equipment, now, to handle anything heavy, even if there'd been any call for it.

It was hardly worth doing—a side line, no profit to speak of. It gave George and Willard an occasional job and kept the old craft of stonecutting from dying out altogether. Not much point—the world had outgrown a good many of the old crafts and skills, like soap-making, or putting together a good flail, or, if you had to admit it, stonecutting. But Elbridge had a feeling about it—the same feeling he had seeing a hayfield grown up to puckerbrush and alders. Something valuable was being lost. That land had been hard to clear. The old-timers had put a lot into what they'd tried to do. And while they were doing it, they'd amounted to something as people. Elbridge had said something like that to his son, Roger.

"Well, look at them now," said Roger.

He was sixteen, inclined to put things strong, and, besides, he was trying to persuade his father to let him take a job over on the mainland.

"Look at them now. Take in each other's washing all winter, and suck up to the summer people for handouts all summer. Not me. I won't clean mud off of anybody's old tennis shoes."

"All right, all right," Elbridge said. "I don't know as I do that, either."

"I know you don't, Pop," Roger said, slowing down a little. He grinned sheepishly. "You do all right, too."

"I guess maybe you use what there is in your own time and place," Elbridge said. "Like last century—" and stopped, aware that he was talking to Roger like a father to a son, which he didn't often feel called upon to do. They understood each other pretty well, he and Roger.

Roger paid him back at once. "Like last century it was granite," he said swiftly. "And this century it's summer people and scenery."

"All right," Elbridge said. "I'm a feeble old man and you've out-shuffled me. Try it if you want to. If you don't like it, come on home and no bones broken. Wouldn't want to go to school over there, along with Rosie?"

Liseo was sending his girl Rosie over to the mainland this winter, to the high school; Elbridge suspected that one reason—maybe the main reason—that Roger was so keen to go was because Rosie was going; but Roger didn't want to go to school. He said it would be a waste of time, and Elbridge was inclined to agree with him. Roger was not interested in books; he was active, too full of restless energy to sit still and read; he liked learning things by doing them. Elbridge himself had taught him a lot, outside of what he'd picked up in the grammar school, which didn't seem to be much.

The teachers who were willing to come to an off-the-map place like Chin Island were, mostly, those who couldn't find a job else-where—either busted-down old maids or young girls just out of school. So far as Elbridge could see, their idea of an education was speaking pieces, or writing little compositions on "What I See In The Sunset," or drawing pictures of sea shells. They weren't to be blamed —probably did the best they could with what they had. But Elbridge and his wife, Jess, themselves taught their children to read and write and figure, feeling that if they had those well pounded in, they'd be able to pick up whatever else they needed to do their work in the world.

"No," Roger said now, "I'll get what I want, without having it poured into me."

He'll be all right, Elbridge thought. He's young, but what of it?

Elbridge himself had been married, his household established, at seventeen.

So he had let Roger go and missed him painfully, for they had been close. And Roger missed him, he knew; in every letter he wrote, he put forth a new argument why his father ought to move his family and his business over to the mainland.

Sometimes Elbridge thought about moving away; but when it came down to the actual going, he found he didn't want to. He was too bound up with the island; he supposed he liked the life he lived here. He and Liseo would never get rich or be even comfortably off, but they'd kept their families comfortable. Through the times of hard-scrabbling, there'd always been enough to eat and wear. The years since Liseo had got back from the war had even been pretty good ones; they'd put a little money by. They both knew that a couple of bad years could bankrupt them, as with any business, so far as Elbridge could see, that ran entirely on credit. The way it worked, people never could catch up—they slaved all summer to pay last winter's bills and came into next winter no better, maybe a little worse, off than they'd been before. It might be a losing game—he suspected that it was—but it was all there was left to hold the place together. If he and Liseo pulled out, everything would go. And, somehow, he didn't want to be the one to give it that last push.

The feeling, he knew, was all mixed up with the past and with old MacKechnie's dreams—a feeling almost as strong as grief, over something worthwhile wasted, lost; though why it should be kept he couldn't say, now that the world had gone on and passed it by.

He walked on through the village, past shut and decaying houses, past MacKechnie's house where Little Sarah, his mother, now lived alone. She was in the front window, watching for him; but he shook his head to indicate there hadn't been any mail for her, and then held up Roger's letter. She'd know that either he or Jess would bring it over later, that now he had to get home to dinner. She'd know, too, from the grin on his face, that Roger was coming home for Christmas.

Little Sarah was sixty-seven this year; she didn't need to live alone; both he and Jess would have been tickled to death to have her with them. But she was strong and capable still, never had a sick day in her life. She liked the old house, she said, liked to be alone with her own things around her, though as to being alone, she wasn't, much. Somebody was always going in to visit, and the kids, his own and the neighbors', were in and out of the house. He kept an eye on her, sent the boys over to do chores, made sure she was comfortable. Another reason, he thought, smiling a little to himself, why he couldn't possibly move away, even if he wanted to.

I'd transplant, I guess, after a while; but I'd sure like to see anybody transplant Little Sarah.

He turned the corner, where the road forked off toward the shore, and started down the slope toward his own house. George and Willard Lowden were coming up, also headed for home and dinner, he guessed, it being the time of day. George walked six paces in front, as he always did, Willard puffed along behind. Seeing them, no one would have guessed that they were brothers. George was a slight, talkative man, with a drooping handle-bar mustache, which, far from making him look sad, seemed to flip when he talked, and gave to his thin, hatchet face a comedian effect. Willard was a mountain of melancholy flesh. He wore a massive sheepskin coat, battered and salt-stained, ripped in places, and he crunched along in creepers—flat metal strips bent downward in sharp points and strapped under the instep of his rubber boots to keep him from slipping on ice or snow. George was in oilskins, and carried in his mittened hand a skinned haddock by the tail.

"Hi," he said. "Going to snow some more, Elbridge."

"Might," Elbridge said.

He hadn't noticed before, but now he realized that the sky, which had started the day clear-blue and cloudless, had lost color—not misted over, it was still blue, but grayed out a little, as if someone had breathed on it.

"Looks like it," George said. "Darned if it don't. That's one thing we don't need any more of, by gorry. Stayed on this winter, ain't it?"

It had; a heavy fall in November hadn't melted a bit; it still lay deep, a foot and a half on fields, two feet in woods. It had stopped everybody's winter woodcutting nearly a month ago.

"I was kind of hoping for a thaw first," Elbridge said.

Willard hove-to alongside George, and stood ponderously breathing. The slope up from the shore was moderate but continuous, and besides, it was icy. Any slope was difficult for a man of Willard's weight. He preferred level ground. He also preferred weather either warm or cool; he hated winter's cold and summer's heat, and had no patience with storms of any kind, feeling that the universe, or the Lord, or whatever power handled extremes, was aiming them right straight at him.

"You can't count on nothing, nowadays," Willard said, between puffs. "Thaw or snow, whatever you don't want, you get."

His voice, a clear baritone, was surprising, for so big a man. In spite of Willard's outlook, Elbridge always liked to hear him talk. Sad observations, glum prophecies poured out of him, but the sound he made was, nonetheless, a pleasant one. He was a fine singer, too —sang in the church choir, and at the school and Christmas entertainments. He had a vast collection of songs—hymns, ballads, westerns, old-time tear-jerkers—and could go on for hours, accompanying himself on a small, aged accordion, without a false note or a wheeze. It was only when he had to move his vast body that Willard lost his breath.

"Maybe have an old-fashioned winter," Elbridge said.

"No, we won't," Willard said. "Nothing like that. Nothing so good. Old-fashioned winter, four-five feet of snow in the woods, you could set home, wait for spring. Rain one day, twizzle round, snow the next, catch you halfway to the wood lot with your ax and saw. Worry, worry, worry, can't get your wood cut, worry, worry, worry, cut it, can't haul it, I don't know why the whole of us don't plain give up."

"Oh, for cramp sake, Wid!" George said. "The wood'll get cut, we'll haul it, same's we always have. Wait till spring, what of it?"

"Then there'll come a thaw, melt *all* the snow," Willard said. "Can't use the wood sled, have to swamp a road in to the wood lot, get the cart in there. Then bust the cart, pounding it over the stumps."

"All right, all right," George said. He spun around to Elbridge, grinning. The volatile ends of his mustache seemed to lift and blow with the energy of his words. "Needs a dost of physic all winter long, Wid does. Wish he'd take one. Sets, from October to April, then worry, worry, worry, for fear he'll get fat."

His imitation of Willard was unmistakable; in spite of himself, Elbridge grinned, and then wished he hadn't.

Willard blushed. His big, beefy face with the folds of flesh and the multitudinous chins turned a delicate pink. He glanced away and then back, and said, with a dispirited air, "My soul, Elbridge, is all that mail *yours?*"

"Miss Greenwood's," Elbridge said. "Thought I'd take a walk over to the Point this afternoon."

"Oh, yeah, meant to tell you," George said. "Liseo said wait for him, he'll walk along with you." His eyebrow lifted, his eyes rolled, in a manner unmistakably lewd. "What you two fellas expect to find, down amongst all them petticoats?"

It was a suggestion so ridiculous that it needed no answer, and George expected none. He went on, "More petticoats, I guess. You know, I counted up one day Imogene was hanging out them Greenwoods' washing, they was fourteen, seven petticoats apiece them two ladies dirt up in one week's time, my Lord, Elbridge, don't make sense, does it?"

"Change their clothes every day, for godsake, George," Willard said. "More'n you'n I can afford to. Two pairs of long johns, that's all I got, going into the winter."

"You're in a hard way," George said. "Sometimes I can't sleep nights for crying."

"Liseo shutting up shop, is he?" Elbridge asked.

"Oh, my Lord, yes, it's rougher'n hell. No boats out. I hauled this morning, went a little ways outside The Pasture, took an awful jouncing. Must be a helmonious old storm making up, off out there somewhere. Funny, too, ain't a mite of wind. Oh, and say, that Novie lumber schooner, that three-master, is laying offshore about three miles, yeeing and yawing around with the tide. I'll bet they're whistling for wind."

"They better," Willard said ominously. "Clawing around out there in that passage, with the weather making on. That's a hell of a way to haul lumber, anyway. Them old coasters, they ain't safe."

George jerked his head. "Listen to him," he said. "Safe, that's all he thinks about. Maybe that's all the way them Novies got to haul their lumber. Safe! Why, I can remember the time when old Nikolaides had the salt store, there'd be three miles of them Gloucester schooners anchored stern to bowsprit off this island, waiting turn to load salt for the trip to the Banks, and for a crack at Aunt Tilson Vira's whorehouse. Me, I wouldn't mind a ride on either one, would you, Elbridge? A two- or a three-masted schooner, I mean. Oh, come on along home, Wid. Harriet's dinner'll be cold and we'll all catch hell."

He set off up the road, swinging his haddock, Willard crunching along six paces behind. Elbridge thought, as he turned into his own gate, If you ever saw one of the Lowden "boys" out alone, or Willard walking in front instead of George, you could be pretty sure one of them was sick, or they'd had a quarrel. George needled Willard all the time, and generally Willard took it, but once in a while he got mad, and then, if he could get his hands on George, he would thrash him. They had been like that ever since Elbridge could remember; George would appear with a bruised face or a black eye one day, and start right in plaguing Willard again. Nobody ever saw the fight.

There were those who said that Harriet, their sister, was the one who did the thrashing, and Elbridge thought that might be likely. Harriet was a big, raw-boned woman, twice the size of George, and lean, without Willard's flesh. She was tremendously strong. She ruled the "boys" with a rod of iron; Elbridge wouldn't have put it past her to take on Willard himself, if she felt there was reason for it.

The Lowdens were all that was left of the Horn family; Harriet Horn, who married George Lowden, both now dead. They were in their fifties, none of them married; Harriet kept house for the "boys" in the old Horn farmhouse at the edge of the village.

Elbridge went up the back steps of his own house, stopping to kick the snow off his feet before he went into the entry. Jess usually left the broom out, but today she'd forgotten it. He was stamping and kicking at a great rate, trying to dislodge frozen lumps from the buckles of his rubbers, when the door opened a crack and Jess's hand came through holding the broom.

"Good," Elbridge said. "That's what we need."

He took the broom and left in her hand Roger's letter.

"Oh, good!" Jess said. "That's what we need, too. Is he all right?"

"He's fine," Elbridge said. "Rosie got A in algebra and they'll both be home Friday on the mail boat."

He finished sweeping his rubbers and followed her into the kitchen, carefully closing the entry door. "The rest of it you'll have to read out loud to me. Stell was talking in tongues over in the post office, and I couldn't take anything in."

"Oh, my," Jess said. She had hauled the letter out of the envelope on her way across the kitchen to the rocking chair by the window, and by the time she got sat down she was already reading it. "Oh, Elbridge, he's—" Her eyes were already going on to the next paragraph, and the words dissolved into chuckles. "Well, there, think of it, and he only—"

She rocked back and forth in the chair a little, lowered the letter and looked at Elbridge, her eyes brimming with glee. "Well, I've got a pair most done, I'll—" flipping over a page, hurrying along the neat, schoolboy-cramped lines.

Elbridge stood watching her, grinning a little, while he took off his outdoor rig and hung it up on the hooks back of the entry door. It was worth the price of a show anytime, to watch Jess read a letter from Roger.

He picked up the letter himself as she laid it down, and sat down to read it while Jess dished up dinner. He found it a little hard to keep his mind on. The kitchen was full of a wonderful smell of chowder and hot bread; Jess had baked cookies and pies this morning, too, which were spread out, cooling, all over the counter top. Presently the kids, Joyce, thirteen, and the twins, Gib and Will, came roaring in, ravenous, from school. Elbridge laid the letter down. Roger was all right; he'd be home soon; the rest of it could wait. Tonight, after the kids had gone to bed, and he and Jess were sitting together, he'd get her to read it to him.

Besides, the kids wanted to read it. They came over, as soon as they'd washed their hands, Joyce first, getting a head start, handing the sheets to the boys as she finished them. They stood side by side, their three heads, one black—Joyce's—and two red, close together, absorbed in Roger's letter.

"Hey, wait, hey, wait," Will said. "I haven't got that page done. Don't turn it *over*, Gib."

Joyce was skimming along, her eyes flying from one line to the next, reading the letter, so much like her mother that Elbridge had to grin. Smart as a whip, like Jess, quick-moving and small-boned, but strong. The twins were more like him, looked like him; big, freckled and sturdy. Will was a little slower than Gib, took him longer to take things in, but once he did, he had them. It tickled Elbridge to see the kids growing up to look so much like him and Jess. Roger was like his mother, too, except there was nothing small about him. At seventeen, he was taller even than his father, and there were times when he almost seemed to crackle with energy, the way Jess did.

Elbridge pulled up to the table, aware that Will, pulling up in the chair beside him, had put off Roger's letter, not because it was unimportant, but because of more immediate matters.

"Hoe in," he said cordially to Will. "You could go a long ways around the world and not find a thing prettier'n your ma's table, right now."

Jess did set a pretty table. On a yellow oilcloth she had put blue bowls of steaming chowder, with, at each place, one of Big Sarah MacKechnie's thin old silver knives and spoons, rubbed shining. The pat of homemade butter, stamped with an oak leaf and acorn, matched the tablecloth. A loaf of bread, pale brown and crusty, fresh from the oven, shared a platter with a stack of crisp brown pilot crackers, beside a glass bowl of mustard pickles and another one full of the spiced crab apples that Will loved, pale pink with brown freckles and stems, in amber syrup. The kids had glasses of milk, yellow with cream; the cream for the coffee, which Jess had just skimmed from a milk pan in the buttery, was clotted almost too thick to pour out of the pitcher. And two kinds of pie to come.

Gib said thickly, "Ma's prettier'n the table," and Elbridge, glancing over at her, saw that this was so.

He grinned. "Shut up, Gib," he said. "I ought to've said that. Would have, if I'd thought of it first."

"Never mind pretty," Jess said briskly. She was pleased, though. Her cheeks were pink, and her soft black hair, dampened with the rush and hurry over the hot kitchen stove, curled back in tiny ringlets from her face. "You kids have got to rush back to school, and I've got a million things this afternoon. So eat up."

"What's so busy about this afternoon?" Elbridge asked, and stopped, aware that all four pairs of eyes were fixed on him in horrified reproach.

"Why, you know as well as I do," Jess said. "The school time at the church tonight. I've been cooking like crazy for three days, and I've still got to make the prize tropic-aroma cake. At least, I hope it wins the prize. That quilt's a beauty. And you've got to freeze ice cream. Where've you been for the last week?"

"Oh, sure, sure, slipped my mind," Elbridge said, and then went on hastily, "just for the moment, that is. I was thinking about the wood lot, darned if it don't look as if it's going to snow some more."

"Pa!" Joyce said. "And I said my piece all through to you last night! You didn't even listen!"

"Sure, I did. Sure, I listened. About a dead hoss," Elbridge said. "Sure it was—about a dead hoss."

"Yes, it was!"

Joyce put back her head and intoned mournfully:

> "Only a fallen horse,
> Stretched out there in the road,
> Pierced by the broken shafts,
> And crushed by the heavy load—"

"That's right," Elbridge said hastily.

He hoped she wouldn't insist on saying the darned piece at the table, spoil a man's dinner, not that he'd hurt her feelings by stopping her if she did. Joyce thought it was a lovely piece, beautiful and sad. She could hardly keep her voice from trembling with grief as she spoke it.

Will said, "Wipe the cracker off your lip," and both boys began to giggle, but Jess shook her head at them firmly.

"Eat up," she said. "It's a pretty piece and Joyce's worked hard learning to speak it. But we've none of us got time to listen to it this noon, dear, it's an awful busy day. You save it for tonight."

Joyce went amiably back to her chowder, and Elbridge breathed an inner sigh of relief. The teacher they had this term went in for sad pieces. She must have a whole book of them tucked away somewhere, for she'd handed them out, according to Will, to the whole roomful of scholars. And not only to the scholars. There were two or three mothers who always liked to speak pieces, and Miss Warren had found good old tear-drippers for everyone.

"Death and destruction," Will said, glumly. "It's enough to kill you."

To Will, Miss Warren had assigned, "Curfew Shall Not Ring Tonight," and there had been a hassle over it. It was a long poem, about a girl whose sweetheart was going to be hung at curfew-time, so she went up into the belfry and hung by her hands from the bell clapper, kept it from ringing. Saved the fellow's life. Will refused to speak it, on grounds, he said, that it was too long; he couldn't learn it in the six weeks before the Christmas entertainment. After Miss Warren had spent a while working on him, she decided he couldn't. So she had assigned him something else.

There wasn't much difference, Will assured his father. The new one began, "Tell me not in mournful numbers, Life is but an empty dream."

Elbridge and Will had been out in the wood lot, a month ago, eating their lunch around a brush fire, when Will had first started to complain about Miss Warren's sad pieces. Elbridge couldn't say he blamed Will much. Having to speak a piece was bad enough anyway, without having to speak one that made you feel like a fool. He suddenly remembered his own embarrassment, at the age of twelve, with "Up the airy mountain, Down the rushy glen."

"Gib don't care," Will burst out. "He's got one, too, but he's learnt it and he ribbles it off and gets it over. I wish I was like Gib."

"Gib's like your Uncle Ralph used to be," Elbridge said. "You're more like me, I guess."

Gib was, he recalled suddenly, quite a lot like Ralph at the age of twelve—heedless, full of the old Nick, active, with a dozen irons in the fire and a hundred fish to fry. His feelings didn't get hurt, either, the way Will's did. Things slid off of Gib.

"You know," Elbridge said to Will, who was disconsolately gnawing a doughnut, on the other side of the fire. "That piece about the curfew's in every school speaker I ever saw. I don't know what there is about a young girl's hanging by her hands from a bell clapper to fire up an old maid schoolteacher, but it always seems to."

"Well, it don't make sense. That girl couldn't have done it, in the first place."

"Shake her up some, I should think," Elbridge agreed.

"And in the second place, they'd hung the feller, whether the bell rung or not, wouldn't they?"

"Likely would."

"Well," Will said. He bounced the remaining quarter of his doughnut hard into the fire. "It takes away my appetite, just thinking about it. Makes me want to puke."

"Does, kind of. Don't waste your ma's good doughnuts, though, you'll come hungry. You know, Will, there's an awful good take-off on that curfew poem, if only a feller could remember it."

"There is? What?"

"Well, it was about a fellow went to call on a girl where there was a bulldog, got his pants tore. I recollect it was called, 'Towser Shan't Be Tied Tonight.' Yes, for a fact, it was."

"What was it? You know it, Pop?"

For the first time in a week, Will perked up, began to show an interest in something.

"Used to. Le'me think."

Elbridge probed back. His mind, Jess said, was cluttered up with all kinds of things, songs and poems and quotations, tag ends that had stuck with him. He remembered cutting the poem out of a paper and learning it; it was a long time ago. Then, suddenly, the page of the paper it was in, The *Farmer's Hearth and Home*, for April 16, 1913, page 4, spread itself before his memory, sharp and clear, like a picture; and he said the poem to Will.

Will began to roar partway through; when Elbridge finished, it was a minute before he could speak.

"Oh, gee!" he said. "Oh, gee! If I could only have that one, instead of that awful crap I've got—" He rocked back and forth on the stump, and his cap fell off, showing his red curls, flattened by the tight cap, but already beginning to spring up, alive and bright and wiry.

Something caught in Elbridge's chest at the sight, just why he could not have said. Old Will, he thought; and aloud he said, before he could stop himself, "Well, why not?"

Will looked at him, awed. "You mean learn that one on the side, and then speak it instead of the one on death and destruction?"

"I don't know as it would do," Elbridge said. "That's pretty deceitful, Will," but in spite of himself, he grinned as he said it. After all, a good entertainment ought to have some light stuff, as well as heavy, in it. What harm could it do, besides taking some of the load off Will? He'd been glum for days. Serve the teacher right.

Privately, though he wouldn't say so out loud, Elbridge didn't have a good deal of use for Miss Warren. She seemed like kind of an odd stick, a tall, willowy girl without much substance, except for very highly colored lips and cheeks. She never had much to say; if you spoke to her, unexpectedly, she would wiggle and gasp around before she answered you, in a sweet, soft voice that, like as not, fell away to a whisper before she got a full sentence out. At Imogene Cayford's, where she boarded, she could sometimes be prevailed upon to sing, accompanying herself on Imogene's parlor organ, but it took a lot of coaxing. Elbridge had heard her once, one night last fall, when she first came; he and Jess had gone around to Imogene's to call, as interested as anyone to meet the new schoolteacher; and there she sat, in the front room, not saying a word for the whole evening, just smiling a funny pursed-up smile and looking off into space, while Imogene coaxed her to sing. At last, when everybody was about worn out, she had—got up and played and sung "Put My Little Shoes Away," in a high voice as thin as a knife-blade, with her wrists arched up like the neck of a swan, and her little fingers stuck straight out. The performance had fascinated Elbridge; Jess had had to poke him to make him stop craning his neck and looking.

A few days later, Imogene reported that that color in Miss Warren's lips and cheeks was natural—some of the ladies had been saying it was too red to be. But it must be, Imogene said, she'd underrun every one of her things and hadn't found one sign of a rouge pot.

"If she's got one, she carries it with her in her corsets," Imogene said. "There ain't a sign of one amongst her things."

Elbridge told Jess privately that he wouldn't care if she painted her head blue, if only she could teach school. Up to now, he hadn't seen any very hopeful signs; and an entertainment, she apparently thought, was something you ought to sit and cry tears through.

"H'm," he said now to Will. "I expect this'd better be between you and me, Will. I don't believe we'd better let even your ma know what we're up to."

"Oh, sure," Will said. His eyes were shining. "I'll get that other fool thing down pat and say it at all the rehearsals."

And so, for some Saturdays after that and nights after school when Will was out and around with him, Elbridge coached him in the stanzas of "Towser Shan't Be Tied Tonight." All in all, it was quite a funny poem; give him something to look forward to the night of the school time; keep him awake, maybe.

He looked down at Will's tousled red head at the table beside him. "You've got your piece learnt, all okay, I hope, Will," and Will looked up at him soberly. "Oh, sure," he said, "if I can get through the foolish thing without puking."

"Ssh," Jess said. "At the table, Will!"

"S-s'cuse me," Will muttered. His eyes, looking at his father, were dancing and Jess glanced suspiciously at the two of them; but she said nothing, merely got up and began to clear away the pie plates. "Run along," she said over her shoulder. "Don't be late to school, and, Joyce, you come home early as you can, won't you, so I can make sure your costume's just right."

Joyce was in one of the tableaux, "Snow Maidens," and Jess had had a time getting some gilt snowflakes to stick to the net on the white dress she'd made for her.

The kids clattered out of the house. Elbridge sat for a moment, feeling the comfort of his good dinner warm inside his ribs, while Jess rattled the dishes out of the way at the sink.

He said, "You got anything for me to take over to Miss Greenwood?"

"I saw you had her mail," Jess said. "I've been putting some things in a basket. I've got lots of extra milk, take a can of that, and, oh, yes, there's that pat of sweet butter I saved out for her from the salt. I thought maybe she'd be in today."

"She was over yesterday. She didn't get this far. The snow's some deep down on that Point road. Tried to get her mail, but Stell was out gadding."

"Oh, that's a shame," Jess said. "Poor old soul, walk all that way for nothing. Stell was over to the church, rehearsing. I wondered at the time if anybody in town had been able to get mail."

"Stell on the program, too, is she?"

"With bells on. She's got a piece to speak, and she's Mother Earth in one of the tableaux."

Elbridge grinned.

"Should think she'd make a dandy," he said. "Who's Father Earth?"

"Stop it," Jess said. She giggled a little. "You'll grow into a dirty-minded old man. Here, take this basket when you go. Tell Miss Greenwood the stale loaf is for her chickadees' dinner."

"My Lord," Elbridge said. "Those two old ladies'll never be able to eat all this stuff in a week, Jess."

"Well," Jess said. "Stuck out on that Point a mile and a half from anybody. Oh, Elbridge, if we could only persuade her to bring her mother over to the village for the rest of the winter!"

"Well, you know all about that. Stubborn's a mule."

Jess nodded. "She won't even talk about it any more. Just gives that funny laugh, says nothing will happen. I suppose nothing will, but it gives me the cold chills, thinking."

"Nothing has so far," Elbridge said.

He put on his coat and cap, hooked the basket over one arm, and leaned over to kiss Jess.

"Dirty-minded old man, eh?" he said.

"M'm," Jess said.

THE Greenwood ladies, Miss Roxinda and her mother, were a mystery to the village and had been from the beginning, though at first, perhaps, no more so than other people "from away." The island was accustomed to summer visitors. Forerunners of the present ones had begun coming over from the mainland as long ago as when the steamboat was running, fascinated by the boat ride and the workings of MacKechnie's quarries; at that time, they boarded around the village with whoever had rooms to let, and some of them stayed all summer. After the quarries closed, and people began to sell shore property, they bought it and built cottages. There was hardly a piece of shore property left which didn't have a summer cottage on it. Others came now, in launches, on picnics for the day; but all of them were gone, usually by Labor Day. One or two families might linger into September, or even October, if they had no children who had to be got back to school.

Miss Greenwood and her mother, at first, were among these early comers and late goers. Their house was open in May, and not until the first spit of snow fell did they close it up and go back to the city. Some said one city, some said another. The Greenwoods had not said. They seemed to have lived in many places, at one time or another. From the beginning, they caused speculation—by not saying definitely where they were from, by the way they dressed, neat and genteel but odd and old-fashioned, by Miss Greenwood's looks, by the kind of a house they wanted built.

Elbridge well remembered when the Greenwood cottage was built. As a boy of sixteen, he had worked on it, helping Luther Mac-Gimsey, who had put in its foundation. The house was on the easternmost point of the island, overlooking the sea. It was set high, on top of a ledge to begin with, a cellar made possible only by building up from the rock with big, rectangular blocks of stone. He remembered Luther's comments when at last he realized where Miss Greenwood wanted her house, all professional advice to the contrary.

Luther was used to having the summer people take his advice; after all, he was the stone man, he was the one who knew. If he said that a house cocked up there on that Point, facing east, with not even a tree between it and the ocean, would get the full sweep of the east and northeast gales; if he said that every mite of water used would have to be lugged from a spring two hundred yards away, because that was where the ledge petered out, and no well could be dug nearer the house, why, he expected people who didn't know—weren't supposed to know—nothing about such things to take some account of what he said. Most people would have. Not Miss Greenwood.

She said she liked easterlies. The bigger the better.

"The bigger the better by thirty-five hundred miles, by the time they cross all that open water from here to Europe," Luther told her.

Even then he was white-whiskered as Father Christmas, and when he talked to the summer people, benevolence flowed out of him smooth as molasses.

Miss Greenwood said not thirty-five hundred miles, surely, Mr. MacGimsey, because of the peninsula of Nova Scotia.

It jolted Luther. He had altered plans for summer cottages all over the coast, using that argument; had set them back a little from the shore, snug among trees, where, to his thinking, they ought to be. A foundation was easier built that way; cut stone was heavy to haul over ledges.

He said, "Nova Scotia or not, I've seen the sea up to this ledge, and over it. Liable to wash right off of there, a house is, in a bad storm. You don't know what them winter storms is like, I guess."

She said, "But surely you can build a foundation wall strong enough? Like a lighthouse?"

And there she had him, because Luther had already bragged to her that he had built lighthouses with MacKechnie, one of them on a

bare rock out in the ocean, where the terrible easterlies had never
stirred a block of their masonry.

Luther said icily that without doubt he could build a lasting wall,
bolted to the ledge, none better, and would do it, if that was what
she wanted. The house would look funny up there on top of that
ledge like a shag on a channel marker.

Miss Greenwood said, oh, she liked the view.

Luther said it would have to have double-strong construction,
heavy stringers and so on. And then he played his trump card. He
said ominously, "It'll cost you."

She said, "But no more than it will be worth to me, Mr. MacGim-
sey."

When the house was finished—and to her own plan—it hadn't even
a gable to split the wind. It had a French roof; a flat expanse of
uncompromising wall reared up to the naked east, pierced by many
windows—an ugly house without a thing to soften it. Raw lumber
color at first, except for the trim which was painted white, it toned
down somewhat through the years. Miss Greenwood was a great
gardener, and her shrubs and flowers, where she could make them
grow, softened a little the rugged outlines.

Gardening on top of those ledges was a chore most people
wouldn't have attempted. The land was, of course, solid rock. Every
bit of what salty earth there was—and there was little—had to be
replaced with growing soil. One of the first things Miss Greenwood
bought, after she got settled in, was a pint-sized wheelbarrow, a little
bigger than a child's—for she was a small lady, not much bigger than
a child herself. She spent hours, every summer, wheeling dung from
barnyards across the island, leafmold and black soil from the swamp.
It took years before she had flowers growing in all those nooks and
crannies.

The flowers were pretty, no one could deny. You would come up
over a shoulder of granite and there would be a clump of harebells,
or a patch of portulaca, sprouting out of a crevice in the rock. It
took her a long time to find the kind of roses that salt spray wouldn't
hurt; but now, on a June day, with the sea wind blowing, you could
smell her hedge of rugosas long before you came in sight of the house.
She had a walled garden—also Luther's masonry—in which the soil
stayed fairly sweet and which went crazy with bloom every summer.
But every winter, in the gales, the sea washed around her house,
carried a good deal of her work away.

In time, she got woodbine to grow across her porch; even that and the soft gray of weathered shingles didn't change the stubborn jut of the house toward the sky and water. Stuck up in the face of everything, as Luther said, as if she would say, "Be damned to all."

The masonry in the house was a marvel, too, high up on the ledge for all to see what Luther could do if he wanted to, if he got mad enough. It had been years since Elbridge had given up being a stonemason; but he could remember now the pleasure it had been to watch old Luther cut out and fit a granite block, working with the grain of the stone. MacKechnie had always said Luther was the best man with stone he ever saw, and Elbridge could believe it. The rock cistern in Miss Greenwood's cellar built to hold rain water caught from the eaves—for she had fooled Luther even on the water supply, having to carry only her drinking water from the spring—was morticed and overlapped until it was as tight as a ship. Luther bragged that if people would let him alone, not pester him with their goddamned notions, he could build any kind of a rock thing and not use mortar; but they wouldn't let him alone. So he used mortar.

"A rock cistern, Luther?" Elbridge asked.

"Yes, by joppy, a rock cistern," Luther said. "Hold water, too, if I set my mind to make it."

Packing up his tools to go home, after he had finished Miss Greenwood's fireplace and chimney, Luther said grimly, "She won't wash off of there."

"I don't see how she could," Elbridge said.

"But by gorry, there'll be times when she'll wring the salt water out of her drawers," Luther said. "And whilst she's hanging them out on the line to dry, she can look at her view." He slammed his plug and feathers into his tool bag. "Crazy as a loon. Cracked as a pot," he said, and went home.

Look at her view she surely could. Her north windows faced the mainland, and the green bay islands—the ones she called the "tame" islands. To the south were other islands, with reefs, ledges, surf-submerged shores. She had the stunted spruces behind her, of the eastern base of MacKechnie's hill, nudging up to her small lawn so close that when she cut the grass she had to lift up their lowest branches to get the edges clean, and the mower was clogged with sprills. But away and open to the east was the thing she said she had come there for—the North Atlantic, stretching from the black ledges of The Pasture to the sky.

She said she liked what she had. Her east windows were always

streaked with salt; in a full gale flowerpots washed off her porch and
the sea sent streaming runnels of foam down across the lawn.

Luther, at ninety, still maintained that Miss Greenwood was crazy.
He lived now from his bed to the rocking chair in the window at
Stell's, spent his time watching people go by.

"There goes Aunt Greeny," he would cry, cackling, as her slight,
black-clothed figure passed. "Crazy as a loon. Cracked as a pot! Look
at the damned old crow!"

She was some twenty years younger than he was; but so much
for her, standing up to him when he should have been the one to
say.

Well, she was certainly odd in a good many ways, but Elbridge
wouldn't go along with anyone who said she was crazy, even cracked.
She was stubborn as a mule, and a defier of custom, who went se-
renely her own way without its ever entering her head that she was
either. It didn't go down very well with Willard Lowden and some
others who made at least a part of their living hiring out to summer
people, that Miss Greenwood wouldn't hire done one speck of work
that she could do herself, take the work right out of an honest man's
mouth. And then, if she did hire a man to do a job, she wouldn't
take his advice, but would come sticking in between him and what
he was doing, right where she wasn't wanted and didn't belong.
Like the time she hired Willard to clean out her backhouse, and
Willard had come back from the Point sweating, profoundly shocked
and embarrassed.

It wouldn't have been no job at all if she'd let him dump the stuff
on the ledges like he wanted to, tide come up wash everything away
nice and clean; no, she made him lug it all out in the woods and
bury it in a pile of old leaves and trash she called her compost pit.
Twice as much work, and when he found out that that pile was
going to be the fertilizer she used on her vegetable garden, he like
to puked.

He was telling Elbridge and Liseo about it, down on the wharf,
and some others standing by, and Elbridge said, "Why, you use cow
on yours, Willard, what's the difference?"

Well, hell, Willard didn't know, but there was a big difference. It
was the idea of it. And what was more, it wasn't any place for a lady
to be, around a backhouse when it was being cleaned out. That was
the time for the wimmenfolks to stay in the house.

Liseo said innocently, "Why, I thought I saw Harriet cleaning out yours, just the other day, Willard, burying it, too, in your turnip patch."

And Willard said, astonished, "Why, I guess likely you did. It's the easiest place to dig, ain't it?"

To Elbridge's way of thinking, if anybody lived in a place as an outsider, and looked, talked and acted different from everyone else, it was bound to have an effect. With anyone like that, ordinary things could be twisted around, quite easily, to look peculiar. Miss Greenwood must have a natural interest in anything that would make plants grow; so did he, or any other gardener. And anyone who had ever hired Willard to do a job of work knew that you had to stand over him if you wanted it done your way. But that was Willard. That was Willard for you.

Elbridge could see that this compost incident was going to be repeated and relished; one more proof that Miss Greenwood was cracked as a pot. Along with others, such as that she talked to herself when she felt like it, ribbling along as if two people were carrying on a conversation; and she tamed the birds and squirrels in her woods, wouldn't let anyone hunt there, or shoot sea birds or set mink traps along her piece of shore line.

That hadn't gone down well either with some. Of course other summer people put up no-trespassing signs, too; but they were only there for three months in the summer when it didn't matter. After they'd gone, nobody paid any attention to their signs. Miss Greenwood's shore line included the small lagoon between The Pasture and the Point, which was one of the best places for ducks along the coast. Millions of birds had been shot there since time out of mind—why, one of the island industries in the old days had been eiderdown, sea birds' feathers. Whole vessel loads had been shipped to Boston every winter and sold to make featherbeds.

That lagoon was public property, the talk went. It belonged to everybody, the way the wharf did. Hell, Elbridge owned the wharf, but he didn't stop boats from landing there, did he? And why? Because he couldn't, it was like a right of way. Nobody could legally close off a right of way that had been used for years, any more than he could stop anyone's using his well, if it was the only access they had to water. Any more than *she* had any right to stop folks shooting ducks off those ledges. Legally, that is. She didn't own below tidemark, did she?

But you let so much as a .22 be fired within hearing of her house, and out she would come, flapping over the ledges in her long black dress.

"Oh, I'm sorry—I can't allow—"

Never angry, always polite, even seeming glad to see whoever it was.

"Oh, it's you, Mr. Gilman," or Mr. MacGimsey, or Mr. Vira. "Isn't it a lovely day? So beautiful out on the water, isn't it? Do come in and have some coffee and speak to Mother. It will *make* her day."

So what could a man do? There would be the flock of ducks he'd been trying to sneak up on high-tailing it off over the water, or swum out of range—she'd scared them, of course, flapping over the rocks like that, might as well have put up a windmill. You went in, and it was always darned good cake and coffee, even if, for a minute, back there on the rocks, you'd felt like letting her have both barrels, as who wouldn't? Or if only she'd been mad, you could have said; but no, there she was, smiling, and nodding like a chickadee, maybe bareheaded and without a jacket, the way she'd run out quick the minute she heard anything, and talking ten to a dozen in her jerky voice with the from-away accent. What could you do?

The thing was, you couldn't help liking her, and most people did, except for the few who had gone on record that they didn't and had shot their mouths off about it and so had to keep on backing up what they'd said. Elbridge did, himself; and he didn't doubt for a minute that her mother and her looks had a lot to do with her being the way she was. The old lady had been totally blind and deaf for years; and Miss Greenwood was the most calamitously homely woman he had ever seen in his life.

He recalled how, as a boy of sixteen, when he had first seen Miss Roxinda, he had stared in disbelief and shock, and then looked away; but in spite of himself his eyes had kept creeping back, painfully, not wanting to look and hoping she did not notice.

Stell MacGimsey, who always seemed to know things, had, in her time, put forth a full explanation of Miss Roxinda. She got it, she said, from a friend of the Greenwoods, who visited sometimes in the summer.

Seems that when Miss Roxinda was a girl, this woman said, or Stell said she said, she was just beautiful, one of the prettiest girls you ever saw—lovely black hair and rosy cheeks, and she was engaged to be married. But just before the wedding—on the day before in fact, since Stell liked her crises clean-cut—she had come down with this awful disease that et all the flesh off of her bones. It was a disease so rare that no other example of it had been seen in the known world, so them city doctors, them specialists, they couldn't do a thing. At first, she'd looked so awful that her family had kept her out of sight for years in the very top room of their city mansion. Then she got a little better, so she could go out; but she always had to wear a veil.

And, said Stell, that was the reason she and her mother had come to a far-off place and built a house in such a lonely spot. Miss Greenwood looked so awful that she wanted to keep out of sight of everyone.

It was one of Stell's best efforts, with little to go on. People swallowed it down, in spite of obvious errors. That is, most people did. There had to be some reason for two ladies to want to live apart like that.

Jess said, "But she *likes* company, Stell. Her friends come to see her every summer, and she enjoys them."

And Fanny MacGimsey, Liseo's wife, said, "Maybe they don't have quite as much money as they used to, and that's why they live here now, and stay the year round, it seems more reasonable."

She guessed she ought to know how much they had coming in a month, Stell said; she cashed their check at the post office every living time. And anybody who could build a summer cottage that wouldn't of cost half what it did, if they'd been willing to set it where Grampa Luther wanted it to set, afford to waste all that money, and who could travel back and forth from away twice a year and entertain all that company every summer, live like queens in palaces whilst the rest of us was slatting our lives out after the all-mighty dollar, well, they couldn't be very bad off. No, sir! When she went off the island to the dentist, she wore a hat veil, didn't she? It just went to show you.

"But a veil goes with the kind of clothes she wears," Jess said. "My mother wore one and so did yours. It's just to dress up, I think, Stell, along with that little bit of white lace."

"Dress up, ha!" Stell said. "You can think so. I know what *I* think."

It seemed possible that some calamity of illness had overtaken the poor lady, though no one in his right mind could believe she had ever been pretty. The skin of her face stretched tight over the bones; the cheeks were sunken, the teeth roundly prominent, as in a skull. Old Dr. Graham, who visited her house occasionally to attend the old lady, blew up one day at Stell when she asked him what on earth

that awful unknown disease could have been. He was crotchety any-
way, and he'd had a long wet boat trip over from the harbor.

"Unknown disease, hell!" he snorted. "Might've had some kind of
t.b., once, got over it. Whose business is it? She's a damn sight
tougher than you are, Stell, for all she has to walk twice in a place
to make a shadow."

Miss Greenwood was slight—slighter than she looked, perhaps, be-
cause of the clothes she wore. The two Greenwoods dressed exactly
alike, always, in the style of the nineties. At first, when the old lady
was able, they often walked to the village together; from the rear,
it was hard to tell them apart. They wore long black skirts which
must have had under them many petticoats; black jackets with
puffed sleeves over white or pale-gray high-necked shirtwaists. Their
black hats perched high on upswept, pugged hair. Through the
years they saw no reason, apparently, to change their style.

Imogene Cayford did their laundry, so the whole village knew
what they wore for underwear. In the beginning, the many stiff-
starched petticoats, deeply frilled, the underdrawers edged with
lace, the eyelet-embroidered corset covers, seemed not too different
from what other ladies wore, except in the matter of quality. They
were handmade, of linen and lawn, with tiny, even stitches, thou-
sands of stitches, hemstitched and embroidered in intricate patterns.

"Will you look, for the luvva God, at old lady Greenwood's
drawers?" Imogene would cry, to whatever caller she might have at
hand while she was ironing. She would spread the fine, soft stuff out
on her ironing board, inviting inspection, and the caller would bend
close.

"Handmade, every stitch, and look at that cloth!"

"My Lord, no wonder that old lady's blind."

"Well, I'm lucky if I get cotton batiste, with a little Hamburg on
it. I've got other ways to spend my time, too, besides finifying up a
pair of lace drawers."

But styles changed with the years. Lace went out and other ma-
terials came in. People nudged each other with delight at the sight
of the petticoats, full-bodied in the breeze, on Imogene's clothesline,
and children tittered on the way to school.

"Will you, for the luvva God, cast your eyes on Aunt Greeny's
washing?"

If people poked fun behind the Greenwoods' backs, nobody ever
did so to their faces. The old lady was senile now—she was ninety,
and never went out any more; but Miss Roxinda came over-town

for groceries and mail every day or so. You couldn't deny that she looked a little like a crow; you couldn't wonder that kids, behind her back, mimicked her shrill, jerky, from-away accent, though El-bridge told his own kids if he ever caught them doing it there'd be works to pay. But people were more or less used to her now. No one was very well acquainted with her, she didn't invite it, not anything personal, that is. Little Sarah probably knew her as well as anyone did, but Little Sarah wasn't one to talk around how well she knew anybody. Not that Miss Greenwood was what you could call stand-offish or stuck up. Her manner to all, young or old, was cheerful and friendly. She always had something to say, speaking in her choppy voice about the weather, about the mail being late, about the beau-ties of nature. Whatever Stell might say about her hiding from the world, she loved company, or seemed to, was never so happy as when someone went to call on her, always made people feel at home and welcome; and she gave four parties a year, one for grownups and one for children, at Easter and at Christmastime. Of course, nobody dropped in casually at all hours of the day the way next-door neighbors did; it was too long a walk, particularly at night, too lonesome, past the old quarry pits and through woods; but people did go sometimes, and Little Sarah went regularly as a clock, once a week, winter and summer, to eat dinner over there and spend the evening, and sit up until all hours talking, though nobody ever knew what about, Little Sarah not saying.

At first, Elbridge worried a little about his mother's coming home late at night along the quarry road, with nothing but a storm lantern to light the way. The road to the Point started out smoothly enough, along the level track of MacKechnie's old causeway. Through the fields, it was safe as a highway, but where it crossed the swamp, its jagged rock foundation was built up eight or ten feet above the mud, with a slant drop on either side, not steep, but enough to give a nasty, rolling fall to anyone who miscalculated and stepped off the level, where the tracks had run. MacKechnie had figured the slope to give his loaded flatcars a head start, not for walking; and walking was hard there, particularly since some of the old ties had heaved up with the frost.

The causeway, of course, stopped at the quarry pits, and then the track, for it was no more than one, went up one side of the granite hill and down the other, skirting the pits. In places, it swung close, no more than twenty feet or so from sheer fall-offs which might be sixty, might be two hundred feet to the bottom of the quarry. The wind, in a full gale, made a funnel of that naked hill, sucking across with blasts that could take a grown man off his feet. Beyond the hill, the road swung down through stunted trees which sheltered it somewhat, but it was little more than a cart track, studded with roots and stones.

Little Sarah said she didn't mind it; she knew every stick and stone of it. She was a great walker anyway, and spent half her time in the woods, berry-picking, or hunting for wild bark and sassafras root, or whatever herb she wanted to find that was in season. She said if she was fool enough to take that walk at night, Elbridge ought to be smart enough to figure she had her reasons for it; and that was all she said. She'd been doing it a long time now, and after a while he stopped being concerned, particularly when he found that if the weather was bad she was likely to stay all night.

The first year November came around, and the Greenwoods did not close up their cottage and go home, the village was agog. What did they plan to do, stay all winter? The idea, two women, one of them helpless, stuck out on that point of rock, a mile and a half from any living soul, with that road the way 'twas, it was flying in the face of Providence!

Elbridge was in the post office the day Miss Greenwood finally removed the speculation. Stell handed her her mail, and said, "I expect you folks'll be taking off for the city pretty soon, won't you, Miss Greenwood?"

Quite a lot of people were there at mailtime, and all over the store you could see the ears prick up.

Miss Greenwood looked up from her handful—she always got a lot of mail—and said cheerfully, "Oh, this is our home for good now. We're not going away."

Stell fairly poked her nose out through the iron grating of the wicket. For a minute, she couldn't think of one thing to say. Then she said, "Won't you be—lonesome, way off down there?"

"Oh, my, no. I've never been lonesome in my life. I have so much to do."

"I guess you will have," Stell said. "The snow gets deep in them woods. You don't realize."

"Oh, I love the snow and the cold weather. I'm looking forward to my first winter here, and so is Mother."

"But how on earth'll you keep warm in that—house?" Stell asked. She'd almost said "fool" house, the way Grampa Luther did, but had caught it in time. "With it twenty below and the wind blowing?"

Miss Roxinda laughed. "Why, the same way you do, Mrs. Mac-Gimsey. Coal stove in the kitchen, airtight in the living room. And, of course, we've had the airtight placed so we can use the fireplace."

"Fireplace!" Stell said, and you could almost hear everybody else in the store saying, "Fireplace!" too. Anyone knew that you might as well have a hole right out through the side of the house into the weather.

"But who'll lug your coal? Who'll fetch the water?"

"Well, I'll tell you," Miss Greenwood said. She was still smiling, cheerful as a cricket. "Roxinda will fetch it."

She always called herself "Roxinda" when she talked to herself. Sometimes she said, "Roxinda, you old fool."

"But what if something should happen? What if you had to get . . . help . . . quick?"

You could tell Stell was pretty excited when she began to slow down and space out her words.

Miss Greenwood at once began to put together her things to go. "Oh, we'll be snug. The worse the storm is, the better we'll like it. Good day, Mrs. MacGimsey. Isn't the weather lovely? This fall sunshine."

" 'T won't last," Stell said. "You better think—"

But the door was already closing behind Miss Roxinda's slim, straight back.

"If that don't make me mad!" Stell said. "Walk right away from you while you're still talking!"

Little Sarah, who was next in line for mail, said, "My land, Stell, I don't know when else that would be," but Stell was so agog she didn't even pick it up.

The village was shocked and uneasy, especially the men.

"My gorry," Luther MacGimsey said, when he heard, "you let a good gust of no'theaster get up under them petticoats, she'll go off of that hill like a kite."

And, in that, there was more truth than poetry.

Besides, it looked as though, after every change in the weather— and there'd be plenty of those before spring—somebody would have to go traipsing across the island to make sure those two helpless women were all right. It was going to be a damned frig all winter long, they said. They were right. It was.

Elbridge, as a selectman, felt the responsibility more than most. He had tried more than once to persuade Miss Greenwood to bring her mother over to the village for the winter.

"There's all those empty houses," he argued. "Wouldn't be much trouble to make one livable, and we'll all turn to and help you bring over what things you'd need. Just for the cold weather, that is."

He put it as strongly as he could, without being impolite, that it was a chore for busy men to have to take time to check up on the Greenwoods all winter; and all of a sudden, he brought up short, aware that she was looking at him, a cool straight look, out of what he'd never realized before were some pretty clear, intelligent gray eyes.

Oh, Lord, he thought uncomfortably. Anyone with the sense God gave a goose would know that there were days on end in the wintertime when no one was busy, when the men either sat with their feet in the oven at home, or yarded up around the stoves in the store or down on the wharf, waiting for weather.

"Well," he said, grinning a little and feeling sheepish; and for a moment he thought, the way she was looking, that he was going to get out of her some kind of a sensible comment on the situation. But all she said was, "Oh, now, Mr. Gilman, you mustn't worry. Mother and I are fine, and the last thing we want is to be a nuisance to anybody."

She began to talk about something else, and all he could feel, outside of being out of patience with somebody as mule-headed as that, was that he'd stuck his nose into a place where it didn't belong.

And so, now, every so often, someone walked over to the Point and checked up, just in case.

Today, Elbridge walked along, carrying her bundle of mail under one arm and under the other the basket of food Jess had fixed. There was no need to take food to the Greenwoods, of course; they could afford what they needed. When there was a really heavy load, like coal, or a barrel of kerosene or flour, they paid Willard to haul it by sled or wagon; but Miss Roxinda carried her day-to-day groceries by hand, or, if there was no snow on the ground, wheeled them in her wheelbarrow. Seeing it was such a jaunt over there, whoever went seldom went empty-handed, lugging along her mail and milk, and, generally, a gift of fresh fish or baked stuff, whatever was handy. Jess always had a contribution of bread or cake or cookies to send along; she and Miss Roxinda were always swapping samples of cooking or recipes—in spite of the fact that it was well known to all the island ladies that none of the summer people knew how to cook worth a hang.

Elbridge grinned a little to himself, thinking of this anomaly. Ex-

cept for Jess, Miss Greenwood was the best cook he ever saw in his
life—maybe, with some things, she was even a little better than Jess.
She could put a brown on a pair of chickens or a turkey that a man
would fairly leave home for. At her Christmas and Easter parties,
the ladies had a chance to sample this cooking and they liked it,
judging by the way they stuffed it down. But let the subject come
up at any time, and the thought was automatic—someone would be
sure to express it, too—the summer people were helpless, they didn't
know how to cook or wash or clean or any of those things that really
capable people knew how to do. Like anything said over and over
often enough, people would believe it, no matter how much proof
to the contrary stared them in the face. Like still thinking of Miss
Roxinda as summer people, an outsider. You did and she was, and
would be, if she stayed forever.

Let's see, Elbridge thought, figuring back. I was sixteen the year
the house was built and now I'm thirty-four. That's eighteen years
she's been here on the island, and for the last seven, she's been here
the year round. And she's still summer people.

It wasn't as if she were standoffish or stuck-up, the way some of
them were. Look at those parties. Kids and grownups went to them,
twice a year, and had a royal good time, felt comfortable, too, at her
house; and that was funny, too, because the island people were
pretty bashful and sensitive with outsiders.

They always went, dressed in their best clothes, and an air of an-
ticipation and holiday hung over the houses, in the afternoon and
early evening before the neighbors gathered with their lanterns for
the walk down through the woods. Miss Greenwood would meet
them at the door in her best black dress, usher them into the bed-
room off the kitchen to take off wraps. In no time, everybody would
be laughing and talking without a hitch. After a little, she would
vanish to the kitchen, where as cook and server she would put the
finishing touches to her dinner. Sometimes they would hear her talk-
ing to herself out there: "Now, Roxinda, you old fool, be careful,
you'll burn yourself."

The dinner would be served on the heavy silver service which
had belonged to the Greenwood family for generations—somebody
had found that out, nobody quite knew who. The tablecloth would
be rich and creamy—pure linen, the ladies said, running their fingers
gently along the smooth material, fingering the big dinner napkins;
and under all that hospitality and graciousness, they bloomed. They
had white tablecloths at home for holidays, nice ones, too; but not

like this. Seated behind the turkey, or the chickens, what she called, "The Bird," at the head of the table with so many extra leaves in it that the dining room looked small, Miss Greenwood would pick up her carving tools and beam at her guests.

"Now," she would say, "which will you have, the light or the dark?" Everybody would have a wonderful time.

Yet Elbridge doubted if there ever was a holiday dinner in the village at which the father, about to serve the meat, didn't pick up his fork and say in a falsetto, imitation-Philadelphia accent, "Which'll you have, the light or the dark?"

He doubted, too, that there was any real meanness in it; it was only for laughs, and anybody who looked different, was different, was fair game. People were used to Miss Roxinda; he guessed some even had a kind of affection for her. He had, himself.

But she was a damned nuisance, all the same, he added hastily, just to make it sound right. Somebody had to look out for her, fritter away time going over there, all winter long.

The thought was automatic; it was the way any island man ended up thinking, or talking, about Miss Greenwood.

At the entrance to his wood lot, which angled off to the left of the causeway, he noticed fresh tracks in the snow, and an ax and buck-saw leaned against a tree. They belonged to his partner, Eliseo Mac-Gimsey, he saw; and Liseo himself was just coming back up the wood road, wading through snow to his knees.

"Hi," Elbridge said. "I wondered where you were. George said you'd shut up shop."

Either he or Liseo had to be on hand at the wharf most of the time, to tend scow and store when the boats came in. Their trade was not only with local boats, but with draggers and lobster fisher-men from a good many neighboring islands who were generally on the way home and didn't want to wait to sell any longer than they had to. When Liseo hadn't shown up at the house, Elbridge figured he'd been held up by a late boat, and hadn't waited for him.

"No sense staying open," Liseo said. "Boats all gone home, any-way. Sea's making up all the time."

"Seems to be," Elbridge said.

He realized now that he had been listening to the sea, off and on, for some time. It was an action so reflex with him that he seldom stopped to notice he was doing it. Some sea sound hung over the island always, so continuous that you had to stop and think before you could hear it, even when the rollers were beginning to boom, as they were now.

"George was the only one went out from here," Liseo said. "Wid wouldn't go with him today. Said he wasn't going to take a chance on starting his liver to rolling over and over."

Liseo's pointed, triangular face took on, briefly, a look of Willard Lowden's habitual bilious melancholy, and Elbridge grinned.

He'd never been able to see how Liseo could do that—how a tall, slender fellow, weighing perhaps a hundred and fifty, could make himself look like Wid Lowden, the fattest man Elbridge ever saw. But Liseo was a born mimic. His flexible features could take on expressions, and his voice intonations which were at times uncanny.

If Liseo had wanted to use this gift maliciously, he could have been an unpopular man; but he did not. His mimicry was always good-tempered and funny; he could have made this one to Willard's face, and Willard would have laughed his head off. The only damage he did, the kids thought Liseo was great—they were always pestering him to mimic someone, and then trying it themselves without Liseo's success; and Elbridge knew that George Lowden's mimicry of Willard, which wasn't good-tempered and was seldom funny, stemmed directly from Liseo.

"Took an awful jouncing last time," Liseo said, still being Willard.

"So would you, if your liver weighed what Wid's does," Elbridge said.

Liseo leaned his shovel beside his ax and bucksaw, picked out of the crotch of a tree a brown paper sack, which he'd apparently stashed there before he went down into the wood lot.

"What would you say Wid's liver weighs?" he asked thoughtfully.

"Forty pounds."

"Oh, Lord, no. Three, maybe."

"I'll bet you."

"How much?"

"I'll bet you a dollar."

"How'll you find out? Kill Wid?"

"M'm. Mine'd go about ten, I'd say, yours twenty. Man like Wid, stands to reason. Forty pounds. Ask old Doc Graham. He'd know."

"No need to," Elbridge said. He set off down the causeway, speaking over his shoulder. "My pig I killed last week weighed over three hundred. I didn't have any forty pounds of liver."

Liseo fell into step beside Elbridge. He dearly loved an argument, but he knew when he was outshuffled.

"That wood lot's a hog-wallow, speaking of pigs," he said. "I got cast in there like an old yo. We might's well give up all thought of cutting wood till some snow melts. The tree stumps'd be two feet high. You hear from Roger today?"

Elbridge nodded. "They'll be home Friday," he said.

"Darn funny we don't hear from Rosie," Liseo said. "Fanny's fussing her head off. The last one we got was two weeks ago, and it was a week old."

"Hadn't ought to take a letter a week to come five miles, had it?" Elbridge said.

Liseo grinned. "Fanny at Stell about it," he said.

"Did? Stell helpful?"

"Well, in a sensitive way. Uncle Sam don't pay enough so's she can put all her time on the mail, and there's a lot of Christmas postcards to mislay."

"Be nice to have the kids home, anyway," Elbridge said.

"It sure will. Lord, do I miss Rosie!"

His pretty daughter, Rosie, was the apple of Liseo's eye. He had two others, younger, whom he loved, and a son the same age as Elbridge's twins, but Rosie had been his first, and she had been in the beginning and still was, a wonder to him. She looked like him —both had crisp, curly black hair and clear olive skin, inherited from the Italian grandfather who had married one of Tilson Shepheard's daughters. They both had heart-shaped faces, with widow's peaks, dramatically dark against smooth foreheads; black eyebrows, expressive above merry black eyes. They were slender, graceful-moving people, deceptively strong, as those who misjudged Liseo's appearance had sometimes found to their sorrow. He had been in the war and had come home with a couple of medals, which seemed strange to think about, because it took a great deal to make Liseo mad enough to fight anyone.

He was a gay man, inclined to practical jokes, and he enjoyed his life tremendously—all the more when Rosie was at home to enjoy it with him. She had been gone since Labor Day, at school on the mainland; and Liseo pined. His wife, Fanny, was quiet and pleasant, and he was very fond of her; but she was inclined to be a sobersides; the two younger girls, Susie and Mary, took after her. His boy, Johnny, was like Liseo in looks, and in some other ways, too; but he was wild as a hawk, always in some scrape or other and he had a fierce temper. It took Rosie to spark the household, turn it into the kind of inspired madhouse, roaring with laughter, that Liseo loved.

"What you got in the basket?" he asked. "Picnic for the birds?" Elbridge nodded. "Chickadees' dinner."

"Why, blast it all," Liseo said, amiably. "Another whole afternoon's work shot to hell. You ever count up how many days, man hours, it's cost the men of this island, traipsing back and forth to see if them two old fairy tales over on the Point is all right?"

"Don't know as I have. A good many."

The fact that Liseo had come equipped with a paper bag which contained, without a doubt, two live lobsters for the Greenwood ladies, showed quite well where he expected to spend his afternoon, but Elbridge didn't mention it.

"It's a cussed nuisance," Liseo said. "Busy man, have to leave his work, can't afford to, wade over here all times of the winter."

"Ought to be a law," Elbridge said.

"Damn right. Deliver me from a bunch of mule-headed old maids. Every time."

Elbridge couldn't resist saying slyly, "I could make out all right, Liseo. If you've got something else—"

"Well," Liseo said. "I ought to be home this minute, killing my pig. Fanny's sore as hell at me because I ain't done it yet. She wanted a roast of pork for Christmas dinner, Rosie likes pork, but it's too late now, got to hang awhile before it's fit to eat, so I figure no sense to kill Uncle Sylvester before Christmas. No, I'd just as soon go along, help you. Man feels a responsibility. It ain't his, but, by God, he feels it."

"I'll trade you a pork roast for Christmas," Elbridge said. "You can give it back when you butcher, later on."

His own butchering was finished, the meat carefully hung in the cold room in the barn annex. He knew quite well why Liseo hadn't done his. They went through this every year. Liseo liked a pig, personally. After he'd raised one, he had trouble bringing himself to kill it. He was always a couple of months late with his butchering, and one year, he'd carried a pig right over through the next summer. By the time he came to kill it, it weighed over four hundred pounds and was mostly lard; and Fanny had made such a rumpus that Liseo had promised not to do it again.

He said now, "Thanks, I'll tell Fanny. She was going to make do with a couple of roosters."

They walked along between the snow-covered fields bisected by the causeway, some of them smooth snow, where hay was still cut in the summertime, but most of them tangled with growth—wild cherry and alder, hardhack and blackberry vines thrusting out of the icy crust below. Ahead of them loomed MacKechnie's hill, the quarry scars sharply gashed against its gray sides, the swamp spread out at its foot, gun-metal color in the windless afternoon. Except for the causeway track, no one had ever tried to clear the swamp; no one wanted the job of it, and there was no real reason to. The big old trees might have been worth something for saw logs, but who would want to put a team in there to twitch them out? The place was mostly bog masked with moss, with boiling springs all over, that didn't freeze all winter long. A couple of winters ago, George Lowden had lost an ox in one of them. By the time he found it, it was dead, and George had had to walk away and leave it there, nothing else to do. A man was in trouble the minute he stepped down off the causeway; What would happen to horses was the same thing that had happened to the ox. So far as Elbridge knew, George, hunting his ox, was the only one who had gone into the swamp in years.

Where the hayfields ended, a wet meadow grew cattails and marsh cranberries for a hundred feet or so; then the wall of trees and undergrowth started, an edge as sharp as if someone had trimmed it off with hedge shears. The causeway went into it in a round, dark hole; looking ahead was like looking up a tunnel, for since MacKechnie's time the trees had nudged close and locked their branches overhead. Here the grade started to climb, and Elbridge puffed a little.

"You want me to come over and kill Uncle Sylvester for you?" he asked.

"Yes, by God, and take him home and eat him," Liseo said. "I tell you, I just as soon kill and eat a human being. Let alone he looks like Uncle Sylvester MacGimsey, around the eyes, anyway, he's got more sense than most men."

"Well, I will," Elbridge said.

It was gray-dark in the tunnel. The branches overhead let in an occasional patch of sky, in places where some big yellow birch or swamp maple had dropped its leaves for a time; through three seasons of the year there was not a place anywhere along here where the sky showed. It was all greened-over and cat-spruced up. Mac-Kechnie hadn't cut any more of the big hardwoods than he'd needed to. The ones left nearest the track had reached out; and the fast-growing cat spruces had done the rest. Some of them, twelve inches thick at the butt, grew right up through the cracks of the rubble foundation. Now that the leaves were off the undergrowth, the swamp showed itself a little; it was dark and cold in there, full of shadows. The big boles went up, black against the snow; occasionally, where their tops had been too thick for the snow to get through, you could see their butts, covered with frost-crystaled moss and clenched down into the hummocky ground.

"How'd it be if you and I was to swap pigs, anyway?" Elbridge asked. "Let Uncle Sylvester hang till Jess can't tell the difference in the meat, then I'll harness up the team and we'll shift pigs. Our folks'll eat Uncle Sylvester, seeing we haven't got any sentiment about him, and you folks eat mine. No difference in pigs to me, Liseo."

Liseo grunted. "Be a damn fool performance," he said. "Anybody got wind of it, I'd never live it down."

"Do it some dark night," Elbridge said. "Nobody be the wiser but you and me."

They walked a while in silence.

"By gorry, I will," Liseo said. "Fool or no fool, it'll be worth it to enjoy a roast of pork again. I ain't for years. Hey, what's that, Elbridge? Hey, look!"

"What?" Elbridge asked, turning around. "What? Where?"

"Ssh. Don't move. Look over there on the far edge of the pond."

The swamp pond, a hundred yards or so away through the tree boles, was still as a slab of glass, its water dark, not so much black as a deep velvety brown against the snowy overhang of the bushes. For a moment, Elbridge could make out nothing in the wild, gray-white tangle that edged close to the water. He took a step back and tried to peer along the line of Liseo's pointing, excited finger; and as he moved, something else moved on the far side of the pond. A great, horned head, which had hung out of a black alder thicket as if carved there, slipped back out of sight. The bushes closed over it without a sound; only a crust of snow dropped from a twig and into the water, where it made a small ripple, quickly gone.

Elbridge blinked; a prickly feeling began below his collar and crept up his neck into his hair.

"Well, I'll be damned," he said softly.

"A buck deer!" Liseo said. "By the God, Elbridge!"

He was standing with his finger still pointing; now he looked at his hand a little sheepishly and let it drop to his side. "If you saw it too, I guess I ain't crazy. Where in thunder d'you suppose he came from? Must've swum over from the mainland."

"Must've," Elbridge said. "But it's been years since there's been any deer here on the island, Liseo."

He remembered hearing MacKechnie tell how in the old days men used to send packs of hounds into the swamp to run the deer, and how hunters, lined up along the causeway, would shoot them as fast as they came into range, until there were no more deer, and never had been any, since. It was quite a wonder that one had come back now; or perhaps it wasn't, he thought, soberly, turning to start again along the causeway. For all there were people here, and a fairly big community in the summertime, up here in the middle of the island you could feel the wildness pushing to come back, and coming all the faster, the more the people seemed to be hanging on by the skin of their teeth.

The old wild, he thought, remembering the crinkled, yellow page of Ansel's diary. And MacKechnie's scratches healed up and haired over.

But according to Liseo the buck deer wouldn't last long. Liseo was trudging along behind him, lamenting every step of the way.

"What wouldn't I give if I'd had my .30-30! Couldn't I have whanged the schnozzle off of him! Oh, blast and damn it, Elbridge, I never used to make a trip over here without a gun, and now I leave it home because them two old pasturages over here don't like guns. If I *ever* come through this swamp again without it, I'll—damned if I ain't a good mind to go home and fetch it now."

"Oh, he's to hell an' gone the middle of the swamp by now," Elbridge said.

"Well, you'll see me staked out tomorrow there by that pond, then," Liseo said. "And I'll have more than my finger to point, by the God."

The woods stopped as sharply as they had begun, where the causeway ended at the base of the hill. The path climbed, twisting between the quarry pits, a bare track on the granite marked only by an occasional small cairn, piled as a warning near the edges. The granite hill was swept clean of snow, except where a scrubby bush rooted in a crack had caused a shallow, dagger-shaped drift, or where patches of lichen held a sharp-edged, crusty scale. At the crest, the path ran narrow between pits that were in some places two hundred feet deep. There had once been a wooden guardrail here, fastened to iron stakes drilled into the ledge, but the wood had rotted and fallen long ago, leaving only the eight or ten stakes near the edge on either side. Down below, the pits now were deep ponds, partially frozen over, the snow-covered ice curving out from the shore to make, in the middle, clear, black-green pools of water. Across them, on the far sides, the abandoned grout piles were jumbled towers of snow-crusted rubble.

"Old MacKechnie could have got a hundred thousand dollars for this view, if it wasn't all pocked-out with quarry holes," Liseo observed sourly. He was still thinking about the deer, and him caught standing with nothing to point but his finger. "Them old men, they gutted the country, Elbridge. Hadn't been for them, some of the rest of us might have had something. Hey, look at that sundog!"

The view from MacKechnie's hill took in sea and sky on four sides of the island, a vast spectacle, leaden-colored now, with the islands looming in mirage toward the horizons, their ends as if undercut by the sea and lifted out of the water. The sun, far to the south and already westering in the short afternoon, swam in haze; it had a companion, a dull blob of light, as if its ghost followed not far behind it in the sky.

"She's a-swimming in it," Liseo said. "There's another snowstorm. Might as well go home prepared to set around the stove another month."

"Might as well," Elbridge agreed. "Look, that must be that three-master out there George was telling about. She's considerable farther out than I thought she was, according to what he said."

"She'd better be, if it comes on to blow before she wears clear of the islands," Liseo said. "I'd have thought the tide would have brought her in some; but maybe she's picked up a breeze out there, seems to have a full suit of sails up. Don't seem to be moving much, though, does she?"

The three-master's sails were small white angles against a horizon so wide that a man had to turn his head a little before he could see land to north or south of her. She looked remote and lonely out there, the only break in the long stretch of gray sky and sea. She was not only alone in these waters, but in the world, for she was very nearly the last of her kind. Only a particularly stubborn brand of sailor, like a Nova Scotiaman, would bother to haul lumber by coasting vessel any more; and maybe a good thing, Elbridge thought, looking down at the big rollers thundering in across The Pasture. Even in his own time, there had been some bad wrecks on those rocks; there was still part of the hull of a Portuguese vessel down there on the shore, rotted away and shifted by storms every winter.

The Portuguese vessel had been driven in across The Pasture on a black night in 1910 and six men lost. A September storm, that had been. She had been loaded with baskets of garlic; and nobody knew anything about the wreck, until the cows began coming home at night with their milk tasting so rank of garlic that no one could drink it. So someone had walked the fenced meadows to find out what in thunder the cows could have got into; and by the shore line had found the tall, woven baskets, flung up by the sea into the edge of the field, smashed open, and garlic strewn in piles and windrows. Elbridge still had one of the baskets at home; Jess used it for a rag basket. Later, they found a piece of the ship's hull, but no men. It took months before word came about what vessel it must have been, and how many lost on her, that wild September night.

"I can't tell whether she's moving or not," Elbridge said.

There was nothing to tell by, only horizon. Maybe she had a breeze out there—he doubted it. Certainly there wasn't a breath of wind inshore. Where those rollers were coming from, there had been wind, all right—they were probably the tailings of a storm somewhere at sea. They were big, glassy ones, heaving up lazily, one after the other, turning over and belting in over the ledges with a dull, thundering boom.

"Oh, well, he's all right, that far out," Liseo said. "Come no'theast, he'll probably head for Port Western. Come on, let's get it over. Can't stand here all day." He started down the hill, his voice coming back to Elbridge grumblingly.

". . . the trouble with this place, huddle up to a coal stove all winter, wait on summer people all summer. Comes to waiting on them all winter, no kind of life for a man."

"That's right," Elbridge said. "No kind at all. It's a damn nuisance. No need of it. I don't know why we put up with it, Liseo."

For two men as put out as they were, they were surprisingly amiable as they went up the back steps of the Greenwood cottage.

Miss Roxinda opened the door at once, as if she might have been standing near it. She had on her usual black dress, skimpy at the waist, descending into yards of material that swept the floor. Her iron-gray hair was piled in a neat pug on top of her head, and she had a piece of white lace at her throat.

"Isn't this nice!" she said. "Company! How do you do? Come in."

"Better not," Elbridge said. "Boots all snow. Dirt up your nice clean kitchen floor."

"Mercy, don't be silly. What's a puddle or two? Come in and get warm, it's raw out. Mother will be delighted."

"Well, can't stop. Just thought we'd drop over, see how you were making out."

Miss Greenwood's eyes, clear as a child's with pleasure, clouded a little. "I do hope you haven't gone to trouble," she said. "You know we don't want to be a nuisance, Mother and I."

Liseo poked Elbridge from behind.

"No bother," he said. "None in the world. Elbridge and me, we started out to see if the snow was too deep to haul wood, figured we were coming that far, might as well bring over your mail."

"That's right," Elbridge said.

He leaned past her and, without stepping his snowy boots over the threshold, set his basket on the table by the door. He said, "Jess sent a few things."

She lifted the clean towel on the top of the basket and peeped in. "I know it isn't polite to look while you're here," she said gaily. "But I can't be expected to wait, Mr. Gilman. Some of Mrs. Gilman's matchless cookies! And sweet butter! Oh, *thank* her, Mr. Gilman. And Mr. MacGimsey, you've brought us two lobsters. Mother will be out of her *mind* with pleasure."

"Well," Elbridge said. He felt himself getting red. No sense thanking anybody all over the place.

Liseo said, "Where's your shovel, Miss Greenwood? Might as well break out a path to the well while we're here."

"That's right," Elbridge said. "And hand me out your water buckets."

They shoveled the path to the well; at least, they widened the existing one she had made, which might have been wide enough for Miss Greenwood, but wasn't any use to a man. They filled up all available buckets and containers with drinking water, brought in coal, heaped the fireplace wood box. Liseo took a can down to tidemark and dipped up enough sea water for her to cook her two lobsters in. By the time they had finished all the chores they could see needed done, the kitchen linoleum was tracked up and running rivulets of snow water. Liseo hunted up the mop and cleaned it up.

Miss Greenwood was not in the room at the moment, and Elbridge stood watching him with a grin. "Liseo," he said, "what would Fanny do, if you was to mop the carpet, after you'd tracked snow from the door to the wood box?"

Liseo lifted an eyebrow. "Fanny?" he said. "Fanny'd drop dead. But what her mind don't know, her heart won't grieve over."

He finished, stood the mop upside down in a corner. "There," he

said loudly. "Now I guess you'n I'd better crawl along home, El-
bridge."

What they expected, happened at once.

Miss Greenwood, coming back, put up both hands. "No, no, no, no,
no!" she said. "I've got cake and coffee all ready by the living room
fire, and Mother will be *so* disappointed if you don't come in."

"Well," Elbridge said. "That'd be pretty nice. We *will* just step
in, if it'd please your mother."

The little, old, incredibly wrinkled lady, Mrs. Greenwood, sat rock-
ing in her corner by the fireplace, on her lips a pleasant, uncompre-
hending smile. She seemed not to know anyone was there, even
though her daughter took her hand and lifted it to touch first El-
bridge's, then Liseo's. The tiny, cold, dry fingers felt frail as a dead
leaf. They did not move, nor did the quiet, blind expression change
on the ancient face. But Miss Greenwood said, "That will make
Mother's whole day. She's been wondering when we'd have some
company. She's been waiting for the crocus to bloom, but I have to
tell her it will be a long time. They're only just coming up." She in-
dicated a blue pot filled with earth, on the window sill, in which
some tiny green spikes were barely showing. "Do sit down, and won't
you take off your coats? It's so raw outside, you'll surely be cold when
you go out."

They sat a little stiffly in the comfortable chairs by the fire, their
sheepskins buttoned, their caps and mittens on the floor beside their
chairs. The fire in the big stone fireplace was crackling and bright,
ruddy on the book-lined walls and on the table laid with a white
cloth, a massive silver coffee pot, thin cups and saucers with beads of
gilt and a wreath of rosebuds, delicate silver spoons, and a chocolate
cake as big as a dishpan, frosted immaculately white.

"I'm generally an old fool," Miss Greenwood said, sitting down be-
hind the coffee pot. "But the Lord, I think, put it into my head this
morning to make an extra cake, when I was cooking for the school
entertainment. So I have chocolate cake today. Let's see, as I re-
member, you both take cream and sugar. You do, Mr. Gilman."

"That's right," Elbridge said, and Liseo remarked hastily that he
did, too.

"And what's the news from the village?" she asked. "I do hope the
weather stays pleasant for the entertainment tonight."

"Don't look like it now," Liseo said. "Looks like snow."

"Oh, I hope not. I do want to go; that is if Mrs. Sarah comes over to sit with Mother. She said she would, but I don't want her to if the weather's bad. Did she mention it, Mr. Gilman?"

Little Sarah hadn't, but that was not unusual. She was independent, sometimes told you her plans, sometimes not. Elbridge knew she didn't plan to go to the school time; she'd listened to the kids' accounts of the program, and had snorted that if she wanted to wring tears out of herself, she'd go peel a mess of onions. Elbridge said, "I think likely she'll be over, if she said she would, snow or no snow, Miss Greenwood."

The coffee, fragrant and nut-brown, filled the cups again. Wedges of cake passed for the second time. The firelight mellowed the backs of books, winked from silver and blue rounds of willow pattern on the plate rail around the wall, on the glitter of the Greenwoods' tall Christmas tree. Outside the gray squares of the windowpanes, the afternoon fell toward twilight, dark on the spruces, leaden on the vast expanse of winter sea. In the corner, the fragile, ancient lady rocked, serenely lost in her silent world.

The men opened coats, shrugged them back from shoulders, stretched out feet a little in the chairs built to hit a man just right in places where it felt good. Bits of village news passed; some town business; Elbridge and Liseo discussed the wood lot, just where, in case they ever had to haul cordwood by wagon, would be the best place to swamp a road through. Elbridge told a modified version, toned down a good deal, of the story of the man torn to pieces by the bear; and Miss Greenwood said it was a most dreadful thing, but if a man kept a wild creature penned up like that, he was risking divine justice, and she wondered if the punishment was out of proportion to the crime.

This idea horrified Liseo, Elbridge could tell. He was shocked, himself, and interested, too, thinking suddenly that this was about the first time he'd ever heard Miss Greenwood say anything outside of being sociable and passing the time of day.

"I guess there isn't much doubt but it was a pretty miserable bear," he said. "But—"

"It was probably insane," Miss Greenwood said. "How long had it been shut up, do you know?"

"Oh, three years or so, wouldn't you say, Liseo?"

"All of that," Liseo said. "But it was a *man* he tore up. A man's life—"

"A bear's life in the wild must be a most private and secret thing," she said. "One seldom sees a bear, I understand."

"Not if he sees you first," Elbridge said, nodding. "Melts right away into the woods, without your knowing he's there, most likely."

"And feeling like that about humans, what must it have been like," she said, "with no place to run to? Penned up, helpless, for a public spectacle?"

"Helpless?" Liseo said. "You call that bear *helpless?*"

"Oh, I do," she said. "I most certainly do. All animals are helpless before guns and traps, Mr. MacGimsey. Why, I found on my rocks the other day a most gruesome thing, steel, set right where the mink goes, and baited with a fish."

Liseo looked uncomfortable. He knew well enough who the trap belonged to—his boy, Johnny. He only hoped she didn't know, too.

Elbridge had heard Liseo say that he'd bought Johnny a set of mink traps. They had cost three dollars apiece.

"I'm afraid I threw it into the ocean," Miss Greenwood went on pleasantly. "You see, I put fish, sometimes, in that very place for the mink. Last year, she had babies there, Mr. MacGimsey, under a rock. Little, tiny things, not tame, but I could get fairly close to them. They expect the fish, but not the trap, Mr. MacGimsey."

"A mink pelt's worth quite a lot," Liseo began.

He felt on shaky ground. He wasn't so sure that she didn't know who owned the trap. He made a note in his mind to shake up Johnny, tell him to get his traps to hell away from Miss Greenwood's. He doubted if it would do very much good. Most of the boys had traps of one kind or another; they all knew that the birds and animals on this part of the shore were more or less tame and easily caught; it was hard, anyway, to catch a mink.

"I can't have it," she said. "I feed the little things, Mr. MacGimsey, so killing them here is only murder. If you know who owned the trap, please send him to me, and I'll be glad to pay."

"I'll inquire round," Liseo said feebly. He cleared his throat. "About that bear, you say he was helpless? Well, I'd help him, Miss Greenwood, let me tell you I would. With a .30-30 rifle!"

"Yes, of course." She nodded. "There would be no other way. Your cup is empty, Mr. MacGimsey, and yours, too, Mr. Gilman. Let me fill them, and do have some more cake."

"I'd like to," Elbridge said, "but I'm up to my marks, thanks just the same. That's about the best chocolate cake I ever et."

"Oh, you say so, and Mrs. Gilman the cook she is!"

"She can't make it like that," Elbridge said. He grinned a little.

"Don't you know the summer people aren't supposed to know how to cook?"

"Well, it's my grandmother's secret recipe for devil's food, you know," she said. "My hand's out now, because Mother and I can never eat up a whole cake, and you can't skimp this recipe without spoiling it, so I only make it now for special occasions." She stopped, flushing a little, and then went on in a great hurry. "Do have another piece!"

Elbridge shook his head. "I'll be called on to eat a baked-bean supper at the school time tonight," he said, "and I don't really know how I'll be able to. And I've got to be getting back, I promised Jess I'd freeze ice cream." He stood up, reached for his coat. "Come on, Liseo. You get to talking again, we'll be here till the cows come home."

Liseo was glad to go. He liked an argument, but this one had got completely away from him before he'd quite seen which way it was headed. "I still say a critter that can jump a man and claw him to pieces *ain't helpless*," he said, getting up.

But Miss Greenwood only nodded and laughed her high, pleasant silvery neigh. "Come again," she said. "And thank you so much for everything. You've done my chores ahead for a week. I won't know what to do with myself." Her voice trailed after her as she passed through the dining room toward the pantry. "I want you to take home some of my kisses," she called.

Liseo lifted ribald eyebrows at Elbridge, though they both knew quite well what she meant. Her "kisses" were famous—sweet baked meringues, light as down, crusty on the outside, soft in the middle. Everyone who happened by her house got a handful.

"I baked a great many today," she said, handing them each a paper bag. "You know, it's silly, but I thought I'd enter them in the prize quilt contest tonight. That is, if I go. If the weather isn't too bad for Mrs. Sarah to come sit with Mother."

She opened the kitchen door for them and saw them out on to the back porch. The afternoon had grown dark. A red squirrel, squatting on the railing, jumped down across the porch and, seeing the bag in Liseo's hand, ran straight up his front from his boots to his shoulder.

Liseo turned white and let out a yell.

"Jesus, Elbridge! Get the cussed thing off of me!"

He began dabbing furiously at the squirrel, not getting his mittened hand close enough to touch it. The squirrel, apparently considered it a game. It ran around Liseo's neck to the other shoulder.

"General Putnam!" Miss Greenwood said. "You bad, bad boy! Come down off the company at once!"

She picked the paper bag out of Liseo's flailing hand, extracted a meringue. "He's harmless, Mr. MacGimsey, really he is. He only wants a kiss."

"Give him one, why don't you, Liseo?" Elbridge said, biting down hard on a guffaw.

She held out the kiss to the squirrel, who ran at once down Liseo and up to her own shoulder.

"My Lord!" Liseo said. He retreated down the porch steps to a safe distance and stood quivering. "How can you—I— Excuse me, but I—rats and mice and them damn things—Jesus!"

"You know what we did?" Elbridge said, as soon as they were out of sight of the house, and he could speak without laughing.

"I know what I did," Liseo said. "I like to jumped out of my skin, there. Br-r-rr! Made me crawl all over!"

He shuddered. "What'd we do?"

"We ate up three-quarters of the cake she'd got all ready for the prize quilt contest," Elbridge said.

"No!" Liseo said. "She give it to us, didn't she? What makes you think so?"

"You heard what she said—her gram'mother's special receet, and all that, and then covered it up quick, by saying she planned to take kisses. Them kisses are good, but they ain't anything special, she always has some around. Every woman in town's conjured up their grandmother's secret something or other to enter in that contest."

"Well, thunderation!" Liseo said. "What she feed it to us for?"

"I dunno. Felt an obligation, maybe," Elbridge said. "You think there's another woman in town would feed her prize cake to a couple gumps like us, come round and did a couple of chores, Liseo?"

"No, sir, by gorry!" Liseo said. "That's hospitality!"

THE Christmas school time started with a bounce and a jostle in the church vestry. The baked-bean supper was a dandy; the ladies had really laid themselves out. The long, plank tables were weighted down with big bowls of beans, plates of brown bread and yeast rolls; a dozen kinds of pickles alternated with platters of cabbage salad. A whole big table over at one side was given over to pies and cakes, a beautiful sight. And outside, in the cool beside the steps, were ten big freezers of different kinds of homemade ice cream.

The cakes and pies were left together on the table show-fashion so that people could see and judge them for the Quilt Society's prize. The idea was to sample as many of them at dinner as possible, and then, afterwards, vote for the one you thought was best. Each offering was marked with a colored cardboard flag and a man's name—"Jack, Joe, John"—to identify it, for no one was supposed to know what anyone else had brought, except Mollie Lessaro, the society's secretary, who had a master list of the cooks, which she would bring out after the voting.

No one could possibly eat a sample of everything, though some of the men, looking at the table, thought they might make a stab at it. This did not matter; it would have been too much to expect that every lady there did not know what every other lady had entered in the contest, and most of the men did, too. Elbridge, for example, knew that a glorious, tan-cream-colored object four stories high, named "Ezra," was Jess's tropic-aroma cake, and he meant to vote for it. As a matter of fact, every husband there had been primed before he came to vote for his wife's cooking. This happened every year, and was considered grossly unfair by single ladies and a widow like Stell MacGimsey, who never had a chance. The society had worked on the quilt at their Thursday afternoon meetings for nearly a year, piecing and hand-sewing it. It hung upstairs in the church, behind the curtains which had been strung around the pulpit-platform for the entertainment, and would be presented to the winner after the program was over. It was a Pine and Willow Tree design, a beauty; and everyone wanted it.

Harriet Lowden's pound cake, as always, was the guessing cake— guess how much it weighed and win it, at five cents a try—though before the greater contest this one paled a little. There was a pound of each ingredient in Harriet's cake, everybody knew that, but how many ingredients nobody knew but Harriet, and she changed the recipe a little every year, or said she did, though in Stell MacGimsey's opinion that was impossible and still have the cake come out the same. Harriet made the cake the same, Stell said, just changed the amount she *said* it weighed. Not that it made any difference, outside of being kind of deceitful, just so they had a guessing cake. Of course other people had receets for pound cake, just as good, but if the Ladies' Aid didn't want to make a change, it didn't.

Elbridge had come supplied with a handful of nickels which he doled out, a few at a time, to the twins and Joyce; and he went dutifully himself to heft Harriet's cake and have a couple of tries

at the grab bag, where he got a small crocheted doily and a china
hair receiver.

"What'd you get?" Liseo wanted to know, as Elbridge sat down
beside him on one of the supper-table benches. "H'm, little dish and
a mat to set it on. Ain't that pretty, though? I got a can of talcum
powder and five pieces of pink candy. Smell all alike, like violets.
I d'no which to eat. Which would you, Elbridge?"

"The talcum powder, if I had to one or the other," Elbridge said,
sniffing. "Try some on your beans, like salt, why don't you?"

The line of people on the bench heaved and settled back, as Wil-
lard Lowden sat down. A small boy on the very end of the bench
popped off on to the floor and set up a howl, as the slack was abruptly
taken up, and his mother, Carrie Hitchman, also stout, pushed back
heartily to regain his lost seat, before she picked him up and stuffed
his round mouth with a buttered roll.

"Lordsake, Wid," she said amiably. "You better take some of that
off, or bring you a kaig to set on, so's the rest of us'll have room to
the table."

Willard leaned his round face, like a pink sorrowful moon, out past
the others to look at her reproachfully.

George, beside him, bawled jovially, "By gorry, Carrie, that's right.
He figured you had that end of the trestle anchored, but I bet he
shifted you six inches. Carrie and Wid's got a race on," he informed
the table, "to see which one of them can get the most chins by the
time they're sixty. He figured she was ahead, but it don't look like it,
does it? Haw!"

Wiggy Shepheard came wandering along the aisle between the
tables, carrying in both hands a plate of smoking hot baked beans.
Wiggy was an undersized, chubby youth, with prominent blue
eyes and a lisp, a little lacking. He was not an idiot, nor was he
foolish; his trouble was, merely, that he did not know enough ever
to be unhappy. He saw life dimly and saw it with unfailing good-
humor through a pair of gold-rimmed spectacles perched on his
lumpy nose. If things went wrong, or kids teased him, as they some-
times did, he grinned and giggled; if things went right, he laughed
out loud. He came along, carrying his beans, an expression of an-
ticipatory pleasure on his innocent, homely face, craning his neck to
right and left, searching for something.

"What looking for, Wiggy?" George bellowed. "A load of hay or a
pretty girl?"

Harriet, George's sister, nudged him sternly in the ribs, and Addie

Shepheard, Wiggy's mother, gave George a resentful glare. One or two of the men grinned a little, but most of the ladies looked down at their plates. It was known to all that Wiggy was indeed looking for a pretty girl, for any girl, and could not find one.

Wiggy, however, grinned.

"I'm looking for thome of my mother'th piccilli pickleth," he said amiably. "Ha, that'th them, right there."

He leaned over Willard's shoulder and stretched a chubby arm toward a dish in the middle of the table. His thumb went to bottom in the dish as he retrieved it. As he straightened up, the plate of beans in his other hand tilted a little, and George, seeing it, reached slyly over behind Willard's back, hooked a finger over the edge of the plate and tilted it a little more. A trickle of scalding bean juice dripped from it down the back of Willard's collar. He leaped from under with a yelp of agony; the line of people wedged on the bench heaved at the impact, and the small boy at the end popped off onto the floor again.

"Thit, Wid," Wiggy said. "I hope I ain't burnt ya."

He turned the pickles upside down over his remaining beans, set the empty dish back on the table and walked away.

Willard, mopping furiously at the back of his neck with his handkerchief, yelled after him. The words, not at first distinguishable, resolved themselves into the threat that he was going to get up there and haul the plate of beans down over Wiggy's head, just let him get the cussed things out of his collar.

Harriet took the handkerchief away from him and rammed it down the collar with a few vigorous swipes. "You shut up, Willard," she hissed in his ear. She was bright red with embarrassment. "Serve you right, whether he meant to or not."

"He meant to, all right," George said, squirming with suppressed laughter. "I wouldn't blame Wid if he killed him."

"All right," Harriet said. "It was an accident, Willard. You ain't burnt to blister, only pink. If you boys don't want to go home without any, you shut up and eat your supper."

"Yes, for heb'm sakes, Wid," Carrie Hitchman said, "and let other folks eat theirs. Every time you spread, poor old Herbie flies off like a bat ball. There, now, Herbie, you ain't hurt. Crawl in here, on t'other side of Mumma. Now," she went on, transferring her son's plate to her sheltered side, "you start me off of here, you'll need more, Wid."

Willard subsided with his sting, and the table got down to real business. Gallons of beans vanished, mountains of brown bread and rolls. Pickle and coleslaw dishes stood empty. With cake and pie, conversation lagged and came to a stop. When Stell MacGimsey, as president of the Ladies' Aid and of the Quilt Society, stood up to make her speech, the vestry was quiet except for an occasional languid clink of a spoon on an empty ice-cream dish.

"Like to have your attention," Stell said. "We're a-going now to vote for the best cake or pie. There's paper and pencils there on the tables, and pass the votes along as fast as you can, because we want to get upstairs to the entertainment and it's getting late." She paused. "We have a new rule this year."

An electric silence fell over the ladies, who had not heard of any new rule at all. Whatever it was, their glances said, it was something Stell had dreamed up for herself.

"Any man caught voting for his own wife's cookery gets his vote throwed out," Stell said firmly, and sat down.

Liseo said softly in Elbridge's ear, "Vote for Jacob."

"Eigh?" Elbridge said, puzzled. "Whose is Jacob?"

Liseo's eyebrows writhed upward toward his widow's peak. He gave Elbridge a sidelong look, and with his tongue pressed hard against the side of his mouth, he printed "Jacob" in large square letters on his ballot. He pushed the pad and pencil on to Elbridge, saying nothing.

Elbridge thought, Oh, well.

Jess wanted the quilt, but if it was a rule not to vote for your wife, no sense to break it. He grinned a little as he wrote down "Jacob," wondering who he was voting for. Liseo had seemed pretty active, before supper, going around talking to this one and that one among the men. He was up to something.

The children, having no part in the voting, couldn't be held down at the tables any longer. Most of them had parts in the program to come and were as nervous as cats. One by one they slid off the benches into groups which, tentatively at first, suddenly exploded into runs and yells, raising a metallic and piercing babble of sound along the stone floor of the vestry.

"Lord, how do they do it?" Elbridge said. He flapped an ineffectual hand at Joyce, who shot by him, a streak of blue dress and flying legs. "The way I feel, it'd kill me."

Liseo grinned. "You've got old," he said. "You et like a pig, too, I watched you."

"Did, didn't I? So did you."

"I ain't been so full since the night we stole the ice cream," Liseo said. His eyes were on Stell and Mollie Lessaro, up at the head of the table busily counting votes.

Elbridge laughed. He remembered well that historic night, and the lickings he and Liseo and half a dozen other young rips of eleven to fourteen had got, when they'd finally been rounded up after the church social. It had been a grown-up social, to which the kids weren't invited, and the freezers of ice cream had stood outside the vestry door, as they had tonight. The kids had got away with three of them, using as eating utensils one iron spoon which had been left in a freezer, a folding pocket-carpenter's rule, and a couple of bleached clamshells found on the ledges behind the church, where they had carted the freezers. They were starting on the third freezer when someone at the social discovered the ice cream was gone. That, if he remembered correctly, had been Liseo's idea, too.

"What a bellyache," he said reminiscently, "and not only a bellyache, Liseo."

His stern, he remembered, had stung for a couple of days from the hearty whacks of MacKechnie's belt.

"Sure was," Liseo said absently. He was watching Stell with a bright expression, his eyes innocent and curious.

Stell had slapped all the votes together in a crumpled pile. She was sitting looking straight in front of her, with a bright red spot on either cheek.

"Now, what in thunder do you suppose ails Stell?" Liseo said.

"Don't know. Looks mad."

"Does, doesn't she?"

Stell got to her feet. She stood for a moment waiting for silence, which, unhappily, the running children did not notice. Then she picked up an empty glass pickle dish and banged it on the table. The pickle dish broke with a crash and a tinkle of glass, and the children stopped in midflight, creating a silence into which Carrie Hitchman's agonized voice fell clearly.

"She has *broke* my cut-glass pickle dish!"

Stell said, "You kids cut out that ranting this minute. This is a church and it ain't no place to act in it the way you act to home. You git and set down, every last one of you."

The children, unaware that they had been creating any disturbance beyond what they always did at a church supper, stood open-mouthed. A shock wave, almost tangible, passed over the vestry, moving between parents and children; then each child sought out his father or his mother and sat down in a scandalized silence. In a moment, according to custom, their mothers would have stopped their racket. To have it done by someone else, to be corrected *in public,* was outside experience.

To give Stell credit, she, too, was unaware of creating any disturbance, or of insulting the manners and upbringing of every child there. She was merely as mad as a hornet. She had been pretty sure she would win the quilt this year; she'd not only sprung the new rule on them, she'd gone all out with an old family recipe, whole walnuts and pink vegetable coloring. Just about everybody else in the society had won that quilt prize, in the years before. This year, it was *her turn.*

She said icily into the thick silence of her fellow members, hovering their injured young, "I wish to announce that the Quilt Society's Pine and Willow Tree handmade quilt has been won–has been *voted* –to Miss Roxinda Greenwood for a batch of *vanilla meringue kisses.*"

Applause, deafening and spontaneous, was started by a small group of men; the ladies sat, thunderstruck, for an instant, before they joined in. Under cover of it, Liseo said in Elbridge's ear, "You ever hear anyone make vanilla meringue kisses sound like rattlesnake poison before, Elbridge?"

Elbridge said, "Liseo, you devil."

He turned to look at Liseo's dead-pan countenance.

Liseo said, "Me? Why, you know I wouldn't do a thing like that, Elbridge."

"Do a thing like what?" Elbridge said, eying him.

"Put people up to it," Liseo said, grinning. "Take a look at Miss Greenwood."

Elbridge hadn't noticed before whether Miss Greenwood had come. Now, following the craning of other necks, he saw her, tiny and erect at one of the tables. She was smiling and nodding, but she had a red spot on each of her high, thin cheekbones, and she was not looking directly at anyone. She did not seem to understand that she was expected to get up and say something, the way the prize winner always did, each year. Mollie Lessaro went over and whispered to her; she shook her head, "No, no, no," but as the clapping increased, she arose.

She said, "Thank you all, very much," and sat down.

"Now," Stell said. She hardly waited for the clapping to stop. "Now, Miss Warren, you'd better get your actors together, start the program upstairs. I, for one, don't want to be here all night."

She turned and went up the inside vestry stairs into the church.

THE program opened with a tableau. Miss Warren announced it, standing outside the drawn curtains around the preacher's platform, and between the two towering Christmas trees that filled all the rest of that end of the church. "Our first tableau," she said in her sweet, dying-fall voice, one hand raised on a limp wrist, "will be 'Sunset on the Rhine.'"

Her cheeks and lips, in the light of the kerosene lamps with their bright steel reflectors, set around the church at intervals, bloomed with high, unnatural color; and every woman there wondered if that was rouge, and if it was, where she kept the rouge pot that Imogene couldn't find it. They forgot this speculation, at the sight of Herbie Hitchman.

Herbie was disclosed, when the curtains parted, a small, round boy in his Sunday pants, sitting on a large, yellow pumpkin, and looking pleased and interested. Herbie had looked forward to his part in the program; to him, it didn't seem like much, but people had praised him for it until he understood that it was something special everyone would wish to see. He was prepared for approval, not for a great sea of large white faces all looking at him.

The audience was unprepared for Herbie. They had just sat down, not yet adjusted to rehearsed entertainment, and knowing Miss Warren, had expected "Sunset on the Rhine" to be something beautiful and drear, such as young girls in nightdresses gazing sadly over a waste of water simulated by sheets. For a moment, they didn't get the point. They stared at Herbie and Herbie stared back. His small, complacent smile began to congeal, his eyes to glaze over with horror.

Then somebody let out a whoop, "Punkin rind!" and the large white faces all opened black holes, roaring. The noise came at Herbie. It was horrible. What to do? He bawled and bawled, sitting helplessly on his pumpkin while the tears flowed, his grief unheard in the storm of clapping and laughter; then he fled to a far corner behind the sheltering curtains, and nothing would persuade him back for an encore. His lament was a hoarse and raucous accompaniment to the tableau of "Snow Maidens," who were young girls in white dresses stuck with tinsel gazing sadly out over a waste of snows simulated by sheets. He did not stop until Miss Warren handed him down through the curtains to his mother, who smothered his hiccups in her ample bosom until he went to sleep there.

Elbridge dozed mildly through a couple more tinsel-stuck tableaux and some pieces spoken by the smaller children; Mollie Lessaro's soprano singing "Silent Night" woke him up, and Jess's elbow nudged him awake while Joyce spoke her piece about the dead horse. He had promised himself to stay awake through "Towser Shan't Be Tied Tonight," just to see how the audience took his and Will's surprise; but it was going to be hard to. He couldn't recall a time when he'd been so stuffed, and the church was warm. He could hear Willard down there now stoking up the furnace—Willard was the church janitor—and the heat was coming in blasts through the register in the aisle. He heard a spatter of sleet against the windows and thought vaguely, through a haze of sleep, Snowing. Wind's out and breezing up. Far off, he heard Miss Warren's voice at the head of the stairway urging Willard to hurry up, he was next on the program, and Willard's boom from below, "Keep your petticoat on, I'll be right up," which got a laugh from the audience, and then Willard's rich voice, accompanied by the wheeze of his old accordion: "Let The Lower Lights Be Burning."

"Send a gleam across the wave," sang Willard. "Some poor sinking, suff'ring seaman, You may rescue, you may save."

Willard was good. His baritone filled the church, rattled the lamp reflectors, drowned out his own accordion. The audience clapped him back and clapped him back; and having got through Miss Warren's selections, he encored with some more to his own taste.

"Oh, we have a ship that sail-ed, Upon the Lowland Sea," sang Willard, "And she goes by the name Of the Golden Vanity, And we fear she will be sunk-en By some bold Spanish ship, As she sails in the Lowlands Low." And "Once I saw a poker, Sticking in the fire-o," he sang. "To take it out and play with it Was my desire-o, Hi-rickety-bye-low, Cocka-doodle-doo." Until Miss Warren closed the curtains and held up her hand to show the program had to go on; and Willard, strutting a little, sweating a lot, came down to take his seat in the still clapping audience, his accordion under his arm.

Elbridge thought, Lord, we could take a lot more of that without going to sleep through it.

He'd had no trouble staying awake through Willard; but now Stell MacGimsey's voice began to declaim, and Elbridge settled himself drowsily again.

Stell, mad as she was, stood up before them all and spoke her piece with gestures.

"There is no death; *the* stars go down
To rise, upon some other shore;
And there in heav'n's jeweled crown
They shine, forevermore. . . ."

The stars went down in a wide sweeping arc of both of Stell's arms, and rose the same way; and heav'n's jeweled crown was a circlet of fingers. At first, she'd made up her mind to go home right after supper, show people; but she found that speaking her piece was a pleasure she did not wish to forgo, not when she'd practiced it so much, throw off Miss Warren's program. So she stayed and spoke her piece, and if her voice was not quite so expressive of deep meanings and her gestures not so fluid as they might have been, it was her neighbors' own damn fault. She sat down, to clapping, and presently rose and bowed, in silent dignity. They were *not* going to get an encore out of her.

Her place was taken by Imogene Cayford, and at the closing lines of Imogene's piece, Elbridge woke up. He realized that for some time a kind of sixth sense had been nudging at him, or maybe it was the half-familiar phrases repeated that knocked against his mind. But he came wide awake to hear Imogene say in tender tones that quivered with emotion, "Curfew *shall* not ring tonight!"

Elbridge jerked. His elbows flew out, and Jess, next to him, leaned over and whispered fierce'y, "*Elbridge! For heaven's sake, stay awake!*"

Elbridge, normally, would have grinned at her mildly and sheepishly and prepared to doze off again; now he hardly heard her.

Oh, my Lord, he thought. I've got to get hold of Will.

He hadn't had an idea in the world that somebody else would speak that curfew piece, let alone Imogene, who was renowned for quivers and throbs, and who, by the way the audience was sitting numb, had put in plenty this time. But how to find Will? The only way would be to get up and walk the aisle in full view of everyone and stick his head through the curtains; and everyone would want to know why, afterward; he doubted both his own and Will's ability to keep the cat in the bag.

It was too late, anyhow. The program was nearing its end; people had had about all the sad pieces they could take and now wanted to get at the presents on the Christmas trees. Imogene got short applause; and Miss Warren, hurrying things up, too, opened the curtain on the next number before Imogene could give her encore, another sad piece which she had all ready.

If, in the days to come, this particular school time was to be remembered as "the Christmas entertainment the devil came to," it was with reason; only the devil could have planned the coincidence which put "Towser Shan't Be Tied Tonight" on the program next to Imogene. Miss Warren, of course, had had nothing to do with it. She had merely felt that Will's assigned piece, "Tell Me Not in Mournful Numbers," would be a fitting finale.

The audience, paralyzed with boredom on the stiff-backed seats, had been suffering for the end. Will, looking very neat in his Sunday suit, with his red curls slicked smoothly down, spoke his first lines into a thick and sticky silence. He spoke well when he was interested, and there was little doubt that "Towser" interested him.

Oh, my, Elbridge thought.

He did not dare to look at Jess, aware that she had stiffened beside him.

For Will was getting into the story of the young man who left his pants with the bulldog a suggestion that was unmistakable of Imogene's tragic lilt.

A rustle went over the audience, as everybody suddenly sat up. The silence, electric as people realized what was happening, lasted through Will's first stanza and into his second. Then someone in the back of the church let out a delighted yelp, and the audience broke down. Nobody heard the end of the torn young man's troubles, because Will, never having been told that a good orator pauses until the laughter dies down, went ahead like a juggernaut. He finished, bowed soberly, and walked out of sight behind the curtains, leaving behind him pandemonium.

Elbridge, roaring and wheezing with the rest, glanced at Jess and saw that she was laughing helplessly, the tears running down her cheeks.

She said, gasping, "Elbridge Gilman, I could *kill* the both of you! But oh, dear, dear—" And she broke down again, mopping at the streams which ran down her face.

Miss Warren had drawn the curtains. She now stood on the platform outside them, with one hand up, flapping it for silence.

"Now, children and everybody, guess *who?*" she kept saying, but nobody heard, and her hand flapped more and more limply on her limp wrist. This was the prepared cue between her and Willard, who had gone out a while ago to dress for the rest of his part in the church vestibule, and unless she could make him hear, she couldn't go on to the Christmas tree.

She gathered her forces and let go with a shrill screech.

"NOW, CHILDREN AND EVERYBODY, GUESS WHO!"

It cut through the racket like a pair of scissors, and everybody looked, astounded, to see what had made the noise. But Willard had heard her at last, and he blew two toots on a fish horn—"toot-toot"— and came stamping in in his red suit and white whiskers.

Santa Claus had arrived.

"Hey," he said, as he came in the door. "What ails Imogene? She come flying by me like a bat out of— Well, here I am, big folks and little folks, right straight from the North Pole, and by criminy, I brought my own weather with me. We had better git out presents as fast as possible and git home and under cover, if we want to git home at all, for a worse snowstorm I don't believe I ever see. Now, I'll take the presents off the tree and call out names, and don't none of you kids hold up matters, because this ain't any ordinary storm."

By gorry, Elbridge thought suddenly. He's right, it isn't.

He had been aware of the weather, in the back of his mind, for some time, but sleepy as he had been, and what with events and all, he hadn't paid much attention. He realized now that snow was slashing at the northeast windows, and that the old church was beginning to creak and shudder in the wind. He slid unobtrusively out of his seat, tiptoed along the aisle to the vestibule, and opened the outside door a crack to look out. To his surprise, the door wrenched itself out of his hand and crashed open on a black, swirling void, which tried, briefly, to suck him out into it before it baffled around, pushed him backwards and filled the vestibule with a stinging blast of snowflakes as it slammed the door.

"My ghost," Liseo's voice said behind him. "What've we got, a Tommycane?"

"Some kind of a cane, Tommy or Harry, I guess," Elbridge said. He rubbed his wrist, which ached where the banging door had wrenched at it. "Look, Liseo, I never had an idea it was as bad as this. I think we'd better get folks started home."

"You'll do well," Liseo said. "Willard ain't near through, and presents is what folks has waited for all evening."

A thundering gust of wind struck the church, rising to a shriek as it passed over. The old building shook deep within itself, and in the belfry overhead the bell stirred with a muted clang.

"My God," Liseo said, with awe. "Rung the bell, didn't it? How rotten is that old belfry, Elbridge?"

"Well . . . it's old," Elbridge said. "Bell rope's slack, anyway. I better go up and take up on it."

"I'll go," Liseo said. "You get folks started home." He went up the belfry stairs two at a time.

Elbridge put his head in the vestibule door.

"Willard," he said. "We've got to cut short and get home. This storm's a bad one."

"I think so, too," Willard said. He too had looked out at the weather. "All right, folks," he sang out. "There's a lot left on these trees, we'll come back and start right in where we left off, tomorrow or next day. I and my family's headed for home. Come on, Harriet. Where's George?"

A few people moved, getting slowly to their feet, but most remained seated, and a concerted bawl went up from children who had not yet got presents.

Stell MacGimsey got up. "Now, you look-a here," she said. "There's been enough done tonight by you menfolks to spoil this entertainment that everybody's worked so hard over. I've stood for it and kept my mouth shut, but when it comes to— Wid Lowden! You come back here and hand out the rest of them presents!"

There was a gabble of voices above which rose Herbie Hitchman's familiar roar.

"It ain't Wid Lowden," he bawled, in disillusionment. "It's Sandy Claus!"

"That's right, dear," Stell said. "Of course it's Santa Claus, don't you fret. *Willard!* You come back up them stairs here!"

"All right, Stell." Elbridge's deep voice cut in over her shrill one. "It's a bad storm, this building's old and nobody wants to spend the night in it."

He stopped, astonished, aware that most of his neighbors were looking at him with faces annoyed or stubborn. They wanted their presents off the tree, weren't going home without them.

"Look," he said, "there's nothing on that tree that won't wait—"

The bell in the belfry clanged twice loudly, and Liseo came tearing out of the vestibule door and into the church.

"Bell rope's busted," he said. "The wind's rocking her like a baby in a cradle. She lets go, she's liable to be right down here amongst us. Come on, Fanny, round up the kids."

"You go on home with your tribe if you want to," Stell said. "We're going to stay in peace and have our presents."

"Oh, don't be so foolish," Mollie Lessaro said. She went by Stell, good and fast, gathering in her three children as she went.

"All right," Stell said. "But I give fair warning. If I go out of this church now, I *stay* out of it."

"Oh, go ahead and stay," Liseo said. "Set down and let the belfry fall in your lap, do you good. What are you, a lot of youngones?" he demanded of his neighbors. "You know damn well the kind of cultch there's liable to be on the Christmas tree. Listen to that wind. Look outdoors and see if you ever saw anything like it."

He ducked down the stairs, and reluctantly his neighbors got up and began to straggle after him.

In the vestry, which was partly underground, the sound of the storm was less evident. People clustered around the cloakroom putting on wraps; mothers hustled children into coats and overshoes; fathers lighted storm lanterns. Nobody said much. Nerves were stretched; nearly everybody was put out for one reason or another.

Willard was in a tearing rage; as he'd come away from the Christmas trees he'd grabbed up a bundle that had his own name on it— he'd spotted that first off, it was a good big one—and brought it along downstairs with him; and he'd torn off enough of the wrapping to see that it was an old chamber pot, hung on the tree for him as a joke. George, again, he supposed. He had got all the way down the vestry stairs before he remembered that his good clothes were up in the vestibule where he had changed, and he didn't dare go back up there for fear the bell would fall on him. He was still in his Santa Claus suit; and the first one down the stairs behind him was little Miss Warren, and he'd given her such a glare of fury that she'd bounced back about two feet and had to sit down, the effect was so awful.

Most families didn't have far to go. The houses were nearly all within a few hundred yards of the church. Bill and Mollie Lessaro, with their three small children, would have the longest walk, since they lived down near the end of the village.

"You make it all right, Bill?" Elbridge asked, as Bill's family passed him, headed for the door. "Might be an idea to all go in company. This is a corker."

"Oh, sure, I'll carry Billy and the rest can hang onto my co'ttail," Bill said. He looked sidelong at Elbridge, rolling his tongue around the inside of his cheek. "Nice entertainment, Elbridge."

"Real tasty," Elbridge said.

"Hell will hoot tomorrow," Bill said.

"You think it will?"

"I know it will. Imogene was setting right next to me. She was so mad her teeth chattered. I don't know as I'd want to be in your place, Elbridge, when she comes around to make sure you tend to Will."

"I don't know as I would, either," Elbridge said.

"And Stell's got a pretty good idea about Liseo and Miss Greenwood's kisses," Bill said. "Or I'll miss my guess, the way she was swallowing down bile." He grinned. "Oh, well, a good fight'll help us get through the winter." He waved a hand and went out through the vestry door, followed by his family.

A good fight, Elbridge thought glumly. He sounds as though he might enjoy one.

That was just the trouble. Too many people, in the beginning, thought they might enjoy a fight, not figuring ahead to where it might end. Well, tomorrow, he'd go around and see Imogene, explain to her, see if he could smooth her down. This was all pretty silly, this business here, tonight.

Just silly enough, his mind said, reaching back through the years to times gone by. Just silly enough to be the beginning of a dandy.

He stamped his foot into his remaining overshoe, and stood uncomfortably, wishing Jess and the kids would hurry up. It was while he was standing there that he suddenly saw Miss Greenwood.

She was over by one of the vestry tables, her lighted lantern beside her, composedly buttoning her coat with black-gloved fingers.

He made his way over to her.

"You aren't thinking of going home in this," he said to her.

Miss Greenwood smiled and nodded.

"Oh, I'll be all right," she said. "I have my lantern."

"You can't make it over the hill by the quarry pits tonight," he said bluntly.

"Oh, yes," she said. "Surely I can, Mr. Gilman."

"You come home with us, sleep in our spare room. That'd be a terrible jaunt, and you mustn't think of trying it."

"Well, thank you," she said. "That's very kind, but Mother would worry."

Where was Jess? Some of the womenfolks, somebody who might be able to stop her, because she had to be stopped, even if they had to tie her down.

"Listen," he said desperately, "you can't—"

A great spurt of smoke and steam and a ferocious hissing burst from the furnace on the other side of the vestry, and he spun around, along with everybody else, to look. Carrie Hitchman screamed and there was a general surge away from the area among the few people left in the vestry. The furnace stood wreathed in vapors, out of which presently emerged Willard Lowden, his face and hands smutted, his Santa Claus suit covered with soot.

"Godfrey mighty!" Liseo said. "What did you do—come down the chimney?"

"It's all right, folks," Willard boomed. "No need to be scairt, no need at all. I've just doused the furnace fire, that's all."

Willard had just poured a bucket of ice water into the almost red-hot furnace. The flare-back had blown into his face and scared him half to death; he wasn't so sure he hadn't been burned, and he was shaking, in spite of his reassurances.

"Willard," his sister Harriet said. "Are you crazy? I'll bet you've cracked that hearth."

"Well, what in hell do you want?" he said, banging down his bucket. "That belfry lets go the bell, falls down here and squats up the furnace, you want a fire in it, burn down the church? I don't want fire to fight, night like this. Maybe you do."

He glared around at his neighbors, who glared heartily back. They had been scared, too.

"It's all right, Willard," Elbridge said pacifically. "That was a good idea. Just so you didn't get burned. You didn't, did you?"

Willard had already decided he hadn't got burned, but things had gone too far. He had had enough.

"I'm the janitor of the church, my responsibility," he said. "But burn down, burn flat, see if I give a good goddam."

He slammed out of the vestry door into the storm.

Elbridge turned around to find Jess and the kids standing behind him. "Well, thank the Lord," he said. "Let's go home. If one more thing happens tonight, I'm going to fly into pieces."

Jess looked him up and down and glanced sternly over at Will, whose face, surrounded by the turned-down ear flaps of his cap, was sober and a little strained.

"If you two jokers and Liseo MacGimsey don't get *torn* into pieces before this quaker's over, I'll miss my guess," she said.

"Now, don't *you* start in," Elbridge said. He felt suddenly, unreasonably annoyed with Jess, and pulled himself up short. Whatever was loose in the air, outside and in, he seemed to be getting it along with everyone else. He grinned down at Jess, aware that the grin was slightly stiff, and said, "Let's get out of here. The next thing, by gorry, if things keep on, that belfry *will* fall down." He stopped. "Hey, where'd she go?"

"Where'd who go?"

"Miss Greenwood," Elbridge said.

"Why, she was right there by the door. She must be somewhere around."

She wasn't. She wasn't anywhere in the vestry. As the last of the crowd gathered by the door, it became apparent that Miss Greenwood, under cover of Willard's flare-back, had taken her lantern and gone along. Where, there was no doubt in anybody's mind. She'd gone along home.

"Oh, Elbridge!" Jess's eyes met his with quick concern. "Oh, she couldn't have been such a fool! What on earth had we better do?"

"Do?" Elbridge said. He couldn't remember when he'd been so mad. "Blast and damn it, follow after her, I s'pose. Somebody'll have to make sure she gets home."

At the bare thought of it, he felt as if he would like to fall right down flat under one of the vestry tables. He was tired all over, his eyelids gritty, and he thought of his bed at home with longing.

Jess said, "Elbridge, not up past those quarries tonight! I can't let you. It doesn't make sense. Elbridge—"

"Will," Elbridge said. "You and Gib make sure your ma and Joyce get home all right. I'll have to get Liseo. Shoot, Jess," he went on, seeing her face and pulling himself together enough so that he could grin at her. "It's nothing but a snowstorm."

LISEO said, "Goddam a mule-headed old maid. Four weeks out of a month I'd rather deal with a chimley afire. If she don't end up in the bottom of the quarry and have to be drug out piecemeal, it'll be the God's living, dreaming wonder, and us on top of her, laid arm by laig."

He walked along the causeway ahead of Elbridge, carrying his storm lantern. His voice came back in wheezy gusts, the words torn apart and flung by the wind. It had been bad, crossing the flat above the village; they had had to lean forward driving into the wind blindly, letting the tops of their caps break the blasting snow particles which cut like sleet. Here in the swamp, they were sheltered a little from the wind, though Elbridge wondered, hearing it scream and thunder through the branches above them, how long before a tree would be down on their heads. The big spruces were thrashing and whistling, and underfoot he could feel an uneasy tremor, deep down, as if all the tough roots under the causeway foundation were being yanked like teeth and giving up hard. The walking was terrible. The heaved ties of the old causeway were out of sight already, under snow; every third step or so, a foot would meet one or slide off with an ankle-jarring thud.

"And what we are doing," Liseo said, "out here in the dead and middle of the night, the little match girl in the prime of her life and up to her changes, wouldn't know. I—"

His arms flew up as one foot slid into a hole, and Elbridge saw his lighted lantern describe an arc, flying against the seething snow-flakes, before it landed somewhere in the thickets and went out. Liseo, floundering on his hands and knees, said something which blew back on the wind as "bawling children down a rat hole."

"You all right?" Elbridge said, holding up his own lantern to see.

"No," Liseo said. "But if you mean, have I broke anything, I ain't."

Elbridge bumped into him, feeling his coat, snow-caked and stiff under his own frozen mittens, and hauled him to his feet.

"What'd you throw the lantern at?" he asked. "See that deer?"

He took a bearing from where Liseo was, and went over to the side of the causeway to look for the lost lantern, hoping, as he groped around in the snow-laden underbrush, that it hadn't gone down the side of the rubble foundation. Going more by his sense of smell than anything else, he found it. It was reeking of hot kerosene, but not broken so far as he could tell, and kneeling at the edge of the thicket, with his opened coat as a windbreak, he wiped it off with his mittens and managed to relight it.

"Daniel Boone," Liseo said. "And them. They got caught in a bliz-zard, all they had to do was scoop out a nice, warm buffalo. Crawl in and there they was, snug as tripe, till spring."

"Bill's got a cow," Elbridge said. "Not too far from here, if you're cold, Liseo."

"Oh, hell," Liseo said. "Suggest something sensible, why don't you? Bill wouldn't like it, it's his cow. No sense going out of your way to make people mad, Elbridge."

"That's right," Elbridge said. "That's a fact."

He started to grin and stopped it halfway, aware that if he let his teeth get started chattering, they probably wouldn't quit.

At the foot of MacKechnie's hill, they stopped a minute to rest before starting the climb. The wind went in long, shrieking gusts across the sky, over the woods behind them, and somewhere, not far away, a tree went over with a muted thud, as if a giant foot had stamped once, heavily, on the snow.

"Noisy," Liseo said.

He held the lantern out, watching its thin circle of light, pale and drowned in the flickering swirl of dry, tiny flakes.

"Don't know as I ever saw it snow any harder," he said. "What did you do in the great snowstorm, grampop? Sonny, I spent the whole livable, damnable time of it chasing an old maid." He pointed downward, where in the wan light a series of small depressions led up the slope of the hill. "Yonder she went," he said.

"She got this far, anyway," Elbridge said.

They started up the hill, stooping forward to ease the sting against their faces. At the top, the bald crest open on all four sides to the sky, it was worse than anything Elbridge could have imagined. The wild trumpeting gusts tore down out of an immense blackness, with a sound in his ears like ripping canvas. One moment they bore him backwards, the next they let up, with a suddenness that almost flung him flat on his face. He bored into it, aware of the pits twelve or fifteen feet away on either side of the track, and the track itself unmarked here, swept clean of snow, the smooth granite scoured, nothing to show where the path was; easy to lose bearings, walk right off over the edge. He raised his head uneasily to spot Liseo's light ahead of him, shielding his eyes with his arm, and thought for a reeling moment that he had gone blind. There was nothing ahead of him but pitch blackness.

Elbridge let out a yell which he did not even hear himself. He got down on his hands and knees and crawled slowly, holding the lantern off and out to one side to give his eyes a better chance, trying to see some sign of Liseo's tracks, making sure, with each careful movement, that the rock ahead of him was solid. But there were no tracks, nothing on the granite except an occasional gray-green rosette of lichen, rimmed with crystal.

One thing about MacKechnie's quarry pits, they had straight edges, sliced as clean and true into the rock as a cut in a pan of fudge. If he got too close to one, he could likely feel the edge in time. He moved at a snail's pace, flattened down, stopping to feel ahead of him. Once, his hand encountered a sharp edge of cut stone with nothing beyond it as far as his arm could reach; he sensed, rather than saw, the black void below, full of wild, full of blown snow streaming and coiling almost as if it were being boiled in a pot.

He thought crazily, Old Ellick. Cocked back like a snake, and his hand, groping, touched one of the iron stakes that once, long ago, had supported a wooden railing to guard this drop-off.

Why in hell we haven't fixed that railing, I don't know. Could at least have put ropes up—saved all this—

Well, he had a leeway of maybe thirty feet to the other edge, he had his bearings now. Go back maybe fifteen feet, then crawl straight, ought to hit the downhill soon, one way or the other. He backed up carefully, sheltering the lantern, and, turning, found himself nose to nose with a wild, staring visage, eyelashes and brows fierce streaks of snow-caked white, the eyes, glittering in the lantern light, six inches away from his own.

"Jesus!" Elbridge said, recoiling.

"What we doing?" Liseo yelled. "Playing snake?"

The wind bit the words out of his mouth, sent them whistling past Elbridge's ears, so that they sounded like "Wha-wha-ache."

He bawled, "What say?" inching sideways so that he could creep past with the lantern, feeling his knees weak with relief that Liseo was up here on the hill, not down in the snow and freezing water at the bottom of the pit.

"I said are we playing snake," Liseo yelled in his ear.

"That's what I thought you said."

"Well, it's a hell of a night for it. Keep on straight. Ahead of you's downhill."

Elbridge felt the granite sloping away in front of him, knew that he was past the crest now. He went on down, feeling at last the wind slack off a little as he reached the spruce thickets at the bottom of the hill. For a moment, he could do nothing but stand still and breathe.

"What happened to you?" he said, after a while.

"Damn lantern blew right out of my hand," Liseo said hoarsely. "Straight up into the air. Didn't you see it?"

"Didn't see anything. Thought you'd blown to hell an' gone down into the quarry."

"That was a good lantern," Liseo said. "Oh, well. It's probably to Port Western by now. It's a wonder *we* ain't." He stopped and panted, his breathing a curious wheeze, with a slight whistle at the end of each breath.

"You all right?" Elbridge asked.

"Sure. *I* am. But we're on one hell of a wild goose chase, Elbridge."

"I guess likely we are," Elbridge said soberly.

If he and Liseo had so nearly come to grief on that hill, something a lot worse could have happened to Miss Roxinda, and probably had.

"We'll have to get out a possy in the morning," Liseo said. "Have to shovel around them quarries, then won't find her, likely till spring, maybe never, if she lit in one of the ponds. Oh, hell, Elbridge, that's going to be one awful frig."

"Well. The only thing we can do is keep on out to the Point and make sure. Ma's over there with the old lady. Better see, anyway, if everything's all right with them. Maybe she made it home."

"All right. We can. But I don't believe once in the living God's world that old tumbrel ever got over the hill."

They went on, able to walk steadily now that the road led again through trees. Up in the center of the island, deafened by wind, they had not been aware of the sound of the ocean, but here toward the eastern shore, The Pasture was making itself heard in vast, tormented thunder, and the air was full of the bitter taste of salt spray. The sound was like being in a barrel beaten on with mauls.

They came at last to the end of the woods, where the storm took them in the face again. They had no breath and it was hard to see, but beyond the last thicket of spruces was the Greenwood cottage, and they could make out a light in the living room.

The windowpanes were blind with snow, but the light shone across Miss Greenwood's porch, down the steps, and made a yellow cobweb on the deep pool of sea water which filled the low place between the house and the woods. As they looked, a wind-driven crest of spray slammed against the house, washing down across the windows and across the porch, down the steps in a waterfall, clearing them of snow. A long slither of water spilled into the pool, the web of light broke up in squiggly lines of sparkling bubbles. Two big dollops of snow went sailing, surrounded by cream-colored foam, whipped fine as meringue. The splash from the spent wave slapped Liseo's boot and he retreated hastily, peering at the cheerful lighted window with bleary, snow-stung eyes.

Miss Roxinda was there. In a warm white dressing gown, her hair braided in two braids down her back, she was sitting by her living room fire, serenely reading a book.

"Why, the damned old curiosity!" Liseo said. "She ain't even out of breath."

The spark was nearly gone out of him. He stood for a moment wheezing, before he said, "Well, she must've waded that pool, but I'll be goddamned if I'm going to. Be up to your waist, wouldn't it?"

"Damn nigh," Elbridge said. "Probably wasn't so deep when she got here. That flood tide likely came in pretty fast."

It was past time for high tide, he knew. The ebb hadn't showed up yet, wouldn't for a while, with that wind piling the water in over The Pasture onto the Point. But it was bound to start soon. The sea wouldn't go much higher, and Miss Greenwood's house, set up high on the rock and reinforced by Luther MacGimsey's stone work, was as safe as a lighthouse. Right now, it was on an island of its own, with water on four sides of it, but it was all right.

"Think we ought to go in?" Liseo said, eying the cold water distastefully. "See if they're scared? Three wimmenfolks alone, and all?"

"Scared?" Elbridge felt a sudden, hot rage. If it had been Jess, any of the womenfolks he knew, he would have waded the pool to his neck, gone in there and got her told so that she would have been teetering around on tiptoe for a week. Little Sarah was there, of course; in bed, asleep, if he knew her, you couldn't wake her up with a cannon. It took more than a snowstorm to scare Little Sarah. "Oh, to hell with it," he exploded. "Come on home, Liseo."

They went home by the shore path, the track made by trappers of mink and hunters of sea birds along the south and western shores of the island. It was rough going, and the long way around; but it was in the lee and sheltered by trees; better than MacKechnie's hill tonight. It went past the beach where, a few hundred feet offshore under the seething water MacKechnie's old donkey engine rusted quietly away into the sea bottom, past the Passamaquoddy spring and the cellar with the rock marked "A," and, turning inland there, skirted the forgotten field of the Red Paint People, its row of shallow holes leveled and drowned in snow. They made it home, stumbling and exhausted, at three in the morning. Elbridge's house was nearest, with a light in the window, and Jess waiting up.

She said, "Oh, thank the Lord!" and hustled to help them off with their frozen outside gear. She had a fine fire going, the kitchen hot enough to roast a camel, a big pot of coffee steaming on the stove, and the rum bottle set out on the table along with the coffee cups.

"Yes," Elbridge said, in answer to her unspoken question. "She's all right. She got home."

And Liseo, leaning his face over the stove to melt the icicles out of his eyebrows, letting the drops fall on the hot metal covers with a fine sizzle that was the sound of all comfort, said, "Ayup. She flew there. On a broom."

IN the house on the Point, the light had gone out. For a while the windows kept a reddish glow from the falling fire, then that, too, died, leaving the panes white and blind. Inside, the three occupants of the house slept unafraid: the old lady, deaf and blind, who knew no more of a winter storm than of a summer day; Little Sarah, who thirty years ago had learned that too much lost meant nothing more to lose and since had disciplined her life accordingly; and Roxinda Greenwood, who, before sleep, had said her private prayer to the God of her solitude, "Thank you, O God, for my good life," and laid her grotesque head serenely on her pillow.

Before the turn of the tide, a balk of new-sawed lumber washed up over the ledges into the pool between the house and woods, and, surrounded by fine, whipped-cream-like foam, nosed gently to rest at the foot of the spruce thicket above the lawn. All along the drowned and screaming rocks, from The Pasture to the water meadows, where, long ago, the sea had scattered tall, woven baskets of garlic for cows to eat, the new lumber, gouged, splintered, rubbed furry on its undersides, began to come ashore.

The house, on its island within an island, thrust toward the sky; its stubborn jut of wood and stone beetled into the vast streamers of the storm. They came choked with snow and the hard, bullet-driven surface of the sea, ripped like a material not of air and water, but something thick as canvas and as tough; the house, unshaken, split them. Integrity of work, of craftsmanship, had put it there; integrity of spirit kindled its fires and kept it going. Without either one of these it was finished, done; but it had both. It said as much to the Old Ellick loose in the world tonight; to the old wild, to the come-and-get-you; to the harm, whatever it was, lying in wait under the secure face of the world to trip the steps of man and bring his proud works down.

THE alarm on Stella MacGimsey's bedside clock went off at four, not waking her, for she had been lying, dozing, waiting for it. Every morning, that last half-hour, she could feel herself coming up through layers of sleep, fighting to drop back, until at last, something neither awake nor asleep would say tensely, "Now!" And then the bell, splitting the thick darkness like a scream.

She put out her hand, groping on the stand for the clock. It never seemed to be where she thought it was. Almost as if someone always came in in the night and shifted it, so she would have to feel around while the squalling bell sandpapered her nerves. This morning, she couldn't seem to find the clock at all. Her spread hand, patting around in the icy darkness over the table top, moved with faster and faster jerks, struck the tumbler in which her false teeth were. The tumbler upset and rolled. She heard it hit the floor with a solid thud and a tinkle of glass.

My land, if I've *ever broke* them teeth! Twenty-five dollars gone to glory. And the Lord only knew when she'd get enough saved up for another set.

Her hand encountered the small, cylinder shaped dish with its card of matches. She broke one off and struck it, yanking it along the match scratcher glued to the head of the bed. The match sizzled with a stinking whiff of sulphur and a growing blue spark, which threw off no light except a smoky illumination of the insides of her lined, knuckly hands, cupped around it.

Portland Star matches, they weren't no earthly good, but cheaper, there was that whole match safe of them in the store that nobody would buy, might as well use them up, got to save somewhere, save on little things have something left for the big, and oh, that *cussed* clock, and I bet I've broke them teeth.

The tiny blue flame turned yellow as the matchwood caught. It lifted the black over the table top enough so she could see the clock and the glassy glitter of the kerosene lamp beside it.

First things first, no use to waste matches. She reached for the lamp, turned up the wick—was that up or down?—lifted off the chimney and held the match to the wick. It was down. The wick sputtered, did not light. The match scorched her fingers and she slatted it out, fumbled for another.

In the bedroom next to hers, she heard Grampa Luther turn over and cough, the loose, phlegmy cough he always had now, winter and summer.

"Stell!"

She found the match, turned the wick the other way, lit the lamp.

"Stell! Goddammit, you dead? Turn off that clock, wake up the whole neighborhood!"

Glass on the floor, that tumbler broke, be careful. No time to cut a foot, the dead of winter.

She put her bare feet out of bed, feeling cautiously down on the crocheted rug, cold as the pelt of some dead and frozen animal, no glass, and lifted the lamp to peer down behind the stand.

The glass tumbler, broken but not shattered, lay split around its contents, which had frozen solid in the night. The teeth grinned safely within a clear cylinder of ice.

Well, there, if that don't beat all, it must've come off awful cold sometime in the night.

"STELL!"

She picked up the tumbler-shaped block, set it carefully down on the stand. That wasn't going to do them teeth one mite of good.

The clock, looking as it always did, like something alive and malevolently jumping up and down, faltered, and Stella reached out and shut it off.

The silence caught Grampa Luther at the top of the long breath he'd taken to let out another holler. He listened a minute and then breathed out in a long wheeze.

"Stell, you git the fire a-going, warm up the house. I'm cold. The pump'll freeze up. It's come off way below zero."

She fumbled around under the bedclothes for her underclothes and corsets. They'd got pushed over against the wall, somehow, in the night; they were cold, the corsets like ice. She could see her breath against the feeble light from the lamp.

"Stell? Stell, you up? You never turned it off and went back to sleep, did you?"

Who'd have thought, with that blizzard, it would have turned cold so quick? She'd been too beat out, when she got home from the entertainment, to stoke up the stove; but last night hadn't seemed like what you could call real pump-freezing weather. Tired and mad, and getting home a terrible trial. She'd never seen *anything* like that wind and snow to beat through. And she could have died right there on the main road, for all her neighbors cared, going off, all in company, and leaving her sitting alone, up there in that church.

"Stell, you build my fire first, you hear me?"

She had sat there, stiff and upright in her pew—the MacGimsey pew—until every last soul had gone home, and then she had gone down front and picked her own presents off the tree. Gone off, they had, one and all, never so much as put out the kerosene lamps in the church. That Willard, he was the janitor, he was going to hear about that. Not that she cared. It would be many the long day before she set foot in that church again. Someone else could do all that hard work she did; see how they liked getting along without her. She'd got home, no thanks to anyone. Them that had families had each other. You'd thought someone would have made sure she got home all right, helped carry that heavy basket. Why, last night after she'd got in bed, even, she'd shook and shook; and for a while it seemed as if the roof was going to fly off the house in the wind; and if it had, there she'd have been, nobody but one helpless old man.

Well, the storm had blown itself out, come off clear and cold, likely, the way it did sometimes; though, as she went by the east window on her way to the kitchen, carrying the lamp in one hand and the block of ice with her teeth in the other, she couldn't see out. The window looked to be blocked with snow, and the whole house was as still as a tomb except for Luther's wheeze following behind her.

"Stell, you build up my airtight first, now. It's freezing in here, it'll bring on my asthma."

Stell hit the pump handle a couple of bangs as she went by. All right, so it was frozen.

The stove in the kitchen was cold; a smell of icy soot came out as she took off the lids. She got the fire going, putting in pieces of crumpled paper and split boxwood kindling to make it heat up fast; when it was caught and roaring, she filled the stove with dry cat-spruce limbs and shut the drafts.

They can have all their hardwood they want, but if you need a quick hot fire, give me dry cat-spruce limbs.

Last fall, getting her winter's wood, she had cut a-plenty of them.

She hefted the teakettle—thank goodness, one thing, she'd filled it, and pumped the bucket full on the sink drainboard. They had skimmed over, weren't frozen hard. She set the teakettle on the front of the stove. Then she rooted in the cupboard for a double boiler, put some water in the bottom half and the cylinder of ice with her teeth in the top half. The potbelly stove in the store would be hotter, for a while, than the kitchen stove—she always kept a coal fire going in the store so the canned goods wouldn't freeze. Carrying the double boiler and the lamp, she crossed the icy entry and unlocked the door to the L room where the store was.

Warmth hit her in the face like a blessing. She set the lamp on the counter and the double boiler on the stove, and spread her purpled hands to the heat.

My Lord, I don't know why I don't bring my bed right out here winters and *live!*

But there, she couldn't, not while she had Luther. If only he could have been the one to go instead of poor Warren. But the able-bodied went, nine times out of ten, left the old and puny who weren't any good to anyone.

Poor Warren, if he'd lived, we could of took comfort together, I wouldn't have the outdoors work and the heavy, and somebody to help me lift Luther, and he not even my own grandfather.

The best husband who ever lived, she thought mournfully, leaning her face toward the drowsy warmth of the store stove. It wasn't his fault he didn't leave me with three-four children to help me out with the work now.

Poor Warren, he never cared for *that*, in any way, shape, nor manner; he got more, any time, he used to say, out of a good bowel movement. Poor Warren, it wasn't his fault that he was barren.

She caught sight of herself in the mirror that hung on the back of the closed store door. The mirror was one that some wholesale company had sent as a prize to the customer that bought the most of its goods, but somehow nobody had ever won it, and Stell had kept it. It didn't seem quite honest to take it into the house as *her* mirror, besides she didn't have a place for it in there anyway; so she'd left it in the store. The company had written about it a couple of times, so long ago now that she'd even forgotten which company it was. Anybody who ran a store got things like that, every once in a while. It wasn't *her* fault if the company never got it back. She didn't ask them to send anything.

The mirror showed her a lean, powerful woman of forty, black hair in braids down her back showing no trace of gray, wearing a shapeless flannel house dress and a tie-on apron.

She was not too different, she thought, from young Stella Lurvey, whom Warren had married. Older, of course. That was bound to be. A hard life showed up on you sooner or later, and she guessed the world would admit she'd had a hard one. But, for an orphan girl, the ward of the state, that Warren MacGimsey had picked up at a dance over on Shell Island, proposed to that same night and married the next day, before she'd had any idea that he had funny-troubles and been thunderstruck when she found it out, she guessed she hadn't done so bad. There were lots of Lurveys over on Shell. They were a very fine family, some of them could belong to the S. and D.A.R. if they wanted to; and she could, too, if only that lazy town clerk over there would bother to look up the records, instead of writing back that there weren't any. Poppycock, he just didn't want to take the time to thumb back, not that it mattered. She was certainly related to the Lurveys, which was all she needed to know.

Now, in her store, at four-thirty on a winter's morning, warming her hands, with her hair not yet done, she wasn't much to look at, she thought. But when she was dressed up, she was.

She always kept herself up, studying the hair-do's in the catalog, and the styles of dresses and hats; if her own were made over out of last year's, it was not because Stell MacGimsey didn't know just what was going. If she ever did get new, it was *new*, and calculated to knock eyes out. She would put a wreath of roses, or a bird, ordered out of the sales catalog, on an old felt or straw that people had forgotten she ever had, and wear it to church; and give out that it had just come yesterday; and if people asked her what catalog she'd ordered it from, she'd say Bellas Hess, or some of them, that no one else had had a catalog yet from.

She lifted the lid of the double boiler and stirred the teeth with her finger. The ice fell away from them, and she fished them out and put them in. A sharp sliver bothered for a moment; she thought, Oh, Lord, they've been harmed! But it was only ice, melted at once; she bit down feeling the plate settle solidly and comfortably against her gums.

I ain't a yuman being in the morning till I get my teeth in, she thought, and took the lamp back to the kitchen.

The kitchen fire was glowing hotly in the stove, and Luther was still wheezing, "Stell, you git my fire built, I'm cold."

There was just time to milk the cow before Orin Vira came, at five, after the mailbag.

She put on her barn clothes—an old sheepskin coat of Luther's, and his old rubber boots—and tied a scarf over her head. Then she lighted a storm lantern and went out through the shed to the barn.

Cold mornings like this, it was a blessing to have the house and shed and barn all connected, so you didn't have to go outdoors, much as sometimes in damp weather the barn and privy smelt in the kitchen.

The privy—might as well get *that* over, not have to come out again after breakfast, when she had so much to do. She sat down, gasping, as the ice-cold wood met her clenched flesh.

After breakfast, she'd open up her Christmas presents she'd got off the tree, and if there were any of them that weren't worth anything, didn't amount to much, she was going to wrap them up and put them into the mailboxes of the people who sent them, show how she felt about the whole matter.

That Liseo, I'll get back at him if it's the last thing I ever do. And saying there was nothing but cultch on them Christmas trees that we all worked so hard over. When it wasn't what you got, at all, ever, it was the *spirit* of Christmas that mattered. Some little thing, show how you felt, even if it wasn't the most expensive item in the whole catalog. The idea. What does he think, people going to lay out a lot for just neighbors, when they couldn't afford to buy for themselves or for their own family? I'll have him know we ain't all rich lobster dealers, to flang around money as if 'twas dirt, spend it on that girl that ain't half what he thinks she is, if there's anything behind, two and two together, in them letters she writes. Her and that Joe Farleigh, whoever he was. Her and Roger Gilman.

Nothing but cultch themselves. That Liseo, what was *he?* Nothing but a— She tried to think of a word bad enough and suddenly one came to her.

Nothing but a cussed wop, she said to herself. And Elbridge, himself, his own wife's got nigger blood in her from old John Cloud. Well, there, that explains it, nobody's thought of it for years, but there it is, and what can you expect. Niggers and foreigners took over, and us good honest Americans git the dirt end of the stick. I guess if the summer people found out some things, there'd be some jobs go flying. And them twins of Elbridge's and Jess's played with Mr. Wynn's kids all last summer. People like them, they're pretty careful who their kids play with, if they only knew.

She got up, banged down the seat, and started for the tie-up.

Must be an awful dark morning. There wasn't one scrap of light showing through the barn window. She held up the lantern to the window, and was surprised to see that it was blocked with snow.

My land, must be some deep drift out there on the east side of the barn.

There was, indeed, she discovered, when she opened the wooden slide window in the tie-up, to shovel out behind the cow. The window had to be pried with the shovel; the opening was a smooth rectangle of snow, packed so thick that she couldn't break it away. She hated to leave the cow not cleaned out, meant she had to take time and do it later, but no use, she'd have to go around and break through that snow from the outside.

Stella sat down on the milking stool, leaning her head against the cow's flank, and began to milk, the two streams drumming hard into the bottom of the galvanized pail. The cow, except that her flank was warm, seemed hardly alive; she stood flat-footed, not moving, giving up hard her few quarts of milk.

"Well, there, let down, you old besom," Stell said impatiently. "I know you're thirsty, but I can't do a thing about it till I get the pump thawed out."

She finished milking, set the bucket and the lantern by the barn door, while she climbed to the loft to pitch down some hay. She pitched some extra for bedding—not much. It was cold in the tie-up, with a dead, icy chill; but the cow had better be cold than as hungry as she would be before spring, if Stell ran out of hay.

She picked up the lantern and milk pail and carried them back to the kitchen.

Luther, hearing her shut the shed door as she came in, said, "Stell, you build my fire, now. Stell?"

Stell set the milk pail on the cupboard, blew out the lantern, hung it on its nail in the entry. Then she washed her hands, using a meager dipperful of water out of the bucket on the drainboard, got out the coffee pot and canister, and made coffee.

Well, see about the pump; she could do that next. She poured half the teakettle of boiling water from the stove down the pump, began banging the handle. Up and down, up and down. The pump gulped, wheezed; to her astonishment, it began belching up water, mixed with a few slivers of ice. It hadn't frozen hard at all, thank the Lord. Now she could water the cow, unless Orin came. Funny where he was. He was late. It was half-past five already.

Luther, in the bedroom, started pounding.

Now, sir, he could stop that. He could holler all he was a-mind to, but when it came to pounding, she wasn't going to put up with it. She started for the bedroom, then realized that it couldn't be Luther, the sound was coming from the direction of the front door. My land, somebody was crazy, coming to the *front* door, this time of the winter.

The closed up parlor and front hall were dark and dead as a tomb. It was useless to try to heat more than the rooms she needed to live in, and Stell never did.

"Hold on," she called, hurrying along the hall with the lamp flickering in her hand, "you'll have them hall lights stove out. Come round back, can't you, like a yuman being? That storm door ain't been opened all winter."

Whoever it was only pounded harder, calling out something she couldn't hear.

My Lord, it's Orin, she thought. What's he way round here for?

She turned the key in the lock, shot back the inside bolt. The front door was stuck and she had to set down the lamp and use both hands to yank it open. Then she unhasped the storm door and pushed at it; it, too, was swelled shut.

"For the Lord's sake, Orin! This door's swole tight."

Orin managed to spring the door back enough, so he could get his fingers in the crack and pull. The door opened with a crunching sound, a creak of frozen boards and rusty hinges. Stell saw he was covered with snow from head to foot.

"I been trying for half an hour to poke a hole through that snowbank over the store door," he said, panting. "It's clan up to the eaves, Stell, must be dag-rabbited near twelve feet deep drifted in there."

Stell's mouth dropped open. "You couldn't get in the store door, for the land's sake? I never heard of such a thing!"

Beyond him, through the open door, she caught a glimpse of clear, starry sky, beginning to lighten with morning, and the fields stretching from her front door to the shore, smooth as a bedspread, all the humps and nubbles deep hidden under snow. Beyond the shore, the water in the bay was black as ink.

Orin came in, hauling the door to by main strength and hasping it.

"Come off colder'n a dog," he said impressively. "If it hadn't been such a gale, we'd have had upwards of seven feet on the level. As 'tis, I never see the beat of them drifts."

"Well, don't leak snow all over my front hall," Stell said. "It's bad enough to have the back of the house tracked up all day long, people coming and going, without having footprints all over your nice. You hyper for the back entry, sweep yourself. Seven feet, my Lord," she went on, preceding him with the lamp.

She went on through the dining room to the kitchen, past Luther's door and his voice going on monotonously now, "Stell, now, Stell, you come build my fire," and out into the store and post office. Orin followed her, shedding gobbets of snow at every step, still full of news.

"Awful gale, regular South American hurricane. Joe's boat sunk."

"No!" Stell said. Behind the post office wicket, she was checking the mail drop, not surprised to find it empty, for who'd have come with letters, last night like it was? "Joe's *boat?*"

"Sunk at the mooring," Orin said. "And them boats that was hauled up there by the wharf, the tide come right over, washed them around there scandalous. No knowing what the damage is, they're all a mess of ice and snow."

"My Lord, Orin!"

"I couldn't find my punt, had to borry Liseo's, shovel it out, it was full of snow to the gunnel, and I rowed off aboard my boat, had to chop upwards of six inches of ice off of her, wonder she hadn't sunk, too. Wonder they all hadn't."

Orin, standing as close as he could get to the potbelly, was melting snow all over it. Stell could hear it sizzle and an occasional soft thump as lumps fell to the floor. More puddles to mop up.

"I don't see how so much snow fell in so little time," Orin said. "Wind come off nor'west, ker-whango, round four o'clock, cleared off cold, thermometer must've dropped twenty degrees, still dropping. For a while there, it blowed harder nor'west than it did no'theast, I don't know's I ever saw it blow so. Down there in the main road by the wharf, there's a punt. I don't know whose it is, could be mine, it's buried up in a snowbank, but it's a punt, and right slap in the middle of the main road. And them big trees along the road is gone as if they'd never been, whether blowed out to sea or buried up in snow, no knowing, every last living one of them."

"Why, Orin, it ain't possible!" Stell said. She handed him out the locked mailbag. "A punt in the main road! No!"

"That's what it was. I like to broke my laig on it. What's in here? Two letters and a postcard?"

"Just about. Imogene's Sears order. And Jess's sending a package of socks over to Roger."

"Why don't she wait and give it to him, he'll be home Friday," Orin said. "What's the sense loading *me* down with it, time like this?"

"Oh, they had a letter from him yesterday, said he'd come to holes. But you ought to know the *mail*, by this time. Something free, people don't have no consideration, none whatever."

"Darn right," Orin said. "Find a mailman froze deader'n a clam in the snow, what's liable to be in his bag? Picture postcard with 'Wish you were here' on it."

That was Orin's favorite story—the one about the mailman in the Arctic. Stell had heard it many times. Orin had carried the mail, winter and summer, the four miles across the bay, for fifteen years, and had never missed a trip. Once he almost did—in a spell of weather one March, when a thaw started the ice moving out of coves and inlets to the westward, and then a sudden cold snap froze the mov-

ing floes, so that around the island, fields of treacherous salt-water
ice alternated with strips of open water. Orin had made it across by
lashing a skiff to a couple of sleds, and he and his boy, Allen, hauled
across, navigating where they had to. Orin said he wouldn't want to
do it again, though. Them sleds made the skiff logy in the water.
Been any wind, she'd have swamped, sure as God, and he'd have
been as dead as the mailman in the Artic, the one with the post-
card.

No, sir, what was in the mailbag was never worth a man's time to
carry; the only thing being, it was the U-nited States Mail.

Orin took the light bag from Stell, made sure it was locked, and
set off without further ado back through her kitchen, dining room,
parlor and hall, trailing tracks and splashes of water, and Stell fol-
lowed him with the mop.

By Luther's bedroom door, they heard him say, "Now, Stell. Stell,
you come build my fire, you hear?"

Stell went back to the kitchen, stood the mop in its bucket behind
the door. She got out a spider from the cupboard under the sink,
then, still carrying the lamp, went to the cellarway for stuff for break-
fast. She sliced streak-of-lean-streak-of-fat into the spider, where it
began to fry, with a thick, mouth-watering smoke. In the oven was a
big pot of beans, brought home last night from the church supper,
already beginning to smell hot. The brown bread was still in her
basket, there on the cupboard. Last night, she'd been too tired to put
things away.

After everybody had gone from the church last night, leaving her
alone, and after she'd got her presents off the tree, she had put out
the lights, keeping one lamp to see her way by down the vestry
stairs. That Willard, some janitor he was, forgetting the lamps and
lacing off, mad, without even waiting to lock up. As for the belfry,
it hadn't fallen down in seventy-four years, and it hadn't while she
was there. After she'd got her hat and coat on, she'd filled her basket.

Usually the ladies auctioned off what food was left from a church
supper, the money going to the minister's fund; but Stell didn't
know as she cared about that, now. There was a lot of stuff left over,
never would be missed. And what a struggle to get home with that
heavy basket!

She unpacked it now. Some of that brown bread was going to go
awful good, with pork fat on it. She took out an apple pie, a big, un-
cut layer cake—that was Addie Shepheard's grandmother's vanilla
nut, and why it hadn't got cut into, God in his infinite mercy alone

knew, it was awful good cake—two pans of yeast rolls, three jars, assorted, of pickles. In another pan by itself was a loaf of nut bread. The brown bread was in a can, a big one. She hauled it out, sliced some off to warm in the oven.

Most of that stuff, if she put it in the sideboard in the parlor, it would freeze solid and keep. And there would be another problem solved, her and Luther's meals, for a little while to come. Save eating out of the store—of course she got wholesale, but even wholesale was costly, not very much coming in. By and by, after breakfast, she'd have to struggle along to the church. That was Addie's bean pot, she would be sure to miss it, and the cake and pie tins, they'd have to be accounted for if they weren't there.

It occurred to her that there was a lot more stuff in the vestry, freeze solid and spoil unless somebody tended to it. Besides, as president, it was her responsibility to see that an Aid time in the vestry got cleaned up after. In snow like this, she doubted if anybody else would be there.

She ate her breakfast with gusto, stoking it in. The hot food put new life into her; the morning's chores were done, she had a minute to think, before she watered the cow and tended to Luther. She sat at the table, rocking slowly in her Boston rocker, feeling warm and comfortable.

Them! she thought. And that quilt! With all I do and put into that church. They'll be sorry till the last day they ever live.

From the bedroom, Luther said, "Stell—Stell," and for the first time that morning she actually heard him.

She got up, then, and went in to build the airtight fire. She built a good one, carefully watching the draft, closing it up as soon as the split chunks caught. Luther knew she couldn't build his fire early, have to leave it while she went out and tended mail. The dining room chimney had soot in it, a lot; a too-hot blaze was liable to set it afire. The room was already warm, that is, not cold, from the kitchen fire.

She fed Luther his breakfast, the same as she had had; he ate almost as much. But he was still cold and complaining, "Stell, I'm froze to death," just as she'd known he'd be. Fire or no fire, he was always cold. She heated a flatiron, put it to his feet. He wanted to get up, come out by the kitchen fire, he said, get warm that way. An airtight wasn't no good, only the kitchen stove would warm him. But she wasn't going to get him up this morning, except to use the chamber. He was better off in bed, where she wasn't going to be

home. His needs attended to, she left him, warmly covered, dry and
still complaining. The Lord in his infinite mercy knew that once on a
time it would of got on her nerves, but now she was used to him.

She watered the cow, came back to the kitchen and took all the
cooked stuff out of containers, loading the tins back into her basket
without washing them. They had better be found dirty in the vestry.
Then she pried open the front door and closed it behind her, stand-
ing for a moment on the front steps, with the basket on her arm.

The village didn't look natural. It was buried, feet deep, in some
places snow drifted up to the eaves of houses. All along the main
road looked bare, trees gone. One of them she saw, with a little
quiver of excitement which was almost satisfaction, had fallen on
Little Sarah's front piazza, and lay there across the roof, a tree of
snow. That would give them Gilmans something to do besides make
fun of their neighbors. She set out to go in, see what Little Sarah
thought about it, sympathize with the repair bill, of course; then it
occurred to her that Little Sarah wouldn't be home, she'd stayed over
with old lady Greenwood last night.

And I'll bet a night of it *they* had, in that fool house, if it was still
there at all, could have washed right off of that Point, a storm like
this! My Lord, wouldn't that be awful.

It made her whole back prickle to think of it. It was all she could
do, when she plowed past Imogene's, not to go in and say to Imo-
gene, what if, or maybe it had already happened.

What a struggle to get to the church! But part of the way she
could follow in Orin's tracks. The sun was just coming up when she
staggered down the snow-clogged steps and pried open the door to
the church vestry. Nobody had been there. It was all a mess, just
as they'd left it last night. Well, the first thing, get a fire going to
heat dishwater, so if anyone came, she'd be washing dishes, cleaning
up the vestry; and the next thing was to see what there was.

IT was Little Sarah who brought word about the lumber washed up
and lying on the shore. She arrived around breakfast time, having
walked over from the Point, and so covered with snow was she, that
Jess, seeing someone go by the frosted-up kitchen windows, wasn't
sure, at first, who it could be.

"Now, who's crazy enough to travel out in this?" she said, craning
backwards to look. "See who it is, will you, Gibbie?"

She had a feeling, half irritation, half foreboding, that no one
would be out this morning unless there was some kind of an emer-

gency, and she wished for once somebody would be called on to tend to it besides Elbridge. He had slept late, worn out after last night's expedition. Jess planned to let him have his sleep out. He'd have plenty to do after he got up—there was always plenty, after a big storm, though, mainly, she guessed, things were all right down at the wharf. The wharf buildings and lobster scow had been in the lee, and from an upstairs window she could see the *Daisy,* Elbridge and Liseo's smack, ice-covered, but afloat at her moorings, and Liseo's boy Johnny aboard of her knocking off ice.

Jess had slid out of bed quietly and got the kids up; together they had managed to make a path, which was half-tunnel, out to the barn and outhouses. While the twins did the feeding-up and milking, she laid herself out to get a good solid breakfast—a Sunday-morning one, though it wasn't Sunday, with all the things Elbridge liked. She figured he had it coming.

She was just setting back the coffee pot, and he was beginning to stir around in the bedroom, when whoever it was went past the kitchen window.

Gib yanked open the back door in time to see Little Sarah come skidding and sliding down the side of the hole he and Will had worried out of the snow by the back steps. He let out an excited yell.

"Hi, it's Little Sarah!" he called back. "Hi, Little Sarah, come in before you freeze!"

The kids all called her Little Sarah instead of Grammy, she seemed to prefer it.

Little Sarah regarded him tranquilly, as she came up the steps. "Brush me off, Gibbie. No sense scattering snow all over your mother's clean entry."

"How'd you get over from the Point?" he demanded, making the snow fly from her skirt and rubbers. "Why, there's four *feet* of snow on the level!"

"All of that," Little Sarah said.

She revolved slowly in front of his vigorous broom strokes, so that he could get at the snow on her back. "Deeper in places. Lots deeper."

"Atta girl!" Gib said. "Hey, she's *walked* through it, all the way over from the *Point!*"

"There, Gib, stop it," Jess said, coming out into the entry. "You'll have the coat right off her back. Come in, Little Sarah, for heaven's sake! What possessed you? Wasn't it a terrible—" Jess stopped. "Are they all right over there?"

"They're fine," Little Sarah said. "A window blew in in the night, but they're all right."

She shucked her coat and head shawl in the entry, and took off her rubbers. She was breathing a little fast and her cheeks were pink, but otherwise she didn't seem much the worse for wear. She did go over, though, and sit right down in the rocking chair.

"A window blew in!" Will said. "Hey, a window blew in!" He stood in front of his grandmother, his hands on his hips, savoring it—the wild night, the lonesome house on the Point, a window blowing in. "What did you do, Little Sarah?"

"Why, I was sound asleep," Little Sarah said. "First thing I knew, a slop of salt water took me in the face, ran down under the bed-clothes." She stopped, looked over at Jess. "No, Jess, leave your biscuits be, I don't want to put my feet in the oven. I'm warm as toast, walking. Elbridge out to the barn, is he?"

"He's just getting up," Jess said. "I let him sleep. He had a night of it."

"Well, what?" Joyce said. "Tell us, Little Sarah. Did the ocean come right into your room?"

"Heaven's sake, let your grandmother alone," Jess said. "Let her get her breath."

She spoke more sharply than she meant to, but she was worried. Something must be wrong. Little Sarah wanted Elbridge, and she wasn't one to do foolish things without reason. It had been foolish to wade all the way over here through that snow, unless she needed to, when she might just as well have stayed put in a warm house until somebody broke trail. She glanced at the three children, who were looking at their grandmother with great approval. You could tell that they were all wishing they'd done just what she had done. Some kind of communication was passing silently between the four of them.

"Atta girl, Little Sarah," Gib said again, and Will, nudging close up to her elbow, said, "You know that big elm tree fell flat down on your piazza?"

"I saw, when I came by," Little Sarah said.

She didn't seem overly put out by the disaster. She smiled at Jess over the heads of the three youngsters, and Jess felt better at once. When Little Sarah smiled, her round cheeks, just now rosy and taut with cold as winter apples, made dimples. It was a pleasant thing to watch happen.

"For the Lord's sake, Ma," Elbridge said, coming in from the bedroom. "I thought I heard you out here. Couldn't believe my ears. What in thunder? I thought at least I didn't have you to worry about."

"Well, you don't," Little Sarah said. "I'm here, all in one piece, Elbridge, so no need to flurry up. If I hadn't come, Miss Greenwood would have, so I figured it had better be me. That lumber schooner's come to grief somewhere, either that or slipped her deckload. The back shore's piled up with lumber like jackstraws."

"Oh, Lord," Elbridge said.

On the way home from the Point last night, he'd thought of the lumber schooner, wondering where she was, how she was making it. Considering how exhausted he'd been, he hadn't thought of her since, not that there'd been anything, of course, that he could have done.

He said, "She's not in sight anywhere, over there?"

"No. Just lumber. That's why I thought it might be only the deck-load," Little Sarah said. "There isn't a sign of smashed up wreckage anywhere."

She went on to say that she'd noticed the schooner when she'd walked over to the Point in the late afternoon—thought how nice it seemed to see sails again. And then, seeing how the weather'd looked, she'd kept watch out Miss Greenwood's east windows, until dark. Just before dark, the sails had gone down behind the horizon. She'd figured the skipper'd found some wind, and had thought no more about it.

"I walked round shore, part of the way over this morning," she said. "There wasn't a sign of wreckage. A lot of that lumber was hove up over the rocks onto the bank, some of it right up into the trees. I never saw such a sea. There's the ends of two-by-fours sticking out where the tide went down, but I expect a lot of whatever there is is buried up in snow."

Elbridge nodded. It would be. A lot of snow had dumped last night, after the tide had started to go down.

He was eating his breakfast, stoking it in—he'd have a lot to do, no knowing when he'd get home for another meal, probably not until suppertime—and making careful notes in his head of everything Little Sarah said.

With her usual good sense, she had found out and was telling him the main things he would need to know—where the vessel had been, approximately, at dark; that her wreckage wasn't on the Chin Island back shore; that there was no one crippled, needing help, at least alive, and not buried along the rocks, there, deep under snow.

Most women, he thought, looking at his mother with pride and affection, would have taken out through the snowbanks on the dead hyper, knocked themselves squalling, and had to be put to bed with hot flatirons for a week. Not Little Sarah. Instead of wallowing through the woods, she had thought of coming partway by the rocks, below tide line where she could, finding out what searchers after the wrecked vessel, if it were wrecked, would need to know. With what she'd told him, he had some starting points that he wouldn't have to take the time to find out himself, not that there were very many things anyone could do.

A vessel with her holds full of lumber would have been more likely to capsize, pound to pieces, or go ashore somewhere, than to sink. She'd probably lost the deckload first, which was what had come ashore here on the island. She herself might be afloat somewhere— upside down, right side up, anybody's guess—or she might have gone ashore on one of the islands to the south. There were two likely ones, and nobody lived on them. If any of the vessel's crew had got ashore alive on either, they would freeze to death wandering around the shores, unless they were hunted up and found fast.

Well, he and Liseo could start the engine in the *Daisy*. She was about the only boat, outside of Orin's mail boat, that probably wouldn't have its engine frozen up tighter than a drum.

His mind went over the possibilities, making plans and tautening them, while he put away as much as he could of Jess's good break-fast—the ham and eggs, the creamed potatoes, the hot biscuits, the coffee—until he became aware of the silence around him in the room, the kids staring at him, big-eyed and sober, Jess with set lips a little white at the corners, his mother concerned, all five waiting for what they knew he'd have to say.

Well, no sense scaring everybody to death.

"Somebody'll have to take a look around the islands," he began, with his mouth full. "Probably the best thing would be to go over to the harbor, get George Farleigh to phone Port Western for the government cutter."

He and Liseo wouldn't do that, he knew; at least, until the last. He guessed, glancing at Jess and his mother, that they knew he wouldn't do it, either. If it were any use at all to look around the islands, it had to be done in a hurry, and no knowing where the government boat might be, just now, probably miles away, or how long it would take to get her up from Port Western.

"That's still a pretty high sea," Jess said.

Well, it was. They could hear it through the thick walls of the house, banked with brush and rockweed, through the panes of the double storm windows. The surf, rolling in over The Pasture with a dull, measured boom.

"Well, there's no wind, anyway, to speak of," Little Sarah said.

It was not the sea itself which was to be feared today so much as the cold. With no wind to speak of, the old *Daisy* could handle anything in the way of swell; she was a load-carrier, sloppy to handle when she was light, but built for all kinds of weather. The mercury must be below zero now, still falling, from the looks of the bay, which was already smoking with salt-water vapor. The *Daisy* was blunt-bowed; she would throw spray. And the spray would freeze wherever it landed.

"Likely that sea'll go down some, no wind," he said. "It has already, a little."

It hadn't; after a storm like that, it might take a couple of days to go down. Elbridge got up from the table, began to haul on his heavy outdoors gear.

"You better take it easy today, Ma," he said. "Stay here and keep Jess company, why don't you?"

"Well, I ought to go home, see how much of that elm tree's in the setting room," Little Sarah said.

"Oh, take a rest. It must've been quite a clamber over those rocks this morning."

"Well, it was hard going," Little Sarah said. "No one'd care for it, I guess, who didn't like to walk in the snow." She went on, thoughtfully watching Jess. Jess was over at the kitchen counter, cutting and making sandwiches, filling the thermos of his dinner bucket with hot coffee. "Hardest was in the woods, where the snow was soft. Out in the open, where it hadn't all blown away, the drifts were packed hard, so I could walk right over the top of them."

Jess handed Elbridge the dinner bucket, and, reaching up, tucked in the ends of his wool muffler, so that it was warm around his throat. She put up her face for a kiss.

"I'll plan to have dinner tonight," she said.

"That's good." Elbridge grinned down at her. "I might be a little late, at that."

"You better not be," she said. "I'm going to have pork roast, and I don't want it all dried up. Be—be careful, won't you?"

ROGER GILMAN leaned against the window sill in the Harbor post office, his heavy overcoat opened and thrown back on his shoulders, as far as he could get from Lombard's potbellied stove, which was red hot. He was waiting for the island mail boat to leave, and everything was late, on account of last night's storm. The mail stage from town hadn't got in—nobody really expected it, people said. The snow was drifted six feet deep in places on the main highway.

Orin had arrived from the island on time; he was sitting over in the corner now, breathing fire, because he was thrown off schedule.

"By the God," he had said to Lombard when he came in, his coat covered with salt rime, icicles frozen in his straggly mustache. "If I can wrastle a powerboat in from the islands today, the way 'tis out there, that young feller ought to be able to run a Ford truck twenty miles over dry land."

He sat down behind the stove to thaw out, grumbling and growling. Every once in a while, he would think of something new to say about the town mail-truck driver, and then he would stick out his underlip and blow, and the melting icicles would fly from his mustache, sizzling on to the stove.

"I better tie a kaig of rum around my neck," he said at ten o'clock. "Track out and hunt, like a St. Bernard dog. That feller's prob'ly froze to death under his mailbag, like the feller in the Artic."

He was too put out to pay much attention to Roger, or even to talk to Lombard about the effects of the big storm, which anybody knew would be a damn sight worse off on the islands than inshore here, to hell an' gone up this harbor.

"Good God, yes, you can ride acrost with me," he said in answer to Roger's question. "If I ever go, you kin. But you better swop that city overcoat for a sheepskin. My boat ain't got a furnace in it, like a drugstore."

Roger grinned at him. He was too happy at going home two days earlier than he'd expected to mind Orin. Right now, Orin was the enemy of anything under fifty-five years old, the age he was himself. Older people, they didn't live in the same world.

"How'd they make out in the storm over there?" Roger asked. "Is everything all right?"

Last night, when he had taken Rosie MacGimsey home from the basketball game, and had seen how bad the storm was, they had both got to wondering how it was over on the island. It was bad enough here at the Harbor, this morning—trees down, a couple of barns over, boats adrift or sunk. And the Harbor was sheltered by hills behind it. Roger and Rosie had decided to try to go home today, instead of waiting for Friday.

"I guess they had it really rough over there," Roger said, now, to Orin.

Orin grunted.

"What do you care? You was over here snug, wasn't you? Ought to been to home, helping your pa, instid of flapping round town in a city overcoat. Trouble with you young fellers, your blood's thin, stay undercover too much. Godalmighty, when us old-timers is gone, I be damned if I know who'll do the outdoors work."

Roger grinned again. There wasn't anything personal in this—the fellow who drove the mail stage was young. If anything had been too wrong over on the island, Orin wouldn't have been able to keep from telling it. He was an inspired carrier of bad news, never missed a chance; and his bad news was often worse news, due to his gruesome sense of fiction.

Roger felt a load lift from his mind, having found out what he wanted to know. Last night he'd been worried, and no way to find out until Orin got in this morning. Well, the old grouch had told him, hadn't meant to either, and now Roger felt good again, for a number of reasons.

This morning, when he asked Mr. Caddell at the drugstore if he could go home two days early, the old man had all of a sudden pulled out a ten dollar bill.

"Why, sure, son. Buy your ma a present and go home today. You've worked good for me, and I appreciate it."

Well, that had been a pleasant surprise.

Sometimes, through the fall, Roger hadn't felt as if he were learning his job very well, wondered if Mr. Caddell even liked him. Homesick as a goat, at first, and lonesome, week nights when Rosie had to study—no date and nowhere to go except the movies, Westerns, for goshsake, if you saw one, you'd seen them all. Working undercover, he'd felt as if his muscles were cramped and slack. Days in the fall, when the leaves were yellow and the sky that color it gets, and the air blew down over the town, cool and crisp and all but snapping, he felt like taking off for some place back of beyond, at a dead run—run and run until he got back that lean, limber feeling he'd had all his life, up to now. All at once, the island which he'd been so crazy to leave, had seemed like heaven to him.

He'd wake up nights, thinking about it; sometimes the color of the water behind the breakwater, that deep green where it lay in the shadow; or the sound the ducks made as they scaled down into the pond in the swamp. It would come right between him and what he was doing in the drugstore—that was what had happened the day he'd mixed the god awful soda, hitting the wrong syrup spigots, until what came out was something the kidders around the fountain still called "Roger's Special," when they remembered it.

But, shoot, that was back in September. He was a pretty good soda jerk now; could even juggle ice cream balls, when Mr. Caddell wasn't around, of course—the old man didn't like horsing around behind the counter. Mr. Caddell was letting him mix a few simple pastes for pills and powders now, too, though not prescriptions, that was against the law. You had to be a registered pharmacist, and the more he thought about that, the better he liked the idea.

You get a good drugstore in a place where there wasn't one, and you really had it made. Mr. Caddell's store served the harbor and all the islands. He had the only drugstore within thirty miles, and he coined the money. He had a Buick sedan, which he'd taught Roger to drive so that Roger could make deliveries; it was older than God, but a dandy engine—a real power plant in there, purred along; not that he himself, Roger often thought, wouldn't have something a little snappier, if he had stowed away what Mr. Caddell had. The old man's wife was dead and he had neither chick nor child, lived alone in an apartment over the store; he had nobody to spend his money on but himself, and he sure did spend it.

He had a workshop fitted up in the basement, with every kind of a woodworking tool a man would want to name—planes or chisels ordered from abroad, with Swedish or German steel blades. Not that he ever used the tools. He was busy in the store, daytimes; evenings he spent with his feet on the stove in his apartment, listening to his radio—a dandy big one with a set of headphones extra, so that Roger sometimes got invited to listen, too, and hear the old man get Dallas or Havana, Cuba, and once a thin, squealing jabber of static, which he said was Paris, France.

Mr. Caddell never listened very long to one station; he just liked to get a lot of them; had a long list of places he'd tuned in, and listened to long enough to hear the station announcement. If he found some place new, he was as pleased as a kid with a new toy.

At first, he didn't invite Roger into the basement workshop; then, after a month or so, he did, one night; and it was seeing the rows of tools, oiled and shining and unused, hanging neatly on racks around the wall, that gave Roger the idea of making Rosie a hope chest for

Christmas. She'd seen one in the furniture store window—a big cedar chest, varnished and red and shiny—and had practically drooled over it; and Roger who had been with her, had looked it over and thought at the time that it wouldn't be too hard to make one. He wanted Rosie to have something pretty nice for Christmas, and the Lord knew, he wasn't going to have much extra cash to buy her anything. He had his clothes and his board to pay for—the new winter overcoat had made a big hole in his savings—and if you wanted to keep up with the high school gang Rosie traveled with, you took your girl to basketball games and dances and the roller rink. He hadn't any place to work on a chest, evenings, though, unless Mr. Caddell would let him use the basement.

But when he mentioned it, the old man went right up into the air.

"There isn't a seventeen-year-old boy living I'd let use my tools," he said. "Damned destructive young devils!"

Even his bald head with the white fringe around it, turned red. Roger turned red, too. "Oh, gosh, I've got my own tool box, Mr. Caddell," he said. "But never mind it."

Shoot, after he'd worked so hard to get in solid with the old man, and now he'd probably kicked the underpinning right out.

But after a few days, when Roger didn't mention it again, the old man said grudgingly, "Well, bring your own tools. I guess you can use the workbench," and when Roger still didn't, he said, "Go ahead and make your Christmas presents, why don't you? I'm not using the bench."

Roger was pleased to see that when he did bring his tool box, Mr. Caddell was pretty impressed with some of the tools.

Elbridge had fitted up the box, the year Roger was twelve, as a Christmas present. It was pine, the joints dovetailed and fitted so that you could hardly see where they went together. Elbridge had bought a few new tools for the box, but mostly he had pieced out with duplicates from his own set, not giving Roger the worst of the deal, either. Most of the things had been MacKechnie's, and, Roger happened to know, Elbridge had hated to part with them.

"There," he had said, watching Roger unwrap the tool box on Christmas morning. "Now, you've got your own set, and it's just as good as mine, some ways a little better. So for heaven's sake, let's leave each other's tools alone, hanh?"

The first evening Roger took the box into Mr. Caddell's workshop, he had to grin to himself at the sight of the old man's face. Mr. Caddell had been stumping around the shop, nervous as a cat; he was dying to go upstairs and listen to his radio, but you could see he was worried to death for fear Roger would touch something on the racks. Now he leaned over Roger's box, picked up MacKechnie's old jack plane, and stood there looking at it.

Well, the tools did look good, oiled and sharp and taken care of. Roger supposed he had given some of them a beating up when he was a kid, the way a kid does with tools, but now he knew better; he knew what he had.

Mr. Caddell said, "You do that sharpening job yourself?"

Roger said, "Yup."

The old man put the plane carefully back into the box. "Damn fine plane," he said, and without another word went back upstairs to his radio. He didn't show up for the rest of the evening; nor did he bother around all the rest of the time Roger was using the shop.

Roger had fun, building the chest. He went over to the mill and hand-picked the cedar boards, and planed and smoothed and sanded until the wood got that kind of soft shine that a lot of good elbow grease will give cedar. He almost hated to varnish it, knowing that varnish would give that hard, pinky-red finish; but it was Rosie's chest, like the one she'd seen in the store window, which was what she wanted. His dovetails weren't as good as Elbridge's, but they were good enough so that he wanted his father to see them.

It was great to be going home for Christmas, with his suitcase stuffed full of presents—he supposed he shouldn't have spent all of Mr. Caddell's ten dollars, but he'd got to thinking how the twins' eyes would bug out over those Scout knives, and how much Jess liked silk stockings, and how probably little old Joyce had never seen a lipstick in her life; and what with one thing and another the ten was gone before he knew it. So here he was, waiting for Orin, wearing his new winter overcoat, the first he'd bought with his own money; and outside, on the post office steps, wrapped in carton cardboard and three or four burlap bags, the cedar chest for Rosie's Christmas.

Rosie had come down with him, early, but when it seemed certain that the mail stage would be late and Orin would wait for it, she had gone back to school. She could see the stage when it went past the high school, she said; there was no sense hanging around the post office answering everybody's questions. Everybody knew that vacation didn't start until Friday. She had permission, of course, to go home two days early; but she didn't know as she wanted to explain that to every Tom, Dick and Harry who might come into the post office. It seemed funny to Roger that she'd spend a morning in school when she didn't have to; Lord, he wouldn't have. But Rosie liked school. She was on the honors list, the only one in her class this term who got all A's, and she was having a fine time, too.

Rosie would have a fine time anywhere; laughter and gaiety rayed out all around her, like streaks of light. She was busy as a bee. Evenings she had to study; nights after school and Saturdays, she worked, clerking in the five-and-dime. She didn't have to—Liseo had tried to talk her out of it, saying he wanted her to come home to the island week ends, but Rosie told him she needed the extra money for this and that; she kidded Liseo until he let her stay. Privately, Rosie told Roger that the island, a week end, without him, would be a howling wilderness. Besides, Friday and Saturday nights were the best times, when all the high school dances were. And so neither of them had been home since September.

Old Rosie. She always stopped in to the drugstore on the way to work to say hi to him.

"Hi, Roger," she would say, standing in front of the soda fountain, her cheeks pink above the collar of her coat, the pink knitted cap with the big white pompon she wore on the back of her head, so that it showed the widow's peak, smooth black against the white skin of her forehead. Half the high school would be right at her elbow, making a racket you could hear up and down the street, and Roger would be spinning on his elbows, mixing sodas. "Hi, Roger."

Old Rosie. Life without her anywhere would indeed be a howling wilderness, and if she felt the same way, why, then, they both sure had it made.

Getting it made. They'd talked about that a good deal, when they'd first come over from the island, not knowing anybody too well, the aloneness bringing them closer together. Rosie would finish high school, maybe teach a couple of years until he got his pharmacy course; meantime, he would learn everything he could at the drugstore, get in solid with Mr. Caddell. Who could know what would happen, when Mr. Caddell died? He had no son, no heir. Not that Roger had it in mind, exactly like that; put that way it sounded lousy. But somebody would have to take over the drugstore; and why not him, if he was handy there, and knew the business?

Rosie wanted all the things, clothes and a car and a nice house with a bathroom, and so did he.

"Gee, a bathroom!" she would say, and her eyes would shine, on Sunday afternoons when they would walk along the main street, window shopping, Rosie picking out all the things she wanted, for some-

day. "When I think of the way we always got along, brr-rr! Look at
that one with the water lilies, Roger! Now, I think that's real pretty."

The water lilies were painted in profile around the inside of the
porcelain toilet bowl, so that when it was installed, they would seem
to be floating at water line. Roger thought, at first, it was funny;
then he saw that this particular set of bathroom fixtures was the
store's de luxe offering, and he found himself impressed.

Well, why not have things like that a little bit nice? He had
cleaned out a rotten old backhouse often enough to appreciate that.

"And look at the price!" Rosie said, marveling. "That set's twice
what the others are, Roger. Oh, boy, wait till you see what we'll
have, when we really get rolling!"

Oh, it was fun, over here at the Harbor. A little hard to get
acquainted, at first, but now he knew most of Rosie's high school
gang. Joe Farleigh, the harbor master's son, he had known before,
and now Joe was his best friend. Joe was a basketball player; the
school even had a special cheer for Joe at the games—"Joe, Joe, good
old Joe!" For if anybody could bring the team up from behind, win
a losing game, it would be Joe. Flashing around the floor, tall and
limber, blond hair flying, he was something to see. Out of town
games, Joe would take Helen, his girl, and Roger and Rosie, maybe
another couple, in his father's car; and after the games, they would
go eat somewhere, and then to a dance or the roller rink. Oh, it was
fun, now that he'd got a place, was acquainted. Fun to be going
home for Christmas, to the island, but he knew now he'd never want
to stay there. Not when he and Rosie really had it made.

And everybody did seem to think he had it made, a beginning
anyway, with Mr. Caddell.

Joe said, one time, "More power to you. Old Caddell's been look-
ing for years for somebody to leave that drugstore to. He's damned
well off, too, the old man is. Stick with it, you'll be sitting in a but-
ter tub. Better than sucking up to some old pot of a summer man,
hoping he'll leave you his toenails when he dies." Roger could see
Joe envied him, and that was good, too.

Gee, it was hot in here. Lombard kept that potbelly red hot. Rosie
would be down again at noon. They had a date to eat together, if
Orin didn't go before then. It must be nearly noon now.

He heard someone come up on the post office steps and craned
back to look through a clear space in the frosted windowpane. It was
Rosie, and Joe was with her, carrying her suitcase. Well, thank the
Lord. Now they could go eat, pass the time quicker.

"Hi, Roger," she said. Her cheeks were pink, the little knitted cap perky on the back of her head.

"Hi," Roger said.

He grinned at Joe, and Joe grinned back.

Orin, behind the stove, cleared his throat with a bumbling sound. He was thawed out now, ready to talk a little, but still mad. He wanted his dinner. If the stage had come, he'd be home now, sitting down to Almeda's biscuits.

"Well, what'd you think you're doing, hanging round down here with a couple fellers, when you're supposed to be in school?" he asked Rosie, querulously.

Rosie winked at the two boys.

"Don't tell Pa, will you, Orin?" she said. "I'm skipping school."

Orin's peevish face, over his dank, sheepskin collar, took on a righteous look.

"*Somebody* ought to tell him," he said.

"I'm a bad girl," Rosie said.

She was in roaring spirits, happy to be going home, showing off a little, too, for the two boys.

"Well, you sure sound like it," Orin said.

Rosie laughed.

"Oh, I'm headed straight down the merry road to the little old bow-wows," she said. "Dances and honky-tonks and roller rinks. If Pa but knew!"

"If he did, he'd take a stick to you. What kind of talk is that, for heb'm sake?"

"Save me from it all, Orin. Take me home to Pa. That stage isn't going to come today. Come on, let's go."

"I ain't never yit gone home without the mail," Orin said. "And I ain't going to now." He got up, stumped to the door. "Right now, I'm going over to the restrunt, git me a hamburg," he said. "You better go on back to school." He closed the door firmly behind him, then opened it and put his head back in. "Or I *will* tell Liseo," he said, and went.

Lombard, the postmaster, behind his wicket, took up where Orin left off. Lombard fancied himself with the ladies, always had; he liked a pretty girl as well as the next one, and if this one was what she talked like, he about guessed he'd know what she was. At least, in his time, if a girl talked like that, you'd know.

"What you in such a hurry to go home for?" he asked. "Come on in here and while away the time with me."

"Oh, I'll be glad to get away from this dump," Rosie said. She winked again at the boys, spun around and sat down on the window sill next to Roger.

Lombard's face appeared at the wicket, that is, his nose did. They could barely make out his fat, rosy cheeks, bald head and heavy, horn-rimmed glasses, in the shadow. But the nose stuck out through the thin bars into a full ray of sunlight from the window—a big nose, red, fleshy and shining, and on the end of it a clear drop, which caught the sun and sparkled like a diamond.

Rosie stared, gulped, and then in spite of herself let out a yelp of helpless laughter.

"Maybe I ain't quite so funny as you think," Lombard said, offended. "And I don't think much of hearing this Harbor, or the U-nited States Post Office, so be that is what you mean, called a dump."

The drop wobbled, sparkled, almost fell, and the three youngsters stared fascinated.

"Not by you Chin Islanders," Lombard said. "Not where you come from."

Rosie's eyes snapped.

"Well, dump, heaven, anything you like," she said. "What we usually call it is Hungry Corner."

"No!" Lombard thrust closer to the wicket. His jaw sagged with astonishment, and the drop, finally, wobbled off and fell. "Over *there* they do? *They* call the *harbor*— Well, I'll be damned!"

The outside door opened to let in old Doctor Graham and his dog, and Lombard transferred his attention to them.

"Doc!" he bellowed. "You know what these Chin Island kids just told me? Over there, they call the harbor Hungry Corner! Why, my God, that old, busted-down, dragged-out quarry hole, why, half the people over there ain't got a full set of rafters! You ever hear of such a thing?"

The doctor grunted. He said, "Gi'me my mail," and stood flatly in front of the wicket, while Lombard handed out a batch of assorted newspapers, magazines and envelopes.

"Today's mail ain't come," Lombard said. "But you got plenty here. How come you ain't picked it up for so long?"

"Been busy."

The doctor took the bundle of mail and started opening it, standing as close as he could get to the stove. The smell of his old coonskin coat and his hound, as both warmed up, joined the memory that always lingered on in the post office of wet rubber boots, damp coats and long johns. Lombard didn't believe in airing out, he said, in the winter; likely to get pneumonia that way.

The doctor was tall and raw-boned; the coat, which came to below his ankles, looked to be three feet broad and seven feet long. The coon hair was rubbed off behind, where the doctor's stern for winters innumerable had pounded around in his buggy or his pung. He was old-fashioned, he wouldn't learn to drive a car.

"Anybody wants me that fast, they can come get me," he would say. "Everybody's got a car. House fall down, kids' teeth drop out, wife needs to have her tubes tied, but hell, everybody's got a good car. 'T hell with one."

The rasp in his voice made him seem impatient most of the time. This morning he looked tired. Under his cap, a fur pillbox affair with long earflaps hanging down, his cheeks were lardy and pinched, his eyes bleary from lack of sleep. The bushy eyebrows, beetling out from under his cap, mingled with its fur, so it was hard to tell where one left off and the other began. His chin was covered with gray stubble. With the earflaps, he looked more than ever like his hound, which sat on its haunches beside him.

The dog, too, was bony, with earflaps hanging down, and a long, irascible, melancholy face. In fact, some said that when the two of them were driving along, the dog, sitting upright on the buggy seat beside the doctor, it was hard to say which was which, except the doctor held the reins.

Roger saw that Joe and Rosie, now, were noticing this resemblance, Joe nudging Rosie. For all you liked the old doctor, it was hard not to notice it. They knew him well—he was always called when anybody needed him over on the island; he had, as a matter of fact, brought all three of them into the world. He did not appear to notice them, though, reading his mail, dropping piece after piece of it, unopened, toward the coal hod, the papers fluttering all over the floor.

"Cold after the storm," Lombard said.

"Ayup."

"Lettie have her baby, did she?"

"Ayup."

The doctor ripped open an envelope, glanced at the contents, let them fall.

"Good for Lettie," Lombard said. "Boy or a girl?"

"Twins."

"No!" They could all hear the crack, as Lombard slapped his thigh.

"Haw! By gorry, twins! That's one on Enoch, that is! How many's that make, Doc? Nine, ain't it?"

"Don't bother to give me any more of this advertising trash. Heave it into the wastebasket," the doctor said.

"I'll write to Uncle Sam," Lombard said.

He winked, through the wicket, at the youngsters. It was said around, generally, that the doctor was old-fashioned, didn't bother to read up on the new discoveries in medicine, and here was proof of it, Lombard's wink said, throwing away all the modern stuff that came in his mail. "How *is* Lettie?"

"All right."

"Is Enoch—?"

"Oh, goddam Enoch!"

" 'S trouble? Ain't he paid your bill?"

"Bill? Hell, I haven't sent a bill in this town since 1900. Cost him more to bury two dead babies than it will to pay my bill."

"Oh, my gorry, Doc!" Lombard's nose bumped up against the wicket. They could see his eyes goggling. "You lose them twins, Doc?"

"Hanh," the doctor said. He let the rest of his mail go toward the coal hod, turned around and made for the door. "*I* lost them, hanh? Blast and damn! Anybody dies around this town, it ain't their fault, hanh? Old Doc Graham lost 'em. No, I didn't lose them twins. Enoch lost 'em. Told him last summer if she got in the family way again to be sure and come see me. What can you do? If I'd had a little help, but who bothers to learn? Had to deliver them with—"

He stopped, suddenly, coming face to face with Rosie, who was staring at him, fascinated. "Whose kid are you?" he said, not bothering to soften the rasp in his voice, and then, before she could answer, "How's the folks wintering over on the island?"

"I haven't been home since—" Rosie started to say.

"Wiggy Shepheard had any more fits?"

"I guess not, I—"

"Hanh. Told Addie and Jack he'd outgrow 'em. Told 'em ten years ago it wasn't epilepsy, more like convulsions from a blueberry stomach ache. How's old lady Greenwood? Hanh? Remarkable woman. Most people been dead. Going home from school, Christmas vacation. What year school now?"

"First," Rosie said faintly.

"Hanh? Liseo's girl. Remember you. You looked like a tadpole." The boys laughed, and Dr. Graham grunted deeply, buttoning his coat. "And don't think you two didn't," he said. "You all do. I grow any older, I better die."

He turned and went out, slamming the door behind him.

The hound, suddenly realizing it had been left behind, made a dash after him, but the door clapped to an inch from its nose. It set up a tremendous commotion, howling and scratching at the panels, and the doctor opened the door again.

"Come on, then, you damned old fleabag," he said, and turning, bumped into Orin Vira, who had just stepped up on the post office steps. Orin side-stepped, and the doctor went past him.

"What ails old Doc?" Orin said, aggrieved. "Ain't he speaking?"

"He's headed home to get drunk," Lombard said. "He's tore out. Been up all night with Lettie Doyle."

He favored Orin with a running account of the short life and times of Enoch's twins, spliced together with some comments of his own.

"If he'd ever learn a little something," Lombard said. "Read up on the modren stuff, instead of heaving it out—look at it, coal hod's full, never even opened some of them envelopes. If he'd read up on the modren, stay off of the rum, he might cure somebody once in a while. If you ask me, they wasn't no need, in the living God's world, of them little twins dying. Lettie's had seven all right, ain't she? Old Doc was prob'ly tight, hand so shaky he couldn't function. Know what he'll do? He'll get tanked up today, a good one, and then he'll go round town saying he needs somebody to talk to, there ain't a soul in the whole town a man can talk to. Well, I guess we all know how a thing like that'll end up, the booby hatch, if you ask me."

"Don't that beat the Dutch," Orin said. His ears were pricked up to get every last detail to take home to Stell and Almeda. When it seemed that Lombard had run down, Orin shook his head glumly. "Poor little duffers," he said. "What's that out on the steps—the casket?"

Lombard stuck his nose out through the wicket.

"Casket? What casket's that?"

"Well, by gorry," Orin said. "Enoch's kind of ahead of himself, ain't he, getting the casket down from town this quick? Or, maybe he knew beforehand, had an intimation, you s'pose he did, Lombard?"

Joe grinned and gave Roger a sidelong look. Joe knew about the hope chest; he had admired it when Roger was building it. Roger wasn't at all sure that Rosie hadn't guessed about it. He felt himself beginning to turn red. Now those two old windbags had got their eye on that chest, they wouldn't rest until they found out what it was. He did not look at Rosie, but he knew she was looking at him, and all at once she said, "Us islanders are going to give ourselves a real treat for Christmas, Lombard. That, out there, is a bale of hay."

"Hanh?" Orin said. "A bale of hay? Now, I ain't going to drag no bale of hay acrost there, the weather like it is."

Rosie shrugged, lifted her hands palm up, as if to say, What can you do? Both boys knew well enough what she meant. Older people, they didn't live in the same world.

Joe said, "Let's go down to the wharf. Pop's got a fire in the office down there."

Joe's father, George Farleigh, owned the wharf; he was also harbor master.

They went down the path shoveled between the white snowbanks, Roger with the chest balanced on his shoulder, taking deep breaths of the tingling icy air. Without mentioning it, but all three aware, they had moved close together, presenting to the world a solid front.

Older people, the messes they got into. A bunch of half-wits would know better. Lombard, Orin, the doctor; some rotten old man who couldn't keep his hands off his wife, so they lost two babies. Blatting about it in public, goggling and sweating. Older people, who treated *you* as if you weren't people at all, only kids; who thought they had a right to nose into your business, tell you what, tell you how. Older people, look at them.

But no one said anything. They came around the shoulder of the wharf buildings in time to see the *Daisy*, Elbridge and Liseo's smack, covered with ice, inches thick, just warping in to a berth at the head of the wharf, with Jack Shepheard and Bill Lessaro aboard and Liseo at the wheel. Elbridge himself was getting ready to jump to the dock.

"Oh, look!" Rosie said. "Oh, Roger, don't they look *nice!*"

She took off down the gangway at a run, and meeting Elbridge head-on, planted a hearty kiss on his frosty, astonished cheek. "Oh, Elbridge! I'm so glad to see you. Merry Christmas!"

His father did, Roger thought, he looked darned nice.

"Hi, Pop," he said, grinning.

"I'll be darned," Elbridge said. "Where did you fellers come from?"

The kids, he thought. Old Roger. He couldn't remember when anything had looked so good to him. He stood beaming from one to the other, and hugged Rosie, feeling, as he did so, the ice crackling off from his frozen oilskins.

"What do you think you're doing?" Roger said. "Hugging my girl?"

"You look out for your girl," Elbridge said. "I hug all the ones that look like strawberries and cream."

"That's *my* girl, I'll have you jokers know," Liseo said, coming along behind them. "How are you, Roger? You going back with us today, thank God, Rosie? We didn't expect you till Friday. Your ma'll be tickled pink."

"We got off early," Roger said. "How is it over there, Pop? Didn't blow away last night?"

"Not quite," Elbridge said. But his face sobered and Roger saw there was something.

"What happened?" he asked, and Rosie glanced up apprehensively.

"The folks are all right," Elbridge said quickly. "Lot of damage, bound to be, a storm as bad as that one. That Novie schooner may be lost—we're afraid so. You hop aboard the boat, Liseo'll tell you about it. I'll be back soon as I see George and get him to make a phone call."

He went off up the gangway, his rubber boots clumping, while the youngsters stared soberly after him.

In the office at the head of the wharf, Elbridge talked to George Farleigh, and listened while George rang up the harbor master at Port Western.

"That you, Henry? This's George. Yeah, oh, fine, how are you? Look, Henry, that Nova Scotia lumber schooner, did she make Port Western last night? She didn't, hah. Yeah. Chin Island had a lot of new-cut lumber wash ashore. Yes, it does. It looks damn bad. No, no sign of her on the shore or on any of the islands, far as they can tell. They been out looking. No, nothing. Sea's high, yet, outside. All right, you do that. Yeah. About five miles off Chin Island, just before dark, last night. Oh, yes, sure. We'll take care of this end of it. Chin Island's already gone out around Chandler's and The Scrags. Not a thing. Okay, Henry, so long."

Elbridge came out of the office, feeling cold, and walked slowly down the wharf. He'd done what he could. He and Liseo, with Jack and Bill along to keep ice chopped off the boat, had circled the islands to the south, Chandler's and The Scrags, running the smack as close inshore as they had dared, which wasn't too close, because of the high surf. They had found no sign of a wreck.

In the back of his mind now, if he closed his eyes, he could see a clear picture of those islands, how they looked; remote, wild, lonely, buried under feet of snow; no wreckage, no tracks; nothing moving on them but the gulls.

Well, he ought to have known. Nobody, yet, had ever smashed up on The Pasture and made it ashore alive. Not that anything was sure, yet. The schooner might have made port somewhere farther down the coast, after losing her deckload; or maybe she was wallowing around out there over the horizon now. Henry Jones, in Port Western, would get the government cutter out and send word to the schooner's owners. But, likely, somewhere in Nova Scotia, there'd be folks who'd have a damned tough Christmas.

The kids were standing, back-to, talking with Liseo, when Elbridge stepped up on the rail. He saw Roger's new overcoat, and the young, broad shoulders under it, the sturdy set of the head, so like MacKechnie's; and he grinned, feeling the icy prickle leave his spine for the first time that day.

TWO days before Christmas, Miss Greenwood got ready for her children's party. The snow was deep along the causeway, but a track had been broken through it, first by men going to and from the backshore to search for wreckage, and then by Elbridge and Roger, who went over to the Point at the first opportunity with tools and some squares of glass to repair the blown-in window.

For a while, Little Sarah said, they had had a wild time that night on the Point when the window blew in.

"I put out of bed," she said, "and for a minute I thought I had stepped slap into the outdoors. It was snowing in the room and the rollers on the rocks sounded as if they were right in there with me, salt water and rockweed a-flying. Miss Greenwood woke up and came in, and we managed to get the blinds hauled to. I never was any hand for blinds—squeak and rattle on a house like the-devil-a-witch-and-a-gale-of-wind. I'd rather have good, tight storm windows. But *she* don't like storm windows, says they streak up inside and she can't clean off to look at her view. I was some glad we had blinds to shut to, that night. Then we blocked up the window with a mattress, pushed the bureau against it and went back to bed."

"Weren't you scared, Little Sarah?" Joyce asked.

"Well, I don't think I'll let on I was, Joycie. I am ashamed of being so sleepy though, through all that big storm. My goodness, seems as though I ought to have stayed awake to watch something you don't see twice in a lifetime."

Two storms, it had been, according to the report Orin brought back from the harbor. It was two storms—they had it in the paper—met overhead, head-on, smashed it out together, with, like, a clash of gongs and cymbals.

Elbridge and Roger fixed the window. They had to take it out of the frame and carry it down to the kitchen by the stove, so the putty would stay soft enough to work. Elbridge thought likely the job would have to be redone in the spring, since fresh putty would probably freeze and crack. But it was weather-tight for now.

He packed up his tools to go home, dropping them one by one into his box. Putting the frame back in had been a one-man job, and Roger had left him to it, going out along the shore somewhere to see if he could scout up a flock of sea birds. It was nice out along the shore today. The weather had warmed up after the cold snap, so that it was only a few degrees below freezing, and the sun was bright in a clear sky. Elbridge and Roger had brought along their shotguns, leaving them out of sight in the woods, so as not to disturb Miss Greenwood; but that was all right, they didn't plan to shoot anywhere near her shore line. There was a rocky cove on the shore road which was a likely place, and some black ducks were pretty sure to scale down into the swamp pond, along about early lamp-lighting time.

It was all very well to be nice to the birds, but Elbridge's mouth watered, thinking what Jess could do to a brace of fat black ducks. There were lots of birds around this winter; the storm and cold weather had driven them into the sheltered coves and ponds; right now, a flock of eider floated just beyond the shore, in The Pasture lagoon. Looking out the newly puttied window, he could see the birds rise and fall as the swells came up under them; he leaned forward, bracing his arms against the window sill. They were out of shotgun range, but near enough so that he could see they were eider, big, almost-white birds, with black on their heads and wings.

Pretty darn things, he thought.

It was a pretty day, too, the ocean deep blue, beginning to darken now with afternoon. A lot of water stretched out to that horizon, one island away off there to the southeast, a blurry purple in the distance, another just beyond, and close to it; for all the rest of it, only sea and sky. The rocks below the house went down in tumbled terraces, pink-gray above tide line, deepening to coppery red, then to brown, almost black, where rockweed covered them. It was about half-tide, on the flood. Lazy rollers, beginning far out, lifted and broke over The Pasture's underwater ledges, sucking back to show rounded, shaggy shapes, slashed fiercely against the curled green and foaming water. Beyond the rollers, the raft of white birds rose and fell.

Lord, look at it today. You wouldn't think it ever did any harm, or meant to. Even the sound it made, hushed by the house walls and the closed windows, was peaceful.

Yet somewhere out there was a dead ship, vanished without a trace, the certainty growing with each day the lumber vessel stayed unreported. Maybe she was afloat somewhere; Elbridge doubted it. Didn't seem as if her skipper could have managed to claw very far offshore in the time he had; from where he was, at about ten o'clock, the wind had started to blow dead on the land. Sometime her wreckage might show up on one of the islands or it might not. Probably nobody would ever know what happened.

What a man ought to feel, standing here, was the treachery under all that shine and blue-green, as if he saw a smile on the face of a murderer. Grandfather Ansel would have, Elbridge thought suddenly. Ansel would certainly have had a feeling of his Old Ellick here.

Well, I do, too. Any man would. Only I don't feel the way he did, that the Old Boy was top dog. Ansel's nerve ends were out; he didn't have the defense against it that most people do. Must have been the hell of a way for a man to be.

You felt it at times; you had to. A train of circumstances got set up and aimed, deadly as a rifle. One event followed another to a logical end, which seemed to be, to some men, their own personal destruction. So far, if it hadn't happened to you, you were lucky. You weren't such a fool as not to know. Nobody was immortal; day after tomorrow, tomorrow, now, you might be undercut, wiped out, from a direction you least expected and hadn't prepared for, the way MacKechnie was, when he fell off the stone pier and crippled himself for life. Treachery, evil, Ansel said, Old Ellick—the come-to-get-you.

But there weren't, actually, any words for it except the words used to apply to men that, for this, didn't make sense. It wasn't good; it wasn't bad; it was, merely, there, behaving in the same way whether a man was in its way or not. You had to think of it sometimes; it was natural to.

But without being more unfeeling than most, Elbridge guessed that what he felt now, looking out over that sky and water, was ironed-out, rested, as if, deep in his muscles, little tight springs were beginning to unwind. He hadn't felt so peaceful since the night of the storm, when everything had seemed to trigger off at once. It wasn't peacefulness, exactly; he was still worried over things; but something, almost as if it were in the air around him, said, "Hush, now. Let go."

In the house, too, he thought, with surprise, glancing over his shoulder at the room behind him.

Miss Greenwood had fixed up the room, after the window had blown in, lugging out snow, mopping up water; but marks still showed, damp and streaked, on carpet and wallpaper. The wallpaper was a soft, salmon pink, a pale silver figure, with faded pictures of old-fashioned ladies and little girls with poodle dogs hung here and there. A bureau of dark wood, polished to a dull sheen, threw back highlights to the window; the bed was a four-poster, of the same wood. It was made up with a deeply ruffled white spread and what looked to be a bolster covered with pillow-shams. The spread and pillow-shams were embroidered with a spidery letter "G," enclosed by a wreath of white leaves. The bureau scarf was embroidered to match, and on it was a little, silver-embossed box.

It was just a room. One of the summer people's rooms, the kind they fixed up, like their bedrooms at home in Philadelphia or Boston or Baltimore, probably. Elbridge had seen a lot of rooms like this— they all had them.

It's just been cleaned; nothing in it outside of that, maybe, to make a man feel better, but he did, he realized, for almost the first time since the night of the school entertainment.

If he had been able to go around and see Imogene Cayford the next morning, before she'd gone on record all over town with how she felt, what she was going to do and so on, he might have been able to smooth her down. Or maybe not, since Jess hadn't been able to. Jess had gone over to Imogene's that day; Imogene, seeing her coming up the walk, had locked the door in her face. For two days Elbridge hadn't had a minute to spare from the search for the lumber schooner, and in that time, Imogene had really circulated.

She was never, she said, going to speak to Elbridge or any of his tribe again; so long as Jess was a member of the Ladies' Aid and the Quilt Society, Imogene would not go to the meetings. She'd *slaved*, she said, learning that piece out of Bronson's *Public Speaker*, just exactly the way it said, *with gestures*. The fellow who wrote that book showed pictures of a lady speaking "Curfew Shall Not Ring Tonight," told when to keep your voice up, when to let it fall. Imogene guessed *he* knew more about it than some common, ordinary folks. But if such things were to be made a laughingstock of, Imogene was all done. She was never going to speak another piece; she was never going to set foot inside that church again; and, what was more, if she got hold of that Will, she was going to beat his ears off.

All this she said in the post office and in other places; and there were plenty to tell her what Will, in the flush of his triumph with "Towser," had told Gib, and Gib had told Johnny MacGimsey, and Johnny had told around among the other kids: that it wasn't Will's idea, entirely, but Elbridge's, too.

Well, you couldn't blame Imogene, when all her life she'd prided herself on being a speaker of pieces. Elbridge could see her now, years back in the grade school, curls and blue hair ribbon and Sunday dress, and all her elders admiring around about how nobody could speak a piece like Imogene. She'd grown up thinking it was a kind of creative art, and maybe it was; at least it was to her, and all of a sudden the whole town had laughed their heads off at it. No wonder she was mad, and had gone around saying things she couldn't back out of, even if she wanted to.

It was, of course, a tempest in a teapot, but Imogene and Stell were a team, when they had grievances, and Stell, too, figured she had plenty. It wasn't the quilt, she said, though everybody knew it was her turn to win it, but she guessed she knew now what certain members of the community thought of her in spite of all the church work she'd done. As for Liseo, putting the menfolks up to vote against her, that was malicious; she'd never speak to him as long as she lived, and she'd get even with him if it took a lifetime. And if Carrie Hitchman was putting out around town that she'd caught Stell stealing left-over food from the church supper, then Carrie was a bare-faced liar.

It was a little early in the game, Elbridge thought soberly, for people to start calling liars and thieves.

There was no doubt that Carrie had caught Stell red-handed.

"Stealing," said Carrie, "right out of the mouths of the minister's little children."

Ordinarily, this wouldn't have mattered. Stell always toted home a lot of cooked stuff from a church time; everybody knew that. The Ladies of the Aid put up with it because they figured she needed anything extra she could get, for Luther; besides, Stell was the hardest worker they had and a good organizer, which was the main reason they'd elected her president. But some of the ladies were put out because she'd made a new quilt-contest rule without consulting anyone; others were good and mad at the way she'd clawed out at their children; and Carrie Hitchman, in particular, was all burned up in the first place over the destruction of her cut-glass pickle dish, which had been an heirloom.

So Carrie and Stell had had it, there in the church vestry, that morning, covering all the angles. There wasn't much about each other's appearance, families, actions and way of life that they had left out. In the Aid, some believed Stell, or said they did—all she was doing was neatening up the vestry after the entertainment, said Stell, though everybody knew better—and some believed Carrie. Jess had reported that among the womenfolks two well-defined sides were lining up for battle, one side headed up by Stell and Imogene, and the other by Carrie. The feud hadn't as yet spread to the men, but old grievances could be raked up any time. No one would have to set his mind on finding a grudge or two to smolder over, the island being what it was, people living for years in each other's placket holes.

Town rows. Sometimes they got better, sometimes worse. There was a time, years ago, when a town row had ended in a killing— old Nick Pumlow had cracked a fellow over the head with a maul. Ward MacGimsey, it had been, old Luther's boy, only nineteen or twenty at the time. He hadn't been killed outright, but he might as well have been, had lain unconscious a long time before he died. In the meantime, Nick had pulled stakes and gone, and most people had been horrified back into their senses.

The thing was, that particular town row, when it started, hadn't had a thing to do with the Pumlows and the MacGimseys. It had been an argument over a property line between some of the Viras and old Harriet Horn. Everyone had taken sides, that was all. The thing grew like a tumor. And when a row really got to rolling and hate and violence took over, you couldn't stop it; it had to run its course. Usually, when it was over, you found more damage had been done than anybody could afford. For himself, Elbridge hated a row of any kind. What bothered him most, right now, was he and Liseo were probably responsible for setting off this particular one. Unless he could think of some way to head it off, it was going to be a nice thing, a pretty thing, for respectable people in a decent town.

It was a decent town. Elbridge was proud of it. He didn't, of course, have many illusions about his neighbors. Some might think they weren't so tough and competent as the old-timers who had built the town, but he was a long ways from believing that. You had to

take into consideration what worry and being in debt and scraping
along on the skin of your teeth year in and year out would do to a
man; three-quarters of the time, no work and no prospects, sand-
papering away at him till he wore thin; until, if he didn't say to hell
with it, he acted as if he might, any time, and the summer people,
seeing how he was, wagged heads as if at a funeral, saying it was
too bad, a fine old solid section of the country was petering out.

But let those who said so see what Elbridge saw from time to time.
Let some project come up where a man felt he was useful and
needed, or an emergency, like the one of the past few days. You
would see the old toughness, the old competence, the old skills come
out overnight, and none of them rickety, either, from lack of use.

Elbridge grinned a little, thinking of old Willard, with his potbelly
and his creepers, careening around over the icy rocks, walking shore,
hunting dead bodies or a sign of wreckage, until his ankles swelled
up and he had to quit and go home to bed. Poor old Wid, his liver
must have taken quite a jouncing.

In the ghost towns of the West, when the ore gave out, the people
picked up and went; there were places there now, you read about
every so often, houses, stores, hotels, standing there empty; not a
soul.

Maybe that's what we ought to do, too, pick up and go while there's
time, while there's something left of us.

We could, he thought soberly. The summer people loved the is-
land. Nobody would have a lot of trouble selling out, if he wanted
to put his place up for sale. He and Liseo, for example, had a stand-
ing offer from Mr. Wynn, one of the summer men, who wanted the
wharf and breakwater for a yacht club and basin.

But somehow, I don't think we'll go. There ought to be some foun-
dations built to last, and our folks have stivered it out here for a
long time.

Elbridge straightened up from the window sill and turned to pick
up his tool box, aware, again, of the room behind him, of the house
and the people in it. The sound of surf, hushed, was like peaceful
breathing. A quiet stir, an occasional clink of dish or pot or pan came
from the kitchen, where Miss Greenwood was cooking for her chil-
dren's party, and sending up the stairs a smell of fresh, sweet baking
and warm spices. In the living room, the old lady's rocking chair
moved with a soft creaking sound, steady and serene.

This house, he thought.

This house was a part of the strong foundation of the town. The same men built it, the same skill went into it. Good, square-cut granite, bolted into rock. Maybe that was what he had been feeling about it. Might be that. All the same, there was something else.

Well, I don't know what it is, he thought, glancing curiously around the quiet room. All I know is, I feel better.

Down at the cove, he and Roger'd have a fine time gunning; all of a sudden he was looking forward to it.

Poor old Roger, I haven't had hardly a word to say to him since he got home. He must think I'm turning into an old man.

He started down the stairs, his mind picking up automatically where any island man's mind picked up, when he thought for long about Miss Greenwood.

Won't have a storm window put on, because she can't clean it off to look at her view. Just as soon freeze to death, so long as she can look out the window. Well, I'd rather be warm. This fool house, no place for a couple of women.

All the same, something inside his mind kept nudging at him. All the same . . . not the foundation, but what you put on it.

ROGER was waiting for him, sitting on a stump where the track branched off toward the cove. Seeing his father, he waved a hand.

"What did you do—get bogged down in cake and coffee?" he asked. "I thought you'd never come."

"Took me a little longer than I thought it would," Elbridge said. "I see you fetched the guns."

"Yup. Thought I'd better. Save time."

He sounded impatient, Elbridge thought. It wasn't like Roger to be impatient, but Elbridge could see how a man might be, who'd worked undercover all fall, and now had to wait for his chance to hunt duck.

"That's a nice house of hers, you know it?" Elbridge said, as they started off down the snowy path. He wondered if he could tell Roger exactly what his feelings had been, decided he couldn't.

"It ought to be," Roger said, over his shoulder. "Enough money went into it."

"Well, I don't think it's that. At least, not all of it."

"Sure, it's that. A little spondulicks makes a lot of difference," Roger said. "If you don't think so, Pop, think where people like the Greenwoods would be without it. Pretty useless in the world, two old girls like that."

"Well, there is that. But I'm not too sure. They put out something else, I don't know what it is. Every time I go into that house, I come out feeling better. I like to go there."

"I do, too. Always did. She feeds you," Roger said. He grinned back at his father. "Cake. Coffee."

"They put out peace and quiet," Elbridge said. "And something else, like—" He hunted for the word.

"Shoot, Pop. They put out money-smell. All the summer people do. Whatever else it is, you darn well want to remember they can afford it," Roger said.

He went along down the footpath, his gun in the crook of his arm. "I thought the snow'd be so deep in here we'd have to crawl," he said. "But it looks as though a herd of buffaloes had been along."

The search parties hunting the shore had broken out some of the woods trails—this one, for example, which was the shortest way to the cove—though, mostly, the men had walked, where they could, on the shore below tidemark.

"Does look as though the whole town had been along here, doesn't it?" Elbridge said.

He came thoughtfully along behind Roger, thinking how much he had missed the boy, how good it was to have him home. They went together as comfortably as a pair of old shoes, he and Roger, enjoyed each other's company. He couldn't think of anyone he'd rather have around, except, of course, Jess.

"What you weigh now, Roger?" he asked, as they went down the rocks toward the duck blind.

"Hundred and sixty, thereabouts," Roger said. "Don't worry. I can't put you on your back. Not yet."

Elbridge grinned. "Any day now, wouldn't surprise me," he said.

"Hey, look," Roger said, coming to a stop at the edge of the bank by the cove. "Somebody's been piling lumber."

The snow on the bank had been trampled flat, a path made down to tidemark. At one side, lying in the snow, was a big pile of new lumber, apparently all that had washed ashore into the cove.

"Didn't know anybody'd taken time to salvage that," Elbridge said. "Nice lumber, isn't it?"

The Nova Scotia lumber was mostly two-by-fours and two-by-sixes, with a few eight-by-twelves, rough sawed. Some of it had been splintered by violent passage over the ledges, but mainly it was as it had come from the mill. Water had darkened its yellow newness, furred over in spots with crystals which might have been salt or frost; the ends were fringed with milky icicles, sparked here and there by the sun. It still had a wild, forest smell of resin and pine cones.

"Some white pine there," Roger said. "Wonder why they didn't finish it. They must have a lot of pine."

"Likely they do. The buyer would plane it, probably," Elbridge said.

He stood looking thoughtfully at the lumber, wondering which of his neighbors had taken the time to stack it. With all the searching there had been to do, since the storm, it looked as though someone had hustled to make hay while the sun shone. Not that it made sense to let good lumber go adrift, as it would if it weren't piled out of the tide's way. A man could always use cut lumber. But Lord, first things first; it did seem as though they might have spent a little more time hunting, before they started salvaging.

There were no ducks in the cove as yet, but some might come in around dusk. It was nearly time. The sky was a deep, quiet blue, lightening white toward the eastern horizon; in the west it was coloring up to a clear yellow. The duck blind, which he and Roger had built years ago, when Roger was Will's and Gib's age, and which Elbridge and the twins now repaired each year with brush and sticks, was all but buried up in snow, like an igloo. Roger cleared away the loopholes. Inside, it was snug as a cave, with an old log to sit on, and no drafts at all through the snow-thickened walls. They sat for a while without saying anything. Occasionally, Roger leaned over and peered cautiously out through a loophole, at the empty, slowly darkening water of the cove.

"How is it over there, Roger?" Elbridge asked at last. "You like it?"

"It's fine."

"You look a little thinned out. Lost your tan."

"Oh, sure, undercover. Don't get much chance at the outdoors."

"But you like it, just the same?"

Roger glanced over at his father.

Elbridge was sitting on the old cat-spruce log, which had been in the duck blind so long that its ends were crumbling away. His feet, in their heavy felts-and-rubbers, with the legs of his old, warm woolen pants tucked down inside them, were stretched out comfortably. His sheepskin coat hung open, showing the dark blue flannel work shirt, red tobacco tin in the breast pocket, his knitted muffler with dangling ends. In one mittened hand, he held his corncob pipe, the one with the bubble in its stem, the pipe which, Roger remembered, never seemed to be new. Elbridge's face, under the battered cap with rolled-up earflaps, was a rich, red-bronze, his eyes crinkled at the corners from squinting into sun and wind.

"Well, I'll tell you," Roger said. "I don't ever seem to get stretched out straight over there. I think maybe this spring, when the good weather starts, I'll probably bust. This is what I *like*. This duck blind. Watching the cove for birds, even if they don't come. Even if we don't get any. You and your stinking old pipe."

Elbridge was touched. "Never will get used to having you gone," he said. "Or that seeing you at all is vacation stuff, now."

"That's right, I guess, Pop. That's what it is. Vacation stuff."

"Sure you don't want to come home?" Elbridge asked. "There's always a place with your ma and me. Or, when you get married, with Little Sarah. She rattles around in that big house. It'll be yours, anyway, when she goes. She's said, two-three times, she'd be tickled to death to move into the summer kitchen, time comes you want to bring home a wife."

There was a silence. Roger stood looking out through the loophole of the blind. So like MacKechnie, the set of his head, his shoulders, though MacKechnie had been a small man.

"Work for Liseo and me," Elbridge went on. "There's room for you. Or if you want to be on your own, I've got enough laid by to start you out with a boat and gear." He said, now, what he had wanted to say. "I'd like to think of MacKechnie's great-grandson living in his house. Kind of take over, where the old man and I leave off."

Roger swung around. "Take over what?" he said. "Look, Pop, I know you like it here. So do I, in a way. I don't like working undercover. But look, in a drugstore you've really got it made. Old man Caddell, he—well, he coins the money. If I can get a course in pharmacy, I can take over."

"Lordsake," Elbridge said. "You want to be a druggist?"

"No, I can't say I *want* to. I want to make dough. I'm like anybody else, I want to pile it up. Over here, living over here, you don't have any idea. Look, I don't want to live hand to mouth. I want a car. I want a radio. I want a movie handy, and a chance to go to it when I want to. I want money enough saved up to marry Rosie, when the time comes, and I want a new house, in a town. A house with a bathroom."

Elbridge said, "Well, you aren't to be blamed for that, I guess."

"I only want the things in my time that MacKechnie wanted in his, Pop. He did it with a granite quarry, that was what *he* had.

I might like to do it with a quarry, but I've got no choice, so I take
what's for me, and that's a drugstore."

"You're good with your hands," Elbridge said. "That chest is a
dandy."

"I can't make a living building hope chests."

"No, maybe you can't."

"The old-timers," Roger said. "I've grown up hearing about them.
What they were, what they did. I respect them, all right, who
wouldn't? But, look, Pop, I'm no different from them. They waded
in here when the country was new, that's all, everybody got his hands
on something. MacKechnie, he had a project, sailed in here and built,
made something on his own. Well, that's what I want to do. Get my
hands on something, wrench it around, make it fly. Only, where's my
project now? What is there for me?"

"Well, you say it's a drugstore."

Roger stuck out his jaw, and in that moment, Elbridge saw he
was like MacKechnie. A lot like MacKechnie.

"What's wrong with a drugstore?"

"Nothing's wrong with it. I don't want you to think I think so. All
that's wrong with it for *you*, you've just said. You don't like it. You
don't like being undercover. I think the old man kind of liked what
he did, Roger."

"I don't think it cuts a whole lot of ice," Roger said, "whether you
like it or whether you don't. The fun's in making the money. Heck,
how you do it, that's secondary. You can get interested in anything,
just so the money comes in. That's why I think a drugstore."

It was beginning to get dark. The sun had set, leaving behind it a
clear, lemon-colored west. The water in the cove reflected it, sending
back slick coils of pure yellow, on which a mat of dark seaweed set
adrift by the storm floated lazily.

He's grown taller, Elbridge thought. He was taller now than El-
bridge was; he towered over his mother. His hair was curly, a crisp
black, like Jess's, and he had Jess's straight, forthright nose, her gray
eyes and stubborn jaw. MacKechnie, yes, sometimes; but when you
looked at him, casually, you saw Jess. It had always fascinated El-
bridge to see Jess's looks coming out in the kids; as for his own, he
never figured he had any worth mentioning. Red hair and freckles.
Of course, the twins had a lot of his looks, but enough of Jess's to take
the curse off. It seemed, in a way, wonderful.

You made kids, they were the spit-and-image, but with a differ-
ence; so that your kid wasn't you or your wife, or any of the people

back of that; and you made a big mistake, if you thought he was. He was something new under the sun, and valuable in a way that had nothing to do with you. You might have made him and you cherished him, but the heft of it was, you'd be a fool if you didn't take into account that it was the kid's own; it belonged to him, not to you.

Roger said, "There's a wharf for sale and a business like yours and Liseo's over at the harbor."

Elbridge nodded absently. "Joe Blake's," he said. "Joe decided to sell, has he?"

"Well, he's old. He'd sell reasonable, I think. But I don't guess you'd buy him out. Not the way you feel about this place."

"Me? Buy out Joe Blake?"

"No. Skip it, Pop. I guess you wouldn't. I'm sorry I don't feel about it here the way you do. Over there, I get homesick. For the way it looks, for the things we do here, for you and Ma. I can't wait to get back. But the thing is, I come back and for a day or so, it's great, and then there isn't anything here."

He seemed surprised when his father said nothing. He looked around, and saw that Elbridge was poking thoughtfully at a rotten place in the log; the old, punky wood gave and crumbled at a touch.

"With your brains!" Roger said forcibly. "You could have done anything. Only you look *back*, Pop, at what a lot of old men did once, that's dead and gone and ended. Not ahead, at what's to come—"

He stopped, wondering if he'd hurt the old man's feelings, and was relieved when Elbridge grinned.

"Brains? Oh, average, I guess. If you've got any extra, likely the heft of them came from your ma."

Roger grinned back. This was more like it. This was the way he and his father used to talk. "Oh, I always tell people my old man's dumb," he said, "so they'll know I'm under a handicap."

"Well," Elbridge said. He went on, after a moment, "If you want to study pharmacy, you'll need high school, won't you? I can help you, if you need it."

"I'll stick with Caddell a couple of years. He's teaching me a lot. I'll be able to cram down a pharmacy course in jig time. I can't arse around four years high school. Rosie and I talked it over. And Mr. Caddell, he's old, got nobody in the world, maybe he'll leave me the store. I've kind of got things planned, Pop."

"Seems as though," Elbridge agreed. "Well, it's up to you, Roger."

He puffed on his pipe. Not that Roger's point of view was new to him. He guessed a lot of people felt the way Roger did, and why not?

It was what you had to expect of the times, and who was he, El-bridge Gilman, to set up the example of his own life against the feel-ing of the times? What did he have to offer in argument? What did he have to show? Not a damned thing, in terms of money or getting anywhere in the world.

A house he'd built, a one-horse fish-dealing business, a family of kids, clothed, warmed and educated with the means of education there was at hand. A certain talent for handling the problems and the failing finances of a bankrupt town. But in terms of success in the world, as the world thought of success, not a damned thing.

"Why, gee, he lets me take over the soda fountain right now," Roger said. "Gee, Pop, no birds. Ought to be getting along, hadn't we, if we're going to stop by the pond."

"Ayup. Your ma'll have supper ready, too, before long."

"Hey, who's that?" Roger said, peering out the loophole.

Someone had come past the duck blind and was headed down the path toward the shore. The footsteps must have been muffled by snow, for neither of them had heard anything. Elbridge got up, peer-ing out the other loophole, and saw the fellow, back-to, rubber boots pulled up, a battered mackinaw and sou'wester—looked like any man from the town, going down the path and stopping by the stack of lumber. It was Jack Shepheard, Elbridge saw, and was about to call "hi" to him, when he stopped, puzzled by what Jack was do-ing.

Jack was picking up sticks of lumber and heaving them down over the bank of the cove.

"What the heck—" Roger began, stopped by his father's touch on his arm.

After he had heaved down eight or ten big sticks, Jack went down the bank and hauled them below tidemark. Then he came back, took a long look behind him up the path to the woods, and began heaving down some more.

"What's that for, Pop?" Roger asked in a low voice. "If he leaves it down there, it'll all go adrift."

"That's what he wants it to do, I guess," Elbridge said thought-fully.

As long as the lumber was stacked on the bank, it belonged to the man who had stacked it there, evidently not Jack. Lying on the rocks below tidemark, or adrift, it belonged to anybody.

"That'll all drift over to the other side of the cove tonight, the way the wind is," Roger said.

"And Jack can pick it up tomorrow and it'll be his lumber," Elbridge said.

"Gosh, what a dirty trick! Whoever piled that there must've worked like a dog. Let's show. Let him know we've seen him."

"Wait," Elbridge said. "Hold up, while I think."

For a moment, he didn't know what was best to do. So far as he had ever known, Jack Shepheard was a decent enough fellow, no better, no worse than most, and Elbridge's friend. If he found out someone had seen him up to a mean trick like this, he'd never get over it. Things were bad enough, right now, in the town, without making them worse. With the women all ready for battle, it wouldn't take much to set the men going, too. So far, the men hadn't mixed in too much. But something like this would surely do the trick. On the other hand, Elbridge knew quite well what he would have done if it hadn't been for the row. He would have walked out of the duck blind and said "hi" to Jack, and no more; and Jack would have been sore at getting caught, and it wouldn't have mattered a damn. He saw Roger looking at him curiously, and thought, Well, better go out there; but just then, the matter was taken out of his hands. Somebody else went by the blind on the dead run, with a muffled sound of feet scurrying in the snow, and George Lowden appeared on the cove bank, hollering and shaking his fists.

"We thought you was down here, tracked you, you thieving bastard, you! You put that lumber back up here on the bank. That belongs to me, that lumber does!"

Jack spun around; he was a big fellow who would have made two of George, but here behind George, puffing and panting, came Willard. They could hear his creepers crunch in the snow.

"That's what you think," Jack said levelly. "It belongs to anyone can get it. I'm getting it."

"No, sir, by God, you ain't!"

"You try and stop me," Jack said. "Come on down here, the both of you and try and stop me." He pulled his head down into the shoulders of his mackinaw, and stood there, his hunched outline black against the still, yellow water of the cove. "You thought you was smart, didn't you?" Jack went on. "Let on you was walking shore looking for dead bodies, and all the time you was down here piling up this lumber, just so's to get ahead of us, whilst we was out pounding around them islands, hunting. Figured you had the edge on us, didn't you? Well, by God, it was a dirty trick. You ain't getting away with it."

"That's quite a spiel," George said. "Quite a spiel."

"Yes, and I mean it. You try to bother me down here, I'll bend one of these two-by-fours over your head."

George reached down, picked up a short end of new two-by-four. "We'll see who'll bend a two-by-four," he said. He turned, thrust it, like a club, into Willard's hands. "Go on, Wid," he said, standing out of the way. "Go on down there and hit him."

"Yes," Jack said. "Come on, why don't you, Wid? If your ankles ain't too swole up from walking the shore hunting for dead bodies, like you said. God knows they ought to be, but it warn't from hunting, was it?"

Willard hefted the two-by-four in his hands. You had to know Willard to know there was real fury behind the sounds he was making. He was humbling and bumbling like a kettle lifting its cover when it starts to boil, and every few seconds his breath went out through his teeth with a hiss. He lifted the club and lowered it, and he began to paw the snow with his feet, shifting from one to the other.

It was quite funny to watch, but Elbridge had seen this happen to Willard once or twice in his life. Once, years ago, if Willard hadn't been pulled off of a man, he might have killed him. Elbridge knew —he had been the one who'd pulled him off, and it was like trying to stop a bull.

He sighed a little, motioned Roger out of his way. He thought, Here goes the town, leveled his shotgun out through the loophole, aimed it at the snow-laden tree over Willard's head, and pulled the trigger.

The tree was a young cat spruce about thirty feet high, with thick branches so loaded with soft snow that they were already slanted toward the ground. The charge of bird shot at close range started a cascade in the upper part of the tree, which fell with a *whush*, cleaning off the lower branches as it came, a great cloud of flying white down over Willard, so that for a moment he could not be seen. Then he heaved up out of it like a snow-topped mountain, buried to his knees, a tower of snow on his hat, on his arms and shoulders, on the two-by-four, which he held in his two hands, as if he were presenting a pile of snow on a platter.

"Bub-by Jesus," Willard said. "Did somebody take a shot at me?"

Elbridge strolled out of the duck blind. "God, Wid, I'm sorry," he said. "Damn squirrel, I don't believe I touched him. Here, goshsake, let me brush you off. I didn't have an idea in the world that would do that."

He hadn't, he realized, thinking only that the gunshot would stop the fight.

He picked the two-by-four out of Willard's hands, tossed it into the bushes and began brushing snow from Willard, knocking it off his hat, digging it out of his collar. Willard's hands jerked blindly; one of them found the lapel of Elbridge's coat, clamped there and pulled, and the lapel came off, ripped clean down the front of the coat.

"Take it easy, boy," Elbridge said.

He went on carefully brushing, using his hands for that.

"No need to tear my coat. Hold on, now, let me get that lump off your collar. God, I'm sorry. Damn careless thing to do. Wonder I hadn't hurt you. You're about soaked through, you know it? You come on up to the house with me. Jess'll feed us hot coffee, get you dried out. Come on, now, no sense risking pneumonia. Man's got to be careful, this time of year."

It seemed to him that he went on brushing and talking for ten minutes, though it couldn't have been more than two, before he saw some answering sign of humanity in Willard's face. The mouth, wrenched with fury, relaxed, and two fat tears squeezed out from under the clenched eyelids.

"That's the boy," Elbridge said, with relief.

Thank God. Wid would be all right now. At least, that was the way it had been, times before.

He stepped back to find Roger directly behind him, his face white, his shotgun cocked and aimed directly at Willard's foot.

"Hey, put that down!" Elbridge said. "What in hell do you think you're doing?"

"I wouldn't have, unless he—" Roger stopped. "I saw him tear your coat."

"Well, it's all right now. Put it down."

It wasn't all right, because Jack was still standing down there, his shoulders hunched, his big, homely face set in lines of stubbornness and fury. As for George, George was gone, hot-footing it up the snowy path to town. George wouldn't fight anybody, not if he could get Willard to do the fighting for him.

"What to hell, Jack?" Elbridge said. "There's a lot of lumber along-shore still. What's the use of a cussed row?"

Jack looked Elbridge up and down. "Let 'em get away with it, would you?" he said. "Wid and George and Paul Cayford and Allen Vira and them was supposed to *hunt*. And what did they do? Spent the time stacking up lumber, so as to get ahead of the rest of us. All right, we won't stand for it. You can side with them or side with us. Which is it?"

"You cool off a little, you'll see they didn't stack up so much," Elbridge said. "There's lumber to burn all over the east shore, Jack." Out of the corner of his eye, he saw Willard going off up the path, stumbling a little as he went.

"That ain't the point of it. It's the dirty trick," Jack said. "What a batch of hogs thought they could get away with." He stood glaring at Elbridge, suddenly turned and started to stump away, his rubber boots slipping and sliding over the icy rocks. "All right," he said, over his shoulder. "If you won't either fish or cut bait, then you mind your own goddamned business."

Well, Elbridge thought soberly, watching him go, if the men of the town are bound to fight, shore salvage is as good a rock as any to split on.

So far back as he could remember, there'd been squabbles, off and on, over shore salvage. Tide currents setting down across the bay brought all kinds of floating objects, not only from the bay, but from the river mouth on the mainland, twenty miles away to the west. In the old days, when the big sawmills were going full-tilt, up that river, there had always been a lot of loose lumber floating around the bay, a godsend to islanders who had to boat or raft across water every stick of sawed lumber they needed. It was traditional to walk-shore, particularly after a storm, to see what you could find; everyone, including Elbridge, liked to, and it had always involved considerable rivalry, because whoever got there first got first pickings.

Most people respected the salvage law—if a man found something on the shore and hauled it up out of the tide's way, it could stay there on the bank until doomsday unless he came and took it away himself. A salvage stealer found out sooner or later that no loot of his own would ever be safe from anybody, and Elbridge had known only a few such in his time. Jack Shepheard had never been one; to his own way of thinking, he wasn't now. He had a grievance; he was seeing justice done.

Quite a lot of the men had spent time out in boats, hunting the bay, making sure nobody, living or dead, had been cast away on any of the islands—Elbridge, himself, and Jack, and Bill Lessaro and Orin Vira and Joe Hitchman and a couple of the Nikolaides kids, probably some more he didn't know about. And Liseo.

Liseo, he reflected, pacing along behind Roger, as Roger headed eagerly up the path toward the duck pond. If that bunch had got together, hashing things over, and they must have, Liseo would have been there, too, with his word or so to say. The idea of setting the lumber adrift to be picked up all over again, had a fine flavor of Liseo. There was a kind of justice in it, you couldn't deny.

Still, if Liseo had had a finger in the pie, the lumber would have gone adrift on a dark night with a high tide, innocent faces all over the place, and nobody the wiser. Only old Jack, single-track mind, was so burned up he couldn't wait.

Too bad, Elbridge thought, with a wry grin to himself. Liseo and I could have fixed that, slick as a whistle, and no fat in the fire at all.

But it was too late now. The circumstances, whatever they were, were set up and aimed. They'd be a lot easier to deal with, too, if there were a single living man on the island whose grandfather wouldn't have been happier to find a new two-by-four lying on the shore than he would a five dollar bill.

ADDIE SHEPHEARD, that afternoon, had walked up the road to call on the Lowdens. She wasn't overly fond of Harriet, though they were cousins—Addie, before she had married Jack Shepheard, had been a Horn. She had grown up with Harriet and had found, even as a child, that you might as well try to be pleasant to a needle. The best of intentions, and *prick!* you got scratched. So a social visit once a twice a year was all Addie felt called upon to make on Harriet, and she wouldn't have gone today except it was church business and she hoped to find Willard at home. She'd waited until nearly supper-time, for that reason; besides, if Harriet was busy getting supper, Addie would have an excuse for not staying very long.

The Church Council, of which Addie was chairman, had met at her house last night to see what had best be done about the vestry furnace. When Willard had dumped the bucket of ice water into it, he'd ruined the hearth, cracked it in three places, so that no fire could be built and no services held in the church through the cold weather until the furnace was fixed. The Council, including Addie herself, was good and put out with Willard, all except Jess, that is, who seemed to feel Willard had something on his side.

"Oh, no, Bill!" she'd said, when Bill Lessaro proposed a motion that the Council assess Willard twenty dollars, make him pay the repair bill. "That isn't right! Everybody was excited that night."

Council Meeting had been awful uncomfortable, anyway, all evening. Bill and Carrie Hitchman had sat there looking right through Paul Cayford, because Paul was one of those who'd sneaked in ahead of his neighbors piling up that lumber; and Paul, being Imogene's husband, had spent *his* time staring right through Jess. Of course, the Cayfords were all terrible put out with the Gilmans.

The atmosphere had got so thick that Jack's aunt, old Aunt Mary Shepheard, nigh eighty, who lived with them, had noticed it and she'd piped up, "For heb'm sakes, what ails them men? They'll be at it. Look out, now!" And Addie would like to have gone right through the floor, she was so embarrassed.

She was having a time, herself, because she hated to vote opposite sides from Jess, who was as good a friend as she'd have in this world; but there, Willard did break that hearth. And he was in on that lumber, too, Jack said so. Serve him right to have to pay out twenty dollars. She didn't doubt for a minute that Carrie and Bill had the same thing in mind when they voted "yes" along with her. And then Jess voted "no," and that left Paul hanging and dangling. He was mad at Jess, so he couldn't vote "no" and be on her side; and if he voted "yes," then he'd be in with Carrie and Bill, who were mad at him. It was real painful to watch. And then Paul got up and resigned from the Council and went home.

Addie wouldn't have had it happen for the world, but there. Up to now it had been a real good Council.

The motion had passed, and here Addie was with a bill against Willard for twenty dollars in her pocket. Not that she meant to bring it out, before Harriet, if Willard wasn't there. Everybody in the world knew how Harriet was about money. Chaw down on the nickels and dimes, and grab Willard's, *whisk!* right out of his pocket, the minute he got home every day.

Willard wasn't there, nor George. Harriet was getting supper. She was civil, but she kept glancing over at Addie with that you-want-something-or-you-wouldn't-have-come look. It made Addie's scruff rise up on the back of her neck, but before anything happened to put your finger on, in came George, all a-puff as if he'd been running, and sweating like a vinegar cruet.

"Heaven's sake, George," Addie said. "What ails you?" and George, who had started to say something to Harriet before he'd noticed Addie was there, sat down in a chair and opened the *Daily News*, spread it right out in front of his face.

"Well, Addie, Jack and the boys gone somewhere, have they?" Harriet said.

It *was* suppertime, but she needn't make so plain she wanted you to go home.

Addie said, "Not that I know of," and sat on for a few minutes, just to show she wasn't going home until she got ready.

"Oh, you plan a late supper, then," Harriet said, and she began to dish up, without ah-yes-or-no.

"Well, I wouldn't want to have to set here and watch you eat," Addie said. She got up, feeling the red come up her neck in spite of herself. "Or make you put back supper on account of my being here. I had some church business with Willard, that was all. I s'posed likely you'd wait supper for him."

That'll hold her, she thought, starting toward the door. Everybody knew George and Harriet never waited for Willard, that he got the pickings-up and the leavings-over in this house.

Thank heaven, there he came. She could hear his creepers, like walking on bones. Ker-unch, thump. Kerunch-thump.

"If the Council," Harriet said, "has sent him a bill for that hearth, you can take it home with you."

"It beats all how private business gets around," Addie said. "I don't know who told you that, but I can suppose it was Imogene. All I can say is, it's a good thing she wasn't born a boat. With her leaks, she'd never of grown up to woman-size. You can tell her I said so, she'd sunk years ago."

"I will," Harriet said. "Count upon it."

"I'm sure," Addie said. She met Willard in the door, and she knew she ought to have led up to the bill, but she was so mad she couldn't. She just put it into his hand, said, "The Council sent you this, Willard," and went on by.

She caught one glimpse of his face and felt real sorry. He just stood there, looking at the bill in his hand with that kind of foolish expression he had sometimes, and he was wet, too, coldlike, as if he'd been rolling over and over in the snow.

George said, "Blood from a stone, Addie. Blood from a stone," without even putting down the paper, and Harriet said, just as Addie closed the door, "Wid, I've told you and told you, that I'll tear the feet off your legs if you so much as set one track of them creepers on my kitchen floor."

LATER that night, as George was coming in, unsuspecting, from the outhouse, Willard came out of the barn, grabbed him and thrashed him, gave him the hiding of his life, so that the next morning George couldn't stir out of bed, and Harriet had to send for Doctor Graham.

The old doctor plastered up George's cuts and bruises, put out a bottle of liniment to rub on; he was furious at having to make the trip over to the island, in the winter, in Orin Vira's boat, for any such cause.

"God, you two fellows!" he said, slapping his instruments back into his bag. "I've got enough to do without having to patch up a mess of foolishness. Somebody ought to bat your heads together, knock some sense into you."

"Nothing to do with me, Doc," George said, out of one side of his mouth, because the other was covered with plaster. "Charged out of there like a wild animal, had me down before I knew what to make of it. I never done one thing to him."

"What were you thinking of, Wid?" the doctor said. "This is no way for a grown man to treat his brother. Next time, it'll be the sheriff, it won't be me, and serve you good and well right."

Willard stood there, looking off sideways, not saying anything. George had managed to give him a black eye, a dandy, but that was all.

Harriet said, "You tend to George, doctor. I'll tend to Willard."

She stood there, watching the doctor, her thin lips tight. This doctor's visit was costing her three dollars. She would tend to Willard.

THE moon was just beginning to rise when the caterpillar of children, of all ages and sizes, from Herbie Hitchman, five, to Bubber Cayford, fourteen, came up MacKechnie's hill and crossed the top by the quarries. The sky in the west was clear gold-green from the sunset still, translucent as a cat's eye. Stars were coming out, big and quiet, and the tip of the moon lay as in a niche in the place where the sky met the ocean, making a faint squiggle of reddish fire across the water. Below the hill, the island spread out, savage and cold, swamp and pasture and water meadow buried white. Tonight no wind blew, but the sound of the sea still hung muted in the air.

The children had formed Indian file where the causeway crossed the swamp, because the track through the snow was narrow. They yelled and stamped and snowballed each other; sometimes, where the snowbanks weren't too deep, the ones on ahead made side excursions to hide behind trees and shake a laden branch so that dollops of snow would fall on someone, or jump out with a boo to scare the little kids. Night was falling in the woods, deep blue shadows growing cold and lonesome. Nobody noticed, or minded if

the raucous and hearty noise they made seemed small and muffled
under the sea-shell sky. Tonight was the night of the Party.

They went through the silent trees with a sound that was like a
flock of birds, part twitter, part scream; and deep in the swamp, in
his thicket behind the pond, the big buck lifted his head a little from
his long dream of cold and heard them go.

Tonight was the night looked forward to for weeks, like Christmas,
like the Fourth of July; the Party, of a kind they didn't know except
in this one place; the night they were let to walk across the island
by themselves, when dark woods were not scary and quarry pits no
danger, being only incidentals on the way to Miss Greenwood's
Party.

At ten-thirty, two grownups would come from the village with
lanterns—tonight it would be Roger Gilman and Rosie MacGimsey—
to make sure everybody got safely home. But that would be after
dark, and it wasn't dark yet, not *quite*. They crossed by the quarry
pits, big children at either end, little ones in the middle, holding to
each other's belts and coattails, as they had promised their mothers
they would; but screaming, laughing because Bubber Cayford, up
front, yelled that he was Big Chief Rosy-Belly and Joyce Gilman, at
the rear, was his Heap Biggest Injun Squaw, and all the rest pa-
pooses; even Herbie Hitchman, the custard of all, stumped gaily
along in the middle of the line, his eyes shining as if with visions of
sugarplums.

So they went down the hill and through the woods on its far side,
where the trees were so thick that not much snow had got through
to the path, only a few inches on the level and one spotless, gleaming
snowbank, drifted three feet high, flat-topped like a table, where
Joyce Gilman lay down on her back and flapped her arms to make an
angel with wings, printed on the snow. And then, when she got up,
Bubber Cayford went up the snowbank and just made the prints
of his knees and his hands on either side of the angel; and the big
kids screamed laughing, because that was nasty, and the little kids
laughed because the big kids did. Only not Joyce. She was mad. She
tried to slap Bubber and he ran off, hollering and hooting.

And then they came to Miss Greenwood's house, set high on the
point of rocks, yellow warm light from every downstairs window, and
she standing in the open door. And the full moon had pulled itself
up, floating free and clear above a vast slice of silver light across the
black-ink water.

Miss Greenwood was in a dress-up dress, gray, with lace at the neck, long, floppy skirt, covered with a little white lace apron in front. Her hair was in a puffy roll, gray above her forehead, neat pug on top. Smiling, talking, greeting everybody, she showed them where to put their wraps, in the small bedroom off the kitchen.

"Big ones help the little ones, please," she said. "And then go into the living room. I shall finish setting the table, and then we'll play games."

Away she went to the dining room, where, if you listened, you could hear her rattling silver spoons and talking to herself. You would almost think someone was in the room with her, even when you knew she was there all alone. Joyce, helping Herbie Hitchman off with his rubbers by the dining room door, heard her say, "Twenty, twenty-one, two, three. That's right, I think, but I must count again. I'm such a fool about numbers. It would be dreadful, Roxinda, if somebody got left out."

Herbie, standing on one leg while Joyce pulled at his rubber, let his foot go limp. A look of deep amusement passed over his face.

"She's *talken* to herself," he said, giggling.

It was one of the things they waited for; it was one of the joys of the Party to hear Miss Greenwood talk to herself.

"You shush, Herbie," Joyce whispered to him.

Suppose Miss Greenwood heard him?

"I *heard* her," Herbie said loudly.

"Well, what of it? Stiffen out your foot, Herbie, it's like a dishcloth. How do you expect me to get your rubber off?"

"But she *wos!* I heard her, Joyce."

"Well, if she hears *you,* she won't give you any ice cream," Joyce whispered fiercely.

This was a mistake. Herbie began to pucker.

"But she didn't hear you."

She gave him a little shove toward the living room.

"You go in and look at the Christmas tree," she said. "See if you can tell which present's yours."

Herbie's pucker cleared up at once. "Oh, yes," he said. "Oh, yes. I will."

Joyce saw him go, thankfully. She put his rubbers down behind the kitchen door, so that she would know where to find them. Always, when it came time to leave a place, Herbie would be sure his rubbers were lost, never to be found, and have a spell of bellering. Joyce didn't want to go through with that. Not on the night of the Party.

Coming over, she had felt so happy that she hadn't really got mad when Bubber Cayford messed up her snow angel. It was no use to pay any attention to him, he was always doing and saying something nasty anyway; and just now, he and his sister Gladys were laying for her and the twins, because Imogene was so mad. But nothing was going to bother Joyce tonight. She felt foamy inside; if she opened her mouth wide, she thought, out might come a big colored soap bubble; and the air in Miss Greenwood's house was as if full of Christmas spangles and smelt most beautifully of cake.

The crowd had mostly cleared out of the small bedroom, leaving the couch piled with snow-damp coats and caps and the floor cluttered with assorted wet footgear, each piece making a separate puddle where it sat. But Bubber and Gladys were in there, still as mice by the far door, which was shut. Over by the couch, taking off his rubbers, was Will. The light was dim from a single kerosene lamp in the bracket by the window, but Joyce could see they were all three staring at the closed door.

She put her own coat and cap on top of the pile. "Come on, Will. What are you hanging around in here for?"

Bubber said, "Shut up. Listen."

From behind the door, there was at first no sound, then a soft, thin, gentle wheeze.

"That's old lady Greenwood," Bubber said. "That's where she sleeps, in there. That's her, snoring."

For a moment, Joyce, too, stared at the door with awe and curiosity. Old lady Greenwood, so old she wasn't any longer a person. Never spoke, never looked. Just sat.

Gladys said, in an important whisper, just as if, like her mother, she knew all there was to know about anything, and no doubt her mother was the first one who had said this, "She only breathes once in every two minutes. Pretty soon, she's going to die."

Gladys was eleven, two years younger than Joyce, a quite pretty, slender girl, with a small nose and a bright, inquisitive face. Her clear blue eyes, long-lashed, stared avidly at the door.

Joyce said disgustedly, "Aw, how do *you* know? I'll bet she isn't in there at all. Sounds more like the cat. Miss Greenwood's probably put Richard in there to be out of the Party."

Richard, Miss Greenwood's cat, didn't care for children, or parties either, and was seldom seen, unless encountered unexpectedly. He was never seen on the night of the Party, although sometimes the little bell he wore on a leather collar around his neck, to keep him from being able to creep up on birds, could be heard tinkling from some other part of the house.

"We know she sleeps in there," Bubber said. "That's her room. Once I peeked in the window in the daytime, and there she was, asleep. Mouth wide open. Round, black hole."

Bubber giggled, opened his own mouth, to show how old lady Greenwood slept.

"Hurry up, Will," Joyce said. She gave Will a poke. "It's nobody's business how people sleep."

She saw at once that she shouldn't have poked Will. He always hated to be hustled, liked to take his time; he was taking it now. Also, she'd made it sound as if he were one of the snoopers. She hadn't meant to. She tried to better things and only made them worse. "Somebody that can't help herself," she said. "Couldn't even know if people sneaked and peeked and mocked you while you were asleep."

"Shut up, Joyce," Will said. "I'm only taking off my rubbers."

What had happened, the crowd of kids had pushed into the bedroom, carrying him along, and he had waited in a corner until some had cleared out and there was room to take off his outdoor gear without having an elbow stuck in his eye. When he got to his rubbers, he had glanced up, and there were Gladys and Bubber with their noses glued to the door. Will hadn't thought much about it, except to wonder what for. He had been avoiding all Cayfords studiously, since the school time; he supposed that sooner or later, some of them would catch up with him. It would probably be Bubber, and he would have to fight. Bubber was older and bigger and no doubt would lick him, but Will knew he could put up enough of a scrap to make Bubber think twice about starting it. It was unthinkable, anyway, that anybody would start anything in Miss Greenwood's house on the night of the Party. Will went on methodically unlatching the catches of his overshoes.

"'Taking off my rubbers,'" Bubber said, mocking him. "I thought you was learning a piece, maybe, to speak to Aunt Greeny."

Will said sturdily, "It's no skin off your ass."

Bubber doubled his fists. "Oh, is that so?"

Will kicked off the second overshoe and stood up with an overshoe in each hand. He said, "Your nose'll look worse'n it does when somebody slams the window on it when you're peeking in."

Oh, no, Joyce thought, horrified. Not a fight, not in Miss Greenwood's bedroom!

For all he was slow-moving, Will was a terrible fighter. He wouldn't give in, ever. She cast around for something, anything, to stop it.

Behind them, Miss Greenwood said, "Oh, here the rest of you are! I was sure I hadn't miscounted, and then I could only find nineteen children. Now I'm *all* mixed up. Joyce, would you count for me, and then count the places at the table? I'm such a fool about counting. And the rest of you go into the living room, please, where we need you all for charades."

They all started to move. Behind Miss Greenwood, as he went by, Bubber made a horrible face at Will, pulling down the corners of his mouth with one thumb and forefinger, pushing on the tip of his nose with the other forefinger. Will didn't turn a hair.

The table set in the dining room, with extra leaves in, stretched almost from wall to wall and was covered with a creamy lace table-cloth that nearly touched the floor. On it were thin, delicately colored dishes—pink-rosebud plates, little cups for cocoa, silver gleaming softly in the lamplight. Lace napkins to match, each place a little pattern! Miss Greenwood always used the little cups, because the children loved them, though the boys could drink the contents of one at a swallow, and it kept her busy jumping up to fill them.

Oh, lovely, lovely table, lovely dishes! It made you feel like somebody good and great, just to see them.

Joyce couldn't resist pausing to look at the things. Not for long—it wasn't polite, of course; she couldn't help just a glance or two as she went by. Here, alone in the dining room, she felt the fizzy, bubbly feeling inside start to come back. Out there in the bedroom, she'd thought everything had been spoiled. But no. Through the living room portieres, she caught sight of the Christmas tree.

Joyce went in. The Party was starting slowly, as it always did, the children sitting stiffly in best clothes, talking in low voices, taking little peeks at Miss Greenwood's things when she was out of the room, but mostly, stealing sidelong glances at the Christmas tree.

Trees at home were trimmed with strings of cranberries and pop-corn, oranges when your family could afford them, last year's tinsel and angels cut from colored paper; sometimes if everybody promised to sit still and be careful, lighted candles in holders that clamped to the twigs of the tree. Not many parents would allow candles for fear of fire. They let them burn only a moment and then blew them out, just before the presents went around. Joyce remembered one time, most particularly, when she was a very small girl, and had poked at a candle which wasn't burning right, hoping to fix it, with a celluloid comb, and had had to be smothered out with a rug.

Miss Greenwood's tree had no candles. It needed none. It was gleaming glitter from top to bottom, covered with shining ropes of tinsel, colored balls, make-believe icicles, small bright fragments of many kinds, and miniature toys. Each year Joyce looked for three things on Miss Greenwood's tree, which were always there—some tiny colored dolls, like fairies, in bright dresses, a doll's trumpet that would really blow, and a pair of mittens not much more than an inch long. With Little Sarah, Joyce had already gone through the agony of learning to knit. Oh, how small must have been the needles, how patient the fingers, to have knitted such tiny mittens!

And under the tree, snuggled in a space where some of the lower branches had been trimmed artfully to make room for it, was always a little tableau of Mary and Joseph and the Wise Men around the crib of Jesus—tiny wooden figures, so real you almost expected them to move; sheep and cows and a dog and hens, and one hen had chickens. All these things could be handled, picked up and admired. Miss Greenwood never minded, even when you touched the gift of the Third Wise Man, which was a tiny, thin blue-glass jug, no bigger than your fingernail.

There were thousands of little things on the tree. But the toys, above all, seemed wonderful and romantic and from far away, because, as all the children knew, they came from places like Germany, and South Africa and the Pyrenees, places Miss Greenwood had been when she was a child and had traveled all over the world. She had said so, one night of a Party, when some of the children were asking about the toys.

"I guess you must have been to a lot of places."

"Oh, yes. Yes. We were great travelers, once, Mother and I. When we were younger. When I was little, too."

"Have you been to London?"

"Oh, yes. I've been to London."

"Paris, France?"

"Yes. Paris, France."

"The North Pole?"

"No, not the North Pole. Only Admiral Peary has been there. And Santa Claus."

And she laughed and began to take the presents off the tree.

The presents were never anything expensive, but they were always beautifully done up in colored paper, with silver stars and ribbon bows. You could see that Miss Roxinda had spent a good deal of time making a pretty package for each child. One year, Joyce had got a little silk handkerchief that smelled of some kind of strange, woodsy cologne; after it was washed, it kept its scent, so that even now, with its pearly blue color faded white from many washings, she could hold it to her nose, and there still would be the smell, far-off, delicate and cedary, as if it were remembering itself.

Another time, she got a tiny wooden donkey, with a saddlecloth of colored brocade, beautifully embroidered with little stitches; once, a box painted with bright scenes; again, a doll's thin cup and saucer. Whatever it was to be this year, she knew it would be different, a surprise; not what you would get at home. Among your parents' sensible presents of wool stockings and underwear, tablets and pencil boxes, Miss Greenwood's gift always stood out—something utterly beautiful and utterly useless.

Joyce looked, as soon as she could get close enough to the tree, for the three things—the dolls, the trumpet, the mittens. They did not seem to be there.

The tree was the same as always—a big one, floor to ceiling. You always wondered how Miss Greenwood had managed to cut it, get it home from the woods, set it up and trim it, all by herself. But she had—she said so, and seemed quite proud that she had done it. She was so tiny, she must have stood on a tall box. Spangles. Glitters. Tinkly icicles. Puffy cotton Santa Claus. Angels. It looked the same. The things must be there, hidden by other decorations. But, of course, you couldn't go and stare, hunting over a Christmas tree; everybody would think you were looking, greedy-greedy, for your own present, for what was for you.

First, at a Party, you played games. Miss Roxinda knew wonderful games.

"Now, perhaps you would like to play—" she would name the game. "The children in Spain play this. This is the way they do in a little town in the Pyrenees," and she would show how to play the game. Each year she tried to have a new one, though she was running out, she said, and it didn't matter, because at each Party, the children called out the old ones that they wanted to play. This year, it was Charades, which they had played before. She herself, she said, had played it as a child. You dressed up for it; and in a pile, out in the kitchen closet, were masks and dresses and tight, colored pantaloons, all smelling of moth balls, funny, musty, old-atticy, but wonderful to dress up in. There was even an old sword in a scabbard.

Johnny MacGimsey was a soldier, wearing the sword and brandishing it over Gib, who was a horrible, creepy dwarf, so awful that Herbie Hitchman started to cry. So then Miss Greenwood suggested another word, and she and Will, who were on the same team, came creeping on all fours through the living room portieres, squeaking. They were, unmistakably, mice. Everybody almost fell down, roaring laughing, and Herbie laughed until he got the hiccups and couldn't stop, and so cried again. With Herbie, you couldn't win.

But every time Joyce came near the tree, she looked and looked; and at last, she realized. It was the same as any other year, decorations and many colored packages, each marked with a child's name. But no little toys. No little toys at all. There was not even the crèche.

She thought, with a pang, Where can they all have gone?

She found out, just before supper, when everybody was out of breath and sat down to rest, and Miss Greenwood said it would be just the time to have the presents off the tree.

This year, she had given the tree's toys as presents. Herbie had the little mittens; the dolls, the wooden animals from the crèche were wrapped in the packages, two or three to each child. Not the people-figures, the Wise Men, or Joseph and Mary, or the Child, but the sheep and cows, the little hens, the chickens, the dog.

Joyce closed her eyes and prayed. "Please, please, let me get the doll's trumpet that will blow."

She did not know why she wanted it so much—a big girl of thirteen, and it was a doll's toy—but she had loved it ever since she was five years old and first had started coming to the Parties.

But even as she prayed, she heard the trumpet blow. Bubber Cayford had it; it had been in his package. He was blowing it funny; you could see, watching him clown, that he thought it was a silly present.

She opened her own package. It was a big pine cone, tied with red ribbon, and a small white card, which said, in old-fashioned writing, "Big Pine, California."

Who would want an old pine cone? For a moment, Joyce couldn't believe her eyes.

She held it down by her side, so that nobody could see. When nobody was looking, she stole out to the bedroom off the kitchen and slipped the pine cone out of sight in her coat pocket, keeping the ribbon in her hand, so if anyone asked, she could say she'd got a hair ribbon.

Miss Greenwood was in the kitchen. She had dished out the ice cream and now was pouring cocoa into a big silver pot. She was standing back-to by the kitchen counter, tilting a heavy kettle; a rich, thick brown stream smoked down; the whole kitchen smelled of chocolate. The kettle was heavy for her, Joyce could see, by the way it wobbled. As she tiptoed by, she heard Miss Greenwood say clearly, "Take care, Roxinda. That pot is hot."

To her horror, Joyce found herself smothering a giggle. She ducked into the pantry.

Oh, dear, Miss Greenwood did look funny, back-to! That floppy skirt, and her waist so small you could have met your thumbs and forefingers around it, if you ever thought of such a thing; that puffy roll of hair, that pug; talking to herself as if she were two people.

Yet, there was something . . .

The giggle went far away. Yes, there was something that tugged inside your chest, as if to hurt, but what was it, what could it be? Miss Greenwood wasn't anybody you could think of loving, being fond of, like other people. Such a thing would never enter your head. She was here, had been here since Joyce could remember—a part of the things at the island; a wonder for living where she did in this lonesome place; a nuisance to the grownups who had to check up every so often, see she was all right; somebody to show off poking fun at, because she looked strange and different from other people. There were the Parties, of course, everybody loved them. But Miss Greenwood herself—

You couldn't talk to her, like to the people you knew. Oh, if you met her on the Point road, or maybe dropped by at the house, if you were on a walk round shore, she was always glad to see you, gave you cake or kisses, called in General Putnam, the squirrel, let him run up the front of your dress, and that was fun.

But to talk to her—it was exactly as if Miss Greenwood had a phonograph record she played with her voice, about the weather, about her garden, about and what are you studying now in school, as if she cared. It wasn't very interesting; you never felt as if you were you at all, but just somebody, anybody at all Miss Greenwood was playing the record to.

Only once, Joyce could remember, had it been different. She had taken the mail over to the Point, and on the way had noticed a headline on a newspaper. RICHARD HARDING DAVIS DIES, it said. So when she handed the mail to Miss Greenwood, she said—because maybe you weren't fond of Miss Greenwood, but somehow it seemed important to impress her that you were somebody who read headlines, who knew about the world—she said, "I see where Richard Harding Davis is dead, Miss Greenwood."

And to Joyce's astonishment, Miss Greenwood looked at the headline and blinked her eyes, and two tears ran down.

Frozen with embarrassment, because she hadn't even known who Richard Harding Davis was, and maybe he'd been one of Miss Greenwood's relations, and how awful, Joyce said timidly, "Was he someone you knew?"

And right away Miss Greenwood had laughed, as usual, and said in her everyday voice, "Oh, no. No. Not at all. No acquaintance. He had *been* so many places."

She stood in the pantry, peering out at the slim back, at the tiny, bony, old hands moving among the cocoa things, thinking, It's awful bad manners to snoop on somebody; and at the same time, feeling the queer, puzzling tug at her chest, as if it were full of something, and what it was, no way to tell.

All those years of Parties, as far back as she could remember, something to look forward to every Christmas, every Easter. Was she *that* disappointed, she thought, because she'd got a pine cone, when she'd expected a something-better? Was it because she'd wanted the doll's trumpet? Was it because all the tree's toys had been given away, never to be looked for again?

From the living room behind her, she could hear the trumpet being blown. Already it had a doleful sound, fuzzy and tinny, where it had been blown too hard.

Whatever had Miss Greenwood given those things away for? She must like them; she'd had them for years and years, memorials of places she had once known.

An awful thought came to Joyce. Suppose Miss Greenwood didn't have money enough this year to buy presents for everyone? Could that be why she had given the trees' toys? Why, the summer people always had lots of money! She put the idea out of her mind at once, it was unthinkable; but it left a tinny feeling behind, almost like the sound, now, of the doll's trumpet.

After all, Miss Greenwood didn't need to give anyone anything. She wasn't related. And she was out there now, dishing supper; she had made cake and cocoa and frozen ice cream for twenty-three kids.

Joyce went straight back into the bedroom and got the pine cone out of her coat pocket. She came out, carrying it in plain sight, in her hand. Miss Greenwood noticed her this time; she turned around and smiled.

Joyce said, "Thank you for my present, Miss Greenwood."

"Oh, it's not much, I'm afraid."

"It's an awful pretty one. Did it really come from California?"

"Oh, yes. Yes. A mountain top. On one side, mountains, and on the other a cliff that dropped seven thousand feet to the Mojave Desert. You must see it some day, Joyce. It was there—" She stopped, and then went on gaily, "It was there that Richard Harding Davis was pointed out to me. Such a handsome young man. I brought the pine cones away as keepsakes."

Joyce gulped. It was a keepsake, the pine cone. Something Miss Greenwood liked, herself. That was the best you could give, something you liked. She wanted to say, "Oh, did you *want* to give it away?" but the words stuck. Instead, other words came out with a rush. "Would you—can I help you carry in the cocoa?"

"Oh, no. No. You go and have a good time with the others. I'll be the bridget."

Back in the living room, Joyce found that Gladys Cayford had got a pine cone, too, exactly like hers, only it was tied with green ribbon instead of red. Gladys was as mad as could be, her face screwed up, her eyes snapping. Gladys didn't want a pine cone. She wanted something better.

Bubber blew a derisive toot on the trumpet at Joyce.

"What'd you get, Oozy-locks?" he asked.

Joyce said, "Pine cone and a hair ribbon."

"I got this tooter," Bubber said.

He had been playing hard and sweating. He was all boy-smell, like old sneakers. He held the little trumpet up, snapped it into the air, caught it when it came down.

"Look at that thing," he said. "Oh, baloney!"

Joyce looked him in the eye. She put her head up high.

"My pine cone came from *California*," she said.

"It did?"

Bubber was impressed, and some of the other kids came crowding around to look at the California pine cone.

"Hey, Glad," Bubber said to his sister, "where'd yours come from?"

"No place," Gladys said sulkily. "Out behind somebody's backhouse, probably."

"How'll you swap?" Bubber held out the trumpet to Joyce.

Miss Greenwood was right in the next room, the dining room, putting cocoa on the table.

Joyce thought, She couldn't help but hear him.

She said, loudly, "No, I won't swap. It isn't everyone that's got a pine cone *straight from a mountain in California.*"

The supper was lovely—all the ice cream and cake you could hold, big china bowls of kisses, cups of cocoa. Everyone was tired afterwards and full; some broke down and had bad manners, like Johnny MacGimsey, who all of a sudden dipped his napkin in his glass of water, wadded it up and threw it across the table at Gib. For a minute, Joyce thought Gib was going to throw it back, but he saw her glaring at him with the look that he always said was the "I'll tell Mama" look, and didn't. Miss Greenwood didn't seem to mind; at least she didn't say she did. Roger and Rosie, who were coming over to sponsor the Party home, were late. It was ten-thirty. Everybody went back into the living room.

"Shall we sing Christmas carols?" Miss Greenwood asked, "or shall we play more games?"

Nobody said much, everyone was too full, except Gladys, who said in a low voice, "We ought to play Ugly-Mug."

"Why, yes," Miss Greenwood said. "That's a good game to settle supper, too. I remember Ugly-Mug. How does it go? 'I put my right foot in—'"

Gladys looked shocked. She hadn't meant to be overheard.

It was a game for little kids, like a dance, forming a ring and saying a rhyme together.

> "I put my right foot in,
>> (Stamp!)
> I put my right foot out,
>> (Stamp!)
> I give my right foot a shake, shake, shake,
> And turn my body about."

It started slowly, with an after-supper lethargy, but it picked up as it went through several stanzas—"'I put my left foot in,'" and so on, and "'right hand,'" and "'left hand'"—until everybody, except one or two of the big boys, like Bubber, who thought the game beneath them, was shouting and stamping, shaking the floor.

Then, at the beginning of the last stanza, the thing hit everybody at once. Nobody had seen it coming, except perhaps Gladys, and probably not even Gladys.

> "I put my Ugly-Mug in,
>> (Stamp!)

I put my Ugly-Mug out,
        (Stamp!)
I give my Ugly-Mug a shake, shake, shake,
And turn my body about."

As one child, the entire roomful froze into silence. In a kind of
numb embarrassment, they stood flat-footed, watching Miss Green-
wood, who went on, alone, through the stanza to its end. She shook,
shook, shook her Ugly-Mug in and out, and finished up with a twirl.

"What's the matter?" she said. "Everybody tired?"

As if to add a period, over the sounds of all rose the familiar full-
bodied bawl of Herbie Hitchman.

"Why, Herbert!" she said. "I expect you're up too late. Come, all
sit down now, we'll sing carols."

Over in the corner, behind the weary, quavery strains of "The
Little Lord Jesus laid down his sweet head," Will whispered in
Joyce's ear and slipped something in her hand.

"Bubber swapped it to Johnny and I swapped Johnny my sheep
and lamb for it," he said.

It was the trumpet, but it was bent and it wouldn't blow.

"I can fix it, I think," Will whispered, "or, if I can't, maybe Pop
can."

She said, "All right, Will," and slipped it into her pocket.

And then she heard Roger's voice in the kitchen, and there was
Rosie by the door, pink cap and pink cheeks, looking lovely; and
the Party was over and it was time to go home.

THE reason why Roger and Rosie were late, and why Rosie was
looking so lovely, was, they had stopped for a while on top of
MacKechnie's hill, to talk about plans and things to come. There the
old and cold moon, riding high in the sky, silvered the mysterious,
empty pits and the lichen on the ancient frosty stone, and silvered,
too, Rosie's smooth cheeks and her gay eyes, bright with promise;
and looking ahead, they saw the moonpath leading to the horizon,
as if it had been the radiant path of the years to come—for Roger
and Rosie, engaged, now, with a ring for Rosie as soon as Roger could
afford one; and walking hand-in-hand down from the crest of the
moon-bemused hill, with their lips tingling.

PART THREE
Easter

IN the spring, the cold comes out of the ground slowly. The frost gives up hard. Jess's snowdrops bloomed in March, under snow; they pushed their blossoms through little ice-rimmed holes as the snow melted, indestructibly blowing in the crazy winds of spring. Coming back from taking a plate of table scraps to the hens, Jess knelt to smell the snowdrops, and felt the edge of ice, harsh under her knees, cold and hard as stone.

In the night, a quick freak storm had blown up from the east, snow at first, changing to sleet and freezing rain, with two or three hard claps of thunder and dazzling flashes of lightning. The racket waked Jess up; she thought she had never seen lightning so bright. The flashes were a steely, metallic blue against the darkness; they seemed almost to make a snapping sound. The wind and sleet were pounding against the house with a noise almost as loud as the thunder.

Jess watched the storm from under the shelter of Elbridge's warm broad back; thunderstorms made her nervous, but nothing like that ever woke him up. This one didn't last long. It was traveling so fast that she didn't hear the thunder die away—just the three hard claps, and then the drum and rattle of the sleet.

She thought sleepily, Well, here's a change in the weather coming, maybe we'll get some spring now.

The storm did bring a change. This morning the wind was north-west—cold again, and blowing fit to tear out roots. The sun was dodging in and out of big fluffy masses of cloud tearing over, making huge, deep purple-blue shadows that sliced across the muddy gray-green water where the storm had roiled up the bay. Big rollers were thundering in on the rocks of the bay islands, with their tops blown back in long smoky plumes.

It was too cold to stay knelt down on the edge of a frozen snowbank, but Jess lingered, smelling the frail, wildwood sweetness of the snowdrops, watching the little things blown every which way, sometimes so flat that they streamed straight out on the snow. The purity of their white bells made the grainy snow look dirty. The whole yard was shaggy with spring; there never was a time of year when everything seemed so unkempt, dead stems of things sticking up, sloppy, gray-tan tufts of grass.

Behind her, Elbridge said, "What are you doing—catching your death of cold?"

She smiled around at him and got up. "M'm," she said. "Snowdrops. Get down and smell."

"You think I'm crazy? Br-rr! This wind would skin a pig," he said. But he got down on his hands and knees and shoved his nose close to the flowers, his big stern sticking up into the air.

He had been out in the lee of the shed, bucking up cordwood, and his heavy white woolen mittens, spread out while he balanced himself with his hands, were stiff with pitch. Jess could see the two neat patches she'd sewed on the seat of his work pants, and two more on the elbows of his blue overalls frock. Something gave her a catch in the throat. You wouldn't think to look at him, the man he was, that every once in a while you'd wish you could look after him better, as if he needed it, stand between him and the things that were turning him wrong side out. She knew she'd done everything she could; there ought to be something more.

All winter he had worked his head off trying to patch up the town row. Jess had, too, but it seemed that anything either of them did only made things worse. In January, the row had branched out, exactly as both of them had hoped it wouldn't. It had so many ramifications now that a man needed a pencil and paper to figure out which neighbor wasn't speaking to which, or what he could mention that wouldn't be, unbeknownst to him, a sensitive subject. Jess had never known a time when the town had been split so many ways. In some cases, it was brother not speaking to brother, as with George and Willard Lowden, who had looked right through each other all winter.

Apparently, after his fight with George, Harriet had tended to Willard, because, since January, he had taken to spending most of his time down at the wharf, buying crackers and cheese at Stell's for

his meals, and going home only after Harriet had gone to bed. Late
at night, Jess would hear the forlorn sound of his creepers crunching
up past the house as he went home in the dark. And George and
Willard were no longer seen together, as they always had been, Wil-
lard stumping along six paces behind.

Poor Willard, he was really embattled with about everyone, and
Jess thought it was too bad. All the Church Council members, except
herself, were furious with him and he at them. The bill they had
sent him he had mailed back to them, torn into shreds.

"In an envelope *without even a stamp on it!*" Carrie Hitchman
said. "That ain't even *legal!* But Stell let it go through the mail that
way, just to show where *she* stood. It's a slur, that's all."

Outraged by this belittlement, Carrie refused to be calmed down
when Jess suggested that the whole thing might have been Harriet's
idea, or Stell's. Anyway, it didn't seem like Willard. And to Jess's
surprise, Bill and Addie, the remaining two Council members, re-
fused to be calmed down either. Over her own vote of "no" they
passed a motion firing Willard as janitor.

Down at the wharf next day, Elbridge had talked to Bill, and to
Joe Hitchman, Carrie's husband. But they were burned up over the
lumber row, felt that anything Willard got, he had coming.

"Shoot, you must know George talked Wid into that," Elbridge
pointed out. Normally, everyone would have agreed with him.

But most of the men had piles of salvaged lumber sitting on the
shore which they were brooding over like hens, waiting for the snow
to melt enough so they could haul it home before somebody stole it.
Several of these piles, in the more accessible places, had vanished—
whether set adrift or whisked away by night to someone else's pile,
the owners couldn't tell. Nobody paid any attention to the law of
salvage any more. Even men like Bill who had respected it all their
lives, felt that under the circumstances, it didn't apply.

"No sense to blame poor old Wid for George's shenanigans," El-
bridge said. "Nor for Harriet's, either."

But they did blame poor old Wid. After all, he and George had
got caught red-handed, not that Joe and Bill weren't equally mad at
the other fellows.

"It wasn't a bad idea to put out that furnace fire," Elbridge said,
approaching things from another angle. "What if the belfry had come
down, and a hot fire going in the furnace? I wish I'd thought of it,
I'd have done it myself."

"That ain't the point, if you follow me, Elbridge," Joe said stiffly.

"Willard stove up church property, refuses to pay for it. As far as Carrie's concerned, he's fired and he stays fired."

"For all of me, too," Bill said. "He can afford to pay for a busted furnace hearth. His pile of lumber's bigger'n mine."

"Oh, blast that lumber!" Elbridge said. It was like trying to kick a sofa pillow, and he was sick and tired of it. But he held on to his temper. "What'll you use lumber for? Nobody's building anything, or plans to, far as I can see. Unless you want to donate some to fix the church belfry."

He stopped, aware that both of his neighbors were glaring at him, outraged.

"Well, I don't know as I asked you for skin," he said mildly.

Telling Jess about it later, he said, "But I guess I might just as well have."

A few days later, he got the duplicate keys of the vestry door from Addie—Willard hadn't yet turned his in; he had paid no official attention to the Council's note firing him—and went himself to assess the damage to the hearth. He found it to be serious, but thought it might be fixed, temporarily, with stove cement, if he could think of a way to keep the cement from freezing. Addie had in her attic an old single-burner oil stove which she smuggled out to him—Jack, of course, was on the outs with Elbridge, so Addie had to be careful.

She was torn right in two, she said. Jack had put his foot down on her being friends with Jess.

"Well, I just had to tell him to take it up again," she said. "I told him, heaven's sake, *I* wasn't mad at you and Jess, and he ranted around like a sore bull. Why, we haven't had a fight like that in all the years we've been married, and the kids was just about scairt to death." Addie's voice shook. She shivered, standing in the back entry with a shawl over her head. It had been cold, rummaging around up-attic. "But there's Aunt Lucy's old oil burner. It burns good, or did, when I put it away. You tell Jess to fill it, be sure to adjust the wick. I would, I am *ashamed* not to, but Jack's due home any minute, and I guess he better not find you here, Elbridge."

"That's right," Elbridge said. "Thanks, Addie, and I'm sorry. Jack'll calm down, give him time."

"My soul, I hope so. I've seen some town rows, Elbridge, but this beats all I *ever* saw, brother against brother. Can you really fix that hearth in time to get the church het up for Mr. Franklin?"

Mr. Franklin, the minister from the mainland, got over for services once a month. He was due in a week's time, on the last Sunday in January.

"Oh, sure. If I can fix it at all," Elbridge said.

"Because if you can't, I've got seven dollars egg money I could donate towards a new one," Addie said. "Though," she finished forlornly, "I'm sure I don't know what Jack would say."

"No need of that, Addie," Elbridge said. "I'll cobble up for now, and maybe this spring we can have a rousing old church supper and raise the money for a new furnace."

Shivering in the icy vestry, while he waited for the ancient single-burner to warm up, if it could, the area around the furnace, Elbridge reflected that his hollow comfort probably hadn't helped Addie much. Jack was mule-stubborn. Elbridge had tried three times to talk him around, getting in return only surly grunts and glares. Addie was, without doubt, getting the same treatment, and would, until she gave in. She had always said, laughing, but only half in fun, that that was the only way to get along with Jack—know when to give in.

As for a church supper, the Ladies' Aid couldn't be counted on to organize one. Not now. The day the ladies had met to clean up the vestry after the entertainment, the Aid had split wide open. Stell had said outright that it was all very well for Carrie Hitchman to accuse her—*her*—of stealing out of the mouths of babes, but there were others in town she could mention who lived in glass houses—stained glass, if you asked her—like them that had faked a whole handful of ballots in the voting for that quilt.

"Stuffed the ballots," she said. "Which in some places is a state's prison crime."

That, of course, made Fanny MacGimsey, Liseo's wife, mad; but Fanny always came slowly to the boiling point, and before she said anything, Mollie Lessaro duffed in. She had helped count those ballots, she said, and anyone who said there'd been more than there ought to've been was a bald-faced liar. Whereupon Stell said she hadn't been going to name names, but if Mollie wanted her to, she could say in words of one syllable which ones were hand-in-glove, and always had been.

It had ended up in a fine old free-for-all tongue-lashing all around, some ladies having a fine time, others, like Jess and Addie, trying to stop it. Jess had come away discouraged and disheartened. Telling Elbridge about it, she had cried. Some had sided with Stell, of course, because they had their winter's bills for groceries running at the store, and they needed the credit. Others had gone out on a limb they couldn't crawl back from.

"Well, their husbands have got bills running with Liseo and me," Elbridge had pointed out, trying to comfort her.

"Yes, and they know you won't do anything mean about it," Jess said, mopping away the tears.

The Aid hadn't had a meeting since, while its members stayed home and licked their wounds.

Elbridge patched up the hearth as best he could. He guessed a fire could be built in the furnace now, without burning the church down. But it was a temporary job. Something drastic, like a new furnace, would sure have to be planned for in the spring.

Getting ready to go home, he realized he was chilled to the bone. The vestry seemed a lot damper than it ought to be, smelled funny, too, kind of musty like an old tomb. On the way out, he noticed, on one of the trestle tables, a big puddle of ice and water, apparently from a leak down through the church floor.

Oh, blast! he thought. Darn an old building!

Upstairs, he found not a leak but an eastern window wide open, in just the spot where passers-by outside wouldn't be likely to notice it. Must be, when Willard had cleaned up, chucked out the Christmas trees, he'd forgotten to close the window. Still, that was a darned unhandy place to chuck trees out of. Whoever had opened it, had had to pry it up from the inside with a pry bar, looked like. You could see the marks on the sill. Not like Willard, to bother with a frozen-down window when there was the front door nearer and more easily opened.

Well, it had made a fine mess. Winter was in the church, as bad, he thought sadly, as in the island's deserted houses with the smashed-out windowpanes. Snow was heaped in the aisles on the eastern side, crusted on the seats, melted and refrozen, icicles hanging down. A long icicle hung even from the warped binding of the big Bible, left spread open on the pulpit.

He went downstairs to Willard's tool closet for a snow shovel and some rags. Once, of course, it would have been Willard's job to clean the mess up, but not now. Nobody was responsible now, for the simple reason that nobody had been found who would take the janitor's job.

It was too bad. A mess of foolishness. Because Willard had always done a good job, and he'd been janitor for a long time. Got mad, once in a while, but who didn't?

Elbridge shoveled out and scraped off what ice and snow he could, closed the window and fastened it. He put the Bible and the worst-damaged hymn books into a box to take home and dry out by the kitchen stove. The exercise didn't warm him; he felt chilly and hot at the same time, and his nose was stuffing up as if he had a cold coming on. Downstairs again, he checked the single-burner, made sure it was all right to leave, locked up the vestry and went home. Nothing more could be done till he could get a fire going in the furnace, melt off and dry up the rest of the damage.

Jess, at the sight of him, hauled out a tub and hot water for a mustard foot-soak, which he had, shaking and shivering with chill, by a roaring fire in the sitting room airtight; but that night he went to bed with the worst case of the grippe he'd ever had, and didn't get up for a week.

Liseo took over the janitor's job, temporarily—tended the single-burner, and in a day or so built a fire in the furnace which he kept going, though he said it was lowering the church woodpile something scandalous.

"Someone opened that window on purpose," he reported to Elbridge. He had come in one night to commiserate, see how horrible the grippe was by now.

"Well, that I don't believe," Elbridge said. "What makes you think so?"

"Well, it wasn't Willard. I asked him."

"He speaking to you, is he?"

Liseo grinned. "No more than necessary, out of a sense of outrage," he said.

Willard was not speaking to anyone remotely connected with the Church Council. Jess, of course, was on it; Elbridge was Jess's husband; Liseo was Elbridge's friend.

"But he did say," Liseo went on, "that after the womenfolks mopped up their blood in the vestry, he went in and checked. Doors and windows all fastened up tight, he said. That particular window hadn't been opened all winter."

"Oh, blast and cuss!" Elbridge said. "*Now* what have we got?"

"War," Liseo said laconically. "The big one I was in, we smashed around regardless, anything to hurt the other feller. You know that." He went over to the stove, stood for a moment back-to, warming his hands. "How's your grippe? You sound like a dead rat in a foghorn."

"I feel like one," Elbridge said glumly.

That had been late January. The first Sunday in February when the minister came over for services, Elbridge was still moping around the house. He felt too rocky to go to church that day; even if he had been there, Jess didn't see how he could have prevented what happened.

Mr. Franklin, the minister, had never been too popular with some, because he didn't preach hell-fire and brimstone, he talked more on ethical questions. There wasn't anything to get your teeth into, if you liked a sermon to sizzle and fry. He was a serious-minded young man, with a turn for writing poetry, a family man with a wife and children and a big parish. Besides the island church, he had three other small churches over on the mainland, neither one big enough to support its own minister, so he had to divide his time and his Sundays, taking each church in turn. It was a grueling schedule, which ran him ragged and gave him little time to assimilate undercurrents.

He had, for example, not long ago, preached a red-hot sermon on cooperation and brotherly love, which had for its message the combining of the mainland churches into one, not realizing that, years back, they all *had* been one, but a couple of rousing old church wars had split the parish; each time certain offended members had resigned and started a church of their own, so now there were three. The sermon caused quite an uproar. He was waited on by committees, and had to say that he hadn't quite realized the situation, had been thinking of it from a practical point of view, as well. With one church, he could give everybody his services four times, instead of once, a month, to say nothing of other advantages. Poor Mr. Franklin. Being from away, and a little oblivious anyway, he had walked right into that one.

The lumber schooner, vanished somewhere off Chin Island, had fired up his imagination, and he had really laid himself out on his February sermon there. He'd used the Bible, and he'd used poetry; he'd even written a short poem for the occasion. Jess, watching him deliver, realized that he felt he was doing a pretty good job. So did she. It was a stirring and an appropriate sermon.

But toward the end, he drew a picture of the casting away of the schooner. "Their vessel split," he said. "Their cargo scattered on the shore for wind to toss and rain to spoil, as thieves in the night steal the unguarded treasure of worthy hands."

What he meant was that the wind and the rain were the thieves, but the church was still damp and chilly and a lot of coughing was going on at the time. The phrase about the thieves came out rich and full-bodied, but even Jess, for a second before she had time to think what he'd really said, thought he'd said "and" instead of "as." It certainly sounded, at first, as if Mr. Franklin were accusing the islanders of robbing the dead.

Somebody gasped; there was a frozen silence. Then a rustle started up, as heads turned and people looked to see how others were taking it.

Bill Lessaro and Joe Hitchman exchanged grins—slight and sedate grins, since they were in church, but none the less gratified. Jack Shepheard turned on George Lowden a ferocious glare, which plainly said, "I guess that'll hold you, bud." Willard wasn't there; he hadn't come to church.

Then Paul Cayford, who had sat turning first white and then red, nudged Imogene and got to his feet. He walked down the aisle toward the door, and Imogene, with a slight pause while the idea penetrated, gathered up Bubber and Gladys and followed him.

You could see Mr. Franklin thought it must be some kind of a personal family emergency—one of the children sick, or something. He staggered in midflow, and two words of his next sentence came out, before he stopped and waited sympathetically for the Cayfords to get to the door.

"O thieves—" he said, aimed right at the back of Paul's head.

Then he went on with the poem he had been at great pains to write as suitable for the occasion, which began:

"O thieves of man's endeavor,
Lurking by the windswept shore—"

And then he stopped, astonished. People, all over the church, were getting to their feet to go.

Too much thief-calling had gone on already about that lumber.

As Jess watched it stunned, she thought, You can tell now, if you want to, exactly how the town's lined up.

All the men who had been too previous about salvaging lumber went, with their families—George and Harriet, Allen Vira and his wife, Emily, Orin and Almeda, who had to side with their son; part of the Nikolaides family, and assorted relatives of all; Stell and her faction of the Ladies' Aid, following Imogene, and of all people, Jack Shepheard. Jack had a difficult choice to make—you could see him making it. If he stayed, he would be on the side of the Church Council; he would be giving in to Addie. If he went, he would be with George Lowden and the others. But Addie was the one he wasn't going to give in to. He got up and tiptoed, as most of the others had, to the door. Even if they were leaving, it was, after all, the church.

Jess, looking sorrowfully over at Addie, saw that Addie was sitting there in tears.

AFTER services, Jess tried to explain the whole matter to Mr. Franklin.

"If Elbridge hadn't been sick," she said, "I know he'd have warned you beforehand. Come home with me and talk to him, stay to dinner. I've got a couple of chickens in the oven."

But he said no, he thought he had better get back at once to the mainland.

"Please stay," she said. "You know you might be able to help us."

But he was buttoning his overcoat.

"Mrs. Gilman, I've got a prayer meeting at three o'clock, thirty miles from here," he said. "Across water. I am sorry I am not a mind reader, I could foresee these things."

Well, he was hurt and put out, not that she blamed him, and probably he was still stinging from his hassle with the church committees over on the mainland. He was a stuffier young man, too, than she'd had reason to reckon on.

He went down and stood on the float by the wharf, waiting for Liseo who was going to take him back to the mainland in the *Daisy*, standing back-to, holding in his hand his little black satchel. And Bubber Cayford, who was fooling around behind the breakwater in his father's powerboat, started up the boat and ran it full-tilt, close-in past the float, so that the bow wave rolled up over the low timbers and wet Mr. Franklin's feet to the knees.

As soon as Elbridge felt well enough, which he did in a week's time—it seemed to have been a pretty nasty variety of flu bug—he went over to the mainland to see the minister. He found him still put out, and in some doubt as to whether he'd try to get over for a March service. It was a strenuous trip, he said, and of course he had a great deal to do.

And then the third week in February, a big thaw came, so that everybody could cut and haul firewood—the depth of snow remaining in the woods was exactly right. The island men spent every day from dawn to dark in their wood lots, and Elbridge was stretched out straight getting his own supply and helping to haul his neighbors'. Since he and Willard Lowden owned the only two teams of horses on the island, they were in demand; sometimes they worked side by side, loading the wood sleds, Willard not speaking, and maybe, Jack Shepheard, making up like a thunderstorm on the other side of the sled. Working together, they hauled the lumber piles, too. Good hauling conditions you had to grab, unless you wanted to risk getting caught, in March, with all the snow gone and twenty cords of wood still out in the lot.

On the last Sunday in February, Elbridge was out in the woods, in the middle of a blustering snowstorm, hustling to get the final loads in before the new snow got too deep. He couldn't have laid off work and gone to services even if there had been any; but early in the week Mr. Franklin had written Addie that the trip, in the winter, was too much for him, and with all he had to do, he guessed he'd wait for warmer weather. In a way, Elbridge was relieved. He wasn't sure what would happen when Mr. Franklin came back, whether people would go to hear him or not. Some wouldn't he knew. The offended members were already making an issue over Mr. Franklin. They had met at Stell's, voted not to go to meetings of any kind until they had a different minister. The Church Council hadn't been notified of this, nor had Elbridge. He had tried, on one sled-loading occasion, to talk about it to Willard.

"We don't care for his sermons," Willard said.

"All the same, the whole town's concerned with the church," Elbridge said. "We all own it. Every family here, their folks built it, each one paid for a pew."

Willard didn't look at him. "Majority rules," he said. "Don't it? Well, does it or don't it? Live in a democracy, do we, or where they's just a few runs things, regardless of what the most of the people want?"

This was all Willard would say; it was more than he had said to Elbridge all winter.

Now, in March, the wood was all hauled; everybody's lumber pile sat safely in his back yard, though nobody, still, planned to build anything; today, earlier, Elbridge had been again to the mainland to see the minister, and had come back, Jess knew, feeling bad.

"Oh, Elbridge," she said, as he got to his feet on the edge of the snowdrop bed. "What's got into people?"

"The Reverend Archie Snow would have said, The Devil," Elbridge said, grinning at her, but his eyes were sober. "Br-rr! Let's get back into the lee. I'm frozen."

She followed him around the shed, where, out of the wind and in what warmth there was from the watery sun, he was finishing up the last of the firewood.

"What about Mr. Franklin?" she asked. She hadn't asked him before, knowing he would tell her when he got ready. "Is he coming for Easter services?"

"He can't seem to forget his wet feet," Elbridge said briefly. "He says he's sorry. He'll try, but he doesn't think so."

He took a couple of swipes with the bucksaw at the cordwood stick on the sawhorse, put the saw down.

"I don't know as I blame him," he said. "But I set out to ask him if he'd ever heard of the Reverend Archie Snow. In the days when this was the place, the Reverend Archie used to go over there to give *them* services, and in a good no'theast snowstorm, he used to help bail the boat all the way with a bucket, calling on the Lord. The Reverend Archie, according to what I've heard tell, would have had all the sinners back in church inside of ten minutes, too, and he'd have et their lights out. Sometimes I wish we had somebody like him."

"You don't, really, Elbridge."

"Well, no. I don't suppose so. Hell-fire and brimstone's kind of a side line, I guess, compared to some other things. Me, I *like* to hear something about the Golden Rule."

"Me, too," Jess said. "Hard as it may seem to live up to."

Elbridge grinned. "Come to think of it, I don't know as it's ever been done," he said. "Outside of a few folks using each other decent, which is all I can seem to make myself do."

"I'd settle for that."

Elbridge picked up the saw again. He was nearing the end of the big tier of four-foot sticks, she saw. It had been a big job—twenty cords of wood, it took, to keep running the four stoves that kept their house comfortable all winter.

Last year, she thought, we had a chopping match.

Last year, everybody had had a chopping match, families meeting at each other's houses, the women, inside, cooking up dinner while the men at the woodpile performed miracles of wood-chopping in the contest to see who could cut the most in one day and get the prize for it. A chopping match was always a lot of fun. You had a royal good time, and you got the wood cut up—the pile that was a lonesome, tedious job for one man alone.

"Hell!" Elbridge said forcibly. "People don't want to hear about using each other decent. They'd a damn sight rather sit around and shake over the idea of a puddle of hell-fire waiting for them, or for the world to come to an end. It's more fun. It's easier. Besides, to be decent means a certain amount of give and take. Most people would rather see everything smashed up than *give* one goddam inch!"

Jess looked at him with concern. It wasn't often he got stewed up like this. With most things, his easygoing good humor came back after a while and helped him out. But he thought a lot of the town. In his time, he'd done a good deal for it, without, she thought, ever getting much back, either, except the satisfaction he got over seeing things run right.

He had been first selectman for years; he had worked at the job even as a boy, at MacKechnie's, helping the old man keep the records of the town; in a good many other ways, too, he had been an unofficial leader; he had always been a man whom people came to.

True, the office didn't amount to much now, the town had gone down so; this year, there had been only nineteen people to town meeting; but even with the town row going on, they had automatically had the moderator cast one vote for Elbridge Gilman, as first. The other selectmen were Liseo and Jack Shepheard, but it was Elbridge who always did the work.

Jess thought of the town records in the little room off the kitchen that Elbridge called his office, and she called her sewing room, where they carried on their projects, side by side. Long ago, on the winter's night when the town hall burned, men had risked their lives saving those records. Some of the old ledgers still showed scorch marks that nearly obliterated MacKechnie's crabbed writing. Now they lined the walls of Elbridge's room. Each year he added to them his own columns of neat figures, set down in orderly fashion—what the town collected and spent, every penny accounted for. Each year, with satisfaction, he tucked a new Town Report—now, hardly more than a couple of double sheets of folded foolscap—into the shelf beside the long line of others, which went back through the years to the yellowed sheets on which Robert MacKechnie and Ansel Gilman had first written down the annals of the new town. Assessments, road funds, school funds, births and deaths. Times ago, there'd been enough money to have the Town Report printed; but now Elbridge's folded sheets of foolscap made one, and it was there; the continuity was not broken.

"Look," he would say, taking down a ragged Town Report near to the left end of the shelf. He knew those pamphlets from end to end, by heart and backwards, carried them in his memory, along with his tag ends of poems, quotations from the Bible, bits of this and that he'd picked up worth remembering. "Look. Here it tells where Sherebiah MacGimsey—that's Liseo's grandfather—got married. And here, in this one, it tells where he died. Eighty-four years old."

He ran his finger along the backs of the shabby, yellowed little pamphlets, picking out one here and there. "In 1870, he and his wife lost four kids. Diphtheria. For twenty years, he paid for a weir privilege over on Bay Island, six dollars a year. He was town clerk three times, 1883, 1884, 1887. He paid his taxes every year, except 1900, when he was on the delinquent list. I'd give a lot to know what happened to him that year. The next year, he paid; but that same year his wife was committed to the asylum, and the year after that, he died."

"Look," Elbridge would say. "You can look at figures like this and see figures, or you can see the running record of a man's life, the scratchings he made on the face of the earth; his doings. His history. One town, this size, it doesn't amount to much; but the world, after all, is only a mess of towns, some big, some small. The history of the world's nothing but town records of one kind or another, records of government. And government, when you boil it down, is decent people getting together and making decent laws for themselves to live decently by. If you have it, you've got the best there is so far; if you don't have it, you've got nothing—a mess of thieves and pirates."

So, Jess thought, looking at him mechanically working the bucksaw up and down and not getting much of any wood cut with it, it's a life's work to him, and not only his own, a lot of other men's, too, all lost if anything happens to the town.

Elbridge put down the bucksaw.

"God's little children," he said, "is what they'd rather be, all sitting in a row, waiting to be walloped with the Old Man's belt. It's more fun that way than to learn how to work things out, like God's grown-up men and women."

"Maybe they can't," Jess said.

"They could try. Maybe what they get in school is 'What I See in a Sea Shell,' but the old boys who organized things, a lot of them didn't have even that."

"They can't do anything at all," Jess said, "while they're mad at each other."

"Goes in a circle," Elbridge said. "Like the hole in the roof, when it's dry weather you don't need to fix it, and when it rains, you can't."

He saw her concerned face and grinned. "I've sounded off," he said. "And I feel better. You got any doughnuts in the house? Well, go on in and put on some coffee."

"You come, too. It's cold out here."

He followed her into the kitchen, hung over the stove while she put on the coffee pot.

"Take your outside gear off," Jess said. "You'll be cold when you go out."

They sat companionably at the kitchen table, drinking coffee and munching doughnuts, nobody saying anything for a while. Jess could see that he was feeling better; at least, he was beginning to think about something besides trouble.

"The twins want to run a string of lobster traps this summer," he said meditatively. "What'd you think about it?"

"Why, I guess so. Roger had his traps when he was twelve."

"They could do it, all right. Only thing, they want to go partners with Johnny."

"Oh, dear," Jess said.

Johnny, Liseo's boy, made you think a little. He wasn't what you could call bad, but he wasn't steady either. He got into a lot of trouble.

"He and Gib together, I'd say no," Elbridge said. "But Will'll balance it a little. Might do Johnny good."

"We wouldn't want to hurt Fanny's feelings," Jess said.

Liseo was inclined to be stern with Johnny, but Johnny was his mother's white-headed boy.

"The twins have got it all figured," Elbridge said, grinning. "The idea is, Liseo and I'll sell them the trap stuff on tick, and they can pay for it as they earn."

Jess laughed. "They aren't the only ones in town have got that idea," she said.

"M'm," Elbridge said.

She knew as well as he did that he and Liseo were carrying nearly three thousand dollars in unpaid bills for gear on their books, credit extended not only to the fishermen of the town but to off-islanders who traded with them.

"They'll pay up when the spring fishing gets under way," he went on. "I think I'll let the kids go ahead with it, Jess."

"All right with me," Jess said, smiling. "You know the three of you have got it all decided."

Elbridge grinned back at her. "I suppose we have. Decide it first and then tell the women. That's standard procedure. You care if it is?"

"Nope. So long as you don't care if it kicks back sometimes. Why don't you go along to the post office, see if there's a letter from Roger? There surely will be, where we didn't hear from him last week."

"Funny we didn't. He must be busy."

"He must be. Roger always writes. You know it might be kind of fun if you and I and the Liseos took the kids and made a trip over this Saturday."

"By gorry, it would. Go to a movie, maybe. Anyway, see Roger and Rosie. Liseo's like a bear with a sore head. Rosie'll take his mind off his troubles. He and Fanny haven't heard from her, either. He was raring, this morning."

Elbridge pushed back from the table, reaching for his coat. "Go over in the morning, Saturday, do some shopping if you want to, take in the movie, come back at night. If it's good weather."

"Better let Roger know. He might have plans."

"Sure. Drop him a line now. I'll mail it."

He went off down the walk and along the road toward the post office. He felt better. The warm kitchen and Jess's hot coffee had driven away his chill, and her company, the way it always did, had given him a new grip on things.

At the fork of the road, he met Liseo, steaming along for the post office, his one idea a letter from Rosie. He greeted Elbridge with a grunt, and they went along together.

"Sure," he said, when Elbridge proposed a trip to the mainland to see the kids. "I'm going anyway, if I don't hear, today. Fanny's about wild. We haven't had a letter for two weeks."

It wasn't Fanny, Elbridge thought, it was Liseo who was wild. Fanny took Rosie as casually as Liseo took Johnny.

"Kids are always busy," Elbridge said. "Well, you tell Fanny, Liseo. She'll want to bake up stuff to take the kids. I know Jess will."

"Oh, Lord, you know Fanny," Liseo said. "She'll probably take along a pork roast. How did Uncle Sylvester eat, anyway, I meant to ask you?"

Uncle Sylvester, Liseo's pig, had met his doom long ago. Elbridge had done the butchering, and unbeknownst to anyone, he and Liseo had shifted pigs, as they had planned. Liseo had enjoyed his pork all winter.

"Damn good," Elbridge said. "As good pork as I ever ate. You must've fed Uncle Sylvester off the top of the barrel."

"Well, turn about is fair play," Liseo said.

Stell wasn't in the post office, but the store door was unlocked, so they knew she couldn't be very far away.

"Probably had to go in and tend Luther," Elbridge said. "He's getting pretty feeble. She'll be along."

Liseo fidgeted. He hated to be kept waiting for anything.

"More like she's doing it on purpose," he said. "Seeing you and I ain't on the side of light."

"Could be."

"My God, this place!" Liseo said. "Keep on, it won't be fit to live in."

He had poked his nose through the mail wicket and was craning sideways, trying to see if there was any mail in his box.

"You know that lap-streak skiff of George and Wid's?" he asked.

"M'm-h'm."

"Well, Wid decided she ought to be painted, but you know he ain't speaking to George. So he up and took a foot rule and measured off, and painted his half of her exact to the inch. Figured George would know from that that Wid thought she ought to be painted. But George, he took up arms, didn't like the color green Wid used. So he painted his half bright red. Funniest looking skiff I ever saw."

"Oh, for godsake!" Elbridge said disgustedly. He knew he ought to laugh, that Liseo expected him to, but somehow it didn't seem funny.

Liseo looked around at him, his eyebrow writhing upward toward his widow's peak.

"Why take it hard?" he asked. "It's nothing but childishness."

"Sure. I know. About fourteen years old. But did you ever stop to think what would happen if fourteen-year-olds were let loose with nothing to stop them?"

"They'd do a damn sight better running things than some old men do," Liseo said. "Got cleaner minds, for one thing, and they like each other better."

"Well, maybe, but you can lick a kid, if you have to, learn him some sense. A grown-up fourteen-year-old you can't lick and you can't learn. This whole mess here is nothing but a kids' squabble, but it can do harm if it goes on much longer."

"Ah, nuts!" Liseo said. "Let 'em slam it out amongst themselves till they've pounded it out of each other. They can't harm us, El-bridge."

"Maybe you think so. But George and Willard are brothers."

"George and Willard are damn fools," Liseo said. He stiffened, suddenly, his face thrust close to the wicket. "Hey," he said in a hushed voice. "Come here, Elbridge. See if you see what I see."

"What?" Elbridge leaned and peered past Liseo. "I don't see anything."

Liseo pointed a shaking finger.

The drawer of the wooden table in the post office was cracked a couple of inches. A bar of light from the window fell across it, showing a welter of stamps, money-order applications, penny postal cards, insured mail slips, all mixed together, and in a corner a slender pile of letters, the top envelope addressed, with a canceled stamp.

"By God," Liseo said. His voice choked a little. "That's a letter from Rosie. Fanny and I thought it was funny we hadn't heard. Rosie always writes—"

He spun around, past Elbridge, past the candy counter and the scales, stamped into the cubicle and yanked out the drawer. He picked the letters out of the mess of stuff, ran through them quickly, glancing at the addresses. Without a word, he thrust two of them through the wicket at Elbridge. The others he put in his pocket. Then he came back out of the cubicle.

The two letters, Elbridge saw, were from Roger, one dated last week, the other yesterday. The flaps of both envelopes were smeared, fresh glue on the latest one not yet dry.

That was why they hadn't heard from Roger, then. Stell had been holding up the letters. It was too much to believe from the looks of them that she hadn't steamed them open and read them. He glanced over and met Liseo's eyes.

The expression on Liseo's face was wooden. He said, jerking his head, "Yonder she comes."

Stell's high heels were clicking along the entry, outside the door. She came in, shutting the door smartly behind her, went past the two men as if there were nobody there and into the cubicle, where, still maintaining the tradition of not speaking to anyone who was not on her side, she thrust a couple of newspapers through the wicket.

Liseo said softly, "Is that mine, Stell? Or is it Elbridge's?"

She couldn't resist. "Won't cost you nothing to look."

Liseo moved over to the wicket.

"Yours," he said politely to Elbridge, pushing the newspapers aside. "And here's mine. Looks as if I'd got the sales catalog today. Let's have the rest of it, Stell."

"That's all."

"My goodness. Every bit?"

"You can come in and look in your mailbox," Stell said, disdainfully."

"No letters? Well, well. You're all dressed up today, Stell. You going to a party?"

Elbridge glanced at him, concerned. He had heard that purr in Liseo's voice before.

"Why, I don't know as it's any of your business," Stell said. "But I'm going to a meeting of the Ladies' Aid."

"Well, isn't that nice. The Ladies' Aid starting up again. I hadn't heard Fanny say."

"It wouldn't surprise me if *Fanny*," Stell said, "hadn't been told."

"No?"

"No. There's those of us Americans feel we can get along better by ourselves."

"I don't doubt."

"What we are starting is a Society of American Christians," Stell said. "No foreigners or niggers need apply."

"What in hell—" Elbridge began, but Liseo's soft voice stopped him.

"Keep it Christian, by all means," Liseo said. "By gum, Elbridge," he went on. "I've got two letters from Rosie here, one of 'em last week's. Now where in time do you suppose that's been?"

Elbridge heard Stell gasp, saw her whirl around before she could stop herself to glance down at the table drawer, which was now tightly closed.

"I see you've heard from Roger, too," Liseo said. "Is one of yours last week's? The kids must've got together on it. Either that, or something's gone flooey with the U-nited States Mail, and we'll have to write to the post office inspector. Well, so long, Stell. Have a nice time at the Christian society."

For a moment, Elbridge hesitated, looking after Liseo's stiff back as he went out the door. It had been in Elbridge's mind, this morning, to try again to patch things up, if he could. But glancing at Stell, frozen-faced behind her wicket, he wondered, now, how he could have imagined anything ever could be patched up.

And if they're as bad as this, he thought, anger at last getting the better of him, I don't know as I want them to be.

He followed Liseo and caught up with him. Liseo was plugging along, his head down. For a few steps, nobody said anything.

"We'd better tell the kids to register their letters, with a return receipt," Elbridge said at last.

Liseo stopped in his tracks. His face was pale under its olive tan; his black eyes burned bright with fury.

"Register, hell!" he said. "You've got to write to the Post Office Department. It's up to you. That's a federal crime, frigging around with the mail. Rosie sticks pretty private business in those letters of hers. I won't put up with it."

"No," Elbridge said. "I don't guess anybody could."

"Well, are you going to stop it?"

"I expect so. Give me time, Liseo. I've got to think."

"Think? About what?"

"Stell needs that post office job. She's got to support Luther. The store isn't enough."

"She ought to have thought of that."

"Look, Luther doesn't deserve what would happen to him, if Stell had to let him go. A state institution somewhere—I've got to think, Liseo."

"You think too goddamned much," Liseo said. "You're too easygoing. That's the only thing that's wrong with you, Elbridge, and always has been. You ought to crack down, once in a while. Everybody says so."

"That so?" Elbridge said.

He could feel his face getting red, the heat starting to rise under his collar.

"If you and everybody else think you can do better, you elect another selectman," he said.

"Well, by God, I don't know but we need to!"

Liseo glared at him and Elbridge glared back, feeling his muscles tense up. For a moment, he wanted to hit out. It didn't matter at what, or that the one he wanted to hit out at was Liseo. Hit out at Liseo and get Liseo to hit back at him, and thrash the big-mouthed son-of-a-gun within an inch of his life. He hauled back his fist and saw, with satisfaction, that Liseo was all ready, too. But somebody was coming along the road behind him.

He heard the steps and turned, his rage cooling, thinking wryly that, in an hour or so, it would be all over town, people laughing their heads off because at last the town row had caught up to that impregnable combination, him and Liseo, chortling because someone had seen them chested up to each other like a couple of roosters, right out in the middle of the main road.

But it was only Miss Greenwood coming along, her full black skirt flopping across the frozen, muddy ruts, her incredible pancake of a hat perched on top of her gray pug.

She said, "Good day, Mr. Gilman, Mr. MacGimsey," and they moved politely aside to let her pass, but as they moved, she stopped.

It went through Elbridge's mind, as it hadn't for years, he was so used to her now, how painfully homely she was, how grotesque and odd a figure. She had her pocketbook that she always carried, a brown, bag affair with two big amber-colored balls at the clasp, which she was looking down at; and as Elbridge tried to pull himself together enough to say something pleasant or decent, feeling the sweat of his fury evaporating on the back of his neck, she opened and shut the clasp with a sharp little click.

She said, "I need help, Mr. Gilman. My mother has just died."

OLD Mrs. Greenwood had died in the middle of the forenoon, sitting in her rocking chair by a sunny window. The people who went over from the village, Jess and Little Sarah, Fanny MacGimsey, Imogene Cayford and Emily Vira, George Lowden and Harriet, and Jack and Addie Shepheard, found her still sitting there, a square of sunlight falling warm and yellow across her folded hands and across an inside window box of crocuses in bloom on the sill. She looked small in her neat black dress, and serene, her white hair combed smoothly, as it always was, the bit of lace spotless at her throat.

"I didn't wish to leave her alone there," Miss Greenwood said. "But moving her was beyond my strength. So I thought, perhaps, by the crocus . . . she always liked them. They give off a green smell. It was one of the few things left she could really enjoy. I thought . . . for company . . . and, of course, I had to go for someone."

She stopped, as if she felt she had said too much, and she said very little for the rest of the time, until Elbridge and Liseo got back from the mainland with the undertaker and the doctor. She went about the house quietly, directing what needed to be done. And this puzzled Addie Shepheard.

Addie was generally sent for in time of death, to do what laying out was needful before the undertaker got there—not that much was; it just seemed more seemly for a woman to wash a dead person. Almeda Vira usually helped, but Almeda, Orin's wife, was off-island visiting just now.

Addie wasn't used to having the relatives underfoot at such a time, she said, didn't consider it fitting. Miss Greenwood should go and lie down and have witch hazel cloths on her head and cry. Addie wasn't exactly put out, you couldn't be, of course, with someone who had suffered a loss; but she came out of the bedroom where the menfolks had put the old lady, shutting the door behind her with a firm little click.

"She won't let me do a thing," Addie said in a fierce whisper to Little Sarah. "She says her mother isn't used to anybody but her. But *she* isn't doing a thing, either. Just sets there. At least, I ought to wash—"

"Never mind, Addie," Little Sarah said. "You've done what you could."

"Well, it passes me," Addie said. "You wouldn't think to see her that she cared one hoot. Acts just the same as she always has. I guess she must feel something, but—"

Little Sarah said, "You don't grow crocuses for people to smell of, Addie, if you don't care about them."

"Well, you know her better'n anybody else," Addie said. "You eat dinner with her once a week."

"Nobody knows her, Addie," Little Sarah said. She sat down in a rocking chair beside the closed bedroom door. "I expect we'd just better wait for the boat to get back, Addie. There isn't anything we can do."

Fanny MacGimsey said, "My Lord, I know it. Look at this house, spotless. Not one livable, namable thing for the neighbors to do. If people had to come to my house, unexpected, it wouldn't look like this, I can tell you."

Fanny's neighbors smiled a little at each other. They all knew this to be true, and they also knew that Fanny didn't care. She was a comfortable person, believed that, so long as the meals were good and on time, a house was for people to live in and not for.

"Well, no kids," Imogene said. "Nothing but a cat to do for. Look at that furniture—not a brack on it. Why, my kids tear up the furniture faster'n Paul can fix it. But it's all what you can afford, I guess."

"Even when my house is red up, it doesn't look like this," Addie said. "My Lord, china plates finified up around the room. I dread to think what Jack would say, if I asked him to put up a little shelf around the setting room to stand what's left of my wedding set on! Or how long the boys would leave a single solitary dish on it, if he did!"

The ladies, some of whom had not spoken to each other all winter, smiled, each thinking what her own husband would say, and went on conversing, in a gentle community of interest. Each one had come to do what she could, and more of them had come than were needed, no one wishing to hold back in a time of emergency.

Jess, listening, almost held her breath. Oh, lord, she thought. It's awful that it should take something like this, but maybe it would anyway, to bring them back together.

She glanced at Little Sarah and saw that Little Sarah was thinking the same thing. She gave Jess an almost imperceptible nod of understanding. Neither of them said anything.

Addie kept glancing at the closed door, behind which remained a deep silence.

"Now, I really think I ought to go in there, try again, Little Sarah."

Whether Little Sarah's rocking chair had walked as she rocked, or whether she had moved it, Jess couldn't have said, but it was now squarely across the door to the bedroom, so that, to get in Addie would have had to move Little Sarah. So Addie sat down by the window. She was fidgety. She kept twiddling her thumbs. Poor Addie, she wasn't anything, really, but conscientious; she just wanted to be sure she was doing everything she could, and she always had a hard time when things didn't follow their usual pattern.

"Well," Addie said suddenly. "One thing, the funeral. We'll have to have it in the church, and Mr. Franklin will have to come over, and all of us go."

The low buzz of conversation cut off sharply. The ladies glanced at Addie, then back at each other. Imogene reddened, and Harriet's neck grew perceptibly stiff. But it was not the time nor the place. There was a short silence; then Fanny MacGimsey said, "What on earth do you suppose anyone would want to have all those books for? It must take forever to get them dusted."

And presently, they began talking again.

Oh, dear, Jess thought. Trust Addie! All she meant to say was she wished we could all bury the hatchet, and a funeral would give everybody a reason for going back to the church, without having it thrown in their faces that they'd sworn they'd never set foot in it, as long as Mr. Franklin was minister. Oh, poor Addie! She did mean so well, and she was the salt of the earth.

But when the boat got back from the mainland and Doctor Graham and the undertaker took over, Miss Greenwood went upstairs by herself and packed a suitcase. She came down, carrying it, and with her coat on and the hat with the veil.

"I shall have to take Mother to Baltimore," she said to Little Sarah. "Our family vault is there. Could you see that Richard is looked after, Mrs. Gilman, and that somebody puts out the bird seed? I do hate to trouble anybody, but—"

"Of course," Little Sarah said. "Don't you worry, Miss Greenwood."

"And when I can get it, I put out a fish for the mink," Miss Greenwood said. "But I wouldn't expect you to do that, Mrs. Gilman."

"We can always get a fish," Little Sarah said. "I've got some apples, too."

"Oh, thank you, Mrs. Gilman."

Just what the communication was which was passing between her and Little Sarah would have been hard to say; Jess knew that there was something. She wished that she herself could think of a thing to say.

Miss Greenwood leaned down and patted the cat, who was in his basket by the fireplace, his blunt old battler's muzzle thrust out over the edge. He purred and pushed his head against her hand, and the bell on the leather collar he wore gave forth a frail jangle.

Bell or not, he was a terrific hunter, killed birds and mice and squirrels all over the place, the children said, though Miss Greenwood might not know it. Jess thought of this, irrelevantly, watching the black-gloved fingers against Richard's sleek yellow fur.

"He hates gloves," Miss Greenwood said. "Now, you be a good boy, Richard. Don't you dare to chase General Putnam while I'm gone."

It was worse than if she had cried and carried on, the way Addie felt she ought to. Jess felt herself puddling up, and to hide it, she picked up the suitcase and carried it out to the front porch. She put it by the steps, where the menfolks would be sure to see it when they started back to town.

She saw that Willard had harnessed up his team and driven his farm wagon over. The horses stood there with hanging heads, resting idly in the bright sun. Over by the trees, in the lee, Paul Cayford, Jack Shepheard, and George Lowden and Liseo, sworn enemies all winter, were sitting side by side, coats open, deep in conversation. Only Willard sat apart, on the wagon tongue, holding the reins. He sat back-to, the set of his head stubborn, not glancing around when Jess closed the back door behind her with a click of the latch which he must have heard. For a moment, she thought of going over and speaking to him. She had always liked Willard.

With all his oddities, his rages, his conceit, his blues, his angry and stubborn prejudices, she thought him to be, at heart, a man of considerable kindliness, one who would take endless trouble, if let alone, over little things, anxious to please, anxious to be well thought of. From childhood, George had plagued him, put him up to mischief for which, nine times out of ten, Willard alone got the blame, which he took, nine-fold, from his raw-boned, icy-bitter sister Harriet. No one ever had known quite what was wrong with Harriet; she had never married, never had seemed to want to; she ran her brothers with an iron hand; wouldn't let Willard play his accordion or sing around the house because she said it made her head beat in and out, when probably it was only because singing was the one thing Willard had which she and George didn't. Neither of them could carry a tune, and of course, the whole town took it for granted that what Willard had was a gift.

> "Let the lower lights be burning,
> Send a gleam across the wave,"

was what Willard always sang first, whenever he got a chance to sing; and thinking of that, Jess felt her eyes blur over.

No, now wasn't the time to speak to Willard, not when she was all rucked up like this. He probably wouldn't answer anyway, the way the back of his neck looked. Of all the neighbors who had forgotten differences in this, the greater emergency, Willard was the only one here whose hurt had gone too deep, it seemed.

And it's a shame to us all, Jess thought fiercely, that it takes something like this to make us use each other decently again.

She stood in the brilliant sunlight by the porch until the blur went away from her eyes, and, looking down, saw that Miss Greenwood's bulbs were coming up, thick as a spatter, in the black earth in her walled garden. The wind was still cold, but it was warm in the lee of the wall, the sun there almost hot for early spring. The sharp spears of the daffodils were tipped with yellow, already turning green; the tulips a clear, maroon-red; one or two crocuses showed color. Other flower beds were snugly covered still, where Miss Greenwood had banked them with spruce boughs for the winter. The lawn was not yet greening, and probably wouldn't until it was replanted, for the salt water running over it had killed the grass.

The work she's done here! Jess thought.

Looking at the outcrops of bare granite, the gravelly soil showing, she thought, appalled, of the labor—wheeling loam, digging out rocks, planting, and just plain tough rooting—that had gone on here through the years; what it must have been like to take this place in the beginning, and make something out of it that roots could cling to and the frail, sweet-smelling blossoms come out of in the spring.

Jess thought of herself how it might be, alone, without Elbridge and the children; would she ever, could she, do anything like this? The thought of it turned her cold to the bone; she knew, at once, that she never would.

You couldn't live without people, without your own. No. It wouldn't be possible, unless you had something wrong with you.

She pulled up short, looking at Willard. He hadn't moved. The back of his neck was red and stubborn in the light of the sun. Willard, who had a lot of things wrong with him; and most of what was wrong had been caused by other people, by his own. Hadn't she just been thinking to herself how Willard might be, if only people let him alone?

Yet Miss Greenwood, when you really thought about her, didn't seem to have much of anything wrong—oh, of course, odd and stubborn, and that homeliness which might do more than you could guess, if it hadn't happened to you. But look at her house, it was beautiful in there. Not a woman in the whole town, and they were critical, too, could find a thing wrong with Miss Greenwood's housekeeping, the decent way she lived, or the way she'd taken care of her mother. She had, it suddenly occurred to Jess, the things people were brought up to think worthwhile—dignity, self-respect, willingness to work hard and take responsibility. And courage.

The courage it took to stand up to this wild place alone, with nothing but an old, blind woman for company. The old lady must have been a little company; somebody to come home to; somebody to be there through the black, wild nights and the winter storms. She had been what there was, and now she was gone.

Jess felt cold; she felt bewildered. There just wasn't any way to reason it out.

Of course it wasn't fair to compare her life and Willard's, because she's always had money and he's had to scrape along. But—

Oh, I don't know. It isn't any of my business, anyway.

Except it kept plaguing at her.

Somebody whose actions you couldn't account for at all when you compared them to the rest of people's.

If she does like it here, if it isn't that she's just hid herself away, like Stell and them say she has, then it's the worst of all.

Because it was unthinkable that Miss Greenwood should ever come back here to live alone.

Jess heard a stir and some bumping sounds from inside the house. She realized that they were through in there, ready to start for the village. She moved away from the steps, over to the side of the porch, and stood with her back turned, so as not to see them come out, carrying the old lady.

Elbridge was with them, and as they passed her, he said, "Don't stand out here without your coat on, Jess," and she said, "I'll get it, Elbridge."

She didn't turn around, just waited until their footsteps went heavily down the steps and across the lawn to the wagon.

But at the sound of Elbridge's voice, at the sight of his ruddy, sober face, she felt all the tumbled upside down start to go right side up again, and she felt warm, even standing there without her coat in the spring breeze.

Fanny and Addie and Harriet and Imogene, ready to go, came right out behind them. Imogene was saying, "If Little Sarah's got apples left at this time of year, I wisht she'd give them to me, not to a darned old mink. Our folks ain't had an apple pie since February."

"I never knew a mink *liked* apples," Fanny said.

She was buttoning her coat over her ample stomach, amused in her mild way at the idea of feeding anything to a mink. Not very many things upset Fanny; she was placid of mind. She had to be, being Liseo's wife and the mother of his children.

"Well, I suppose Sarah'll get a penny or two out of Miss Greenwood for 'em," Imogene said. "More'n our folks could afford to pay."

She glanced up and saw Jess, remembered that she was mad at all the Gilmans, and walked away with Harriet down the steps without another word.

"You coming along with us, Jess?" Fanny asked.

"I'll get my coat."

Her coat was in the kitchen. Putting it on, she glanced through to the dining room. Miss Greenwood and Little Sarah were coming along out, and Miss Greenwood was saying, "Oh. Thank you, Mrs. Gilman, that's very kind. And you mustn't be sorry for me. I have known for years that sometime this must happen."

STELL said, "Well, I guess we've seen the last of them Greenwoods. My Lord, I'll miss the old crow, won't you? It won't seem like the same place, not see her flapping over from the Point every day or so, and, you know, before I thought, this morning I strained out her quart of milk just like I always do. Well, habit is a cable. Every day you weave a thread until it becomes so strong you cannot break it. What d'you suppose'll become of the property?

"They ain't got chick nor child in the God's world, and between you and I and the bedpost, there ain't too much money there, either. I guess I can read the handwriting on the wall. Them same scrimey old skirts and jackets for years—of course, good Lord, if you or I had a check come every month regular as a clock, regardless of it's smaller now than it used to be, we'd feel as if we was made; but you know the summer people, if they haven't got solid gold placket holes to flout around amongst us, they feel it. What?

"Now, you listen to me. I've cashed that check right here in this store, every month for the past eighteen years, more times than you've got fingers and toes, and I know! I used to send over to the bank when it was for two hundred dollars, so as to be sure to have enough on hand. Oh, she must have some laid by, they all do, holes in their houses stuffed full of it, but that last check was for a plain sixty-five dollars. I guess none of us would sneeze at it, not if it come regular, and us not turning a hand over, would you?

"Well, as I was about to say, if you or I or the tomcat was to turn toes-up, we'd have services in the church and be buried in the cemetery, right here on this island, like yuman beings. But not them. Addie asked her, made her the offer— What? No, I *ain't* speaking to Addie. Addie told Almeda and Almeda told me. Made her the offer that we'd open up our church, get the minister, if she'd like to have a funeral, and she said, 'Oh, no, no, thank you, Mrs. Shepheard, it's very kind and she'd appreciate it, but Mother was an Episcopalian and would have to be buried down to Baltimore in their family vault.'

"H'm, I got to thinking of *my* old family vault, down there under the thistles and the hardhack, the bare ground is all 'tis, but I guess once you're gone you don't care whether it's thistles and hardhack or gold bricks on top of you. I got to go down there, the Lord only knows when I'll find the time, either, and dig that hardhack off of poor Warren's grave, it's growed up so you can hardly see the stone.

"But, there, might's well face it, there ain't nothing you or I could offer good enough for *them.* Offer the skin off'n your back and it'd still be dishpan hands.

"That poor old soul, I see them jolting her up out of them woods in that wagon, and *wouldn't* you thought they'd of took the casket over there, lugging a dead body around them woods in nothing but a barsket, it wasn't decent.

"Well, *of course* a casket's heavy! Heavy or not, the Lord knows there was enough of them to lug it. That whole crowd, Elbridge and Liseo and them and the undertaker. They could of lugged it. Been willing to put out a little stren'th, showed the poor soul some respect, her an old lady ninety-four years old. But there, that crowd run it, never asked *us*, you'll notice. How Imogene ever got in on it is more than the mind can compass. You can guess without busting your brains what kind of a rig any of them'd run, foreigners and niggers.

"Well, as I was 'bout to say, I see them lugging her by here, and I set down right by the post office window and watched them out of sight, and I got to thinking that poor old soul, going off of this island heels first after all them years, and dying the way she did, strangling alone and neglected in the night, no need of it at all, except she swallowed her tongue—

"Why, yes, didn't you know that? Imogene said Addie was the first one there, and she said she didn't want it talked around, so don't you say nothing, but Imogene said when she walked into that bedroom! Black in the face and the black blood, and the smell of death on her, it was a sight! And her tongue was turned right wrong-sid-out. If she hadn't of been neglected, someone to give her the care I give to Luther, she'd be alive to this day. I keep my eye on Luther, sleep with it half-open most of the time, and many a time I've heard him start and gone in there with a spoon and hauled up his tongue. It was just the same as murder, if you ask me.

"No, I don't know how long she plans to be gone or if she'll ever come back. I wouldn't show *my* face here again, I'll tell you. Some says she'll sell the house, but who'd want the fool thing, and I hear she ain't give the cat away, Little Sarah and Elbridge and them goes over there every day and feeds it, the way some people suck up to the summer people, it'd knock a dog off a gut-wagon.

"But as I was going to say, I see them lugging her by here and I set right down by the post office window and before I could stop myself, I got to howling. Why, the tears run right down my cheeks and splashed on to the blotter, you can go in there right now and see the spots, they ain't dry yet."

MISS GREENWOOD was gone for three weeks. At the end of that time, she came back to the island one day on the mail boat. Orin Vira, telling Stell, said that she sat in the stern of the boat all the way over and snuffed of the air. Sat there and drawed it in like perfumery.

"Come back to close up and pack, I s'pose," Orin said. "She never said."

"Never said to me, either," Stell said. "I asked her, whilst she was waiting for her mail and milk, just said, Oh, my, my, how lovely the island was, and I asked her, said what did she plan to do, and she said, 'Why, I'm planning to go home, Mrs. MacGimsey.'"

That Stell. She was a card. She could sound just like Miss Greenwood, funny accent and all. Orin couldn't help laughing. All the same, it was a peculiar situation. He didn't feel right about it.

Miss Roxinda had walked up from the wharf with him; she'd waited in the store while Stell sorted the mail, and then she'd taken off for the Point, loaded down with groceries, her mail and her milk can.

Only Imogene was in the store, waiting for mail. It wasn't the way it used to be, with a whole storeful of people talking and passing the time of day, while Stell sorted. He'd thought at first that old lady Greenwood's death might bring folks back together, in a manner of speaking, but it hadn't. Some people spoke, but they were distant; you still had to be awful careful not to give offense.

Orin felt it. He was a sociable man and the high point of his day had always been when he got back with the mail and was the center, like, because he had the mail and the news. If he'd thought, he wouldn't have been so quick to side with Allen in the row, last winter, though he dreaded to think what life would have been like if he was on the other side, the way he had to go into the office and talk with Stell twice a day. Why, half the town wasn't speaking to him on account of Allen, without his having done a thing. Orin felt it.

He'd got to thinking about that, what a shame it was, now, for people to be distant, not come to the office when the mail got in, made life hardly worth living; so he hadn't given much thought to Miss Greenwood, standing by the stove and quietly greeting Imogene, who purred and chittered and took on about her getting back, and asked questions so fast Miss Greenwood didn't seem to get a chance to answer them. At least, she didn't answer anything, beyond being pleasant and polite.

But when Orin left to go home, she was just going out of sight along the causeway, walking along upright and fast, her skirts going flippety-flip; and Orin got to thinking that it was kind of nice, nowadays, to see a skirt like that once in a while, the kind his own mother and old Aunt Hannah used to wear; and then he thought of *her* mother and the lonesome house she was going home to. It gave him a turn.

He said so to Almeda, his wife. It gave him quite a turn. "Why, I wouldn't live over there if you paid me. I sh'd think that house would be haunted."

Not having had a good audience for days, Orin was gratified when Almeda's jaw dropped and she stared at him.

"My Lord, Orin, so would I! You don't suppose 'tis, do you?"

Orin filed the item away to tell to Stell, not thinking, of course, that it really could be, nobody had ever seen a ghost. The idea gave him a pleasurable twinge of horror, however, and the next morning it brought Stell right up standing.

"Mind you, I don't believe in 'em," Orin said. "But if there was such a thing, it'd certainly be a likely place."

"And old lady Greenwood a likely one to appear," Stell said.

ORDINARILY, Miss Greenwood's return would have been all over town in hours, or minutes as the case might be. But the fact that people were mad with each other held up news, nowadays. It was, in many ways, inconvenient.

Elbridge didn't find out that Miss Greenwood was back until the next forenoon, when he took over some fresh milk for Richard and a fish for the mink.

For nearly three weeks Richard had been a nuisance to him. Elbridge couldn't see Little Sarah traipsing over there every day, and he told her so. It was too much for her. Though Little Sarah protested that she didn't mind and would certainly go, a few days after Miss Greenwood left, Little Sarah developed a grippy cold.

"All right, now, you can't go," Elbridge said. "I'll tend to it, Ma. Just tell me what she wants done."

"Feed Richard," Little Sarah said, sneezing. "Fill up those little hopper things with birdseed. You have to let them down with a string, pull them up so the cat can't get to them. And put the fish down on the rocks by that crevice."

"All right," Elbridge said glumly.

She looked at him, one eyebrow raised a little, and he could see she was amused at the idea of his tending to all this monkey business. He grinned himself. It *was* kind of funny.

"How about apples?" he asked. "Jess was saying Miss Greenwood's mink's developed a taste for them, too."

To his astonishment, Little Sarah looked annoyed and snapped at him.

"I took those over," she said. "Don't bother me about it, Elbridge."

"What's the matter with you?" he asked, looking at her.

"I've got a cold in my head. Go along. And Elbridge—"

He stopped, halfway out through the door. "What?"

"Don't you dare to take your gun over there."

"Why not? Couldn't you use a mess of sea birds?"

Of course he had planned to take his gun. It was the only consolation he had for having to trot over through the woods with a chickadees' dinner. He'd had his mouth all puckered up for a chance to shoot off into the lagoon by The Pasture for once, without hurting anybody's feelings.

"Yes, I could. But there's other places to shoot them," Little Sarah said. "And you can let it be known around town that I don't want to hear of anyone's going gunning over there while she's away."

"Oh, good Lord, Ma," he said impatiently. "Have you hung around so much with her you're catching it, too?"

"You heard what I said," Little Sarah said ominously.

He went out, shutting the door good and hard behind him. This wasn't at all like Little Sarah. For one thing, she was famous for minding her own business. She could certainly stand hair on end if she wanted to; she seldom wanted to.

It was one of the few times in his life, he thought, as he went along through the woods, carrying his shotgun in one hand and the food basket in the other, that he'd heard her make a noise like Mac-Kechnie. For some reason, it made him feel pretty mad and stubborn. She ought to know what effect anything he said would have, right now; if he said not to, there'd be twenty people over there gunning, inside of a day.

He shot five sea ducks in the lagoon before he even went up to the house to feed the cat.

He found he didn't feel comfortable about it, though. The ducks weren't tame, but they didn't act wild, either. He'd sneaked down on a big flock of them that was bunched up, diving close in on the rocks, and let go and got his five with one barrel; the rest flew. But while he was waiting for his kill to drift ashore, within reach, the flock circled and came back, lighting right in his face and eyes, about where it had been before. They started feeding as if nothing had happened.

A damn foolish way for wild ducks to act, he thought, staring in astonishment. He almost let go with the other barrel into the middle of the flock before he reflected that five was plenty; no sense to shoot more than you needed to eat, and anyway, it would be slaughter. The only time he'd ever known birds to act like that was, years ago, when, once or twice as a boy, he'd been allowed to go with old Uncle Sylvester MacGimsey, who made part of his living shooting birds for their feathers. Uncle Sylvester used to "corn" the ducks, as he called it; he would dump a peck or so of hens' corn into the water, near the shore, and then set up his scatter-gun behind a rock, and wait. He used to get twenty or thirty ducks at a clip, and the ducks, after a while, came back to the corn. Five ducks Elbridge had got, but it had been like shooting fish in a barrel, all the fun gone out of it.

Oh, hell! he thought. Why not let the wild things alone? They're wild; why try to make human beings out of them?

The whole thing suddenly made Elbridge furious. He picked up a rock and heaved it out into the middle of the flock, and was gratified to see the sudden frantic splash and scrabble.

"Git!" he yelled. "Shoo! You goddam pullets!"

Up at the house, he filled the bird feeders, then took the fish he'd brought down on the rocks and gave it a heave into the mink's crevice. He fed Richard.

Then, still fuming, he decided he'd be damned if he'd frig around this way again. The wild critters could fend for themselves; they always had. Richard could, too, if he had to, but no sense to starve a cat. He'd take Richard home, keep him in the shed. Nobody'd need to know a thing about it. As for Little Sarah, what the mind didn't know, the heart wouldn't grieve over.

He waited until Richard was nearly through eating, and then, leaning down as if to pat him, scooped him up and tucked him under his arm.

Richard straightened out into wire. He spat; his eyes turned green and venomous. He let Elbridge have it, a whole set of claws in the face, raking down his cheek and narrowly missing his eye. Then, he squirmed to the ground and went to earth in his hole under the porch.

Elbridge went home.

Spring was his busiest time, when he was stretched right out straight, town taxes and town books added to everything else he had to do. The next day, after school, he sent Gib and Will over to the Point with Richard's meal and a covered box, and instructions to toll Richard into the box and bring him home.

"Don't you fool around over there," he warned them. "And no. You know you can't take my shotgun."

The twins had been deeply impressed by Elbridge's five ducks. But they knew they couldn't take the gun unless he was along. That was law until they were thirteen.

Richard, however, wouldn't be caught. He stayed out of sight every day, until whoever brought his food had put it down and departed. It took the boys a week to get him, finally, into the box and the cover down and fastened.

Gib and Will had been growling because they had to walk over to the Point every day—it took all their spare time after school, they said—and Elbridge knew just how they felt. He was about ready to go back to doing it himself—Little Sarah's cold hung on—when, one night at dark, the boys came home with Richard in the box. They were worn out with the chase and with the tote across the island— Richard weighed twenty pounds, he was a big cat. But they didn't growl at all, this time; they had, apparently, found something else to interest them. They were acting pretty important, Elbridge noticed, shooting knowing looks at each other, as they thought, behind his back. He made a note in his mind to ask them what was up—instinct told him something was brewing—but he forgot about it in the hassle that took place when they let Richard loose in the shed.

Richard took one look around, spotted the one windowpane that was cracked and went through it in a flying leap, jumping right over the top of Gib's head. The pane broke like an eggshell. The last they saw of Richard, he was stretched out straight along the causeway, headed toward home.

"Oh, blast!" Elbridge said, disgustedly thinking that now he *would* have to fix that pane of glass Jess had been after him about. "Let him go. Maybe somebody'll shoot him. I hope so."

But all that evening he had a bad time of it, wondering uncomfortably if Richard made it home. Miss Greenwood thought an awful lot of that fool cat; she'd lost enough, without losing him. The next morning, he took time to walk over to the Point himself, put out food, and then went and hid in the trees. He waited, but no sign of Richard.

The tree he had picked to hide behind was a little way from the house, across the pocket handkerchief of ruined lawn. As he waited, swearing a little under his breath at the waste of his time, he thought he heard somebody moving around in the thicket behind him—a sound almost like a stumble, as if a boot heel had caught on a root. He turned around to look and was about to speak—feeling foolish to have whoever it was find him lurking in the bushes watching the house—when the thicket parted and a big buck stepped out into the open, not twenty feet from him.

Elbridge's jaw dropped. He stared at the buck and the buck looked back at him, not frightened, just kind of brought up short, the way Elbridge was. Then it turned around slowly, not in any kind of a hurry, and walked back into the thicket.

"Well, I'll be goddarned," Elbridge said aloud. "Old mister wild himself."

Then he saw, under a nearby tree, the chumbled-over remains of what must have been, in the beginning, quite a sizable pile of apples.

So that was it; that was where Little Sarah's last bushel or so of winter apples had gone. They were pretty fairly fresh, too, quite a lot of them untouched, which meant that Little Sarah, cold and all, had been over here not too long ago, and more than once, for she surely couldn't have carried them all at one clip.

Apples for the mink, he thought.

Suddenly, he found himself grinning. That was pretty coony. Let the whole town have it over that you're crazy enough to feed good apples to a mink, and their minds so taken up by the joke, just the kind of thing you'd expect Miss Greenwood to do, that they'd never think to question it, and nobody'd come over here and shoot the deer. Which, he thought, his grin fading, would be darned easy to do. There'd be plenty who'd shoot a buck this time of year just for the sake of saying they'd done it, even though they'd know the meat wasn't much in April.

This must be the fellow he and Liseo had caught a glimpse of in the swamp last Christmas, and nobody had seen a sign of since. Liseo had hunted in there around the pond a couple of times, but he'd finally given it up, figuring the buck had left the way he had come, swimming back to the mainland. The reason he wasn't to be found in the swamp was, he wasn't there at all; he was over here, getting tame. Being fed apples. He didn't break for cover when he saw a man, just walked away.

Blast and damn! Elbridge thought. What can you do?

Being wild was the only protection the darn critters had. Blast a sentimental fool of an old maid! And Little Sarah, by God, she ought to know better, too.

A movement by the food dish on the porch caught his eye, and he leaned forward to peer through the tree. There was still no sign of Richard, but a fat squirrel—might have been General Putnam, might have been one of half a dozen others—had come down a porch column and had started to eat out of Richard's dish.

From under the porch there came a flash of yellow fur and a furious bell-jangling. The squirrel took off up the column, so little ahead of the murdering claws behind him that, for a moment, it seemed to Elbridge it was all over with him. A puff of reddish squirrel hair shot into the air and floated down; then the squirrel broke clear and climbed high to the gutter of the house. He sat there swearing, while Richard strolled majestically to the dish and began to eat his meal.

"That'll learn you," Elbridge said, grinning at the squirrel. "Keep your nose out of somebody else's dish."

He started along the road home, and heard something else in the woods. This time, it wasn't a deer.

Gib and Will and Johnny MacGimsey were coming carefully along the path, walking in Indian file, on tiptoe. Gib and Johnny were carrying guns. Gib's gun was Elbridge's big twelve-gauge shotgun, and Johnny had Liseo's .30-30 rifle. So absorbed were they, craning their necks through the bushes, looking toward the pile of apples, that they didn't even see Elbridge.

That was what was in the wind last night, Elbridge thought, remembering suddenly. They had, of course, seen the buck over here yesterday.

Well, too bad to spoil a good time, but all three of them were too young for those big shooting irons; his own boys, at least, had been told times enough not to touch the shotgun. As a matter of fact, Liseo, too, would rather have cut off a finger and handed it to Johnny than let him handle that rifle.

"What did you fellows think you'd find around here to shoot?" he asked sternly. "And what's the idea, not going to school today?"

To Gib and Will, his sudden appearance was disaster. They stood, red-faced and scared, their eyes on their boots. Gib's hand moved furtively, and Elbridge heard the click of the safety on the shotgun. But Johnny looked him impudently in the eye.

"There's a deer over here," Johnny said. "We're going to shoot him."

"That rifle loaded?"

"Darn right it is."

"Take the shells out of it."

Johnny didn't move. His black eyes, beginning to spark with temper, swiveled once at Elbridge, then away.

Will said desperately, "It was a buck, Pop, a big one. We thought if we got him, you wouldn't care about the gun, us taking it."

"What made you think so?"

"Well . . . a buck . . ."

"Sure. A buck. The meat's no good this time of year. He's just got through the winter, he'd be stringy and tough as a bundle of fence posts. If you're any kind of a hunter, you'd know that. Pretty smart, to shoot a buck, just for the sake of shooting him. My shotgun loaded, is it?"

Gib nodded miserably.

"And the safety was off. So you were walking along behind Johnny with it pointed right between his shoulders. Blast it, Gib, the times I've tried to learn you fellers about guns, looks to me as if I'd wasted my time. Take the gun back home. You, too, Johnny."

"You go to the devil," Johnny said.

Elbridge's long arm shot out, caught him by the back of the neck, his other hand picked the rifle neatly out of Johnny's clutch. "All right," Elbridge said. "I'll take this rifle home. When your father misses it, you can tell him where it is."

Johnny, meeting his eyes boldly at first, suddenly realized the implications of this. He turned a little white and backed away. Then he burst into raucous howls, spun around in the road and took to his heels.

The twins, Elbridge saw, were staring at him, round-eyed; their faces, too, white and scared.

"No need to be afraid of anything except a good licking," he said. "You can have one, or you can wait till you're fourteen, before you get a gun of your own. Take your pick."

The twins looked at each other, measuring the disaster.

"I guess we'll wait in the woodshed," Will said dismally.

THE day after Miss Greenwood came home, Elbridge had made the trip to the Point himself. He came out of the woods, went across the lawn, fuming, and saw Richard sitting casually on the porch rail in the sun. Every window in the house was open, the clothesline hung with blankets airing, the porch heaped with rugs. In the walled garden, the flower beds had been uncovered, the old brush that had been over them was piled on the rocks for burning. A bed of daffodils bloomed, like a sheet of yellow fire, against the stone. Richard, who was usually off like a streak of light at the sight of Elbridge, didn't even open his eyes when Elbridge came up the steps.

Miss Greenwood met him at the door. She had on a dust cap and a bungalow apron that covered her from throat to heels, and she cried out, "Oh, oh! You caught me at my spring house cleaning, but I'm very glad to see you. Come in, Mr. Gilman." She shook hands with him. "You've taken your time on a busy day to bring Richard's dinner," she said, relieving him of his bundles. "I don't know how we'll ever thank you."

"No need to. Glad to oblige. I didn't expect to see you, or I wouldn't have come barging in."

"Why, no harm done at all. I should just have taken off my apron, fixed a place for you to sit. Will you have some coffee?"

"Well, thanks, no, I'm in a little mite of a hurry today. You find everything all right? I expect Richard's glad to see you. He and I didn't hit it off any too well."

"He's very standoffish," she said. "I hope he wasn't too much trouble, Mr. Gilman. I found everything in good condition, thanks to you. The house was stuffy—of course, it would be, shut up so long. But it isn't now. I threw every window wide and let the good salt air in over everything. It smells so wonderful. I find I can't breathe any other kind, Mr. Gilman."

She was talking a little more than she usually did, or perhaps faster; otherwise she seemed exactly the same.

"See you've got the brush off of your garden," he said. "I set out to do that, but I wasn't sure it was time."

"Oh, it was time." She smiled and nodded. "The bleeding heart and the delphinium are up and looking white-livered, but they'll quickly take the sun. I came back sooner than I intended, because of the flower beds. Richard, I was sure, would be all right. But you and I don't see eye to eye about the birds, Mr. Gilman. Somebody has been shooting here. I found empty shotgun shells down on the rocks, and I had to throw another of those horrible steel traps into the ocean. I worried all the time I was gone, for fear somebody would kill the mink. But nobody has, Mr. Gilman! I saw her last night. She has babies."

"That's nice," Elbridge said feebly. "Kids, probably," he went on. "Hard to keep track of kids all the time."

"Oh, yes, I'm sure it must have been. The young boys. Grown men, of course, would realize how tame the little creatures are here, and that it's only murder to kill them."

"That's right," Elbridge said. To his horror, he felt himself turning red. "Well," he said hastily, "I'll have to go. You need anything done, before I do?"

"Oh, no, thank you. Now that Mother is not here, I shall have a great deal more time to do things—much, much more for myself, and not have to bother people."

"Yes," he said. "I expect so."

She didn't plan to go away, then; she was settling in. It must have been gossip, all that talk about her selling her house.

Elbridge said diffidently, "You going to manage all right, alone?"

"Yes, indeed. The days won't be long enough, Mr. Gilman. I shall have so much to do."

"Well," he said, starting down the steps. "Call on, if you need anything."

"I shall. Oh, Mr. Gilman, will you be having Easter services in the church?"

"I don't know. I hope so," Elbridge said. "If the minister can't make it, I guess we won't."

He almost added, "But I don't know who'll come to them," and stopped, thinking automatically, No sense having *that* over with an outsider, and then, Oh, of course she isn't an outsider, but no sense bringing it up anyway.

"Mr. Franklin's very busy, isn't he?" she said.

"No man ought to be asked to do so much," Elbridge said. "So if he doesn't come, you can't blame him."

"I think the Episcopalian rector from Port Western would come," she said. "On Easter afternoon. If somebody went over to fetch him. Do you think people would like that?"

"Why," Elbridge said, "people would enjoy having him, Miss Greenwood."

"Well, I'll write him," she said.

Elbridge considered, as he walked home through the woods. The Episcopalian rector from Port Western had held services here on the island once before, coming at the invitation of the summer people, who seemed, most of them, to be Episcopalian. The service had been held in the schoolhouse, and he had, at the time, wondered why,

when the rector could have had the church just for the asking. El-
bridge himself had been off the island that day, which had been a
weekday, and hadn't gone to the services; but he made up his mind
now, that if the rector could come for Easter, he'd make a point of
offering the church to him.

But there ought to be some work done, he thought glumly, as he
walked along.

The old church was already looking dilapidated, needing work
done on the belfry and a coat of paint. Before the row, the Ladies'
Aid had planned to raise some money for that. You couldn't let an
old building go too long, or it would be beyond repair.

He and Liseo and some others would be glad to donate labor, but
paint and nails and lumber cost money to buy. Of course, there was
the salvaged lumber lying around unused in almost everybody's back
yard, already getting weathered and losing its look of newness. But
Elbridge dreaded to think what would happen if he suggested again
that some of it might be donated to fix up the belfry.

That lumber was a point of battle; you would think it was made
out of solid gold, and the only thing of its kind in the world. There
wasn't a stick of wood bigger than a shingle left now on any of the
shores. Men had even snatched out from under each other's noses
a couple of old chunks of half-rotten eight-by-eight that had been
lying buried up in the cove beach rocks for years—so long that they'd
been a kind of landmark. The feeling was out of proportion to any
benefit derived. Just something to focus the fight on.

Elbridge sighed a little. There was the furnace, too. It would all
be quite an expense, couldn't be done unless the whole community
got behind it. He could donate something and Liseo could; the thing
was, it was a time of year when money was short, when about every-
thing they had would have to be plowed back into the business.
And, he had to admit it, business wasn't good this spring, mainly be-
cause some who were put out at him or mad at Liseo were taking
their trade over to the mainland.

From the top of MacKechnie's hill he could see the church steeple
over the trees, and the sight saddened him. It had stood there since
1860, the hearthstone and center of the town. Ever since he could
remember he had been to services there, from the time when his
mother squeezed his feet into his Sunday shoes and made him sit,
red-faced and squirming on the hard plank seat that wouldn't give
an inch to a stern of iron.

He didn't know as he'd ever been overly religious—that is, he couldn't always go along, entirely, with what the minister said. For example, he'd never felt like a miserable sinner—oh, a sinner, sure, sometimes, but not miserable. There was something about the combination of words that took away a responsible man's dignity. He figured that, anyway, to be an interpretation of what the Bible was talking about; there might be more than one way to understand it. If what it meant, there, was humility, that was a different matter.

It had occurred to him a good many times that if he were a minister, he'd lay on the line the part about love thy neighbor until it came out of the congregation's ears, and let the hell-fire and brimstone and the sin and punishment part of it go hang. Most people weren't wicked, anyway; nine-tenths of them were doing the best they could, sometimes with pretty moderate equipment. And God, as an administrator, with a whole universe on his hands, would probably rather see a world full of self-respecting decent people than full of miserable children.

Well, whatever you believed about what you heard in church, a man without it was like a three-wheeled wagon. Let Miss Greenwood invite her rector over. Maybe he'd jolt some people back into their senses. Anyway, it would be interesting to hear what the rector had to say, and to see how many would come to church, if the minister wasn't Mr. Franklin.

But on Easter Sunday morning, when he went into the vestry to build a fire, he found there was no use thinking he could use the furnace that day, or ever. Somebody had mixed up a bucket of cement and poured it into the grate to harden. The interior of the furnace was blocked with a great rough lump. You might have blasted it out with a stick of dynamite—there wouldn't be any other way. Whoever had done it must have been in a hurry. He had left his bucket and his mixing trowel there on the vestry floor.

Well, he thought, dully. A trowel. A bucket. They're mostly alike. No way to tell who they belong to.

But he picked up the trowel and turned it over. It was an old trowel, rusty, and on the end of the handle, incised with a burning iron, letters: "L. MacGimsey."

Liseo? he thought, for a thunderstruck moment, before his mind started to work. Liseo had a burning iron, stenciled with his name. No. Not Liseo. Not conceivably. Never in this world, Liseo.

Luther? Was this from his old tool box?

Stell.

Some of Stell's crowd. Wanting to show where they stood about an

Easter service conducted by Mr. Franklin. He had written two days ago that he wouldn't be able to come, but Addie had had the letter. Maybe the news hadn't got around; likely it hadn't, one side not wishing to have Christian speech with the other.

If people feel this way, he thought, soberly shutting the vestry door and locking it behind him, I wouldn't doubt they left the bucket and the trowel on purpose. Just to show us.

PRACTICALLY the whole town turned out to go to the services at the schoolhouse on Sunday afternoon. The rector hadn't made any bones about coming; he'd said he'd be glad to. That the church couldn't be used had turned out not to matter to him. The Episcopalians, it seemed, had a rule—couldn't hold their services in a church not consecrated to them alone, the rector explained. The schoolhouse was jammed, with people sitting on benches in the back.

Under the circumstances, Elbridge wasn't surprised to see that the two factions of the town row were keeping to themselves, one on each side of the middle aisle.

About what you could expect, he thought grimly, looking at his neighbors. Going on record, showing where they stand. Even in church, maybe because it was in church, nobody was going to give an inch.

He tried to stop thinking about it and get interested in the service. That seemed to be the least a man could do.

The service was altogether different from any he was used to. It turned out to be mostly prayers read out of a book—no sermon to speak of, only a short talk at the end. The rector had a clear, deep voice; his prayers sounded good, except for a habit he had of putting in an extra syllable after a full stop. "The kingdom of God-uh," he said. That might bother you, after a while; of course it didn't amount to much—probably it was the way he'd been taught to read. It seemed odd to see a minister conducting services in long white robes, and Elbridge, to save his life, couldn't tell what the congregation was supposed to do from one minute to the next.

He thought at first that the thing to do would be to watch Miss Greenwood. She, of course, knew the service. She was sitting smack up front, apparently right in her element. Then he saw that, quite a lot of the time, she was kneeling down, and that he couldn't go along with. Stand up to sing a hymn, sit down to listen to a sermon, but kneeling in prayer was something a man did in private, if he did it at all, not where all his neighbors could see him. Apparently, the rest of the congregation felt the same way he did. When Miss Greenwood knelt, they sat quietly in their seats.

That is, they did at first, before Stell MacGimsey got her idea. Halfway through the services, Stell began kneeling, and then Imogene did. The two of them watched Miss Greenwood like hawks, began doing everything she did. Pretty soon, the rest of Stell's faction got the idea, too. The services proceeded with everybody to the right of the aisle kneeling, when the times came, and with everybody on the left of it sitting stiffly in their seats.

Well, that was certainly a new and novel way to spite your neighbors. It must look darned odd to the minister, who wouldn't have any way of knowing that what he was seeing wasn't anything particularly devout.

Elbridge glanced at Jess and saw that she was sitting looking straight ahead, her cheeks a little pinker than usual. His circling glance caught Liseo's, and Liseo slanted his head sideways, with a tiny, almost imperceptible jerk, at Willard Lowden, over on the other side of the aisle.

No, Elbridge thought. Not Liseo. I was crazy even to let it enter my mind.

He and Liseo had got over their spat long ago. Neither of them had mentioned it after it happened; things were back now, so far as Elbridge could tell, on an even keel, the way they'd always been.

But Willard? Someone might have talked Willard into it, and Willard still had the keys to the vestry. Elbridge glanced over at Willard.

Willard was following leader, getting up and kneeling down. He was having trouble. He had one of the eighth-grade seats, the largest size there was, but it was still too small for a man of his poundage; and no sooner did he get wedged into it, than he had to get wedged out again. He was, just now, staring glumly at two big smears of chalk dust from the schoolhouse floor on the knees of his dark blue Sunday suit.

For a moment Elbridge thought he might be going to commit the crazy crime of laughing out loud in church.

Or maybe, he thought, what I want to do is cry. Or get mad. Why don't I get mad?

Except, he told himself, there's been so much of that already that a man can see how far it's likely to get him.

Old Wid isn't funny, he thought.

But he had to bite down on his teeth until the lumps came out on the side of his jaws, and he stared hard at the prayer book the rector had handed him when he came in.

And I'll be darned if I'll believe it was Willard, either, until I've got good reason to. Any more than it was Willard who left that window open.

The rector had brought a big bundle of prayer books with him, knowing, of course, that there wouldn't be any of his denomination's on the island; he had had quite a lot of luggage, what with his robes and altar equipment. He seemed like a nice kind of fellow; he deserved better than this spite-your-neighbor shenanigan, taking place in his services, and the services deserved better, too. They were impressive; Elbridge could see that they might be pretty nice, once you got the hang of them. He stared down at his book.

Easter Sunday, it said.

Well, he'd got up, times enough, in town meeting, before a gathering of his neighbors; he wouldn't mind it. There might be a place, along toward the end of the service, where the rector would mention church announcements.

There wasn't, perhaps because it wasn't the rector's home church; but after the benediction, he turned to go and stand by the door, as ministers do; and in the rustle that followed, people starting to get to their feet, Elbridge got up.

"I've got a church announcement before you go," he said, and was aware of a variety of expressions turned toward him, startled, friendly, sullen.

"We've got trouble," he went on, "as we all know. But when it comes to filling up the church furnace with Portland cement, I don't believe there's anyone here who won't agree with me that the trouble's gone far enough."

Willard Lowden said, in a voice deep with shock, "No, Elbridge! Nobody'd do that!" and Elbridge thought, relieved, Well, it sure wasn't Willard, looking from face to face, to see if any other could make him as sure. But the looks on his neighbors' faces, one and all, seemed to be all of astonishment and outrage.

"Just who," Stell MacGimsey said icily, "are you accusing of such a thing?"

"Nobody," Elbridge said.

"Well, you'd better not!"

"I don't care who did it," Elbridge said. "Kids, likely as not. It's certainly a kids' trick."

That was the wrong thing to say, he thought, seeing Stell's head go up.

"I don't think it matters now who did it," he went on. "What does matter is us all getting together and settling our differences. It's Easter Sunday, and it's a good time to. I've got ten dollars to put down on a new furnace. Will the rest of you help out?"

"I've got seven, Elbridge," Addie Shepheard said. "Only it's to home in my egg-money box. I'll bring it," and she looked straight at Jack. Jack looked back for a moment; then he got up and headed silently for the door.

"Well!" Stell said. "Filling up the furnace with cement, Elbridge, is as smart a way as I can think of for two jokers like you and Liseo to try to get your own way."

She, too, headed for the door, where she was heard to say to the bewildered rector, "That was as lovely a service as I've ever heard in my life, Mr. Martin, and if you've heard what's just gone on, I guess you'll admit we've needed it. You'll surely come again, won't you?"

"Er—yes. Yes, of course," the rector said. He went on shaking hands, in a puzzled way, with the rest of Stell's faction, which was following her out of the schoolhouse, close-packed, in a body.

"Oh, Elbridge!" Jess said, at Elbridge's shoulder. "I thought for a moment it was going to work."

"Yes," Liseo said. "It was a darned good try, Elbridge."

"If I hadn't said all the wrong things, as usual," Elbridge said.

Well, he thought. If they want war, war is what they're going to get.

"Liseo," he said tersely. "You know anybody owns an old mortar trowel with 'L. MacGimsey' burnt into the handle of it?"

"Sure," Liseo said slowly. "I do. Why?"

"Where is it?"

"Home in my tool box, the last I knew."

"No, it isn't. At least, there's one like that in an old green cement bucket down in the church vestry."

"Wooden bucket? Painted green?" Liseo asked.

"That's right."

"My bucket," Liseo said.

His dark olive face began to burn dusky red, his eyes to sparkle with fury. "You got any idea—" he began in a choked voice.

"Not about you. You know that."

"H'm, no. I don't guess you have, at that. I've got two bags of cement in my shed, too, in case you—" He stopped. His face, if that were possible, turned a darker red. "And I've got an idea. If I'm right, I'll—" He turned and headed out of the schoolhouse, leaving an eddying wake through the crowd of Stell's friends, who were six deep around the rector, all but patting him on the back.

All over town, that Sunday afternoon, there were explosions. Up to now, squabbles had been widespread, but more or less personal. Now, larger issues were at stake.

Stell said, "It's going some, when people will stoop to despoiling church property just to get their own way, and then lay it on their neighbors."

Willard had gone, hot-foot, to the church vestry to view the remains of the furnace, and he had reported the bucket and the trowel. He had recognized them, having at odd times in the past worked with Liseo, and his sense of outrage made him blurt out what he thought. Willard felt very bad about the furnace. Talking of it, he sounded as if some female relative of his, difficult in life but sadly missed, had died.

"I had her for eleven years," he said, wagging his head. "Eleven years and three months. She was a bitch, but I was the only one could handle her."

Stell said, "Well, they can fill the whole works up with cement and leave it there for a monument, for all of me. It's about time this island had a real church, not that old dead thing with the belfry half off of it. It ain't Christian the way them folks is acting, and I, for one, will be glad to have something of our own, where we can have some say who's to come to it. I don't know as I ever saw services any lovelier than the ones we had today."

Addie said, "I never thought, as long as I *lived* I'd see people stoop to do a thing like that, just for spite. I don't see how we'll ever get a new furnace, the way folks feel, but somehow we've got to. After today, the old-time religion is good enough for me. All that getting up and kneeling down and reading prayers *out of a book,* in front of an altar, I don't go for, it's worse than the golden calf. People that do it is idolaters, that's all. Oh, of course if you've been brought up to it, like Miss Greenwood and the summer people, and it's your own religion, but to do it for spite, that's idolatry, and it makes me feel sick at my stomach."

She said this to Carrie Hitchman, on the way home from church, and it set Carrie to thinking. Well, *that* idea hadn't entered her head before.

That afternoon, in the main road, Carrie and Stell met face to face.

Carrie said, "A pretty nice thing, Stella, I must say."

Stell said, "Yes, I think so myself."

"I'm not surprised at some wanting an Episcoble church in here," Carrie said.

Stell said, "You won't be surprised, then, to know that I don't give a hoot what you think."

"None of it surprises me," Carrie said. "When you think that most of the summer people are Episcobles. I might of known. Of course, there's always some who'll go to any lengths to suck up to the summer people, but to do it over such a thing as their religion is downright hypocritical."

"You should know what a hypocrite is," Stell said.

"Well, I do. I've certainly had a bellyful of them," Carrie said, and walked away.

Will Gilman came home that day with two black eyes and a deep cut on his chin, and Imogene came over to Jess to complain that he had bounced a rock off of Bubber's head, given him a lump the size of an egg. A wonder he wasn't killed. She was not appeased when Jess pointed out that Bubber was older than Will, stood a head taller, and that Will, too, had been hurt. Jess was worried about Will. He did not, usually, shed tears; but after she had patched up his wounds, he disappeared into the bedroom, lay down on his cot and cried, so she had to wonder what else ailed him.

At Lowden's, George tripped up Willard by means of a string tied between the posts of the back steps, gave Willard a bad, jarring fall; and while he was lying on the ground, half-dazed, George whipped in and removed his wallet and the church keys from his pocket. From a safe distance, George said, "So that's why you kept these keys so long, waiting for a chance to get back at the Council! Godfrey mighty, Wid, a dirty trick like that, you'll be lucky if you don't end up in jail. You ain't bought your share of the groceries here to home, either. So I'll just keep what's in this wallet."

He fired the empty wallet at Willard's head and departed, leaving Willard to get himself up and into the house, which he did, muttering dazedly, "Why, I never done it, and I don't see why anyone thinks I did."

All over town, that afternoon, incidents of rage and resentment took place, people accusing each other, getting each other told, saying things not easily forgotten.

AT dusk, Elbridge heard someone come thumping up his back steps. Liseo, he thought. Well, thank the Lord. But he's either mad or in a hurry.

Liseo had been gone since church time. Elbridge had stopped by his house before supper, but Fanny hadn't known where he was. She'd seemed upset for Fanny, almost in tears, and Elbridge hadn't lingered.

"Hi," he began relievedly, as Liseo came through the door. "Wondered where you'd—"

The look on Liseo's face brought him up short.

"What is it?" he said. "What is it, now?"

"Here's fifty bucks," Liseo said. He dumped a handful of small bills and change on the table. "Twenty-five from me and twenty-five from Paul Cayford. The rest of it'll be forthcoming, just as soon as—" He glanced over his shoulder. "Hey," he said. "You come on in here, out of that entry. We'd kind of like to hear your word on this, too."

Liseo's voice was quiet, but his face was still the same dusky, congested red which Elbridge had seen earlier in the day.

From the entry came not a sound; a mouselike stillness prevailed, then a couple of shuffling footsteps.

Elbridge did not know who he expected to see; but he was not too surprised, he realized, as a sober, tear-stained face materialized in the darkness of the entry door, at the sight of Liseo's boy, Johnny.

"I smelt a rat about something when he sneaked off this morning without telling his ma and me where he was going," Liseo said. "He's done that before when there's been devilish actions afoot and he's been at the bottom of 'em. So I caught up with him, down around shore, late this afternoon, and I found cement dust around the eyelets on his larrigans. It was," Liseo went on, his eye fixed bleakly on his son, "an edifying sight."

Johnny, apparently, had had it. He looked rumpled, as if he had had a good shaking up; his eyelids were red, and as he stared at the floor, he hiccuped.

"It seems," Liseo said, "Bubber Cayford organized a club that had secret meetings in the vestry. Seems they started out going down the coal chute, but that was a dead giveaway—it got coal dust on your pants. So they opened a window, and left it open, so they could go in and out of the church whenever they wanted to. That right, Johnny?"

Johnny nodded. He did not look up.

Elbridge glanced over at Jess. She was white and worried, and

Gib, who had been sitting unobtrusively over in the corner, was as red as a beet. Will was still in his room.

"All right," Elbridge said. "You and Will in on that club, Gib?"

Gib said forlornly, "Uh-huh."

"Knew all along about that open window?"

"We didn't realize it would *leak*," Gib said. His voice, beginning on a deep bass note, broke at the end of the sentence into a kind of hoarse soprano. "We never touched the furnace," he went on desperately. "We never even thought of it. Will and I got mad and resigned from the club this afternoon, and Will tried to lick Bubber—"

"Oh, Johnny and Bubber did the job on the furnace," Liseo said. "You're lucky. Your kids didn't know about it at all. The way I pounded it out of Johnny, Bubber was taking Mama's side in the Great War, and Johnny was sore at you because you took my rifle. Where is it, by the way?"

"Oh, Lord," Elbridge said.

He had meant to return the rifle at once, and had been waiting for a time when Liseo would be away from home, so that he could slip the gun to Fanny and have her put it back before Liseo missed it. Fanny could always be counted on to help Johnny out of a scrape with his father, and Elbridge had figured that a day or two of suspense would be punishment enough. But he'd had so much on his mind that the rifle had gone completely out of it and was still standing in the corner behind the dining room door. He thought how, as the time had passed and nothing had happened, the suspense must have been growing in Johnny's mind.

"You hop up to bed, Gib," he said. "I'll see you later." A little suspense there won't hurt, either, he thought.

"Well, you know, John," he went on, after Gib had gone, "I think I'd better take part of the blame. I was going to hand that gun to your ma after you'd had a couple of days to worry about it, tell her to slide it back into the closet. But I forgot it. I'm sorry. I kind of figured you had a spell of worry coming, but that was all."

"I'll say he did!" Liseo said wrathfully.

"I wouldn't have had it happen this way for a good deal," Elbridge said. "But I had a lot of other things to think about. So, John, I guess I'd better pay for my share of that furnace."

"No, you don't!" Liseo said. "Johnny's got mink traps and he's going to run a string of lobster traps. He's in hock for every cent he earns till that furnace is paid for, and don't you forget it! I went over and waved reform school at Paul and Imogene, and they came up with twenty-five bucks, but it's still quite a bill. Quite—a—bill. It'll take all summer, and then some." He spun around on Johnny. "Well, is that all right with you? Speak up!"

"That's okay," Johnny said. But the look he gave his father was stricken.

"Hold on, Liseo," Elbridge said.

He felt a sudden upsurge of spirits, relief flowing over him like a wave. It had been *kids*, kids all stirred up in one way or another by grownups' foolishness; but kids you could deal with.

"Liseo," he said. "Remember the ice cream we swiped from the vestry supper? Remember the fish oil in the beans?"

"By gum, this was different! This was—"

"Suppose the town had been all stirred up like a hornets' nest at the time? No knowing what you and I would've felt called upon to do. Besides, I recall spending a whole summer paying for windows stove out of the schoolhouse, don't you?"

Liseo brought up short. A slightly foolish look crossed his face. He stared thoughtfully at his son, plainly remembering the time when he himself had been a hellion on wheels.

"Twenty-five dollars," Elbridge said. "And maybe him and Bubber to help us dismantle the furnace. Twenty-five is what Bubber's folks have paid, and if I know Paul, Bubber'll earn it. And that's enough. For the rest, I say those of us who are partly to blame had better chip in."

To his relief, Liseo suddenly grinned.

"All right," he said. "Of course, I'm willing to pay the whole thing, when I can, Elbridge, and I don't know what the town'll say if I don't."

"I know you are. Here," Elbridge said. He reached around the corner of the dining room door for the rifle, handed it to Johnny. "You take this home, shove it in the closet, before your old man finds out you swiped it."

"Okay," Johnny said. His face was still pinched and miserable, but a faint ray of hope had crossed it, as if all might not be lost.

"You better realize what you've done, though," Liseo said, eying him. "Damage untold, fights all over town, this one and that one accusing the other—it'll take months, maybe years, to get people back on an even keel. Elbridge and I'll have to talk it around town who really did wreck that furnace, try to straighten things out. And anything that comes of that, you'll have to take, like if there's deviltry goes on anywhere, from here on in folks are going to look at you and Bubber first, and don't you forget it. You travel home now, put away my gun, and tell your ma to feed you. And then, by godfrey mighty, you go to bed! For once I'll know where you are for the next twelve hours."

"Fanny says George and Willard had another one," he went on, thoughtfully watching his son's mournful progress past the kitchen window.

Elbridge nodded. "Stell and Carrie, too," he said.

"Well, we'll have to get word around. If it'll do any good now," Liseo said. "Some already having waged battle above and beyond the call of duty."

Elbridge reached for his hat. "I'll start in down by the wharf," he said. "You get some supper, and then you go up the road, if you aren't too tired. Stop in at each house. For once, we'll see that information gets around town straight, without any donkey tails on it."

"Okay," Liseo said.

He went off, trudging up the road, not stopping, Elbridge saw, to go home to supper.

A couple of hours later, they met in the main road by the post office. The moon had come up, shining serenely. Normally, at this hour, with four-thirty on a workday morning coming up, everybody would have gone to bed. But tonight, down through the town, there was a light in nearly every window.

"How'd you make out?" Elbridge asked, seeing Liseo, like a tall shadow, coming toward him along the road.

"Had a nice talk with everyone," Liseo said. He stopped, running his tongue along the inside of his lips, looking wryly down the road at the scattered lights. "Looks like a peaceful little town," he said. "Fire and lamplight and all."

It did. Here on the road, where the tilt of the land began, you could smell wood smoke, and see it, curling quietly up from a couple of nearby chimneys.

"You have a rough time?"

"Yes," Liseo said. "Bill and Mollie made me feel doggone good, and Joe was all right. But Carrie—well, she's in a fever, and I kind of think it's got to run its course."

"Same way with Addie and Jack," Elbridge said briefly. "Only, there, it's Jack."

"Uh-huh," Liseo said. "Some it appears don't care to have things straightened out. By Judas, I've listened to more self-righteous clap-trap in the last two hours than I ever stood up hog-tied to in the rest of my life." He sighed. "All on account of that blasted sprout of mine. He's laid me wide open."

He paced along silently by Elbridge's side for a while. He looked exhausted, as well he might, Elbridge thought, the day he'd had and nothing to eat since noon.

"Come home with me, why don't you?" Elbridge said. "Jess has got Sunday dinner left over, and I'll give you a jolt of rum."

"If I had a jolt of rum, right now," Liseo said, "I'd fly into five thousand pieces and each separate piece would start to swear. Fanny'll have some supper waiting. She'll be bawling, too. It takes a lot to undermine Fanny, but anything with Johnny and she's all over the floor. Poor old Johnny," he went on, glumly. "You think I ought to go home and beat the hide off of him, so he couldn't move for a week?"

His voice, making the transition smoothly, had suddenly become Stell's, and Elbridge looked at him, startled.

"I didn't think you'd go to see Stell," he said. "I didn't plan for you to. I was going in there myself, only it was late, so I was leaving it till tomorrow."

"You put it off till last, same as I did," Liseo said. "Oh, yes, I went there. Said my piece pleasant, same as to everybody. I told her Johnny'd had his licking, a good one he'd remember, but that I didn't beat the hide off kids, my own or anyone else's. And she said, through the door—she didn't open it—that if I'd been a little handier with the horsewhip, my kids now might be safe to live in the same town with, and that included that girl over to the harbor that wasn't any better than she ought to be; and I said—you interested in hearing the rest of this?—I said that if any talk started up about Rosie, the post office inspector would be here so fast he'd have singed coattails. Or somebody would. But I said it pleasant, Elbridge. I didn't raise my voice."

Likely he didn't, Elbridge thought. Liseo's voice, now, had the silky purr it took on when he was quietly, murderously angry.

Elbridge grinned. He couldn't help it, thinking how pleasant Liseo probably had sounded, and Liseo grinned back, but the grin was brief, a little more than a flash of white teeth in the moonlight.

"Oh, yes, I covered everyone, up at this end of town," Liseo said. "Except Miss Greenwood. You suppose that old cantata knows, for a minute, how much damage her church service has done, Elbridge?"

"Good Lord, no!" Elbridge said. "How's that?"

Liseo wasn't going to talk any more about Stell, he realized, or the post office business, and maybe that was a good idea. What he meant now, changing the subject, and he might as well have said it outright, was, I won't fight you over it, Elbridge, but I've got to take care of my own. Well, that was all right. It would have to be Liseo's business; if more damage were done, the pieces could be picked up somehow. The way to let Liseo know he had been understood was to go on talking about the something else.

"Miss Greenwood was only trying to get us a minister for Easter," Elbridge said.

"Well, it's true she lives inside of a flower," Liseo said. "Wouldn't understand for a minute a thing like a fight amongst us lovely people."

"Why would she? People don't tell her much, except stuff about the birds and the weather. Maybe Little Sarah's mentioned the fight to her, I doubt it. Everybody puts best foot forward for the summer people, you know that, Liseo, don't even cuss. The only one I *ever* heard cuss in front of Miss Greenwood was you, the time the squirrel crawled on you. Why wouldn't she think we're all lovely?"

"Well," Liseo said. "Unless they cool off, and I doubt if they do, Stell's crowd's going to get up a petition to the rector to make his services over here a regular thing. And you know what that means, right now, as well as I do."

"Ayup," Elbridge said. He hadn't heard that this evening, in his travels around the town, though about everything else had been gone into.

"It means a rousing old church war," Liseo said. "Another little bit added to what we got."

He turned aside to go in at his gate, lifting a hand in good night.

"Sure you won't change your mind about that rum?" Elbridge asked.

"Ayup, guess not. I better go in and pat Fanny. See you tomorrow, Elbridge. 'Something accomplished, something done, has earned a night's repose.'"

It was a quotation Liseo had heard him use at odd times and lighter moments, and Elbridge grinned, turning away to trudge wearily down the road to his own house.

Whatever's accomplished, he thought, and maybe it isn't much, tonight, there's one thing.

Liseo and he were all right now, whatever happened.

THE next day, Monday, was a good fishing day, with warm sun and a quiet sea. The island fishing boats swooped out like a flock of birds to take advantage of it, for good days were scarce in the boisterous spring weather. Catches were profitable, too. But at Elbridge and Liseo's wharf, business was rotten. Some off-island boats stopped by to sell, as was their custom, so there was something. Fully three-quarters of the Chin Island boats, however, made the trip to the mainland and sold their hauls there, apparently rather than give their business to Elbridge and Liseo.

Elbridge, totting up the day's total, saw that it was smaller than any he remembered, even in times when fish were scarce and catches poor.

"Well," Liseo said wryly, glancing at the figures. "Blessed are the peacemakers."

Tuesday was no better, Wednesday worse. In the town, the row blossomed like a tree. Stell's crowd finished up their petition, mailed it to the rector in Port Western. On Thursday, several people, Liseo among them, went to the harbor post office for their mail, leaving instructions with Lombard not to send any more of it over to the island for Stell to mishandle.

"I'm sorry," Liseo said briefly to Elbridge.

"Gossip starting?" Elbridge asked soberly.

Liseo nodded. "Fanny's picked up a few whiffs," he said.

"Anybody'd know it's only gossip, Liseo."

"Anybody knows how I am about Rosie, too," Liseo said.

ON Saturday morning, to everyone's astonishment, Miss Greenwood went around to all the houses in town, saying she would like to conduct Sunday school in the schoolhouse. She didn't mean, she said, to conflict in any way with regular Sunday school, if it were to be held again in the old church, and so she was inviting the children to come on Saturday afternoon. This caused a great deal of comment, since it was not like anything Miss Greenwood had ever done before.

Taking sides, Carrie's faction said. Taking part. Well, didn't it beat all, wouldn't you think. An outsider like that, duffing in. But there, people living all soul alone got funny. In time, they went one way or they went another. Miss Greenwood was going one way—she was getting to be a religious maniac. *Their* children couldn't go, said Carrie's faction, and that was all there was to it, noticing all over town that Stell's crowd was pleased as could be.

They reckoned, however, without the children. So far back as any child there could remember, anything Miss Greenwood invited you to was sure to be fun. A chorus of disappointed howls went up, heard from one end of the village to the other, interspersed with the worried tones of mothers and fathers, discussing it pro and con. A few die-hards put down the foot hard, but as things turned out, most of the children went. Mothers in Stell's faction dressed up their children; other mothers said it wasn't Sunday and it wasn't church, let the kids go in their play clothes.

Anyone could have told, just by looking, Joyce thought, coming up to the schoolhouse door, which side you were on. She herself wasn't dressed up for church, but she had a clean dress and a new hair ribbon on. Some of the kids had on the old pants and sweaters they'd played in all Saturday morning in the spring mud, and Herbie Hitch-man had a cold and a lamb's leg that bobbled in and out of his nose as he breathed.

It was a lovely day. For a minute, Joyce regretted. Warm in the sun, and the air smelling clean, with that little, sharp remembrance of chill behind it, but far away, so that you didn't wear your cap, and your clothes felt prickly on you. Such a lovely day, and horrid, in a way, to be going to the old musty schoolhouse on a Saturday after-noon. But all the same, everyone wanted to go. Not the big boys, of course, they were all off and away somewhere; Will and Gib were down to the shore building traps. But the little kids and all the girls were there. Most of them. Some, of course, their mothers wouldn't let go.

Miss Greenwood stood by the schoolhouse door. She had a pack of paper napkins in her hand; as each hatless little girl came in, Miss Greenwood pinned a paper napkin to the top of her head, with a common pin. Nodding and smiling, greeting each one.

Was it to be a game? All the children had heard talk at home about the old-time religion as against this kind; was the new one this differ-ent, did you play *games?*

Miss Greenwood had put a lovely embroidered cloth over the teacher's desk, and a carved wooden cross and two candles, and some other little, pretty things that you didn't know what were. It changed the teacher's desk. You'd never know it for that banged-up old wooden thing Miss Warren sat to. It made you feel funny inside, almost the same, Joyce discovered, suddenly, as Miss Greenwood's Christmas tree made you feel—as if something mysterious and beau-tiful was about to happen.

Miss Greenwood stood in front of the rows of children sitting at the school desks, the little girls with the fluted white paper napkins nodding and bobbing, expectant, like a field of white butterflies.

She said, "It is out of respect for the house of the Lord that we cover our heads. Perhaps, next time, you will wish to wear your hats, but the napkins look very nice, so it does not matter. Now, when we come in, we kneel down, and this is the way we do; and then perhaps we can all talk together about the gentle Jesus."

PART FOUR
Spring

THE wind blew, the spring came; everywhere the wild apple trees flung out scarves dizzy and sweet with bloom. It was a country of apple trees, noticeable in spring, though much of the fruit was pig apples now, from blends of old varieties, whose seeds the crows had scattered all over the countryside in their ritual of fall.

Every place on the island had had its orchard, once upon a time planted and tended carefully, and a few people still took care of their trees—not many, for the trees were old now and it was less trouble, if you could, to buy apples, or, if you couldn't buy, to go without. On the abandoned farms, the spruces came in, first, through the orchards to close up around the barns and houses, sometimes nudging near enough to a window to shatter, on a windy night, an old and watery pane of glass.

As Little Sarah said, "When once those spruce seeds start to fly, you know well where they'll end up, sister and brother, in amongst your apple trees."

It was hard enough, when someone was living on a place, to keep an orchard clear.

All over the island the tame roots fought a choking battle with the wild ones—the leathery spruce thongs that, in a gone time, the Indians used for rope, that could split rock and did; that could suck substance out of granite to make green spike, gray bole, and stiff, prickly plume, and hurried, hurried, hurried to cover marks and scratches, to hide in a closed rank an open place where none was once and might not be again. The old apple trees gave up hard and slow. In the spruce forest, their rotted boles, set orderly, forty feet on the square and forty feet diagonal, still thrust out, here and there, a bough or two of bloom, flung high and unseen; so that a hunter in the thickets, stopped by a sweet, remembered smell, might look up and catch a glimpse, up there, of pink-and-white drowning in a softly closing sea of green.

"Nick Pumlow's old Bellflower tree," an older man might say. He would remember the flecked yellow skin of the big apple that fitted in his hand, the *crack* when a boy's teeth bit in, the lovely taste on the tongue.

"Wonder why there aren't any Bellflowers any more. You never see any, anywhere. And Nodheads and Tolman Sweets and Kings, too. And sometimes, even Northern Spies are hard to find. The old apples, they tasted good. Seems like the new kinds don't have that flavor any more. The kind you buy, I'd sooner eat a punkin. Wild apples all over the place, too, and all pig apples."

And the hunter would go on, to wherever he was going, seeing everywhere the young trees blooming out of thickets, above old stone walls, along the shore—the pig apples, valued by the crows, who flew off with them in the fall, looking funny with an apple speared on each bill, but as if they had great treasure, the way they went; the small, hard, sour pig apples, from the mingled pollen of uncared-for, untended bloom. Yes, it could truly be said, it was a country of apple trees.

IN the gray, lightening morning just before sunrise, Willard Lowden opened the door of the shack by the wharf and came out to his woodpile. He stood for a moment looking down at the water behind the breakwater and off over the bay, breathing in the quiet, estimating the weather.

The water was glassy calm, a kind of dark green, down in there by the wharf. It was low tide. He could smell rockweed and the clamflat smell that came up from under the pilings. The morning was cool, everything soaked and gray with dew, so still that he could hear the slow drops fall from the wet timbers under the wharf—*plop*, and then quiet, and then, in a minute, again, *plop*—and the sleepy *s-s-s* sound the barnacles and winkles made. The wind, if there were going to be any, would start after the sun rose, he guessed. It would be a few light puffs at first, skittering over the water, getting stronger with the sun, until by afternoon it might blow a good stout breeze from the southwest. That milkiness, low down on the horizon, probably meant fog sooner or later, it was hard to say. Whatever it was, by the time it came, Willard planned to be back at the wharf, his lobsters sold and his money in his pocket.

That firewood was wet with dew; better split some out of the heart, or he'd never get a fire going. He grinned to himself, grimly thinking what Harriet would have said, up at the house, if he'd ever let the wood box go, left the wood out so it was too wet to start a breakfast fire. Hell would have popped; after a while there would have been a good fire and a good breakfast, but nobody would have enjoyed it. Well, he was all through with that, now.

He went back into the shack with his arms full of the dry, split out of the middle of the stove-wood sticks, built himself a fine, hot fire in the stove, and cooked his breakfast.

This shack was the one that had belonged to Aunt Tilson Vira in the old days. It had once been considerably more than it was now. It had had four rooms, a kitchen, sitting room and two bedrooms, where Aunt Tilson and whatever outcasts she'd gathered up or befriended lived. These were usually girls from off-island that Aunt Tilson had run into in her travels—it had been her custom to pick up dunnage every fall and go south to work, she said in a hotel, though since she usually came back in the spring pretty well heeled, there were some who said, bound to, that it wasn't a hotel she worked in.

Anyway, she got a bad name, and stood up to it. She told the minister, once, that if he knew of a way for a lone woman to earn her living, she was waiting to entertain suggestions. For all anybody knew, she went on waiting to the end of her life, and bringing back from away girls who weren't any better than they ought to be. When Willard was a young fellow, just beginning to toot around, Aunt Tilson Vira's place, down here by the wharf, was quite a rig. He had come here himself, had even got quite interested in one of the girls, Mary Salveda, her name was.

Times going to bed here alone, he'd get to wondering what ever became of Mary Salveda. Gorry, she'd been a pretty girl. Pleasant, too, as anybody you'd want to meet, if you didn't know, of course, what she was. She'd had a wood's colt, didn't make any bones of saying so. It was with her folks, up Canada way somewhere. While Mary was out alone in the world, digging, she would say, to make a living.

"Digging, just digging," she would say, her mouth open in a square pink hole of laughter. "If you've got a round dollar in your pocket, boy, don't come near me, I'll have it for my wood's colt."

Well, of course, a decent man couldn't look more than twice, three times at the most, at a girl like that. But lying here, nights, at first it had been hard to go to sleep, a strange place and all, and brooding over how he'd happened to leave his home, the back bedroom where he'd slept all his life; most of his things up there, he hadn't brought much down here except his clothes, his bedding and his accordion, and he guessed George and Harriet would find out how it would be, getting along without him, supported them all his life.

Of course, he went up there every day to tend the horses and milk the cow, couldn't leave the horses to George, he didn't like animals; and neither George nor Harriet knew how to milk, never would learn. But he hadn't seen George and he hadn't seen Harriet for three weeks, not since he'd moved down here. Just went up to the barn and milked and left the full milk pail by the back door, and fed up and combed down the horses, old Bos'n and Matey, they were next to the only living critters on earth would miss him if he was to pass on this minute. And not sleeping, just lying there having it over, he would try to think about something else, make an effort. That was how he got to thinking about Mary Salveda.

It got so all he had to do when he blew out the lamp was to shut his eyes, and there would be this place all over again, even the rooms which were rotted off and fallen down now, just as it used to be—plum-colored plush sofa with carved legs, Aunt Tilson's stove red-hot in the chilly fall nights, and the pot of stew on back for any who wanted some, and a bottle of rum and a poker you could heat in the stove and stick into a mug of, if you liked rum hot—Willard didn't—and pink lawn curtains at the windows, the girls and the laughing and the sound of his accordion and his own voice singing, the way it was when he was a young fellow just beginning to toot around. Until Harriet found out, and made him stop coming here.

Well, that was the way it had been at first, when he moved down here. A man got lonesome, thought up a cure for it the best way he could. For all George hadn't been speaking to him all winter and Harriet had—God, had she!—and treating him rotten, not passing the food to him at meals, just to each other, taking all the best of it themselves and leaving the nape of the fish and the gristle of the meat for him; for all that, they'd been somebody in the house to come home to; it wasn't this blank, this stillness, where there was nobody.

Willard minded that. By the God, it seemed to him he couldn't stand it. Four walls and a fire, that was all he had now; and he a sociable man, liked to talk and have somebody listen, liked to say how he felt and have somebody say back that that was too bad,

Willard. But when it got so that the people you were closest to in the world, all you had, your own, acted like that, something had to come.

If that was the way they felt, after all he'd done for them, then they could go straight leaping to hell, for all he cared.

Some parts of being alone he kind of liked. For one thing, he could eat what he wanted to, didn't have to grab or George and Harriet would get the best. He couldn't cook the way Harriet could, of course, but most things didn't seem too hard to fix so they tasted good. Steak, now. You take steak. He dearly loved a good, thick tender one, held over the coals in the stove, black on the outside, red and juicy within. God, any man not a moron could fix a steak that way. Harriet wouldn't because she said it smoked up the kitchen, but George liked steak cut thin and fried dry as leather. Willard guessed that was why. Tough damn stuff, he'd just as soon eat a heel tap. Biscuits he couldn't make yet, but store bread was all right. Vegetables were easy—just boil till you could stick a fork in.

Seemed at first as if he couldn't get enough steak and boiled potatoes and yellow turnip. Had them four days running, and could have done it again, only it didn't seem right for a man's health. Eat, eat, eat, he must've gained ten pounds since he moved down here from the house.

For another thing, he could play and sing all he felt like, down here, nobody to say, "Shut up that caterwauling, for heaven's sake, Willard!" And for a third thing, he had a cat now. Harriet never would let him have a cat in the house, said they were nasty. Cleanest thing in the world, a lot more so than most humans, for his money.

Funny, about that little cat. He had found her on the bunk when he came in from lobstering one day about two weeks ago. No way to know how she got in. She was about half-grown, a black and white, long-haired female, with all four double paws, and her fur was a sight —matted up and stringy—and she had a sore foot, where somebody had either stepped on it or she'd got into a mink trap. It scared him a little, something alive in the shack when he'd come in—caught a movement out of the corner of his eye over on the bunk, brought him right up standing. He was dearly afraid of rats; in an old shack like this, a man never knew. But it wasn't a rat, it was this little cat, half-starved, and where she'd ever come from the Lord in his infinite mercy knew.

First thing was fix up that foot; she'd licked it as clean as she could, but it still had some dirt in it, a bad wound, the paw looked to be tattered. So he'd soaked it in Epsom salts—thank the Lord he'd remembered to bring his package of that—and put some Mack's All-Heal salve on it. You couldn't, of course, bandage up a cat. Then he'd cleaned her fur as well as he could, cut off a lot of the wuggets, fed her some milk and a hunk of fish, and put her back on the bunk.

In the morning he woke up to find her sitting on the pillow next to his head, her nose about half an inch from his, purring like a mill. She'd licked all the salve off of her paw, and for a while he had a bad time wondering if there'd been anything poison in it; but apparently there hadn't. She liked it, and the foot was starting to heal nice and clean.

He'd wondered all the next day, out fishing, if she'd still be there when he got in. She'd found the way into the shack, she must know how to get out; but at night, there she was, glad to see him. When she purred, it had a little catch in it, as if something went over a ratchet.

In a week's time, her fur began to look soft and pretty—part of that mess in it was winter coat she hadn't had the gumption, being half-starved, to get rid of. Nights when he got home, hauling traps all day from a skiff—and it was some hard to go back to hauling traps from a skiff after you'd been used to a powerboat, but, of course, George had the powerboat, didn't make any difference that three-quarters of it belonged to Willard, had a lot of his savings in it, George had it; and Willard be damned if he'd call it to George's attention, when George ought to, by the God, think of things like that for himself; anyway, Willard had the skiff, and he'd repainted it green all over, so that the whole town wasn't laughing their heads off about that half-red-half-green skiff—nights when he got home, tired, lonesome and wet, there Mary would be. It seemed kind of natural to call her Mary.

Well, there was one soul in the world gave a damn whether he got in all right, hadn't had an accident in that skiff and drowned outright, nobody would know for days if he did. He would come in and, first thing, give Mary her fish and the milk that he always brought a can of down from the barn now, before he even built his own fire and put the kettle on. Then he would sit down at the table—if you could call it a table, it was built out of boards and boxes, hell of a thing for a decent man to have to eat supper to—and turn out his pockets and count his money. *His* money, now, by the God, that he'd earnt from his day's haul, nobody to have to share it with, hand it over, you eat twice as much as either of us, you pay twice as much, or no supper.

After supper, and all cleaned up and shipshape—first, when he'd come, he hadn't give a hoot, let it go dirty, live like a pig, that was all they thought you were, treated you like one. But now Mary; and a cat was a clean thing, couldn't expect one to stay around a dirty place; so he'd given the whole shack a going-over, hoed out and scrubbed; and it was nice now, even smelt good, with his bunk made up and tucked in, the pink quilt from his bed up home on top.

That was a good warm quilt—the "sea quilt," the Lowden family'd always called it, because it was the one grandfather had taken in his chest to the Grand Banks, times he'd gone there with the fishing schooner. A good warm quilt, built long for a big man, he did hate bedding too short; and clean, too. You couldn't say of Harriet that she wasn't a good housekeeper. And them old-timers, decent, respectable people, what they would think to know that this good quilt had come to such a pass, the Lowden family fallen so low that one of them, one of the last of them, a man who was once the janitor of the church, had to live in a shack away from his own, a shack that was once a bad-house, they wouldn't sleep quiet in their graves, and not to blame.

But not to think about that any more, think about something else, make an effort. Because, if he didn't, that heavy grief would come over, like a tombstone, that feeling of all lost, everything gone; our folks that was once good people living in a white-painted house, and their keepsakes so old that nobody remembers now what they were kept for. Don't think, make an effort.

So after supper, Willard would lie on the bunk with his accordion on his chest and play and sing to Mary. She didn't like the accordion much, that is, if he played it too loud. But the songs she liked, some better than others.

"Let the lower lights be burning,
Send a gleam across the wave,"

she was real fond of, or seemed to be.

And lying there, the fire warm—that old range he'd salvaged out of the Cloud house and cleaned the rust out of and blacked up—that was a corker, a real old-time cook stove, with a reservoir for hot water and an oven a man could put his stocking feet into, if he wanted to; them old-timers, they made it real comfortable—lying there, resting, Mary sprawled out along his side, he playing and singing with no clack to stop him; his money, forty-four dollars and seventy-seven cents, now, in the baking powder can on the shelf, and the kerosene lamp burning on the table to light him, and the place neat and sweet-smelling; Willard would begin to feel good again, the way he hadn't for a long time; as if, some day, he might pull out of it, be a man again and not a mountain of misery.

Old songs came back to him he hadn't thought of for years; one night he thought of one really to sing to Mary, like as if it was her song.

"Black is the color," sang Willard, barely making heard the accompaniment on the accordion, so Mary'd be sure to like it. "Black is the color of my true love's hair."

This morning, he was part way through his breakfast—a good breakfast, the kind he liked, eggs and three-four thick slices of ham and bread and gravy and doughnuts, boughten doughnuts, of course, but still doughnuts, and coffee—before he noticed the folded paper somebody had slid under the crack in the door.

Why, walked right over that, times untold, this morning, and never seen it.

He leaned over and picked up the paper. It was from Harriet, he saw, her writing, the Palmer method she'd been so good at, better than him and George, when they were in school, on a folded piece of grocery-store paper bag. He thought, with a little jerk at his chest, well, they've come round, they want me back home now.

But the note said:

> "If you ain't going to put in towards running the house, you ain't got any right to steal the milk. I need all of it to make butter to sell so's George and I can get along. This is a fair warning. STAY AWAY FROM MY MILK, WILLARD P. LOWDEN."

ELBRIDGE stepped up on the rickety platform which made a sort of back porch to Willard's shack, and thumped with his boot toe on the door. Ordinarily, he wouldn't have knocked, nobody did hereabouts, but he had his hands full—in one, a crocus bag of turnips and in the other, a basket of cooked food that Jess had sent down.

"It won't do any good," he had said to Jess, when she suggested it. "The way Willard feels, he'll probably give it the heave-ho off the wharf."

"We can try," Jess said. "At least, we can make the motion."

For three weeks, she had watched Willard go stumping up past the house each day, headed for the Lowden barn, and then, an hour or so later, stumping back, looking neither to right nor left, speaking to nobody, a can of milk clutched in his hand. She supposed what he thought he was giving off was righteous anger, but actually, lonesomeness was sticking out all over him.

It seemed awful to Jess, much the worst of all the foolish squabbles which had racked the town. That old, tumble-down place, it must be horrible inside, damp and buggy, unlived in for all those years, for a man like Willard, too, who had a decent home, one he'd taken pains to keep up. It had always been Willard who put on coats of paint, fixed gutters, replaced shingles. He was a man who liked a house, respected its needs; at least, it had always seemed so.

"You take him a peck of turnips," Jess said.

"Why?" Elbridge asked, surprised.

"He likes turnip. I've heard Harriet complain she can't fill him up on mashed turnip," Jess said. "Nor does she try."

Her voice took on the dry, bitter, metallic clack that was Harriet's tone of complaint, and Elbridge stopped in his tracks.

"Godfrey! Don't do that," he said. "Not you. It gives me fur on my tongue."

Jess smiled at him. "Well, that's why turnips," she said.

"This is the whole of them," he said, grinning at her as he brought the bag up from the root cellar. "Not that I can't do without, myself."

He wouldn't care if he never saw another mashed turnip, but Jess and the kids liked them; and the root cellar, this time of year, was beginning to look empty. There was always a period, from late spring until the garden began to yield, when last fall's vegetables were gone and Jess's shelves of preserves were bare.

"I doubt if we go hungry," Jess said dryly. "If I run out of a vegetable, there's always dandelion greens."

"Pu!" Elbridge said. "And that's the *last* thing."

Not that he hadn't eaten plenty, in his time. Little Sarah had always believed in dandelion greens for her family's health in the spring. Sulphur and molasses and dandelion greens. Elbridge, remembering what the combination had used to do to him, felt his insides give a slight, premonitory roll. "You think I need a dost?" he asked, grinning.

"The whole town needs one," Jess said, grimly. "A good physicking would at least give everyone something to think about."

"Maybe."

She stood holding the ample basket of food she had packed for Willard, watching him while he buttoned his work frock, put on his cap. He seemed to have grown older this spring, and soberer, his laugh less frequent, the lines deepened around his mouth and eyes. The town row had cut drastically into Elbridge's business. Men who had dealt with him and Liseo for years were now taking their trade to the mainland, buying equipment over there, too, and going in debt to the mainland dealers, while a good many hadn't yet paid for last year's gear. This meant that, with new debts to meet, they probably never would; and there were two thousand dollars still left on Elbridge's books, which ordinarily would have been paid off by now, with the spring fishing. Jess knew this.

She smiled at him as he reached for the basket, lifting her face for his kiss.

"I shouldn't have," she said. "But I got to thinking about Willard."

"Sure," Elbridge said heartily. "Of course you should have, if you want to. We've got enough. Plenty. Don't need to worry yet awhile about eating, or go up and try to mine the gold out of the vein."

Jess drew in her breath. It had been years since anybody had mentioned the gold mine. In the old days, when times got hard, that was what the joke was—go up and haul what gold you need out of the mine. The mine that wasn't a mine and didn't have any gold in it.

"If we need to," she said stoutly. "We've seen hard times before, Elbridge. Weathered them, too." She grinned at him. "You like pigweed greens," she said. "It doesn't have to be dandelion."

"Not yet."

"And it wouldn't be the first time that folks here have had to live off the land. Lived decently off it, too. Laughed about it. Oh, Elbridge, I know you can't stop worrying, honey, but I—miss you."

"Good Lord!" he said, stricken. "Am I that bad?"

He set the basket on the floor and put both arms around Jess.

"Times before we've mentioned the mine, we've laughed," she said, her voice muffled against his coat.

"Lordsake, and will again. It isn't so much the tough going, Jess, we'll be all right, we know that. It's the foolishness that's causing it. I know I'm glum, I'm sorry. But I feel as if I were wading a tank of molasses."

"I know," she said. "One foot gets sticky while you pull the other one out."

"M'm."

He pressed his chin against the top of her hair, moved away and sat down in a chair by the kitchen table.

"Look," he said. "The way it is, the whole system here is balanced on a pin. As long as we trade with each other, take in each other's

washing, like, we're all right, we can get by. But now, half the trade's
going off-island. Stell's in trouble—her store's not earning peanuts.
Carrie's crowd won't buy their groceries from her, they go to the har-
bor. Go to all that trouble, just for the sake of the grudge. Besides, the
Post Office inspector was here—"

"He was?" Jess leaned back, her concerned eyes, seeking his.

"Oh, she got away with it," Elbridge said. "She told the inspector
that she was all stuffed up with Sears and Roebuck catalogs, and in
the melee some letters fell into the table drawer, accidentally got
held up."

"She didn't deserve to get away with it."

"No. It was her word against Liseo's," he went on glumly. "I
couldn't see my way clear to back up the complaint. There's a lot of
things to think of. Do we want a post office here, or don't we? There
isn't another soul would take it over. Besides, if Stell goes under, what
about Luther? I told Liseo all that."

"He couldn't see it?"

"He could see it, but he's a fire-eater when he's mad. And anything
to do with Rosie—what's happened, somebody's started talk about
Rosie, her and the Farleigh kid, over on the mainland. Nothing in it.
Liseo says it's stuff Stell gleaned out of Rosie's letters and twisted
the facts around."

Jess's eyes sparkled with anger. "To start talk like that, about a
nice kid," she said. "Oh, Elbridge! No wonder Roger's letters have
sounded so blue."

Elbridge nodded. "He's probably all backed up. Hurt and mad,
can't write any of it home, because we told him to be careful what
he put into his letters. First chance I get, I'll go over and see him."

"Maybe we'd both better go."

"Sure, be a good idea." He hesitated. "Liseo and I've been kind of
holding off on the trip until we get a load for the *Daisy*," he said.

Oh, dear, Jess thought.

Time was when the *Daisy*, fully loaded, made the trip to the main-
land every day.

"We're hustling to rig up a string of lobster traps, too," he said,
and at her startled glance, he went on, "No, it's not that bad, really;
but we've got spare time now, we need extra cash to meet payments
on the bills, and neither one of us wants to sit around doing nothing,
waiting for people to get over the sulks. Traps don't cost us anything
—we've got all that gear lying around the building that nobody's buy-
ing. Figured we'd build it into traps, maybe use 'em. If business picks

up, we can always sell 'em. Scrape some barnacles off us both," he said, meeting her concerned eyes, "to get outside and pound around in the *Daisy* awhile every day."

"People owe you money," Jess said. "They ought to be made to pay it."

"Liseo and I could go to law," Elbridge said. "We could probably collect, some. And that would leave most people without a pot to put pea soup in. So far, we haven't done anything that people'll really remember—Lord, Jess, a couple of hijinks that went sour at a church supper, at a time when everybody was tired and discouraged, and not much of interest coming up till spring! If the devil hadn't come also, that would have all been laughed off, nobody would have cared a hoot. But lawsuits, by the Judas, would put up a monument to Liseo and me that nobody would forget to his dying day. So we talked it over. Sit tight; raise cash where we can. And that means go lobstering awhile, and Liseo's roaring to get the traps in the water before shedding season. That's why I was kind of putting off making an extra trip to the mainland, but we could go any time, if you think Roger needs a boost."

"You could use the backlog," Jess said thoughtfully.

"We talked that over, too. We could, and would, if worse came to worst. But that was put by for the kids, Lord knows, it isn't much, but it'll help, when they want to get married, and I don't imagine—" he grinned slightly—"I don't imagine, the way Roger and Rosie feel about each other, they'll want to wait much longer than you and I did, when we were that age, do you?"

"Well, I'm not too sure. They've got terrific plans—a lot more than we had."

"Not more, I guess," Elbridge said. "Different, maybe. They're different kids, you know that, Jess? Different kids in a different time."

"Better?"

He shook his head. "Neither better nor worse." He stopped a moment, thinking. "More complicated, maybe, because the times are. You know, they must know none of us would swallow any of Stell's squash blossoms."

"Of course they must."

"Liseo was all for rushing hot-foot right over there, make a touse—you know how he is about Rosie. But I was thinking, if we don't make too much of it, let the kids and everybody else think it's rolled right off of us, the whole thing would blow over. God knows, it's too damned ridiculous to do anything else."

"I could write Roger a long letter, do it up inside a package of fudge," Jess said, and seeing him hesitate, she went on indignantly, "That Stell! Somebody ought to *kill* her!"

"Well, she never should have had a thing like the post office to batten on. But it's hard to know what to do. There's Luther. God knows, he's never been much, an old blowhard, but he did a job of work in his time. He wouldn't deserve what would happen to him. He's too old." He stopped. "I got to thinking what MacKechnie would do."

"You know what MacKechnie would do."

"Yup. He'd sail in, hammer and tongs, have Stell fired, clean up the mess, and go on from there, hell tooting. I'd like to, God knows, but it isn't as simple as that. Not now. MacKechnie had something to draw on. He had a town behind him, for one thing, and he had town funds. I've got neither. And besides, I'm not MacKechnie. My name's Gilman, and there's a whole lot of Ansel Gilman bumbling around inside of me."

Jess said, "And I'm pretty glad there is, Elbridge."

"Well, times, it's a devilish nuisance. No one would be gladder than I would to sail in with both fists, and—"

There was a short silence.

Elbridge quoted thoughtfully, " 'We had a bloody fight today, Rocco and Jarvis pounding each other groggy over a jackknife. I separated them, but the fight goes on in each man's mind. Sometimes I think it is not the forces of Nature we have so much to fear, but the ill-will over little things that breaks out of even good Christian men.' "

"Did Ansel say that?" Jess asked, looking at him, impressed.

"Page 94, Volume 1. 1856. Oh, they had it early. It's nothing new. Only in those days, maybe they could afford it. We're too shaky, these times, to have it turn out anything but hell."

Elbridge got up, picked up the basket by its handle. "For a man that lugs bake goods and cats around as much as I do," he said, grinning, "you'd think I'd be a little mite more popular."

"Cats? Besides Richard?"

"Sure. Liseo and I took Willard a cat the other day. Little black and white stray, with a busted paw. It appeared at the wharf from God knows where, maybe somebody'd been abusing it, I don't know. Anyway, we shooed it into Willard's cabin, and I guess he opened his heart to it, I saw it around there yesterday, perky as a chickadee.

Lord, Jess, if I could tell you how much better talking things over with you makes me feel!"

He kissed her again, and then went out the door, carrying the basket and the crocus bag.

Jess watched him go out of sight down the hill. She started to cry, but from the bedroom, she could hear the bumps and rattlings around, where the kids were getting up. No sense taking the joy out of life for them. They sounded like the fun and the happiness of the world in there. So she mopped at her tears and started getting their breakfast.

Will came through the door, knuckling his eyes, and made for the washbasin, and from behind him came a howl of righteous wrath, from a virtuous boy put upon. Gib, undressed, bounced into the kitchen.

"Ma, Will's got on my new underdrawers! Make him—"

"Don't you boys fight!" Jess burst out. "Don't you dare! If you do, I'll tan you both, big as you are!"

She glanced around and saw at once their startled, astonished faces. "Oh, shoot!" she said, laughing. "Have you got on his drawers, Will, and if he has, Gib, do you honestly care?"

"Well, I guess I have," Will said. "But it was a mistake. I got all dressed before I saw it. Take mine, Gib, can't you? They're all alike. I hate to get undressed again."

"Sure," Gib said. "You didn't say you had a pair of clean ones, that's all."

As Elbridge stepped up on Willard's back porch, he heard Willard say in a choked voice, "Who is it?"

"Me," Elbridge said.

He waited, but there was no answer. After a moment, he put down the crocus bag and opened the door. Willard was sitting at his breakfast table, a piece of brown paper clutched in one hand. His eyes, Elbridge saw, had a wild look, the lids skinned back over the whites; his gaze darted here and there about the room, fixing on anything but Elbridge.

Oh-oh, Elbridge thought. Wrong time for sure. But he went on in, carrying his basket.

"Say," he said, glancing admiringly around the small, neat room. "You've worked wonders with this place, Willard. Got it real nice in here."

"No skin off you, is it?"

"Nope."

"Well, what you shoving in here for then?"

"Jess sent you down some baked stuff."

"What for?"

"Why, thought you might like a change, I guess. Lordsake, Wid." Elbridge grinned at him, finding it hard to do in the face of that darting, stony gaze. "What does any woman send stuff around to the neighbors for? You tell me. Wants to show off her cooking, I don't know. You know how the womenfolks are."

"Yes," Willard said. "I know how they are, all right."

He looked down at the crumpled paper in his hand. "I don't want anything to do with any of them. I can cook my own stuff. You can take yours and eat it or shove it, I don't care."

"All right." Elbridge felt the red coming up in his face, but went on, carefully keeping his voice from rising. It was hard to do; he had to work at it. "What ails you, Willard? What's come over you, boy?"

Willard began to get to his feet. It was a ponderous business; Willard was fatter than he had ever been, Elbridge saw, watching the tremors of the big body, the legs scrabbling to get under the weight. He watched Willard come, thinking, I've done the wrong thing and now I've got to be sure he doesn't get his hands on me; but Willard merely thrust the paper, crumpled in his fist, into Elbridge's face. In spite of himself, Elbridge backed up a foot at the sight of the big fist coming.

"Look," Willard bawled suddenly. "That's my sister for you! That's the last of the Lowdens for you! Look what she wrote me, didn't dare to say to my face, got George to shove it under the door. Well, read it! Dammit, read it!"

"Hold it still," Elbridge said. He tried to focus on the paper, found his head swiveling up and down. "Hold it still, goddammit! You're wringing my neck. Oh. Godfrey mighty, Willard, that's too bad. She's in an awful pucker."

"Pucker! You call that a pucker? I go up there twice a day, milk that cow. All I bring back is a quart. Don't even drink it myself, give it to my cat. By the God, that Harriet! Bone selfish, she is. She never thought of anybody but herself all her life, never done nothing to help nobody. Pass the fish to George, leave the nape for me. Eat the chops, leave the bones. I eat too much, says, bones is all I can have. I don't like the nape, Elbridge, the nape of a fish is the last thing God ever made. A man can't—"

His troubles came rushing out of Willard. Backed up so long, mulled over, stewed and steaming, with the dead weight behind them of Willard's hurt feelings, they poured like water; everything came. It took him upwards of half an hour to cover the whole situation.

Elbridge stood for a while, then he eased over to Willard's bunk and sat down, might as well; the little black cat tentatively pushed against his elbow and, finding no resistance, crept on to his knees and curled up to sleep, while above her peaceful head beat the malice, hatred and ill-will, the child's hurts, the little spats of small brothers and sisters stretched back through the years, as if on never-severed strings that grew strong and tangled as a ball of snakes; the yapping of the ten-year-old whose sister pushed him become the steady, grouching complaint of the maimed grown man, whose sister, still pushing him, was now the world.

Appalled and shaken, Elbridge listened, feeling the warm, relaxed weight of the cat on his lap, tangling his fingers absently in her silky fur. He lost track of Willard's discourse—no one could have kept up with the incoherence for long. Instead, a yellowed page of a notebook, covered with old-fashioned writing, kept coming before his mind's eye. His freaky memory again; and could be, this time, there was reason for it.

"It is lonesome, yes. But so is any wild place and I have seen plenty of those. I cannot help but see how foolish I am to feel this lonesome has anything behind it. A place is a place, no more than that. A man can do his work anywhere. But remembered when small, a time when I was stealing apples and looked up to see a hairy head poked out of the bushes. It was only Old Ellick, he owned the orchard, a neighbor who never hurt anyone, nobody to be scared of. Yet, all of a sudden, what there was in the world to be afraid of, hidden but not seen . . . now was here. The old wild, the come-to-get-you."

Not the place; there was nothing in places for a man to fear. The natural disasters—two storms meeting overhead and bashing it out together, lightning striking, the sea rolling up to drown—were land and sea and sky and weather, minding their own business. They were what a man coped with the best he could, but not afraid so much as watchful. Death in its own good time; but in between, breakfast and birds' nests, the buds on the trees, apples and sunsets; grass with dew on it, a winter overcoat, a man's wife and his children, spring coming and fall-turned leaves, a hot buttered rum on a cold night, and clean spruce chips and clam chowder and snow. Not the place, or the dark, or the nightmare of the bears' woods; but the malice, the ill-will, the rancor, running like pus out of the minds of men.

Elbridge said, "You ought to get right away from it, Willard. Take out and go."

And Willard, who had been running down, started up all over again. "Goddammit, I don't want to go anywhere. Them things up there to the house, they belong to me as much as to George and Harriet. By God, they'll find out who's right, they'll come on bended knee—"

"Take a trip, then. That girl you tell about, try to hunt her up, she might be around somewhere. Get your mind off George and Harriet, for a while. They might come around, when they find you've really gone."

"That girl? That Mary? Why, she was a—" Willard brought up short. "Who'd milk?"

"Why, I and the kids could do that, be glad to help out, at least till George learns how."

Willard regarded him stonily. "You want to get rid of me, just like everybody else does."

"No, I don't. I'd miss you. Besides, we need you back as janitor, say we can get the church going again. Nobody else would take the pains you do."

"You never said so, time I cracked the hearth."

"I said then, and you heard me, that it was a good idea to put the fire out."

"I wouldn't go back if they was to beg me. To hell with it."

Elbridge got up. He put the cat carefully down on the bunk, saw her stretch and roll over, peacefully purring.

"You take a trip, see if you don't feel better. You can't believe in anybody's good intentions, Wid, feeling the way you do. Come up and see Jess and me some evening, bring your accordion, why don't you?"

He went out and down to his office on the wharf, where he got out his ledgers and began figuring out how much he and Liseo could spare to meet the demands of the wholesale supply houses, who, and not to be blamed, wanted their money.

Later, going home, he saw lying below the wharf, on the sand where Willard had flung it, the mince pie, tin and all, which Jess had sent down.

Well, that's that, he thought, and clambered down the ladder to salvage the tin. It was one of Jess's good ones; she'd want it back. He washed it out at the edge of water, carefully dumping out the soggy remains of the pie. No use to let Jess find out.

"What damned foolishness!" he said aloud, going back up the wharf.

Stick your nose into somebody's business, get just about what you asked for. A fight was like a teeter-board; you hurt somebody and you went up; they hurt you back, and you went down. It got going faster and faster, winding up tighter and tighter, until what you saw everywhere was ill-will; and you no longer wished for things to be righted, but for yourself to be appeased, to be in the acknowledged right of it, for Harriet and George, for the world, to come on bended knee.

Willard had, indeed, thrown away the pie. He wasn't too crazy, anyway, about mince pie, and throwing it away had helped his feelings.

Let them all, any of them, try to get rid of him!

But the cupcakes and the cookies and the doughnuts looked so good to him that he tried one and was lost; and sat down to them, with a big pot of coffee, and ate them all.

ALL through the spring, as always, the alder swamp had held back, as if winter and silence had become a habit not to be broken. Late April had found the twigs still bare, still turning red in wet weather, and in deep-shaded places, the snow still thick, as if it might not melt all summer. Yet as far back as January 20, Little Sarah had noted signs of change. You could see it, Miss Greenwood said, on the day after the winter solstice, December 21, if you knew what signs to look for—the year, going away, grinding slowly into reverse, turning, to come back again, gathering forces, bringing spring. Little Sarah guessed she didn't know the signs, not in December, anyway, not this past December. It had been a real old-timer. She wrote it down in her Line-A-Day: "December 21. A Real Old-Timer. Big Snowstorm. Thermometer down to 20 below."

She guessed that if Miss Greenwood could find signs of spring on that day, it was because she knew already that December 21 was the low point, the shortest day, and that after that the sun turned north again; and she guessed, anyway, that you found, with most things, about what you wanted to look for.

But on January 20, Little Sarah had gone for a walk along the causeway and found, in the swamp, the trees full of chickadees. She wrote that down, too: "January 20. Woods full of chickadees."

Oh, the chickadees were around all winter, but Little Sarah hadn't noticed them much; anyway, not popping out of the twigs as if they found life pleasant, and making those three or four little trickles of notes, careless-like, as if dropped in passing.

Little Sarah had kept the Line-A-Day for ten years, ever since she and Miss Greenwood had begun to look at birds and such things together. It was pleasant to have a record to glance back over—of unusual things, like the time you saw a robin in January, or what day the first white violet, which days in winter had been stormy, which clear. Such things, for ten years' time; but for ten years only, because further back than that Little Sarah did not wish to go.

Oh, things about the children she remembered—Ralph, dead in the war, and Elbridge's marriage to Jess, the births of grandchildren, the childhood of Roger, who was the light of her heart. But for the black days after Malcolm's going—times when all she had lived on was the hope, alive and moving within her almost like a child, that he would come back, dying hard; so that when it was dead it had to stay so, unless she too died or went crazy—for those times, bury them deep, let them stay deep; for them, if you wanted to remember, you wouldn't look in a Line-A-Day, nor need to. And you must not remember, not while you rebuilt your life, painfully, step-forward-step-back, around the children, around chicks hatching, around the garden, the flowers, the leaves on the trees, the herbs of the swamp, the birds, the weather—the things of every day.

Little Sarah did not know when the change began to come; it took a long time. At first, keeping the Line-A-Day, never did she write down "song sparrow," because that was the sound in the woods that Malcolm liked.

"Hear the cunning little devils," he would say. "Listen, Little Sarah, honey. Isn't that some cussed pretty!"

So not "song sparrow." Until one spring, not too long ago, she found she had written, without thinking:

March 22. First Robin.
March 24. Heard a song sparrow.

And then she thought, and found that Malcolm was indeed gone, so far away she could not recall his face, nor his young, urgent arms around her, his voice saying, "Oh, Little Sarah, honey. I'll find it. Let me hunt. Let me look for it a while longer. I'll find it, I swear I will. And then—and then—"

Not even the turn of a head, the quirk of a worried grin, the echo of a voice receding down the years; gone away.

This was the roster of Little Sarah's days, recorded in the seventieth year of the town her father built, the sixty-eighth year of her age. She told herself she was happity-hazard about it, but no time to write down every day:

February 24. A thaw. Like a spring day. Snowdrops out.

March 29. Some phoebes. Many robins.

April 1. Snowdrops going by. Crocuses showing color. One daff. budded. A strange bird song in the swamp. M. G. says might be migrating mocking bird.

April 2. A cold snap. 18–12 degrees.

April 8. Big flight of grosbeaks. They are in the spruces, tearing cones apart. Makes a pattering like rain, the pieces falling through the tree.

April 11. A day of hard rain—cold. But at ten o'clock at night, the first peeper.

April 13. Two cranes in the swamp pond. The fish hawk's back.

April 14. Snow, for godsake.

April 15. Paper says 40,000 wild geese in Merrymeeting Bay. If I was the birds, I'd go back south.

April 16. Old red hen hatched her chicks—3 pulls., 4 roos.

April 26. White-throated sparrows, "sampeabodying" all over the swamp. That deer is eating anything green that shows up in M. G.'s garden. I told her she hadn't ought to toll him up around the house. When I was to the harbor the other day, I got some blood meal to put around, to hold him off. She says it is mean to "repel" him.

April 28. But it doesn't repel him. He ate half her daffs.

May 1. Willard plowed my garden. Put in peas. Says he heard a whippoorwill at 4 A.M. I, a hermit thrush.

May 2. Planted sweet peas, (cupids).

May 7. Planted veg. garden. Too early, but good weather. So, had to try it. I'll be sorry.

May 11. It snowed. Melted that night. I'm sorry.

May 15. Planted sweet alyssum, calendulas, set out asters. Lilacs budded, but it is a late spring.

May 20. The swamp is not beginning to green up much, M. G. says behind the pond there is still quite a lot of old snow.

M. G., who was Miss Greenwood, went into the swamp, now and again, after baskets of leafmold from alder leaves, which she said was good for lettuce. This had worried Little Sarah, at first, the swamp being so treacherous with boiling springs, one of the places where menfolks cautioned women and children not to go, though what the menfolks' minds didn't know their hearts wouldn't grieve over.

Little Sarah, herself, had made most of her living out of the swamp, for years, gathering medicinal herbs and roots, spruce gum and bark. Some of these she made into home remedies, dispensing harmless and healthful tonics, diuretics and such, among the neighbors; but the bulk of them she shipped to a wholesale drug concern in Boston. She was skillful at digging and drying and she prepared first-class material, and the owner of the drug concern, an old gentleman, with an old-fashioned fussiness about the sources and purity of raw materials, bought everything she sent him and ordered more. He had been a summer visitor to the island for many years, and came, each summer, with a long list.

Roger, as a small boy, had tagged at her heels, fascinated with all the woods-roaming, gathering, stripping, drying and packaging processes; she didn't doubt that the fun they'd had in those early days, not to speak of what he'd learned, had quite a bit to do with his wanting to be a druggist now. Now, of course, that he was really learning to be one, he poked a gentle fun at some of her remedies. "Wild cherry tree *bark*, Little Sarah!" he would say. "It hasn't any *known* healing properties at all! It says so in the pharmacopoeia!"

And Little Sarah would smile, knowing that more cures could be made with wild cherry tree bark, just because people thought they could, than with a lot of other medicines.

So she went into the swamp, often, for a good many things, whenever she needed blue flag rhizomes for somebody's jaundice, or goldthread for a sore throat, or two-eyed plums, which Miss Greenwood called partridge berry, or smallage for gas on the stomach. "Smellage," Big Sarah had used to call that, when she grew it in her garden.

Smallage had somehow escaped from Big Sarah's garden and grew, now, in a sunny, rich, moist place in the swamp. This was a wonder to Little Sarah. She figured that the birds, who doubtless, at times, might have gas on their stomachs, too, had dropped the seeds, times ago, and she wondered how on earth smallage seeds had managed to grow by themselves, and in such a place as the swamp; it was a seventh wonder, without rhyme or reason. She herself had tried to grow the seeds in her own garden, but no luck, too dry. Of course, Big Sarah, who herself had been a seventh wonder with plants, had always said "smellage" was a chancy thing. There in the swamp the big plants grew, some of them seven feet high, seeding themselves, it must be, liked the wet.

Little Sarah had found a place, years ago, where the causeway stones made almost natural steps down; she knew that if you picked your way carefully across the hard, where the tree roots were, you could find solid footing in the swamp. As for the menfolks, anything they thought they might have to bother about, such as children and women going into the swamp and getting lost and having to be hunted for, why, the menfolks made out worse than it was, good and dangerous. On such things, their advice was not to be relied on; you took what of it you could use and let go the rest. But the swamp was not a place to take casually; she cautioned Miss Greenwood.

"Oh, I tittup," Miss Greenwood said. She laughed. "I'm so light that I go right across the top of the moss and don't sink in, just the way I travel on snow, Mrs. Gilman. And I do need the leafmold."

Little Sarah guessed she did. With the gardening problem M. G. had on those ledges, she needed everything. And whatever she put with that swamp leafmold, she grew the best lettuce Little Sarah ever saw.

Coming home with a full basket, on the afternoon of the third of June, Little Sarah saw that overnight—almost within a part of one day, for she had not specially noticed it that morning—the alder swamp had stopped holding back. She had been down into the swamp after goldthread a little earlier than she'd planned to go this spring, because today she'd had a note from Roger saying: "Little Sarah, please come over to the harbor. I have to talk to you." The note had not come in the mail, Bill Lessaro had brought it, sealed in a plain envelope, so Little Sarah guessed that Roger had something pretty important and private on his mind. She didn't believe that Stell, now, would dare to bother people's letters any more; nonetheless, everybody was careful what they put in the mail. Roger was, anyway, and Little Sarah planned to go with the mail boat tomorrow. So she'd gone after goldthread today.

In a place she knew, she had found plenty, and she thought, I ought to tarry and fill up the basket with some other things; but on the way, she had chanced on a tremendous bank blue with long-stemmed violets, and had filled her basket with those. She knew she oughtn't to waste time so, but lots of people liked a bunch of violets. Old Luther MacGimsey might like some, seeing he couldn't get outdoors this spring; and take some to Roger tomorrow, he couldn't get outdoors, either. He'd laugh at her, bringing him violets, but he'd

like them all the same. A lot of people thought that boys and men-
folks didn't care for the pretty; Little Sarah knew better.

She stepped up on to the causeway, above the pond, and saw that,
almost within hours, the green had come—the rich, brilliant, electric
emerald, with the sun pouring down through it, making like a mist
of green, so strong that you could smell it, taste it in the air, and the
water of the pond white with petals where the wild pear blooms were
falling.

ROGER met Little Sarah at the mail boat the next morning, all
dressed up in his best suit, with a fresh haircut and a blue bow tie,
much to the puzzlement of Orin Vira, who didn't see how Roger'd
known she was coming off-island that day.

"You're up with the birds," Orin said. "One of them must've brought
you word from your gra'mother." He was about to say further that
there hadn't been any letter from her to Roger in the mail, then de-
cided not to mention it. People were kind of sensitive, nowadays,
about their mail.

"I sent word off yesterday morning by Bill," Little Sarah said
laconically. "No sense to waste a stamp, Orin, when I didn't need to."

Well, that explained it, then. All the way over in the boat, Orin
had felt about busted, wondering what Little Sarah was coming off-
island for, carrying a basket of some kind of stuff; not that she didn't
come sometimes, but usually she wrote ahead, so that he knew be-
forehand what to expect, and could say to Lombard or Stell, "See
Little Sarah's writ to Roger. Must be going over to see him."

Orin filed away the comment about the stamp—it would make an
item to chuckle over—everybody knew Little Sarah was tighter than
a tick, never wasted so much as a potato peeling; she must have the
first quarter she ever got laid away somewhere, probably the eagle on
it squat lopsided, where she'd held onto it; and, by gorry, wouldn't
you like to have what Little Sarah's got in her sock, everything old
MacKechnie must've left and then some.

"You fellers going somewhere? You're all dressed up," Orin said,
but Little Sarah answered only, "I expect to spend most of the day
off here, Orin. If you can't come and get me, along towards night,
will you tell Elbridge to?" and then she and Roger were already half-
way up the gangway of the wharf, out of earshot.

Well, there! Orin thought, irritably. Them Gilmans is close-
moutheder than turtles. I'm a good mind to charge her what I charge
the summer people for an extra trip. Something's up, all right. That

boy may have on his Sunday pants, but he looks like something come out from under a stump in the spring.

He questioned Lombard at the post office, but Lombard hadn't heard a thing new.

Of course, any young feller was liable to look pindling after a dost of girl-trouble, he said, and he guessed Roger'd had plenty, the rig Liseo MacGimsey's girl had run all winter, round to the dances and the basketball games and the roller rink. Somebody ought to paddle her bottom and send her home to help her mother, where she belonged. It was all dang foolishness to send girls to the high school, anyway, when, you take a woman, you couldn't learn her nothing, only one thing. She didn't even have decent manners, that Rosie, they wan't learnt to her, laugh right in your face, liable to, and Liseo'd better limber up a check-rein, if he didn't want to be head cahoot at a shotgun wedding one of these days.

"Well, that's too bad, she was always a pretty nice girl before she come over here," Orin said, shaking his head mournfully.

"Now, you look-a here, be dang if that don't touch me up!" Lombard said. He put the mail right down and stuck his nose out through the wicket. "Anything she got, she got right to home, she brung it with her, and from all we hear about Chin Island, plenty to bring. My Lord, fights and battles, and beat up the minister so the poor feller was limping around here for a week! If you bring up a kid amongst the savages and the monkeys and then send her over to live with decent folks, what do you expect but tail feathers a-flying, but don't you lay it onto the harbor, Orin!"

"By the gorry," Orin said. "You come out from behind that wicket and say that, Lombard! That there is the kind of a bald-faced lie that I am sick and tired of listening to. Come on!" he howled. "Come right out here into the middle of this post office floor, and I'll be pleased to ram that right back down your throat, where it belongs!"

"Eigh?" Lombard said, astounded.

He had no way of knowing the state of Orin's, or nearly any other Chin Islander's, nerves, these days. He stood frozen at the wicket, staring at Orin, who never in his life had he heard blow up this way.

"By God, I wisht I was the mailman in the Artic!" Orin said. "I hate fights and I hate battles, and the last one I had, knockdown and dragout, was with Jack Shepheard when we was ten years old in the grammar school, over who put a angleworm in my jelly sandwich. But by gorry, I'm working up! I'm working up, Lombard, and you take that back about the monkeys and the minister and Rosie

MacGimsey, or else you git your nose in out-sight where I can't git a-holt of it!"

Lombard hastily withdrew his nose. Standing a safe foot back from the wicket, he said cautiously, "Wan't so about the minister, then? Way I heard it—"

"The way you heard it was wrong, and you know it!" Orin said. "Nobody laid a finger on the minister. And you can start circulating it, Lombard. You hear me? I want to hear you start circulating it, right here in this post office. By the jumped-up, pink-whiskered old godfrey mighty, if you don't, I'll either yank you around myself, or I'll go tell Liseo MacGimsey what you've been peddling about his girl!"

"Well, gorry," Lombard said. "Well, gorry, Orin. Wouldn't want to start no stories around town that ain't so. You know that. I've seen that girl to the dances, even asked her to dance, and she wouldn't, too busy playing the high-school field. Way I heard it, she was two-timing Roger with the Farleigh boy, but now wait, now wait, hold on, Orin, young Joe come out yesterday that he was engaged to My-ron's girl, that Helen. Wan't a word of truth in the gossip, I'm glad to be able to say."

Orin stood blowing into his mustache, which felt hot on his lip, so that it stood out almost at right angles to his face.

Monkeys and savages! Beat up the minister! Why, with Lombard peddling that, it was probably all over the county by now, when everybody ought to know that Chin Island was a decent, nice place, always had been, where decent, nice people lived. Well, it was this cussed town row, it had got around into the gossip, people stretching things, saying a lot of stuff that wasn't so.

Orin felt some old ashamed. He said, "Gi'me the mail, Lombard, you ought to realize I've got a schedule to keep," and stomped out of the post office with it, huffing and puffing.

Might feel a little better for blowing off steam, he thought, but he still wished, by the old holey, that he was the mailman in the Artic.

ROGER had Mr. Caddell's Buick parked up near the head of the wharf. "Hop in," he invited his grandmother. "I've got the day off," he said. "Going for a ride."

Little Sarah looked at the car doubtfully. It was not the time, that was clear, to say that she hated automobiles, would rather ride with the-devil-a-witch-and-a-gale-of-wind. She had, of course, had rides before, enough to know how she felt about sailing along with everything going by you whippety-whip, no time to stop and look at anything. When she came to town, she liked to *see* things; she did dislike anything hustled, too fast, too windy.

Roger usually kidded her about this.

"Why, Little Sarah, you old die-hard!" he would say, laughing at her, unable to understand how she could possibly not like something that, to him, was the breath of life. "I'll bet you'd rather have a horse and buggy!"

"You know I would. You'll never know what a good time you could have with a horse and buggy. I wonder what it would be like, never to have had a sleigh ride, too, Roger. Oh, you youngones, you certainly *don't* know!"

She would think of times ago, when she'd come over here to visit Malcolm's people, or to see Ralph, after he had gone to them to live. Hot summer afternoon, sun on dusty leaves, the road white and deep with powder, the slow *clop-clop* of the horse's hooves, sway and creak of the buggy, sleepy countryside unrolling on either side like dusty ribbons. Or snapping cold, rosy-cheeked days, white, deep snow, sleigh bells; the sting, now and again, in the face, of small, flying pieces of ice! Oh, they couldn't know, they that did their courting racing along the hard in a smell of burnt gasoline!

But Little Sarah didn't mention this, today.

Roger looked thinner, pale without his tan, but he'd grown up, some, the way a boy should grow; his shoulders looked broad and competent beneath the jacket of his Sunday suit. Sitting in the car beside him, while he started the car and sent it—flying, she thought —up the narrow street flanked with houses cheek-by-jowl, so close together that you didn't care whether you looked at them or not, Little Sarah didn't say a word, waiting for him to say. He had something, she could tell. There was some kind of excitement and gaiety showing, under a layer of concern and worry. What it was would come out, if she waited.

He drove looking straight ahead—much too fast, twenty-five miles an hour, she saw, on the little clock that said how fast the car was going. But she said nothing, holding tight to the basket in her lap, smelling the frail, spring smell of the violets which leaked up through its slatted cover.

"Rosie and I want to get married," Roger said, not looking at her, his eyes on the road, watching his driving. He was going slow, poking along at twenty-five, so as not to scare the pants off of Little Sarah, and he wasn't used to it. The big car handled better at a higher speed.

"Why," Little Sarah said. "Good. But I thought that was all settled long ago, Roger."

"That was for sometime. We thought if you'd come over today, come with us, we'd—"

"Roger," Little Sarah said. "Where are we going?"

Roger gave her a brief, worried grin. "We figured I working in the drugstore and Rosie clerking full-time in the five and dime, we can make it. Not be rich. But enough. I'm picking up Rosie at her house. We're going to Port Western and get married."

Little Sarah looked at him. She saw the grin, the Sunday suit, the haircut, all the spic-and-span, and her heart turned over. What on earth am I going to do? she thought. They can't, they're under age, and Jess and Elbridge will want to see Roger married, and Liseo— Oh, Lord, Liseo!

"I went and got a license over in Port Western," Roger said. "I'm eighteen pretty soon. Rosie won't be for a year or so, but I guess we lied some, Little Sarah. Might not be quite legal."

"You know, it won't be," she said. "Liseo can have it annulled, if he wants to."

Roger's jaw came out. "He'd better not!" he said. "Liseo, for cramp's sake, Little Sarah! What's the matter with him? Why hasn't he gone around and batted heads together?"

"What for?" Little Sarah said. "And don't roar at me, Roger. I can't take it in any more than I could when your great-grandfather had a spell of it. Simmer down, and tell me what the trouble is."

"Talk!" Roger burst out. "Gossip! There's a whole bunch of filth steaming around town about Rosie. And Joe Farleigh. Joe's my best friend, Little Sarah. Rosie's my *girl!* The four of us—Joe's girl, Helen —we've been going places together all winter. There hasn't been a thing—I—we—"

Roger hadn't stopped roaring, but the furious baritone caught, momentarily, in his throat on a choke of rage. His foot came down hard on the accelerator. The big car shot ahead.

Little Sarah put both hands up to her hat and closed her eyes. But her voice came out composedly, "Why, I heard something, Roger. I didn't pay much attention to it, it was too foolish. None of us did. I'm sure Liseo didn't."

"Well, I did! And Rosie did. And I'll tell you, it pretty near busted up Joe and Helen. It went all over the high school. There's a lot of girls up there would be pleased to be able to make some time with Joe, and they didn't hold back passing it around, either. Helen was mad as a hornet and poor old Joe was sunk; and it got so people couldn't come into the drugstore without handing me a funny mouthful. So Joe wanted to marry Helen right away, and both their folks put up a yatter—they're too young, finish high school—all right, Little Sarah, dammit, nobody's going to stop Rosie and me!"

"Who's trying to?" Little Sarah said brusquely. "Unless you kill yourself before you get to the preacher."

"Oh," Roger said, and Little Sarah felt the car slow down. She opened her eyes and looked at him; she saw MacKechnie and Jess and Elbridge, and a look, unmistakable and suddenly unexpectedly recalled, around the furious set young mouth, of Malcolm. The four people, of all in the world, that she had loved best, she thought, distilled into one better beloved, now, than any.

"Your father got married young," she said. "I don't see as it ever hurt him any."

Gaiety, which she saw now had not lain too far below the surface, suddenly wiped out Roger's rage. He gave her a dazzling, wide grin. "I guess I scared you, Little Sarah. I clean forgot you don't like to go fast."

"Yes, you did. You horrified me," she said.

"Wait till I take you on an airplane ride," he said. "Someday, Little Sarah."

"Oh, no. Oh, no, Roger," Little Sarah said. "Oh, no, you won't."

He slowed the car again and stopped it at a house where Rosie was waiting on the steps. She, too, was shining, spic-and-span, red cheeks, hat with bright spring flowers, new shoes, best coat and dress. She came running down the steps, as Roger opened the car door, and she slid under the wheel, so as to sit between him and Little Sarah.

"Oh, Little Sarah," she said. "Thank you for coming."

She gave Little Sarah's hand a squeeze, quickly, anxiously looking at her, and Little Sarah smiled.

"I'm pleased to be here," she said. "But, honey, don't you want a real wedding, and your folks to see you married?"

"Well, I would," Rosie said. "I always wanted one. But all this has come up, Little Sarah. Joe and Helen—did Roger tell you?"

"Yes," Little Sarah said. "I told Roger we'd heard a few things, over home, Rosie. Nobody believed anything so foolish. Nobody thought twice about it."

"We've had to," Rosie said. "Oh, Little Sarah, we've *really* had to! It was part my fault, I kidded old Lombard one day, Roger was there, he heard me, it wasn't anything, really, but I said, gee, was I a bad girl, or something like that, and after that, every time I turned around at a dance, there was old Lombard creeping around on the outskirts somewhere, and I wouldn't even look, and after a while I know he got mad. And he's only a nasty old man, Little Sarah, but if Roger ever hit him he'd come unshackled all over the place, and of course I did write home stuff about Joe Farleigh, but that was only to pull Pop's leg—of course Pop knows me, he'd know it was kidding."

"Of course," Little Sarah said. "We'd all know, Rosie."

"And Pop will die if he isn't there to see me married, and I will, too, and Jess and Elbridge— Oh, Roger and I've talked and *talked* it over. But they'd try to stop us, Little Sarah, you know they would, or make us come home to the island to be married, and we don't want to, not with everybody over there standing around hating everybody else, and all the talk there'd be—"

"They'll talk, Rosie," Little Sarah said sturdily. "If you get married in a hurry this way, they're bound to."

"Then they can just wait nine months and see!" Rosie burst out. She stopped, horrified at herself, and blushed deep red, then went on defiantly, "No, sir, I'm going to say it. I won't go there for a thing as nice as my wedding day and know while I'm being married that half the people there are counting on their fingers. I just want you and Roger, and Joe and Helen to stand up with us, and—" Rosie stopped, gulping. "And I won't cry on my wedding day, either. That awful mess of fights and stuff they've got over on the island—well, it's given me Roger three years before I thought I'd be let to marry him, Little Sarah, so I guess maybe I ought not to feel as bad as I do."

Well, Little Sarah thought. Somebody had better be on the side of light, let the chips fall where they may. And three years longer to keep somebody you love might be a treasure beyond knowing, in the years to come.

She opened the basket in her lap and hauled out the big bunch of blue violets.

"A bird must have brought me word," Little Sarah said. "I thought to bring along a bride's bouquet."

PART FIVE
Summer

S CHOOL closed for the summer. Miss Warren organized a school time with sad pieces, but she had to have it in the schoolhouse, without benefit of baked-bean supper. Only a few went to it, mostly mothers of children. None of the mothers had pieces to speak; nobody was in a mood for festival, even a big, seasonal one. Besides, everyone was busy. So Miss Warren had her final entertainment, stowed away the textbooks in the closet, packed her trunk and took the mail boat to the mainland, to be seen no more.

June was always a busy time; in June, prosperity was always just around the corner. Those who were caretakers of summer cottages were hustling, scrubbing and cleaning, putting everything in order, making sure that any borrowed object got returned before the owners got back; the men getting sailboats out of boathouses and dinghys calked and painted, yards raked, and so on, in the general upheaval that took place each June before the return of the summer trade. An air of anticipation hung over the town of people busy and interested and looking forward. Just offhand, two or three people spoke to each other who, all winter, hadn't given the time of day.

Imogene Cayford, excited and triumphant because something had at last been proved to her that she'd known all along was so, was hurrying past Shepheards' headed for Stell's, when she saw Addie out in the side yard hanging out clothes; and before Imogene remembered that she was mad at Addie, hadn't spoken for months, she turned automatically in at the gate.

Addie, glancing up in astonishment, said to herself, Well she must surely have a tiddle-bit, this time, to bring her in here.

Goodness knows, there'd been enough to talk over, what with

Roger and Rosie getting married like that, and Elbridge standing Stell's hair on end, when she started to put out that it was a shotgun wedding.

"A shotgun wedding," Stell said, right out loud in the post office, "and Little Sarah went over there, unbeknownst to all, and waltzed them two kids right to a minister."

Addie had heard about it—oh, there were always plenty to run with a story like that, but just try and get church news around town, like the minister wasn't coming for Easter—and she had felt so bad for Jess that she thought she was going to die, almost as bad as she felt when Wiggy started to grow up and she and Jack found out for sure he was lacking.

But then Elbridge had gone in to see Stell, in the evening it had been, so nobody really knew what had happened, except perhaps Luther, and Luther was getting so feeble now that you couldn't depend on his getting a story straight. George Lowden had visited Luther the next afternoon while Stell was over to Imogene's having *their* Ladies' Aid meeting; something new for George to go visiting the sick, hadn't been in to see Luther all winter, but any half-wit could guess the reason; and George reported that old Luther was lying there in bed laughing his head off, said he felt so much better he guessed he'd try to live through another winter. But George couldn't get very much out of him, except that for once Stell had met her can-uckance.

Well, that didn't happen too often. It kind of tickled people; you could tell some weren't quite so put out with Elbridge as they had been. The story was starting around, now, that it hadn't been a shotgun wedding at all, thank the Lord. Though, of course, there were always those who gave up hard—wagged their heads as if they'd been there, knew more than they'd say, and said that only time would tell. Liseo's and Elbridge's families had pulled right in together, a solid front; you'd never know but what their kids' marrying so young wasn't the best thing that ever happened. Right now, Roger and Rosie were down in Boston, so Roger could go to school and learn to be a druggist. Some said Elbridge and Liseo were paying for it, though where they ever got the money, the shape their business was in, the Lord in his infinite mercy only knew, must have had some put by, or Little Sarah did.

But that was all talked over, long ago. Imogene must have something else.

"Teacher's gone," she said, breathlessly hurrying up to Addie in the side yard. "And it's just as I always said it was, that color *wasn't natural!*"

Addie was interested. Everybody had wondered, all year, about Miss Warren's pink cheeks and lips, since she wasn't a girl who looked to have that high a natural color, kind of anemic.

Addie said, "You found the rouge pot!"

"I did not!" Imogene said. "Nor was there one."

She paused to savor Addie's curiosity.

"Then how?" Addie said. "How in the name of heaven?"

"I house-cleaned that room after she moved out of it and gone," Imogene said. "And if you ask me, between I and the bedpost, for a schoolteacher she wasn't any too neat. I moved out that bed to clean behind, and what do you suppose I found, outside of dust-kittens as big as baseball bats?"

"I don't know. What?"

"Every mite of the red is smudged off the roses on that wallpaper down behind the bed," Imogene said.

"Well, I ask you!" Addie said, amused.

"It's got to be papered over, the whole room, you never saw such a mess in your life. Looks as if she'd spit on her finger and *wiped* all winter long. I looked at it, I couldn't believe my eyes, said, so *that's* where she got it. And down behind the bed, where nobody'd see. Now, I ask you, how is that for sly?"

"Well, I never in my life!" said Addie.

"Nor I. I knew as well as I stand here that that color was off of something, but I never matched it up to the roses on the wallpaper. Well, you never know the lengths to which people will go, do you?"

It struck Addie, suddenly, as sad. She said thoughtfully, "Poor thing."

"Poor thing! What do you mean, 'poor thing'? Nasty thing, maybe, but not poor, not by a sight, Miss Addie!"

"Well, I suppose all she was trying to do was make herself look pretty, Imogene. Maybe she was trying to catch herself a husband. I wonder who?"

"What about my wallpaper, for heaven's sake?" Imogene said. It occurred to her, suddenly, that after all, she was *mad* with Addie. "The expense and all. Well, I like that, Addie, I certainly do." She started to make her exit from Addie's yard, her back stiff, but she was not to the gate before a parting shot occurred to her. "Isn't it lovely about the new church building?" she said.

"New church building!" Addie said. "What on earth are you talking about?"

It hadn't occurred to Imogene that Addie might not have heard about that, why, it was all over town!

"And there's going to be one," she said. "Didn't you know?"

"I certainly *didn't* know!"

"The *summer people's* interested," Imogene said. "Mr. Wynn alone donated a hundred dollars. They've all give money, even some of the rich ones over to Port Western, and Bill Lessaro's sold them a piece of land. There's going to be a nice new little chapel, for those of us who want to go to that church."

"Well, I must say, you've kept it some old quiet," Addie said ominously.

"Oh, no. I guess you just don't keep up with the news, Addie, the way you used to be able to." Imogene swept airily on her way, leaving Addie standing.

Addie was thunderstruck. At first, she didn't believe it. It couldn't have happened, without her knowing it, and she the chairman of the old Church Council. Then she wondered. Bill Lessaro and Mollie, she knew, had been talking, all winter, about selling their land. Mollie had said, more than once, that she and Bill were disgusted; if only they could sell something, they'd move off-island like a shot, go where they could have neighbors again, without having to worry all the time over who you were mad with. Mollie had said that, right in Addie's house, not a month ago. Maybe they had sold to the off-island church people. Well, wouldn't that frost you!

Addie left her washtubs where they were in the middle of the kitchen floor, got on her coat and went over to Mollie's.

It was true. Bill hadn't sold all his land, only an acre of his upper field, in by the causeway, and he hadn't got much out of it.

"But we're going just the same, and don't you think we aren't!" Mollie said. "They're going to build, I know—Bill says there's a whole scow-load of lumber waiting over to the harbor for the weather and tide to serve right. Well, I don't know, Addie, seems kind of a waste to build another church here, us not even able to keep the one we have going."

Addie went straight home. She sat down to the table and wrote a letter to that rector. He had been coming over here, holding services, and Stell's crowd had been going to them, but there were some to whom he was not welcome, though better not tell him so. Not a minister.

She tried four times before she had a letter polite enough to send, explaining as much of the situation as she thought it fitting for a man of God to know, and finished as follows:

> We have our own church here, been here since 1860. We would be glad to offer it to you for your services, if you want to have services here. But two churches is too many for a town of this size, we can't support one as it is, and two is too many. I should think if you people have all that money to spare, you might better use it for missions.
>
> Yrs.
>   Addie R. Shepheard
>   Chairman of the Church Council.

The rector wrote right back. Addie had a letter from him almost by return mail. It was a nice letter, polite; but he said no, thank you, to the offer of the church; he was puzzled to learn that there was opposition to the new chapel, since the island people, themselves, had sent him a petition for regular services, and so funds for a mission to the fisherfolk on the island had been raised, donated mostly by certain generous summer visitors. The new chapel, incidentally, was to be called Saint Somebody-or-other's Mission.

The rector's handwriting was hard to make out, so Addie couldn't figure what the name of the saint was; she didn't puzzle over it. The word that came out and hit her in the face, that she could make no mistake about, was "mission." She flew right up into the air and went over to Jess's.

"I've helped pack too many missionary barrels for that to go down very good with me," she said, between her teeth, to Jess. "Fisherfolk, my eye! I suppose the summer people's behind it, and they can do no wrong."

"I suppose so," Jess said. "Maybe some good'll come of it, Addie."

Jess felt bad, too; but she felt worse at the thought of losing Bill and Mollie Lessaro, who really were going, moving to the mainland. Bill and Mollie had been good neighbors for years, and she and Elbridge would miss them.

"Well, let them build it," Addie said. "I and mine are not heathen to be sent a missionary to, and will never set foot inside of it as long as we live, may God strike me dead." She burst suddenly into tears. "Why, Jess," she sobbed, "Why, Jess, our folks was always the ones who *sent* the missions!"

"WELL," Liseo said. "There it is on the line, Elbridge. What do you think we'd better do?"

They were in the end-building of the wharf, which they had always called the office, Elbridge in the swivel chair behind the roll-top desk, Liseo sprawled on the rickety sofa in the corner, his hands behind his head.

The office was more than an office, actually; it contained the desk and chair and MacKechnie's old iron safe, and Elbridge's ledgers and cashbooks, and all the business gear; but it also contained a good deal of other miscellaneous litter belonging to various people—old mittens and somebody's jackknife and a couple of whittling sticks, and other stuff left casually, maybe to be called for, maybe to be forgotten. Up-ended trawl tubs and buckets, a few wooden boxes were ranged around the walls—places to sit down on and stretch out legs. There was a chunk stove, unused now in the middle of August, and slightly rusted, and there was the sofa. It was an office, but it was also a place to be sociable, a kind of casual men's club in which to sit down and pass the time of day, if you felt like it and had the time of day to pass.

Elbridge said nothing, and after a pause, Liseo said glumly, "There's the ledger, there's the cashbook, and there's the bills."

"I know."

Elbridge did know. He had been over the figures a good many times, until he knew them by heart. Up to last June, he and Liseo had felt they could always pull out of the red by using their backlog of savings, if they had to; but now the backlog was gone, most of it used to set up Roger and Rosie, and the rest of it swallowed by endless bills. Now, in August, hardly a half of the credit extended to various island fishermen the previous winter had been cleared up.

The kids were now in Boston, where Roger was getting the education he needed for his course in pharmacy.

On the day in June, when Little Sarah had come back from the wedding, marched up the wharf and confronted them, in the office, with the news, Elbridge, after the first shock, found himself glad. He felt a clutch at his heart, thinking how Jess was going to feel at not having seen Roger married; well, he would like to have been there, himself. But things like that were in proportion. The kids were right, together, always had been; if they were young, they would grow older, as he and Jess had done and never regretted a moment.

But as Little Sarah's story unfolded, he began to feel something that was entirely new to him. He thought, for a moment, he was going to be sick; then, as if a slow, red coal had started to flare in his chest and was burning upward toward the top of his head.

Liseo said, "I see you're getting mad. It's about time."

He himself looked murderous, his eyes slitted, his brows drawn blackly down in a scowl.

"As far as Lombard's concerned," Little Sarah said, looking composedly at the two angry men, "Rosie herself tended to that by refusing to notice it. She took it for what it was, a nasty-minded old man with the wrong idea, and she held Roger down, too. She's a smart girl, Liseo, and I'm pleased that she's married my grandson. They couldn't, of course, do anything about the talk. Except what they did." Little Sarah got up. She picked up her empty basket and started for the door. "Oh, and another thing, Orin tended to Lombard, too. According to him, he pulled Lombard's nose."

By the time Orin had got back to the mainland that afternoon, to fetch Little Sarah, he had had a day of triumph. He had told Stell about Little Sarah's "secret" trip, and how Roger looked, and what Lombard said about a shotgun wedding; and then he had said about the monkeys and the savages on Chin Island, and how he had got Lombard told, "right in the face of his nose stuck out through the wicket," and Stell had said, "Too bad you didn't pull it," which had tickled Orin just about to death. By gorry, what if he had! So the next time he told the story, he said he *had* pulled Lombard's nose, to the delight of every Chin Islander he told it to; his stock went up, he was popular with everyone. Bringing Little Sarah across in the boat, Orin had said, "Pulled his nose, by gorry," and firmly believed he had.

"We heard," Liseo said tersely. "Nobody thought to tell us the whole story, though."

"Not likely they would," Little Sarah said. "Seems, nobody ever does." Over her shoulder, at the door, she said, "I could, and would, take over the post office, Elbridge, if I had to. I'd hate it, but it wouldn't hurt Stell to know there's somebody."

And so, that night, Elbridge had gone to see Stell.

He couldn't, for the life of him, see what good it had done, now that it was too late to stop the talk. He had left Stell white-faced and, for once, silenced; for the past two months, no one could possibly have complained about the efficiency of the post office, or the hours it was kept open.

For the rest, the situation remained much the same. If the islanders, with the summer's work coming up, had been settling into uneasy truce, they were split apart again, in June, when construction started on the new chapel. Mr. Franklin had taken his regular monthly services through the summer, and the rector had taken his, dodging each other by one Sunday. Half of the island families, set like rock, went to one service; the other half, set like stone, went to the other. Elbridge and Liseo had gone to both and had lost business thereby. They fell between the chairs, people being put out at their refusal to take sides. Since June, they had been running a string of lobster traps, and they still had, of course, their off-island business, with which they had managed to quiet down their biggest creditors. The business was still above water, but that was about all. The future didn't look like much.

"With a good season, we could pull out of it," Liseo said. "But it won't be, not with the church war. Funny. You'd think a church'd be the last thing to aid and abet war, wouldn't you? But shoot, Elbridge, they're good people, they mean well, and I'm told they've got Stell and them so pious they even pray at home, so good's been done, however you look at it." He stretched out his legs. "You going to the consecration ceremony of the new chapel?"

"Why, I expect to."

"Gorry, you'd better," Liseo said. "They've got three bishops."

Elbridge nodded absently. He sat adding figures, only half listening to Liseo's talk.

The new chapel, now finished, was to be dedicated on Sunday. Quite a ceremony was to be made of it; numbers of summer people, not only from the island, but from the resorts on the mainland, had been interested in the new mission and had donated funds to the building, and several boatloads of them were scheduled to appear, along with the bishops.

"Them bishops is on vacation, over to Port Western," Liseo said. His voice, accomplishing the transition smoothly, had become, unmistakably, Stell MacGimsey's. "They're giving their services *free*. You know good and goddam well, Elbridge, *you* couldn't have raked up that many bishops to save your life."

Elbridge grinned. "Did Stell say that?"

"Almeda said she did."

"Well, I guess likely she's right."

"And never will Addie set foot," Liseo went on, his voice now, as unmistakably, Addie's, "never as long as she lives and draws breath, into a building that looks like a garage with the bell stuck up on top like a bird in a cage; and you'd think, with all them rich summer people digging down, they'd have put up something a little more elaborate, it must be disappointing to some. The truth of the matter is, nobody, Addie guesses, dug down very far, unless 'twas Miss Greenwood, and she's put every cent she's got into it, and now she ain't got enough left to buy what she needs to get along on."

"Oh, I don't believe that can be so," Elbridge said, putting down his pencil.

Might as well listen to Liseo. No matter how you figured, the total came out the same.

"Who knows what's so and what isn't?" Liseo said, being himself again. "Miss Roxinda's been about everything else you could name— et by a horrible disease, and all, and now she's a religious maniac. Spends three-quarters of her time flat on her knees, reading prayers out of them books they've got—don't really pray, of course, they *read* their prayers. Got calluses half-an-inch thick on her kneecaps. Fanny had the word right straight from Carrie and Carrie had it from whoever saw Miss Greenwood's kneecaps last. You know how it goes."

"I know how it goes."

Miss Greenwood hadn't been looking very well lately, which was probably what the talk about the kneecaps grew out of. It was not surprising that she hadn't; she had been working day in and day out, beautifying the new chapel.

Elbridge was not unaware of the justice of Addie's criticism of the chapel. Like everyone else, he had been interested in a new building —outside of a summer cottage here and there, it was the only one that had gone up on the island in years. He had gone around to chat with the carpenters from the mainland, who were building it.

It was a simple little structure, set on cedar posts dug into Bill Lessaro's former hayfield at the top of the village, not far from where the causeway crossed the fields. Unplastered inside, and unpainted out, it had offered no problem to the construction company's men, and had gone up in jig time, bare studs boarded over and shingled, and the belfry composed of a spidery structure of two-by-fours which might, conceivably, be thought to look like a bird cage. Except for the belfry, and the three amber-colored windows on each side, you might almost have taken it for a garage, and, inside, it was stiff and raw with new, yellow wood. The thing was, on the day the carpenters moved out, Miss Greenwood had moved in.

At first, she dug flower beds and transplanted plants from her own garden; it turned out, Little Sarah said, that there were quite a lot of plants that would stand moving in August, that is, if you knew as much about it as Miss Greenwood did. She had quite a patch of bloom there, the first week, and a whole hedge of rugosa rosebushes started.

You wouldn't believe, Willard said, how fast that little old woman could dig, unless you saw it. He went up, thinking she might want him to help her, but she said no, and she didn't mention paying him for it, so he didn't insist. A man couldn't be expected to put in his time for nothing.

The next thing she did, she cut the stiff field grass all around between the hedge and the building, with a sickle; and then she wheeled her lawn mower across the island and trimmed the stubby grass, and watered it, so it was beginning to come up fine and green.

But what, most of all rose up and hit you in the eye, was what she did inside the chapel.

Down the middle aisle, between the rows of spidery yellow settees, put together on the premises by the carpenters, she laid a long, T-shaped rug, hooked by hand in intricate patterns, out of silk, in tiny, delicate loops. Over the altar, she put lengths of stiff, heavy cloth, embroidered with religious symbols, in many shades and colors, with millions of perfect stitches.

"Why, she must have been planning it for years," said the ladies of the opposition, the ladies on Addie's side. "There's *years* of work in that hooked rug! And she had the altar cloths all ready, too. Now I ask you, how is that for sly!"

I ask you and wouldn't you think, and well, if I live to be a thousand years, I never.

But they could not keep themselves from going in to see. Curiosity, and word passed about the perfection of the work, drew them as moths to a flame. Even Addie, who sneaked in to look around, one early morning before people were up—just to look wouldn't count, not, of course, in a religious way. She went to see it; nor did God strike her dead.

Elbridge himself had gone in to see what Miss Greenwood had done, out of curiosity as much as anything, he told himself. He stuck his nose in the door, and then, after a moment or so, took off his cap and went in and sat down on one of the settees.

It was a pleasant place to be. The silk rug made a rich stream of color up the middle aisle and across in front of the altar. It brought mellowness out of the thin, tight amber stain of the windows; the new, raw wood was a nice background for bright colors. The place had dignity and quietude, but more than anything else, warmth; and outside, the swallows made a quiet twittering in the summer afternoon.

He had sat there for quite a while.

It was no wonder, he thought, getting up at last to go, that Miss Greenwood looked so frail lately, and thinner, if that could be possible. The work she'd done here, outside and in, would stagger a strong man.

"If you ask me," Liseo said, shifting a little on the sofa, "half of the business we had and a third of the money on the books we'll never see again."

"That's right."

"Well, then?"

Elbridge said nothing. He sat, thinking.

"You're helpful," Liseo said. "Damned if you aren't."

"Don't hustle me."

"I'm not. I'm worried, is all."

"I was just thinking how to say it. There's always Mr. Wynn. His offer for the wharf and breakwater was a dandy."

"Yup. It's more than enough to clean up what we owe."

"And buy out Joe Blake's fish wharf and set up shop over to the harbor. And that's what you think we ought to do, isn't it, Liseo?"

Liseo got up from the couch, which sagged and creaked, even under his light weight. It was the ancient, parlor sofa, salvaged years ago from Aunt Tilson Vira's place, after she died and left no heirs, for though Orin was a cousin, he wanted no part, he said, of anything Aunt Tilson had used down *there*. Liseo, seeing that the office on the wharf was a place where men liked to drop in and sit, a loafing place on stormy days, warm from the fire in the chunk stove, had, when he and Elbridge first set up in business, gone into Aunt Tilson's abandoned place and commandeered the sofa. You needed, he said, at least one comfortable place to sit.

The sofa had caused considerable speculation as to who had sat on it, in its time; many had, there was no doubt of that. Since it had been in the office, it had come apart and been cobbled together more than once; a carved leg was gone entirely and was replaced with a stack of two-by-four blocks; its plum-colored plush was rubbed down to bare fabric, and horsehair stuffing was right out into the world. It was a far different thing from the fashionable parlor piece Aunt Tilson Vira had bought new.

Liseo looked down at it, hauled back his foot and kicked at the two-by-four blocks, which fell down, causing a corner of the sofa to drop to the floor.

"I've been all over the world," Liseo said, "and this country, too, in training, and then the Navy. I've seen a lot of places. I never saw one anywhere as good to live in as this one is."

He crossed over to the door and stood, his hands in his pockets, looking out. The office door faced the village; beyond Liseo, Elbridge could see the road climbing up between the houses, and the gray pile of MacKechnie's hill.

"I was aboard a ship," Liseo went on. "One of the first ones that got into Odessa in 1919. There was a grain ship tied up at the dock, came in just ahead of us. Crowds of people standing there, waiting to see if they could get a little grain. A handful, God, one kernel. Eat it raw, if they could get hold of it, if a grain bag had a hole in it, they'd all get down and scrabble, crazy hungry. One night, coming back to the ship, I saw what looked to be a bundle in a doorway. It was a little girl. About the size Rosie was then, I'd say. She was dead. Starved to death, from the looks of her."

He went on, in a quiet, matter-of-fact voice, his hands thrust deep into his pockets. "A lot of places not so bad, but plenty bad enough. Places I was at, I'd think of this place, where a man can make a living regardless, if he's willing and able. Times you don't live off the fat of the land, you can always find a fish. Row over to Gimbal, and dig a mess of clams. Nobody here ever starved, or even went hungry, far as I can see. This place ain't in too bad a way now; not compared to some of the stinking dumps I've seen. I guess you've got to see the rest of the world, before you realize how lucky you are, if you've got so much as a pot of yellow-eyes in the oven.

"Hell, I came back here on purpose to bring up my kids. Had a good time doing it, too. Couldn't possibly have had it so good anywhere else, even if I was a ball of fire making money, which I ain't. I've worked when I wanted to, quit when I wanted to, nobody hollering at my heels I wasn't earning my day's pay. It's been good."

He spun around, went back to the sofa to sit down, and then, seeing the dropped corner, knelt and began carefully to replace the blocks he had kicked out.

"The night Rosie was born," he said, "and old Doc said Fanny was okay, I went up on top of MacKechnie's hill and hooted and hollered and sung songs. I told all the old ghosts of the MacGimseys and the Clouds and the Gilmans and the MacKechnies, and the Viras and the Nikolaides, down there in the quarry pits, that I had a girl

and her name was Rosie. About everybody in town heard me holler-
ing up there, knew what it was about, too, and when I got ready to
come down, about three in the morning they had everything ready
for me and we had a hell of a party. Remember that, Elbridge? You
remember Willard singing and playing his accordion at the top of
his lungs, and George dancing that cussed hornpout he dances?"

"I sure do," Elbridge said.

He well remembered that night, when Liseo, in a kind of glory,
had come down the hill. They hadn't really planned a party, at three
in the morning; it was just that people had gathered at Elbridge's
house, getting ready to go up the hill and bring down Liseo, who was
up there drunk as a skunk, and make sure he didn't fall into the
quarry; but he had come down under his own steam, not drunk at
all, just as they were about to start up there, and the gathering had
turned into a party, a doggoned good one, too, that everybody in
town, even the kids, had got out of bed and come to, to celebrate
Liseo's baby.

"Well," Liseo said. "If you want to know why I hang on here, it's
things like that. To look at the place now, anybody'd wonder what
there is here a man in his right mind would want to keep. It's like
we'd had a war. All we need now is some killing to make it one. This
is one of the places in the world, now, where a man loses his business
just because he went to church. If you and I'd taken red-hot sides,
set fire, in this church war, instead of going to the services like decent
people, because we liked a good service regardless of the sect, we'd
have kept a full half of the business we lost this summer, you know
that?"

Elbridge nodded. He knew this to be true. Carrie's crowd, now,
was almost as put out with him and Liseo as Stell's crowd was, and
their husbands, too, were taking their trade to the mainland.

"Why, thunderation," Liseo said. "I like a good ceremony. Maybe
because some of my folks, back along, were Italians. You know, when
I was in France, I went to services at Notre Dame de Paree. Nobody
ever made a snide remark behind my back that I was out of place
there because my grandfather was a wop out of Italy."

"That's all foolishness," Elbridge said sharply. "What Stell says
doesn't signify."

"It's so foolish a man could break his jaw laughing," Liseo said.
"But look at what it's led to, all a part of the same bundle. You and I
are scrabbling around on the bottom of the barrel. So is Stell. And
anybody else you want to name, head over heels in debt. I'd be all

ready to pull out tomorrow, if I didn't feel about the place the way I do. Oh, we eat. And we'll go on eating. But I always planned, when Rosie got married, to set her up fancy. Made me feel pretty cheap, not able to."

"That's right," Elbridge said. "Me, too. I miss 'em, too, don't you?"

"Miss 'em! Life's a howling wilderness without Rosie," Liseo said. "But so long as she's okay, and happy, it's all right with me." He stopped, went on a trifle gruffly, "And the day you and I and Fanny and Jess put the kids on the boat for Boston, I saw that it was damn well all right, Elbridge."

Elbridge grinned at him, remembering that day. The kids, starting out, had been delirious with happiness; no one, in his right mind, could possibly have any regrets about what they had done.

Liseo grinned back at him, the cocky, to-hell-with-regrets grin that Elbridge had known ever since he could remember.

"Well," Liseo said, the grin fading, "I won't be the one to say sell out and go, Elbridge. But if you want to, I will."

"If we did sell out, I think it'd be the end of the town."

"No. It wouldn't. Things'd be different, change hands, be owned by different people. All these places here could be sold like a shot, if old Wynn bought the wharf and breakwater, made them into a yacht club and swimming pool, whatever, the way he wants to. At least, he'd repair the wharf buildings, save them from rotting down, which is more in the living God's world than you and I can do. It wouldn't end the town at all. It'd just mean different people owning it."

Elbridge said nothing, aware of the truth in what Liseo had said.

"Everybody here," Liseo went on, "has been twizzling like a wind-mill, for years, hoping he can sell his land to the summer people. You know that. This is the loveliest place on God's green earth, and no better anywhere for folks to live, if they want to try to live and make something of it. Why, people from away come here and pay thou-sands of dollars, just so they can stay three months out of the year. But it's like anything else in the world—if you've got something that's worth something and you don't value it or take care of it, someone'll take it away from you, legally or otherwise."

He turned, looked down ruefully at the silent Elbridge.

"I've shot my mouth off," he said. "God, I know how you feel. In a way, you and I started this tempest in a teapot, but the place was ready for it. If it hadn't been us, it would've been somebody else. Hell, let's shut up shop here, on the wharf, go lobstering, what say?"

"Give it till spring. If we can, Liseo."

"Okay," Liseo said. "And God help all that try to lobster through the winter out of the *Daisy*."

ON the day of the chapel dedication, the twins had summer colds. They weren't really sick, but they were miserable with stuffed-up throats and noses, and Jess, in a way, welcomed the excuse to stay at home. Without her, Elbridge didn't know as he cared to go. There'd be a lot of people. Launches had been arriving from the mainland all morning. The harbor behind the breakwater was full of them, and the main road of the town was colorful with strangers in gay summer hats and dresses.

Elbridge figured he wouldn't be missed. He always took a tramp around over the island on Sunday afternoon; usually Liseo went with him. They would go the shore path, or walk property lines, sometimes ending up at Miss Greenwood's; but today Miss Greenwood would be at the dedication, and Liseo and Fanny were going, too. Liseo, as he said, always liked a good ceremony, and this one was going to be a lulu.

So Elbridge was nearly to the top of MacKechnie's hill, when he happened to look back down, over the top of the swamp, at the town, and saw the three bishops coming along the causeway.

At least, he supposed that was who it must be. Three bishops were scheduled to come from Port Western to help with the blessing of the new mission, and these were three robed figures, in tall headgear, walking in dignified procession, headed for the chapel. Even from this distance, Elbridge could see the color against the drab browns and grays of the town.

Years ago, Bill Lessaro's father, Joe, had fixed steps down the side of the causeway into his meadow, so that he could duck off into the woods, unbeknownst to his wife and children, when he felt like it, he being a man inclined every so often to enjoy his solitude. Elbridge guessed that the bishops found the causeway easier walking than the dusty, rutted road that petered out, in Bill Lessaro's back yard, to the wagon track the carpenters had made, running through tall, uncut hay and puckerbrush in the meadow where the chapel was. The walking on the causeway was probably rough enough, Elbridge thought, and caught himself wondering absently what bishops wore on their feet.

Down there, he could see the new yellow shingles on the chapel, and the spidery belfry with its bell, and the moss-covered roof of

Bill Lessaro's empty house—Bill and Mollie and their kids had been long-gone to the mainland—and below that, the town, stretching to the shore, old barns and houses baking in the summer sun.

There was little enough of it left, he thought, and suddenly wondered what there was, actually, that any man in his senses would fight to keep. It was, as Liseo said, one of the loveliest places on earth. From the top of MacKechnie's hill, where he was now, the vast prospect stretched away, sea and sky and solitude; the green-gold of sun-soaked leaves, dark shine and plumy thrust of spruces, the cupped and lichened granite. Here, once, had been the forges and the drills, the powder houses, and the derricks whose fallen wood was rotting logs now, whose wheels people in time to come would not know how to account for, saying only, with wonder, that here, among these ledges, was a big rusty wheel, and over here, another. As MacKechnie, in his time had wondered about the people who made the paint pits and the rock marked "A."

But if what was here was not enough, now, to make a man feel pride in it, so that year by year he let his house and hayfield slide, and himself slip daily into the querulous complaining which is the voice of discouragement, then better to let it go. If there were those who valued it, let them have it, make their scratches on it.

He turned to go along the crest, and realized, for the first time, that he was not alone. Addie Shepheard was sitting on the top of MacKechnie's hill, on the highest rock she could find. She was in her oldest clothes—at least, they looked to be—a faded pink calico dress with a sagging hem, and a straw flapjack which once had been a Sunday, church-going hat; you could see the bright places, faded-around, where the trimming had been ripped off. She had a bucket, half-filled with highland cranberries, set down beside her on the rock.

It was, obviously, a gesture designed to express, to Addie if to nobody else, what she thought of the ceremony going on down there in the town. To rip the trimming off her Sunday hat, to put it on, with old clothes, and go cranberrying in it, on a Sunday, was an unheard of thing for Addie to do. But she had also brought along Jack's folding spyglass, and she had it focused on the colorful, robed procession, marching slowly along the causeway.

As Elbridge stopped, she turned on him a pair of bright, glazed eyes.

"Idolaters!" she said.

"Well, no, I wouldn't say so," Elbridge said. He tried to think of something. "Anyway, they look pretty."

"Not to me, they don't. Them and their mission! Not when our folks were the people here, once, Elbridge. The ones who *sent* the missions."

"That's right," Elbridge said. He started to say, "Well, now we know how it feels," but stopped in time.

To his surprise, Addie slid down off the rock and came over to where he stood.

"I expect I look some old funny and foolish, up here with a spyglass," she said. "I didn't come for that. I suppose you don't believe me."

"Why not?" he said. "I've known you a long time, Addie. You've never been a fibber."

He had, he thought suddenly, known Addie all his life. She had sat in front of him in school, and many a time he'd dipped the end of her pigtail in his inkwell. Such things. Addie Horn had been a darn nice little girl.

"No," she said. "When it comes right down to it, I haven't been a fibber, Elbridge. I most always take along Jack's spyglass when I go berrying, come up here on the hill awhile and look off over the water. It rests me. I thought it would today, me being out-of-my-mind mad the way I was, and it did, especially seeing that lumber schooner again. And then I turned around and saw *them*, and I got mad all over again—"

"The lumber schooner?" Elbridge said.

"Why, yes." She pointed. "Out there, now."

He spun around, looking off at the horizon.

The sails looked small and far away, about where they had been when Liseo and he had last seen them, nearly eight months ago; but there they were. Sure enough. Maybe not the same schooner, though; at this distance, he couldn't tell.

"Let me take the glass, will you, Addie?" he asked, and she handed it to him.

It was the same schooner; she had three masts so new that they weren't weathered yet, or tarred, three, big, bright-yellow pine sticks; her canvas was all new. Jack's glass might be old, but it was a good one; and Elbridge could make out the light tan color of new Manila rigging, that not yet tarred, either. She had a big, fresh black patch on her hull, for'rard, you could make out the different shade of it on her gray, battered planking. She was high in the water, headed northeast, headed home.

"By the God!" Elbridge said jubilantly. "That makes me feel good!"

"It does me, too," Addie said. "Jack and I, we had them fellers on our mind all winter. Must've been just the deckload they spilt, off here, wasn't it?"

"M'm-h'm. And then they must've clawed off the land and probably blew to hell an' gone, south somewhere. She looks to have been through it, all right, but they've got her fixed up, and now she's going home. Funny, we didn't hear—"

He pressed the eyepiece of the glass to his eye, watching the creamy sails and the battered hull, withdrawing in dignity across the summer sea.

"To do it all over again, I expect," Addie said, nodding. "It does make you feel good, something that tough and stubborn. But, you know, when I first see that, it gave me a terrible turn. I thought, a ghost, a Flying Dutchman-like. And then, of course, I got a-hold of myself."

"No ghost," Elbridge said. "That's as real a thing as you or I'll ever see, Addie."

"Oh, I know it. It was just all this talk about ghosts," Addie said. "Like old lady Greenwood hanting the Point and—"

Elbridge lowered the spyglass to stare at her in astonishment.

"Why, yes," Addie said. "Somebody started that, Stell and Almeda, I guess, and Carrie sent little Herbie down to Stell's the other night after the milk, and he got so scared over Imogene's washing flapping on the line that Carrie was up all night with him. Wasn't even Miss Greenwood's washing, because she don't send it over any more; does it herself."

"Well, it's about time somebody did something for us," Elbridge said disgustedly. "Sending a missionary is as good as the next thing. God, I guess we need one!"

Addie gasped. For a moment, Elbridge thought she was going to haul off and hit him. Then, to his astonishment, she began to grin.

Elbridge began to grin, himself.

For a moment, they regarded each other with great good-humor, then Elbridge burst into a roar of laughter that went on until he had to sit down, wheezing helplessly; and Addie sat down with him, letting out hoots that might well have been heard down the side of the hill, through the swamp and into town.

PART SIX
Autumn

STELL MacGIMSEY woke up in the middle of the night, not knowing what had waked her, only that suddenly she'd come wide-to, the way she would have if she'd overslept in the morning. She sat up straight in bed, all prepared to jump; but the night was as dark as a graveyard, not a crevice of daylight, so it wasn't morning. It was still, too, except for the crickets outside the screen, making that touse they always make in September, drive you crazy.

Well, something had woke her up, something unusual, or she wouldn't have. One thing, thank the Lord, she slept good, nights. She listened. Seemed there'd been a sound, somewhere.

There was. It was Luther. He was making a funny noise.

She called automatically, "All right, I'm coming," and lit the lamp. Shoot, he'd seemed real well lately, almost as if he were getting better. Well, coming on of the cool weather, the getting-up-nights would probably have to start all over again. Them doctors, seems as though some of them could make an invention . . .

Luther was lying on his back, his whiskers pointed up toward the ceiling. He didn't turn his head or ask her for anything, when she brought the light through the door, and that gave her a turn. She couldn't recall a time when she'd come through that door and he hadn't asked for something. But she didn't really suspect anything until she leaned over him and the light fell across his face. Then she saw that one of his eyes was half-closed and the other one wide open, and the one that was open was black.

Why, Luther had blue eyes. She ought to know. They'd watched her from a bed or a chair for nine mortal years.

The pupil of his eye, she saw, leaning down, holding the lamp, was all widened out until you couldn't see the iris, made it black. It was like looking into something bottomless, as no one could tell how deep, or what was there.

Stell felt a queer clutch at her chest, as if her heart had squeezed together a little and then let go. But, she'd seen death before. Dear Warren died in his sleep and she found him in the morning, lying there, couldn't help but think it was the first time in her life she'd ever seen him look at peace, he was a worrier, but such a good-looking man.

She set the lamp on the nightstand, and Luther said thickly, as if he had a throatful, "I'm going."

Well, from the way you look, Stell thought, I don't know but what you are. And I'll bet you'll make a touse about it, too.

She caught back the thought, it was not the time to think such things, but how could you stop thinking something pounded in, year upon year? Luther *always* made a touse.

Aloud, she said, "Don't be so foolish, Luther, it's nothing but phlegm. You've got the horrors. I'll get you a cup of tea."

But Luther didn't seem to hear.

"I'm the last one of them," he said. "When I'm gone, they'll all be gone."

She had to lean over him to hear.

"What we done," Luther said. "What we done. And all gone," and he widened his eyes and looked right at her.

Whatever was behind the blind, black stare, she thought suddenly, was for *her*. It was not kindly, not saying good-by forever, not peaceful like dear Warren, as a death should be.

Why, he's *blaming me!* she thought. At such a time as this, he stops to blame *me!* And she stared back, with a growing sense of guilt and horror at the changing eyes.

It did not occur to her that Luther was beyond blaming anyone, that he was only dying.

She put the sheet up over him and left the room, blowing out the lamp. Daylight was coming, enough, anyway, to see by, no use burning good kerosene. Going to be a good, sunny day, quiet, too, not a breath of wind. Not a sound in the world anywhere, but them cussed crickets.

I'll need help and it'll have to be Addie. I don't know as I want anybody don't know any more than Almeda does to touch someone my own. I'd better go—no. Mustn't leave a dead person alone in the house, it ain't right. But if I blow his old fish horn three-four times

out the back door, the neighbors'll come a-running. They all know
how sick he was. Now, where on earth did I put that horn?

After all I done for him, nine years, he went blaming me, blaming
me for the way the island's gone down, well, it has, no doubt of that,
my business not half what it used to be, and Elbridge and Liseo
lobstering, hadn't been for the summer trade all of us would've had to
shut up shop and maybe will anyway. Well, I wasn't the one started
the fight, he ought to understand that and I'll—heb'm sake, here I
was, all ready to go in there and tell him, and I can't ever tell him
anything now, he's gone. This house is going to be some old lonesome
without Luther.

Well, I'll do what I can. Out of respect for the dead. A funeral's as
good a time as any for old neighbors to get back together, and I'm
tired to death of the fight anyway, the Lord in his infinite mercy
knows, everybody ought to want things back the way they was.
Though there's some that I don't see how they can ever speak to each
other again, and it will take me I don't know how long to get the
store back on its feet.

My Lord, and me baptized not three weeks ago into the new
chapel, and now I'll have to have his funeral in the old church, he
always went there, I better bury him the way he wanted, anything
the living can do to make the dead rest. And after the funeral, I'll
write everybody a postcard.

Of course, there's all the stamps, but there, I'm the postmistress,
I can send without any stamps, just slide a card in everybody's pi-
geonhole, local mail like that, it won't matter. And there's all them
cards the salesman left, that time, of the Boston Custom House that
nobody bought. I can put out an olive branch and it won't cost me.

And, thank the Lord, there's that horn.

Stell stood in the back door, in the bright-streaked morning, and
blew the horn—short, sharp, blasts, the old-time signal of a ship in
distress, at sea.

THE day after Luther's funeral, Stell put out her olive branch. She
spent a long time composing a message to her neighbors, and when
it was done, she was proud of it:

> If you want a store-and-post-office here at the island, you'll have
> to trade with me. I don't have Luther now, so I don't have to
> stay, and if business don't get better, I'm going to move.

Says just what I want it to say, without giving in.

WILLARD had had, all in all, a pretty good season. He had lob-
stered and fished all summer, in spare time from his gardener's job
up at Mr. Wynn's summer cottage, and he had over three hundred
dollars—had had to find a bigger can than the baking-powder one
he'd at first kept his savings in. He had solved the milk problem by
leaving a dime by the milk pail, each night, to pay for the quart he
took for his cat; and apparently that had satisfied Harriet, for he had
heard no more from her. He was used to living alone now—well, not
alone, because now he had Mary, and Mary was fat and sassy. Her
coat was silky, even through the summer, because he'd kept the
briers and tangles combed out of it; though, on the combing, she
fought him every inch of the way, didn't like to be combed.

He had got used to lobstering in the skiff, even taken off a little
weight with all that rowing, though it was nip and tuck, the way he
ate—hungry all the time, and he'd got to be a darned good cook, if
he did say so himself. But anyway, his muscles had tightened up,
and he felt better than he had for years. He guessed maybe this fall
he might even take a trip somewhere, the way Elbridge had said to,
if he could find a decent place to leave Mary, or maybe even take
her with him. He didn't see how he could part himself from her,
even for a month or so. Those cat-carriers in the catalog, the ones
with the cunning little window in one end, he'd bought one of those,
hoping she'd take to sleeping in it, get used to it, just in case he did
decide to go and take her; but she didn't care for it, so far, would
rather sleep on his bed, the way she always had.

So summer had slipped into fall, and still Willard couldn't make
up his mind to go. Didn't know why, just didn't seem like the time
yet. Cottages closed up, summer people all gone, everybody around
with summer's earnings in their pockets, kind of cheerful; and some
people had made up differences, but not all. Some, looked like to
Willard, never would speak to each other again, like him and Harriet
and George. He'd met George face to face more than once this sum-
mer. George never so much as showed by a blink of his eye that he
even saw Willard was there. Well, they could speak first; Willard
wasn't going to be the one.

Changes had taken place, too. Elbridge's boy and Liseo's girl had
got married—shotgun wedding, some said; seemed funny, quite a
comedown for some people if it was so—and in September, old
Luther MacGimsey had died.

The whole town had gone to Luther's funeral, even the ones who'd
sworn they'd never set foot in the old church again. Mr. Franklin

preached Luther's sermon, and it was a humdinger—all about the old-timers and Luther being the last of them, and what the island was and what its tradition meant to folks now. Seemed like that sermon ought to have sent Mr. Franklin's stock up a little. Maybe it did, with some. It certainly had with Willard. But of course there were a lot of people out on a limb they couldn't crawl back from.

Like Stell. Some people said that Stell's sending out that postcard meant she was breaking up a little, *asking* people to come trade; but most of Carrie's crowd said if she sent out a catalog, they'd fry before she or anyone else could tell them where to buy their groceries. Willard himself thought the card had been a peace offering. You had to know Stell. He didn't know whether the postcard had helped her business; she was still running it, so he supposed it had.

But Elbridge and Liseo were still lobstering. They bought what groundfish and lobsters they could get at the scow; they didn't have a lot of business. Some said they had failed. Elbridge and Liseo didn't say.

Well, it was too bad, if it was so. Nice business like that, things were coming to a pretty pass, getting worse all the time. If Elbridge and Liseo couldn't make a go of it, who could? Willard, himself, had gone back to selling his catch to them now, no sense holding onto a grudge. Help them out, if he could, not be like some, who still wouldn't.

Willard was janitor of the new chapel now, but there wasn't enough *to* the building to keep a man busy. No vestry, no furnace to look after, only an airtight you stuffed chunks into and shut up the drafts. That furnace in the old church vestry, she had been a bitch, you had to know just how to run her, or no fire and a cold church.

He guessed he had to admit it, he was one of those out on a limb he couldn't crawl back from. He had this new janitor's job, and like a number of other people he'd got baptized in the chapel during the summer. It had been kind of an interesting thing, an awful good place to see all the summer people, they were a sight all together in one place; but now they were gone, seemed some people had kind of lost interest.

One service, the Sunday when herring were schooling in the bay, and a lot of boats went out to dip bait, there hadn't been a soul go to the new chapel but the rector and Willard and Miss Greenwood. George had taken the powerboat, a man couldn't dip herring, alone, in a skiff, and anyway, Willard didn't care to work on a Sunday. So he'd gone to church, and he'd been some old embarrassed.

He'd tried making some of the responses, but his voice was a pretty heavy one, either drowned out Miss Greenwood altogether, or went mumble-mumble-mumble along behind her; and somehow the sound of just their two voices made him feel as if he'd like to slink out, then and there, go home and never come back. But of course he was baptized now, and the janitor to boot. And nothing in it, any more, not for him; no baked-bean suppers and sociables; never once had he been called upon to play or sing. He hadn't sung in public for nigh a year, and he missed it.

He guessed, with the chapel, a new broom had swept clean. Summer people gone, and that was all there was to it. Oh, the children still went to Miss Greenwood's Sunday school—they liked it, she had a powerful way about her with children. But, looked like, the old days, when he could stand up in front of the whole town at a church time and sing "Let the Lower Lights Be Burning," and have people clap him back and clap him back, until he was singing hoarse, looked like those days were gone.

The town had gone to grass, to Willard's way of thinking, and he wondered why he didn't go away somewhere, at least for a trip. But time passed and he didn't go; and on the first of November, he came home from fishing one night to find the door of his shack ajar, his money can empty on the floor, and Mary not there.

LITTLE SARAH was having supper in her kitchen when she heard someone stumble on the walk, coming up to her back steps. She had been out harvesting the late vegetables in her garden all afternoon —she was one who liked to leave the roots in the ground as long as possible—sorting out the best of the carrots and turnips to put away down cellar for the winter, putting the culls in a pile for Elbridge to fetch for his pig, and carrying the left-over green tops to the compost pit. She was tired, but it was a good tired, the kind that comes from a hard job of work well done and nothing wasted, a job that you got satisfaction from. Time you got carrots and beets and cabbages and turnips sacked up and stored, you felt you had a treasure better than gold. The stumble on the walk outside sounded like somebody drunk; she got up and opened the door, letting out a rectangle of lamplight.

It was Willard Lowden, carrying some kind of a square case with a handle, she saw, and if he wasn't drunk, he was sick.

She said, "Come in, Willard, what's the matter?" and he came up the steps into the kitchen, and stood there holding out the case, which she saw, now, was a pet-carrier. For a moment, he didn't appear to be able to say anything, and she could see the streaks, down his cheeks, of tears.

"Heaven's sake, Willard," she said. "What is it? What's happened?"

"It's Mary," Willard said. "It's my cat. Somebody's half-killed her. I thought you—will you—?"

"Oh," Little Sarah said. "Yes, of course. You sit down, while I see."

Sick animals or sick people, it wasn't anything new; she'd looked after a good many of both, and she glanced sharply at Willard as he lurched past her toward the rocking chair. He wasn't drunk, but something had made him feel awful; his breath was coming heavily, as if he had been running. If he had been, she thought, with all that weight to lug, he'd better sit still for a while, the way he looks, like death warmed over.

"You had your supper, Willard?" she asked, as she undid the clasps of the carrier.

"Ne'mind me," he said hoarsely. "See if—if there's anything you can do."

"Well, have some hot tea. The pot's right beside you."

Willard didn't move or answer, his eyes on the carrier as it was opened and Little Sarah's hands went down into it.

Well, if it was my cat, she thought, as her fingers went gently over the quiet, furry bundle, I'd put it out of the way quick, because that leg's broken; but she did not say so out loud.

"She's purring," Willard said.

She was, the steady, interrupted small sound like a rusty wheel going continuously over a ratchet.

"I always heard tell," Willard went on, "if they purred, they were all right."

"Well," Little Sarah said. "That most always *is* the way, Willard."

She did not know what to do. He appeared to be half out of his mind, more than was rational for a full-grown man over a cat; but with Willard, and with things the way they were, you never knew. She said quietly, "She's got quite a hurt there, Willard, on that leg. What happened to her?"

"Oh," Willard said. He changed color a little, got white around the mouth. "That goddamned George. If she come around while he was taking the money out of my can, he likely kicked her. He don't like animals, George don't, and when I got in tonight, and see my three hundred dollars was gone, I knew it couldn't be nobody else but him. But you fix her up, if you can Little Sarah, ne'mind that. If anything happens to her, I'll tend to George."

He spoke with a kind of dreadful patience, as if he recalled, through years, the rifling of many money cans, and not only money, but other things, too, worth more to a man. His voice was quiet, but nonetheless, Little Sarah, kneeling by the carrier, heard in it something almost like an echo that curdled her blood. Long ago, and buried under a towering pile of days and years, and not returning clearly, but unmistakably her own voice, saying, "I've told Mal and I've told him, and now it's Daze that we can't afford to lose"; and then the red violence in her mind, the explosion.

If I had had somebody I could have turned to, somebody to have stopped me for even a little while, till I could think decent again, I would have had my life, not just years to live through. Somebody to put me to sleep for ten minutes, even.

She said quietly, taking her hands away from the carrier, "I can't do much tonight, Willard. I'll have to have daylight to splint that leg. I can put her to sleep though, so it won't pain her tonight, and then, tomorrow morning, we'll see."

She got up and went to the cabinet over the sink where she kept her medicines, moving around the bottles and the jars—something comforting in the clink of them together on the shelf, because, when you heard medicine bottles clink, you knew somebody was going to do something, at least, try.

She came back with a saucer and a medicine dropper in one hand, and a steaming glass in the other which she handed to Willard as she went by.

"There, you drink that," she said casually. "You look to be about beat, Willard, and that'll pick you up some, and settle your stomach, so's maybe you can eat your supper, by-and-by."

He drank it, she saw out of the corner of her eye, and presently, after she had used the medicine from the dropper, she got up and moved the carrier over behind the kitchen stove, where it would be sure to stay warm.

"If that's made you feel groggy, Willard," she said, over her shoulder, "why, don't worry, sometimes it does, some people."

"Well," he said feebly. "I guess I do feel a mite woozy, Little Sarah."

"Lie down, over there on the couch, why don't you?" she said. "I'll guarantee you'll feel better in five minutes."

He got up out of the rocking chair and headed for the sofa. She saw with relief that the stony look was gone from his face, which seemed, now, to have sagged a little, as if it had melted and run down. She waited five minutes or so before she pulled off his boots and went into the bedroom for a quilt to cover him.

He was just as he had come in from fishing, his clothes redolent of lobster bait, good and ripe. And that quilt, she thought grimly, will have to be washed. But never mind that. She had smelt a-plenty of ripe lobster bait in her time, and, with luck, that dose would keep him asleep with morning.

She glanced again into the carrier, and saw that the cat, too, was asleep.

"Poor mite," she said to it. "If you was mine, I guess I'd have given you something a little bit stronger. But the way it is, you and I'll have to get you well, if we can."

Then she put on her head shawl, blew out the kerosene lamp and went along down the road to talk to Elbridge.

ELBRIDGE, with Liseo a couple of paces behind him, stepped up on the back porch of the Lowden house, and went in without knocking. George and Harriet had just finished supper; Harriet was washing dishes, and George was sitting with his feet up on the stove, picking his teeth. His greeting, which started out to be cordial, broke in two in the middle at the sight of Elbridge's face.

"George," Elbridge said. "Get your coat and hat on. We've got to take you to Port Western to jail."

George's feet came down off the stove with a clatter, and Harriet whirled around from the sink, her mouth an O of astonishment and rage.

"What in God's name you talking about?" she demanded. "George? To jail? What for?"

"Breaking and entering," Elbridge said succinctly. "Come on. Get going, George."

"I never!" George said. "You gone crazy?"

"You broke into Willard's place, stole his money and half-killed his cat," Elbridge said.

"Yes, and after you work out fifteen years in jail the judge hands you for willful larceny," Liseo said, "the S.P.C.A.'ll slap on another fifteen for cruelty to animals. You better pack a valise, George. You'll be gone a long time."

"By God!" George said. His voice rose to a howl of righteous indignation. "It ain't *stealing*, not from your own brother! Willard's my own brother!"

Harriet said sharply, "Shut up, George!" but too late, and Liseo went on smoothly, "And now you've just owned up to it in front of three witnesses, don't forget that."

Elbridge said, "Where's Willard's money? I want it."

Harriet came across the kitchen, each heel coming down with a thud that shook the stringers under the floor, and George, who had his mouth open to say something more, closed it with a gulp as she went by. Even Liseo gave ground, backing up a foot or so until he fetched up against the door behind him; but Elbridge stood stock-still, watching her advance. Brought up short in front of him, Harriet thrust out a forefinger, still dank with dishwater, and shook it under his nose.

"Now, you listen to me, Elbridge Gilman. It ain't none of your business, but that money belongs here, same as Willard himself does, he's supposed to put in to help out George and I, and he ain't, for months. Anything he's got he owes us, and if George took it, I ain't saying George did, but if he took it, it was ours and we had it coming. Now, you git. Out of this house!"

"Any more of that," Elbridge said, eying her, "and we'll take you along to jail, too. I don't doubt it could be proved you put George up to it. Where's the money? I'm going to give it back to Willard, or you both go to Port Western."

"You've got no right—"

"I'm an officer of the town, duly elected. When a crime's committed, I'm empowered to make arrests. By force, if I have to."

He thought, I sound damned pompous, even to myself.

But both George and Harriet, he was pleased to see, looked as he had meant them to, taken deeply aback.

"There's no crime been committed!" Harriet said. "No crime in this God's world. Willard's our own brother, and he's supposed to put in his money—"

"That's for him to say. No man needs to put up with the hell Willard has had from you two. Anyone, twenty-one, has a right to say what he'll do with his money, regardless of how many brothers and sisters he's got. Willard's twenty-one. Either you hand over his money, or put on your hat!"

His voice, which had been quiet, suddenly boomed out in the room, and Harriet gave ground, her face whitening with fear and fury. She sat down suddenly in a chair by the table.

"I will not!" she said. "You'll never get that money out of me, El-
bridge Gilman!"

"I'll get it," George said, in a kind of bleat. "I know where 'tis."

"You don't!" she said, spinning around on him. "You don't have the
least idea in the world—"

"Yes, I have. It's in a can buried in the flour bin. I watched you
put it there."

He went hustling across the floor and banged up the lid of the
flour bin, from which he emerged presently with whitened hands
and a covered coffee can, which he thrust into Elbridge's hands.
"There 'tis, now take it and go. Take it out of the house, back where
it come from. We don't want no part of it."

Elbridge took off the lid of the can, pulled out the fat roll of bills
and counted it. "All right," he said. "It's all here. Now, get your hat
and coat on, George."

George stared at him, stupefied. "But I've give it *back!* 'Twan't
stealing anyway, not from your brother, and I've give it back."

His voice took on a doleful note; he stood looking from one of
them to the other, his head swiveling.

"It's up to Willard whether he wants to press charges," Elbridge
said. "Till he decides, you've committed a crime in the eyes of the
law. I've got no choice. You've got to go to jail."

They marched George, protesting every step of the way, out
through the back entry and down the steps, leaving Harriet frozen-
faced by the kitchen table. They took him down the main road and
out a path which led into Liseo's back field, where there was an
aged root cellar, half-dug into a hillside, pushed him in and pad-
locked the door.

"Now, don't let us hear another yip out of you," Liseo called
through the door. "Or we'll take you to Port Western tonight."

"My God," he said thoughtfully, as they walked home through the
frosty darkness. "I never saw you like that before, Elbridge. You like
to scared me to death."

"Good thing for you to know," Elbridge said absently. "See you
don't start anything, Liseo, you'll set me off again. You think he'll
be all right in there?"

"Oh, sure," Liseo said. "Do the bastard good."

The root cellar was an old one, not used for storage for years. It
was ventilated and brick-lined; Liseo's kids camped out in it, every
so often, slept there when they felt inclined. Johnny had put in an
old chunk stove, which worked; there was a supply of wood and

matches, and before they had gone up to George's they had stopped by the cellar and left a bundle of blankets.

"He'll have a night of it," Liseo said, with relish. "Maybe, if we can cool Wid off, we can let George out, tomorrow."

It had been the only way they could think of to meet the situation. If Willard hadn't cooled off by morning, if Little Sarah wasn't able to bring the cat to life, Willard would start on a hunt for George, and if he found him, would probably try to kill him. But if he couldn't find George, he would cool down; in the meantime, they had his money for him, and maybe the cat would live.

They hadn't, actually, had an idea in the world of taking George to Port Western, or Harriet either. The bluff had been mostly Liseo's idea, though he never could have worked out the details by himself, he said; and he declared modestly that he felt pretty proud of Elbridge, and tomorrow, anyway, was another day.

WILLARD woke up, not knowing where he was. In a kitchen, obviously—for a moment, he thought hopefully it was Harriet's; while he'd been away, living at the shack, she'd had everything done over. But no, not Harriet, she wouldn't spend her money that way; and it wasn't likely she would have let him go to sleep on the kitchen couch, my Lord, in his *clothes!* She would have had him out of there at bedtime, regardless, and so she should. No one ought to sleep all night with his clothes on, it wasn't healthy for a man.

The couch felt comfortable; for a moment, he didn't open his eyes very wide. Then he heard someone say, "Well, he ought to be coming to any time, so hold your horses," and realized that the voice was Little Sarah's.

Something happened yesterday. Little Sarah. Oh, yes, Willard thought. Oh. Yesterday.

He fumbled back the quilt which was over him and sat upright gropingly, and Little Sarah, from somewhere across the room, said, "No, go slow, Willard. Don't harass around too fast, you'll be dizzy."

He *was* dizzy, and his mouth tasted like old boots.

Elbridge was there, sitting by the window, and Little Sarah was in front of Willard, with a cupful of something.

"Here, Willard. Only be careful, it's quite hot."

It was hot, but not too hot to drink. Now, that was nice of Little Sarah—most of women would have handed out that coffee scalding hot, burn a man's tongue off. Willard took a big swig of it, and felt better almost at once, his head clearing, the horrible taste gone from his mouth. But that heavy grief, like, in his mind, that didn't go away.

"Your cat's better," Little Sarah said.

"She is?"

"Yes, she'll come out of it, I think."

"I'll be goddarned," Willard said.

He thought for a minute he was going to bust right out crying, but, Good God, crying in front of the womenfolks! He managed to gulp it back, behind a goodly swallow of coffee. Mary's carrier, he saw, was over behind the stove, in that warm place there always is behind a kitchen stove. The fact that it was there, not set out in the cold shed somewhere, as it would have been if Mary was dead, comforted him.

"By gorry," he said thickly. "I never thought she'd weather it through, Little Sarah."

"She's a sick cat. She may be lame, I don't know. But I've splinted her leg and I expect she'll heal," she said. "You wash and have your breakfast. The basin's full of hot water, and there's the towel. I've got a mess of flapjacks and bacon here, and Elbridge's starving to death."

My gorry, Mary all right, and breakfast in a decent house, at a table, and people waiting to start in till you were ready, having consideration, it was darned good. Willard washed his hands and face thoroughly, with great splashings, realizing with embarrassment that he still had on his old fishing pants, that they stunk of bait. In a decent house, to breakfast, that wasn't right. He felt as if he ought to say something about it, then realized he couldn't, the very idea clammed him all up. He hung up the towel, and stood there, red-faced and uncertain, trying to make up his mind how to pass it off easy about his pants—ought to be some way to say, some joke. But nothing occurred to him.

"Lordsake, Wid," Elbridge said. "If you don't get your deal in here, I'm liable to start grabbing. These flapjacks are driving me crazy."

So all right, maybe they didn't notice it. But *he* did, Willard thought, sitting down to the table, and he made a note in his mind that the first thing he'd do, he'd give these filthy old duds the heave-ho off the wharf. Had them too long, anyway. Man living alone, of course, but no reason to let himself go, like a mushrat in a mud pond. Buy him some new work pants, over to the harbor, today, make an effort.

But, he thought heavily, I can't buy new till I get a day's work, fishing. Not with the money gone out of the can.

He sat looking glumly at the steaming stack of flapjacks on his plate. Take away a man's appetite, thinking about it.

"That goddamned George," he said. "Give me time, I'll catch up with him."

"Eat up," Elbridge said, with his mouth full. He had been watching Willard, waiting for this, hoping that maybe he wouldn't have to start talking until after breakfast. It was a darn crime to have to think about anything but Little Sarah's breakfast, once she set it in front of you. Elbridge sighed, looking down at his plate, with the butter and the maple syrup—he liked lots of both—all but floating the pile of flapjacks.

He said, "Your money's there in the can, Willard. After breakfast, you count it, see if it's all there. But don't let your flapjacks cool off now."

Willard swiveled his eyes from Elbridge to the coffee can. He hadn't even noticed it, and he stared down at it as if it were a snake.

Elbridge reached over, pried the cover off the can, tilted it to show the roll of bills. "See?" he said. He set the can down, picked up his fork. "Eat, now, for godsake, and let *me*."

Willard's face started to get purple, the veins coming out reddish in his eyes. "That goddamned George," he said again. "All I've got to do, just once, is catch up with him."

"No," Elbridge said. "It's out of your hands, Willard. The law's caught up with George. He's going to jail. Matter of fact, he's the same as in jail right now."

It stopped Willard cold. The congestion slowly faded from his face, his jaw dropped with astonishment and shock.

"In jail?" he said. "One of the *Lowdens?* In *jail?*"

"That's right."

"Why, good God, Elbridge! There ain't never been a Lowden in jail! George is—well, George is—well, he's a bastard sometimes, but nothing to call for a jail term, or the like of that. What's he in jail *for?*"

"Breaking and entering. Willful larceny. Cruelty to animals. Quite a list. Means a long jail term, Willard."

"But I'm his *brother*," Willard said. "We can't have—not a *Lowden*, Elbridge. No, sir, by God!"

Little Sarah, coming to the table and sitting down with her own plate, said quietly, "I'd like to have you a little more careful of your talk at my table, Willard."

"Oh, gorry," Willard said. The red flooded into his face, a natural red, this time, and his eyes looked down sheepishly at his plate. "Excuse me, I kind of forgot myself, Little Sarah. I don't blame you."

"That's all right. I don't blame you, either. Tell him, Elbridge, why don't you, that whether George goes to jail or not is up to him?"

"Up to me?" Willard said.

"I'm trying to," Elbridge said irritably.

He flapped his hand at her to keep out of it, it wasn't the womenfolks' business; and she subsided with a meekness which was not her custom.

"I'll make it clear, Willard. As an officer of the town, I had to arrest George, seeing we don't have a constable here. He's committed a crime. But if you don't want to press charges against him, I'll have to let him go."

"Oh," said Willard, in great relief. "Well, let him go, then. Well, thank the Lord. I thought for a minute, there, you meant he was *in jail*. Where *is* George?"

"Where you can't find him," Elbridge snapped, "until you get some sense driven back into you. Five minutes ago, you were ready to kill him. I figure I'd rather have him in jail than dead, though why, I don't know, and considering what he's done, jail is where he ought to go. And Harriet with him. I told them so, last night."

"You did?" Willard said, aghast. "You told *Harriet* that?"

"Certainly, I did."

"Well, I don't think much of that, damn—darned if I do. That's no way to talk to decent people, and there's some things that ought not to be said to a woman. I'm surprised at you, Elbridge. And expect me to put my own brother and sister in jail!"

He picked up his fork and started eating, and a silence fell over the table.

"Why, I wouldn't think of it," Willard said righteously, his mouth full. "It's not necessary. Not necessary at all. Our differences we can fix up amongst ourselves, thank you, but without any mixture from anyone. I could of before, if I'd had some kind of a hold on them. I guess now I have. I guess, maybe, now, I've kind of got George and Harriet over a barrel."

He went on eating. His appetite seemed to grow rather than to diminish. He seemed, before their eyes, to expand as he realized the implications of what had happened, that, if he wanted to raise a finger, George and Harriet would think they had to go to jail.

"Well," he said, at last pushing back from the table. "That was a wonderful breakfast, Little Sarah. Wonderful. I won't say that Harriet don't get a little something extra into a flapjack that I don't find in yours, not quite, but I'm much obliged, all the same."

He paused, running his tongue around over his teeth, with all the preoccupation of an expert judge of flapjacks, whoever made them.

"I'll just take this money, now, Elbridge, and go along and see Harriet. If you know where George is, you tell him to come home, I won't lay a finger on him. After all, tell him, there's nobody like your own."

He got up, pulled on his cap and coat and went out, strutting, and across the breakfast table, Little Sarah's eyes met Elbridge's.

"Comes a pause in the day's occupation that is known as the children's hour," Elbridge said. "Forgot his cat, didn't he?"

"I don't doubt that he'll be back for it," Little Sarah said.

On the way out, Elbridge paused by the carrier and peered down into it. Mary lay immobilized, her leg in a splint and a neat white bandage. He squatted down to admire what looked to him to be a mighty good job of splinting. The ratchety purr started up almost at once, and Elbridge reached out a careful finger to stroke the silky head.

"Well, there, now," he said, in the high baritone croon which large, tender-hearted men occasionally use to speak to cats. "You're a pretty good kitty now, ain't you? A pretty good kitty."

PART SEVEN
Winter

M ISS ROXINDA GREENWOOD, going home with her milk and mail in the early December afternoon, stopped on the crest of MacKechnie's hill. She did this whenever she could, in snow or rain or fair weather. It was a lovely prospect, particularly so today with the season's first snow, and to stand there for a few minutes until she caught her breath enough to say the Collect for the Day, was, also, a kind of memorial to Mama, who had loved it so.

Today was chilly, one of those gray, lowering afternoons so common to early winter, when the wind did not blow, but a penetrating damp went through and through. The sun was breaking out, though —later, it would be clear. The six inches of snow on the ground made walking difficult, particularly up and down the hill. Deep snow she had learned to manage much better. Being light of weight and nimble—though not so nimble as she used to be—she could generally go fast enough over the top of packed snow, so that she did not sink in very far. Oh, of course, there had been times in the past when she had had to crawl on hands and knees, as in the big storm last winter, quite the worst storm she had seen in all the years she had lived on the Point.

What a gale it had been! And how she had reveled, going home in it that night! So absurd for those nice people to have been concerned, or to think she would have missed a moment of it, spending the night in somebody's stuffy spare room, when, even if she had been at home, doubtless she would have gone out for a walk. Such a great storm came all too seldom in a lifetime.

Absurd, too, for them to have thought she might have had an accident on the hill! She, who knew by heart every patch of lichen, the size and shape and colors, so that, on hands and knees, that night, with her lantern hanging from the looped scarf around her neck, she had gone from familiar patch to patch without a falter, without having to wonder, at any time, where she was on the hill!

How wonderful that the study of lichen, its lovely shape and substance, should have turned out to have practical uses, too! Mama would have been delighted.

Wetted to the skin and out of breath, she had got home feeling as if all the lamps of the spirit had been lighted. She had wanted, after she had got dry and warm by the fire, to go out again; but Mrs. Gilman would have been concerned. And, of course, that was the last thing a considerate person would wish to be—a concern and a worry to one's friends.

Roxinda Greenwood could never understand why these dear people here on the island did so fear and distrust bad weather. Even Mrs. Gilman did not really care to be out of doors in the very windy or the very cold; even the men hurried indoors to a stuffy stove at the slightest excuse of a stormy day. It did seem so strange to Miss Roxinda.

Their lore of this countryside went back and back; it was hereditary, almost, like something in the genes, understandable, since their people had wrestled a hard living for generations out of this rock. But if you knew so *much*, if you *knew how* to cope, to handle, to deal with, why should this not make you more confident, why should you not the better enjoy?

Her own lore, her practical knowledge, had been very scanty to begin with, very scanty, indeed. To add to it had been most difficult; she had done so only little by little, slowly and painfully through years of observation, trial and error.

From the first, she had found to her astonishment that the simplest of practical tasks, as, for example putting up a stovepipe, involved complicated technical procedures which took the men who did it a long time, and seemed to be secrets as closely guarded as the secrets of a guild.

She had, at first, asked for simple information, and had found that any such information received would be either unusable or embellished with detail indubitably incorrect. Such as Mr. Luther Mac-Gimsey's arguments against putting her cottage out on the Point, or Mr. Willard Lowden's lecture on cow-dressing. Mr. Lowden had told her that cow-dressing, hauled in small quantities in a wheelbarrow, lost all its virtue in transportation.

"To get the good," he said, "you have got to haul it by the wagon-load. You expose it to sun and air, and all the virtue passes right out of it. Don't ask me why. Cow-dressing's chancy stuff, my grandfather always told me."

A great puzzlement to her, sounding as it did, like honest country lore, handed down by generations of experienced men. Things like this were, indeed, what she most wished to learn, because she did not care to be idle while hired hands did work she herself longed to know how to do; and, too, because she could not afford to pay the high going wages, out of her limited income. Over in the village, she saw again and again, people wheeling manure in barrows, when it seemed to be the thing to do for a small garden; and those great, deep wagonloads Mr. Lowden brought could not be disposed of simply and quickly, unless she hired him to help her. But he did charge a good deal—ten dollars for a load of dressing and ten dollars for his labor. While it was wonderful to have help, still, she and Mama had to be most economical.

She had tried to explain this to Mr. Lowden, asking careful questions, but he had seemed put out and hurt, almost as if he did not believe her or felt that she did not trust him. But dressing should not be so expensive in the village. One man she knew had dumped five wagonloads of it into the ocean, just to get his barnyard cleaned out. It was not as if Mr. Lowden, either, were a terribly busy man, that his labor should come so high.

There were other things—the stovepipe which Mr. Bill Lessaro replaced in her kitchen stove cost a good deal and took a full day to put up. Mr. Lessaro said an elbow was hard to find, and once you found one, most difficult to fit.

Yet, later on, she had been calling on Mrs. Gilman, and Mr. Gilman had been putting up her sitting room stove for the winter. He had a new pipe, with an elbow that looked exactly like the one in her own kitchen; and when she had congratulated him on being able to find one, he had said absently, "Oh, an elbow's an elbow, Miss Greenwood. Buy 'em by the dozen, anywhere." At the same time, he put up the stovepipe in about ten minutes.

So she had gone home and had climbed on a chair, had dismantled her kitchen stovepipe and put it back up again. She decided she would not need help for this particular job again—Mr. Lessaro's bill had been twenty dollars, the cost of the pipe, plus, he said, five dollars for his labor. It seemed too much to pay, particularly since she knew now that she could have done the work herself. She had, of course, asked Mr. Lessaro if he thought she could.

"Oh, mercy, good grief, dear lady, no!" he had said. "It will take *me* all day, likely, and I know the ins and outs of it. Not to speak of it's an awful dirty job. Don't make no difference if I get smut all over *me*."

They were so gallant, such nice manners.

But her income fluctuated with the ebb and flow of prosperity, as invested incomes do. Papa, before he died, had left his ladies well provided for, an ample income, for his day. But building the cottage had taken capital, and perhaps had been a mistake, though that she and Mama would never admit, they loved it so. Mama had always said that the thing to do, since they were two ladies alone with no gentlemen left to plan for the future, was to find the most beautiful place in the world and at last put down there a *pied-à-terre*. *Before* the money was depleted, she had said, and they could no longer afford to travel.

Mama had not, of course, foreseen old age. She had had no reason to at that time. All the Greenwood ladies had been long-lived, outliving their men by decades. Grandma had kept her faculties till ninety-four, finishing, without glasses, a set of embroidered altar cloths, the year she died; and Aunt Lucy was designing and hooking silk rugs, and gaily maintaining her circle of friends, year after year, until she passed on at ninety. Mama had not been so lucky. Old age had come upon her before her time. Never by word or deed did she let Roxinda know she minded; Roxinda, however, could not help but know particularly how Mama must have felt about the blindness— she who had so dearly loved to see. "The wonders of the world," she had always said, "and the generosity of God who has spread them freely everywhere for the seeing."

Years ago, when she and Mama had talked over what there would be in the world for Roxinda to do, this was what they had hit upon. To take some small, simple corner of the earth, as rugged as a corner of the earth might be, and make a place there, make a garden. To put to work the orderly processes of Nature, to see each year the lovely logic come to its seasonal end, to pause, turn and go on, seemed a wonder and a mystery, but more wonderful and mysterious when linked with what could be, with effort, orderly process in the mind of man. But it had been Roxinda, not Mama, who had made the final decision.

"Your genius, if any, is not for people," Roxinda told herself, long

ago, in one of the many conversations she held with Roxinda. "Be-
cause no one will ever be able to see you, past your face. It is not, of
course, normal to live alone. With this face, you will be considered
queer and eccentric. But would you not be, in any case, wherever you
are?"

Thinking back over the part of her lifetime she had spent in the
world, she knew this to be so. She had seen too many times the
curious side glance, the embarrassed looking-away. From a child she
had had these things to know and to get used to.

She had been a strong, healthy child up to the age of ten; then,
one day, she had fallen through the ice of the skating pond in the
park. She had been in the water for a long time, because the children
with her had had to run for help. The terrible chilling had brought
on what at first had seemed to be a kind of rheumatic fever, and,
perhaps, was; but the effects of it lasted a long time, dwindling and
worrying away at her resistance, until, at fourteen, she had had the
bony, emaciated face and body of an old woman. She had been
cured of the disease; skillful doctors and healthy climates all over
the world had given her a toughness.

"So let us see, Roxinda," she told herself at twenty, when she be-
came convinced at last that the miserable plight was permanent.
"Let us see what you and I can salvage."

She had not, although she enjoyed people, ever had to work very
hard to learn to be alone. In time, she ceased even to notice the
reactions of people to her looks.

Mama had helped. Mama had provided the best of private tutors,
chances for study abroad, travel and observation; and she had pro-
vided the gay companionship, the resilience, which had always been
the particular genius of Greenwood ladies. Roxinda had thought,
at the beginning, that she might do something actually useful for
people, like hospital nursing; it had been a disappointment that the
sick, above all, had found her appearance unusual.

She did not discover what she was looking for, until the day she
walked out onto the Point and saw the *pied-à-terre*.

There was the ocean, stretching to the sky, the North Atlantic, the
beloved, seen so many times from the decks of ships. Now, here, it
might wash below a doorstep forever, with serene and lovely sound.
There were the ledges, the pink-gray beautiful stone, the strong,
salty turf in which one could wear fingers to the bone to make a
garden. Here the body could become whipcord-tough, the spirit
flower with gentle, unobtrusive blooms. Failing children of one's

own, there were other people's children; small birds and animals would not care because a face was bony.

It was not the first time the place had beguiled mankind; it might not be the last. Spread out in lovely panoply of green and blue, inscrutable horizon, silent rock, secret tree, it spoke in no understandable tongue; yet it had said to MacKechnie, "power," and to Ansel Gilman, "fear"; to Roxinda Greenwood, it had said, "strength"; and in the end, to all three, "home."

So the house was built. Furniture was sent for, dishes and the family silver which had not been out of storage for years while the last two Greenwoods had traveled the world, came home at last to a dining room and a corner shelf. The books, taken from their boxes, lined three sides of a downstairs room, overflowed into bedrooms upstairs and down. Oh, people living in solitude must have books, the one communication, the strong hawser stretching back to the minds of men!

The Greenwood ladies had always been gay, and, alone, they were. They had guests in summer and parties in winter. They read aloud. Mama, who had no critical sense whatever, loved everything she read. One night it would be, with fascination and great hoots of laughter, *Tarzan of the Apes;* and the next, it might be Browning, or Chaucer, *The Miller's Tale* or the *Balade de Bon Conseil:*

> That thee is sent, receive in buxomness,
> The wrestling for this world asketh a fall. . . .

Oh, when Mama died, Roxinda missed her! She had missed her, of course for years; for years, Mama had not really been there.

She had known, taking Mama to Baltimore, that of course she would come back. Friends were kind and wished her to stay. But at the idea of selling the cottage, she had experienced a vast longing, a *home*sickness, such as she had never known. Better to go back, come what may; better to breathe that air than stifle in a crowded place. If she had responsibilities, they were there, with the flowers and the birds and the small animals she loved.

"As for old age, Roxinda, we will cross that bridge when we come to it."

This year, she was seventy-two.

Lingering on the hill, she saw on all four sides of the island, the gray sea stretching vast and leaden to the sky, the islands—"tame" ones to the north where the mainland was, "wild" ones to the southeast where was the ocean. Out beyond The Pasture, the horizon was humpy—some days, it did look so, not straight, a wavy line; perhaps the sea was rough out there, quite high rollers were coming in. Beyond The Pasture, too, some boats were circling to pick up lobster traps—far out, Mr. Gilman's smack, the *Daisy*, which was one boat she could identify, because of its high, white cabin, and in shore, someone in a rowboat, undoubtedly Mr. Willard Lowden.

"I expect they're chillier than we are," she told Roxinda. "We must hurry home and shake down the coal stove and feed Richard."

Now that she had mentioned it, she *was* chilly. Each bone felt like a separate icy stick standing stiff in her body. Perhaps she had stayed in the chapel too long without a fire there; it had been very cold and damp. But Mr. Lowden had cut only enough wood for Sunday services; perhaps he had been too busy to cut more. In any case, she did not feel it considerate to ask him for wood just for her. She was in the chapel a good deal; it was so nice there. Prayers could be said, of course, wherever one happened to be; God was everywhere and did not take account of time and place. But to kneel before an altar in a House of the Lord gave an added beauty, a feeling of appropriateness and peace, which filled a great need.

She had attended the other church in the village for many years, and had never been able to find what she needed there. It had always seemed to her a bleak kind of worship, without warmth or color, and the building itself—not so much ugly as cold. Much public shouting about sin came from the pulpit, and the wheezy organ seemed to lament rather than to play. It did not seem possible to her that the dear Lord, himself, if he came to church, which was something he might reasonably be expected to do, would enjoy anything so lugubrious.

She had been, in the beginning, delighted with the idea of the new chapel; she had done a great deal of work, writing letters to raise money to build it; she had made flowers to grow around it. And now, she loved it. It was not a lifework; it was nothing so presumptuous. But it was something Roxinda Greenwood had at last found that she could do, unobtrusively, for others, and a great satisfaction.

The pools in the quarry pits, not frozen this early in the winter, were inky against their rims of snow; tree branches were heavy with snow, but it would not last long in this air, which was chilly but damp.

She wondered where the buck was; she had not seen him for a long time. In September, she had encountered him briefly in the swamp, by accident had come upon, in a deep thicket, his cunningly concealed home; but he was not tame any more, having found his own food in the woods all summer. That was as it should be, since tameness was not the proper attribute of any wild thing. She had fed him last winter only as she would have fed any starving creature, not to make him in any way subservient.

That did seem to be a thing so many humans desired to do—to destroy the wild. Perhaps because wildness frightened them, they could not let it be, but must cut down the good trees, shoot the birds and deer. Hunting for food she could understand, but not the imprisonment of creatures for curiosity's sake, or the killing for pleasure, or whatever it was—surely, it was not pleasure entirely which would cause a nice young boy like Johnny MacGimsey, catching sight of the mink, to pursue her from crevice to crevice with a club, the sweat standing out on his face, his eyes reddened in that peculiar way. She wished she knew how to stop him from making war on the mink; he had been doing it for two years now, and she supposed that some day he would succeed, and to what profitable purpose, except to prove that he was the cleverer, the stronger one of the two?

Heavens, of course he was; animals had no recourse against human beings; in the end, the animals always lost. It did seem that mankind, so marvelous in many ways, and Nature's finest achievement through millions of centuries of trial and error, should know what itself was, without having to prove supremacy, again and again, with blood and terror, over organisms weaker and less fortunate.

If the buck had really left the island, she was glad. Doubtless he had gone, this season of the year, to find his lady. Perhaps, some night he had returned to the mainland, swimming the dark tides as he had come.

"Go into the deep woods, buck," she said. "Far away from the sight and sound of men, and go quickly, because in snow like this, your tracks will show."

She went down the hill fast, skidding a little on the slippery downslope, and arrived at her back steps feeling short of breath and still cold, though she would have thought the exercise, hurrying home, would have warmed her.

Richard was not there. His tracks were on the step, pad prints, and two flat places where he had hunkered down on his hind legs, waiting. Now he had gone off, probably wouldn't come home until after dark. His tracks went across the lawn, away, out of sight among the spruces.

"To pay you out," she told Roxinda, "for being late when Richard wanted his supper."

Richard was independent; she liked that. A dog would have been waiting, tail-wagging and head-bowing; and while that might have been a comfort in some ways, one preferred the freedom and integrity of spirit of cats.

The other responsibilities had been taken care of before she had left for the village—the bird feeders were full, the mink had had her fish. She paused on the back porch to wave to Mr. Lowden, who was hauling traps in his skiff, just beyond The Pasture, and then ducked thankfully into the house.

The house, too, seemed cold, though it was neat and orderly, everything dusted and in place. It was so peaceful to come into, the clean solitude. The kitchen smelled of the clothes, newly ironed and airing, hanging on the rack behind the stove.

A very good smell, she thought, cool and fresh, like far-off snow.

She shook down the grate of the coal stove in the kitchen, hearing the clinkers drop to the ashpan—"Mercy, the fire was nearly out, Roxinda"—and seeing the ashpan was full to overflowing, reached in to lift it. It would have to be carried out and emptied into the compost pit. The last few coals were on top, glowing with dark, hotly retained fire. The pan felt warm to her cold fingers. But as she straightened up, lifting it, it felt heavy. The strength all at once seemed to go out of her hands. Far away, she heard a scattering clangor as the pan fell to the floor.

Mercy, Roxinda, bestir yourself, some of those coals might have fallen into the kindling basket.

But it seemed restful where she was, in a peaceful and a growing darkness, with the sound of water receding over ledges somewhere —yes, the sea making up, the rollers coming in over The Pasture to the rocks below the house, going away, becoming still, falling to silence at last.

ELBRIDGE and Liseo, hauling traps in the *Daisy* in the late afternoon headed for their last string, which was twenty traps, two miles or so off The Pasture. They had not done at all well, the catch was meager, and all day the smack had bucked cross-chop—the kind, Liseo said, especially designed to drive a fisherman crazy. The *Daisy* handled it, but she was broad of beam. She pounded. Up she would go on a crest, and then, instead of sliding contentedly down into the following trough, as a well-designed lobster boat would have done, she would hang, her engine going *ker-lunkety, ker-lunkety,* until the next trough came along, whereupon she would slam down onto it with a solid thud, which not only sounded like a barn falling from a height onto a pile of empty barrels, but re-echoed up and down a man's spine and threw a good deal of water. Liseo had stood it pretty well all morning, but now he was wet and cold. The coffee in his dinner pail was long gone, and he had a persistent drop on his nose, which he said he was too goddamned discouraged to wipe off.

"Smack!" he growled, scrambling to his feet, red-eyed with fury, after one of the *Daisy's* more unexpected plunges. "Rightly named, by God! Smack all the water out of the bay, the old wart hog, and look over her shoulder at the ocean!"

Elbridge, at the wheel, looked over his shoulder.

"What's the matter—don't like lobstering?" he asked.

"No, I don't. Not in this old floating bottle full of loose rocks," Liseo said. "Let her fall off a little, can't you? You put her head into it like that, no wonder she pounds."

"Well, I can try," Elbridge said mildly. "I thought I'd tried everything, but—"

Seeing a big green-and-gun-metaled crest bearing down, he slacked on the wheel, letting the bow fall off slightly to quarter it. The *Daisy,* preferring more direct methods, or perhaps unable to do things by quarters when helped by the wind, kept on going around until she was side-to, slid into the trough wallowing, and the next wave came mostly into the cockpit.

Elbridge was too busy straightening up the smack to look around, but he judged, by the clanging sounds behind him, that Liseo had picked up the iron bucket and was bailing.

There was a brief silence, while the *Daisy* bucketed on toward the horizon, and Elbridge strained his eyes out over the welter to pick up the first buoy of the string, which should be along about here somewhere.

"Tide runs hard out here today," Liseo said, appearing at his elbow. "Likely all the buoys are towed under. Well, what say? Come on, to hell with it. Let's go home."

"Oh, ought to look around a little, maybe haul a few traps," Elbridge said. "Seeing that's mostly what we do for a living now."

"Oh, sure, count me in. Maybe find a pot of gold in one of 'em today." Liseo stood glowering out over the hubbled water. "There's one," he said, pointing out a buoy. "If I could see a quarter; one round, silver quarter of a dollar, I'd call it a day."

He gaffed in the buoy, as Elbridge slowed the engine and put the *Daisy* alongside it, and without further comment, wound a bight of the warp around the hoisting drum and brought in the trap, which, as it came over the side, looked like nothing so much as a trap-shaped mound of sea urchins, piled one on top of another.

"Whore's eggs," Liseo said, eying them glumly. "Wouldn't we get rich, Elbridge, if whore's eggs was worth a cent apiece. Man with your brains ought to be able to think up some commercial use."

He put in the bait pockets, closed the slat door of the trap and buttoned it, and let the trap slide smoothly off the washboard, as the *Daisy* surged ahead.

"What we ought to do," Liseo said, peering hopefully out past the coop, "is to haul up this damned old knitting basket, and get ourselves a skiff; lobster in around the ledges, the way Wid does. Then maybe *we* could retire and go south for the winter."

"Oh, that's just talk," Elbridge said. "Willard'll never go. You know him—he always has to have something to put out to people. And for all he's home again, top dog, he's still got a couple of hurt feelings about losing his janitor's job."

"Well, I sure wish he had it back!" Liseo said fervently.

Two weeks ago, they had set up the new furnace in the church vestry. It was not yet completely paid for—in spite of contributions, money had come hard with the congregation cut in half—and it had, as yet, no regular janitor. Elbridge and Liseo had had to take over the job, doing it turnabout.

"And you don't really believe he's top dog at home, do you?" Liseo went on. "You know, some ways, that must be hell-on-wheels up there."

Elbridge made no comment; there seemed to be none to make. The Lowden household was outwardly tranquil; at least, no sound of pull-and-haul reached the town. When the Lowden "boys" walked abroad, they went as they had always gone, George in front, Willard crunching along six paces behind. George needled Willard no more; but he went about with an air of inner smoldering, spoke to Willard in public, when he had to, and that was all. He still kept the powerboat, going fishing in her alone; and Willard had never taken his cat home—Mary was still at Little Sarah's.

He was fussy, Little Sarah reported, about what she had to eat —brought in fish and milk every day—and was as tickled as a young-one when the splint came off and Mary went limping around, a little stiff-legged, but well again. But when it came to taking her home with him, Willard hedged. Didn't think it was fair, he said, where Harriet disliked cats so, couldn't put up with hairs all over the furniture, and George—well, George was awful quick-tempered with animals. If Willard took Mary up there and one day she turned up missing, nobody ever able to find out where she'd gone to, he'd have only himself to blame, so if Little Sarah didn't mind . . .

As for the powerboat, he assured everyone earnestly that he'd got so in the habit of lobstering out of a skiff now that he kind of liked it.

"A man can do awful well lobstering in a skiff, even in the winter," he would say, afternoons in the wharf office. "Say you don't get quite so many crawlers in on the ledges as you do offshore, still you don't have a mess of gas and oil to pay for. Why, I might even take a lay-off, later on in the season, go south or somewhere. I could afford to. I've done well in that skiff, done awful well. Why, come February, you all here freezing to death, I'll be sunning myself on the southern sands. Make an effort, anyway."

But it didn't look like the southern sands, today, in December. The water was rough, in on the edge of The Pasture, where Willard was hauling his traps—not so bad as offshore, but the half-tide rollers were coming in steadily, and there was plenty, in there, to give a man in a skiff a good shaking up. Elbridge had kept reminding himself, all afternoon, to kind of keep an eye on Willard, plan to circle around on the way in and offer him a tow home, in case nobody else did.

"No," he said, now, absently answering Liseo. "I don't guess Willard would ever be top dog anywhere. Unless he could manage, somehow, to make himself a different kind of a man."

And he glanced back at The Pasture to see where Willard was now, and saw the black column of smoke, whipped by the wind, standing off over the water from Miss Greenwood's house.

He started to yell, "My God, Liseo, look!" but the sound came out of him as a half-croak, as if somebody had grabbed him around the throat. Out of the corner of his eye, he saw Liseo whip around from the trap he had balanced on the washboard.

"What . . . what?" Liseo said, his glance darting here and there about the cockpit, because in an old boat, on a day like this, the boat was the first thing a man thought of, something wrong with the boat. But no; and then he saw where Elbridge was looking, and stood, for a second, his ruddy face, wet with blown salt spray, turning gray.

"Jesus! Elbridge!"

Turning, he gave the open trap a mighty heave off of the washboard into the water.

"We've got to get in there—she might be—"

He staggered, off-balance, grabbing for the cheese rind, as Elbridge spun the wheel and jabbed a hard thumb against the *Daisy*'s stiff throttle.

The *Daisy* took it as she had taken everything all day—hard. Banging wide open, head on into the wind, she spanked out a bow wave that looked to be half an acre wide. She threw over herself vast sheets of foam, which, in the low, westering sun at last broken through the overcast, created rainbows; so that the two men in the cockpit were half-blinded by the steel-bright glittering colors, through which they watched the hot, hideous orange flower blossom on the point. They saw the windows of the house turn bright, as if from reflected sun; then, from one of them, a flame like a sword blade shot up, taller than the roof.

"We'll be too late," Elbridge said.

Above the *Daisy*'s smashing and crunching and pounding, Liseo yelled something which Elbridge couldn't hear.

No matter, he thought. They both knew that the best the *Daisy* could do would be another twenty minutes to the edge of The Pasture. Even that close, they would still be helpless, with three hundred yards of ledges buried up in flood-tide rollers between them and the shore. There were no channels between The Pasture ledges for a boat the size of the *Daisy*, nor for any boat on a day like today.

Someone from the town would be getting there soon, surely. They must have seen the smoke by now, they could have, over the hill, about the same time we did. My God, I wonder where she is, if she went to town today.

But he saw, as they drew near, that whoever got there now wouldn't be able to do anything.

The house was gone, no longer even the shape of a house, but a towering mass of fire, curdled orange, black and brown, which poured above the trees, and then, caught by the wind, was laid straight out and streaming above the water. The *Daisy* went in under it as under a cloud; it put out the rainbows, turned the sun to a hazy wafer, plunging fast and dizzily behind the smoke. Elbridge, slowing the engine, saw the black Pasture ledges, the cream-and-green rollers curling over them, along their crests deep-reddish patches of reflected flame.

"Where's Willard?" Liseo said suddenly. He had torn his horrified gaze from the burning house and was peering anxiously at the water, north and south along the white-fringed rocks. "Where's he got to, Elbridge?"

"He was here," Elbridge said. "Just about here, not three-quarters of an hour ago."

He spun around, staring, as Liseo was, at the water.

Willard couldn't have rowed out of sight, in the time he'd had; he couldn't have got a tow anywhere; there'd been no powerboat in here.

And as he looked, and as Liseo, grabbing his arm, pointed shorewards with a yell, he saw the long, narrow, dark-green bottom of a stove skiff, which the water, receding, showed for a moment and then overwhelmed, chumbling it over and over on the ledges.

"Oh, my God!" Liseo choked. "He tried it. He tried to row in there. Oh, the poor, simple, damn fool!"

A big roller gathered up under the *Daisy*, nudging her with a motion almost gentle, in toward the rocks, before its crest curled over to smash, a few yards away. Elbridge tasted the salt of its spray blown back into his face, along with the acrid taste of soot and smoke; he rolled the wheel, swinging the smack out of danger, circling back, skirting in as close as he dared to go.

Watch it, not much water here, the old girl draws a lot; if one of those fellows breaks over us—

The thought, the motions of his hands automatic, handling the boat jigging off and on, while at the same time, past Liseo's tense back and shoulders, he tried to look for some sign in the tumbled waters, a man's head showing, or a hand. But there was nothing. Only the long, dark fishback of the skiff, hustled, tossed, unmercifully pounded, so that, he saw, in a little while there would be not even the skiff.

ON the shore, people from the village had come, black, running figures, seen hazily through smoke. Two of them were tearing down the rocks, waving arms, yelling. Elbridge could hear them, faintly, above the surf pound and the bubble and thump of the *Daisy's* slowed-down engine. Jack Shepheard and George Lowden. They had spotted the skiff.

George, coming now to see what might be done, and with him, Jack—the two who, an hour ago, would sooner have been caught dead than in the same world with each other. Behind them, a scattered line of people strung itself along the shore; out on the water to the east, the two or three boats still out this late were coming in fast, motors wide open. The whole town. Coming together. To see what might be done.

"WE might as well go home," Elbridge said, after a while. The sun had set; it would soon be dark. There was no use hanging here any longer, expecting The Pasture to give up anything. He put the wheel hard-over, heading out around the island for the breakwater, leading the line of boats home.

"Let the lower lights be burning," Liseo said, looking back. His face was blackened where he had swiped away soot flakes, his eyes were red and streaming. "Send a gleam across the wave."